The McClures

Let us be judged by our actions

The McClures

Pioneers from Ireland to Oklahoma

by
Mary Ellen (McClure) Randall

THE EDITORIAL ANNEX

© 2025 by Mary Ellen McClure
All rights reserved. First edition 2023. Second edition 2025.
Printed in the United States of America
ISBN 979 8 218 69464 7 (hard cover)

PERMISSIONS

All McClure family letters and photographs are reproduced courtesy of the author.

Newspaper illustrations and adapted text on pages: 73, 79, 82-84, 88-89, 91-92, 94-95, 135, 141-143, 146-149, 154, 162-169, 182-183, 187-188, 198-199, 203-204, 216-217, 233, 264-269, 274,, 281, 283, 290, 295-296, 300-301, 304-305, 306, 308-310, 316, 318, 328, 352, 361, 398, 408, 415-416, and 418 are reproduced courtesy of *The Daily Oklahoman*.

The following material remains undocumented because the sources are lost in the passage of time: Illustrations 80, 81, 199, 210, 211, 212, 458, 549, and adapted text on pages 178, 205, 210-211, 219, and 359. However, proper credit will be subsequently acknowledged upon written notice
by the valid copyright owner.

All remaining material not in the public domain has a permission credit line.

FAMILY LETTERS

Certain colloquial words and phrases in the McClure family letters have been recast in contemporary English usage for purposes of clarity.

Cover design by Emily Guyer

Produced by
The Editorial Annex
Edmond, Oklahoma

Dedication

*I am bound to them though I cannot look into
their eyes or hear their voices. I honor their history.
I cherish their lives. I will tell their story.
I will remember them for I am the result of the love,
struggle, sacrifice, and journey of thousands.*

—Author unknown

This book is dedicated to the many family members who spent lazy afternoons or long evenings talking about our family and telling the many stories found in this book (I really did listen!).

Their reminiscing took me back in time to the early 1800s to their parents their grandparents, and my ancestors. Their stories made these people come alive for me and I am very grateful. They conveyed the love and respect they felt for the people they had known during their lives. And at the same time, they instilled in me the respect for and the importance of the lives lived before me.

Let us be judged by our actions

The McClure family crest
A domed tower implanted with a flag against a yellowish-gold background denotes power and generosity. A banner unfurls the family motto: *Spectemur agendo (Let us be judged by our actions)*.

The McClure family name
The McClure surname appears as early as the 15th century A.D. Most European surnames were formed in the thirteenth and fourteenth centuries. For the most part, people of the tenth and eleventh centuries had only first names; whereas, by the fifteenth century most everyone had acquired a second name.

McClure is a name from the ancient Dalradian clans of Scotland's west coast and Hebrides Islands. In the Scottish clan system, the McClures are a branch of Clan MacLeod (of Dunvegan). In other words, the McClure clan is a part of the larger MacLeod clan.

The McClure heraldry
Family coats of arms originated as a practical way to identify knights. With his helmet covering his face and armor encasing him from head to foot, a knight needed some way to identify himself to his followers in battle and tournaments. He solved his problem by designing an insignia, a graphic badge exclusively his. He painted his coat of arms on his shield and embroidered it on his surcoat. He brandished his shield and wore his surcoat over his armor for all to see.

Table of Contents

List of Illustrations		viii
Preface		xi
Acknowledgments		xiii
Introduction		1
Chapter 1: Thomas McClure	1796–1878	7
Chapter 2: William John McClure	1842–1899	41
Chapter 3: Mary Ellen (McClure) Kennedy	1852–1923	99
Chapter 4: Guy Vincent McClure	1877–1918	157
Chapter 5: David Victor McClure	1879–1944	171
Chapter 6: Grace Anna (McClure) Jones	1889–1974	223
Chapter 7: Veta Ellean McClure	1881–1963	255
Chapter 8: William John McClure	1907–1970	331
Chapter 9: V. Chrystel McClure	1913–1985	363
Chapter 10: Veta Ann (McClure) Meals	1912–1948	393
Chapter 11: Guy Victor McClure	1925–1961	405
About the Author		421
Appendix 1: Who Are These McClures?		423
Sources		427

List of Illustrations

1. Family Bible 1
2. Handwritten cursive in family Bible 2
3. Thomas McClure 7
4. Passenger and immigration list 16
5. Manifest of brig Florida 17
6. Certified copy of brig Florida's manifest 18
7. Family record..............................18
8. Expanded family record 19
9. Thomas McClure's descendants 19
10. Birth record of Jane McClure 20
11. Family group record 20
12. Ancestral file 21
13. Individual birth record of Mariana McClure ..21
14. 1830 U.S. census..........................22
15. 1850 U.S. census..........................25
16. Thomas McClure 27
17. Extended family...........................28
18. 1860 U.S. census..........................30
19. 1860 U.S. census genealogical form 31
20. Thomas McClure at home..................32
21. Newspaper report of Thomas McClure's murder....................................33
22. Newspaper report of Thomas McClure's murder....................................35
23. Monument of Thomas at Table Rock, Nebraska.................................38
24.. Close-up view of McClure monument 38
25.. Individual record of Daniel McClure 39
26. William John McClure......................41
27. 1856 U.S. census Appanoose County, Iowa ..45
28. 1860 U.S. census..........................46
29. 1860 family census 47
30. William John's Civil War enlistment paper....48
31. William John's Civil War enlistment paper....49
32. William John's Civil War card 49
33. William John's Civil War muster record......49
34. A friend's voucher of William John..........49
35. Jefferson Barricks Army Hospital, St. Louis, Missouri..................................50
36. William John's Civil War discharge papers...51
37. Application for pension.....................51
38. Civil War pension 52
39. Notice of pension termination 52
40. Marriage Certificate: William John and Mary Ellen Kennedy............................53
41. Bill McClure's 7C Ranch cowboys 54
42. Bill McClure's 7C Ranch cowboys 54
43. 1870 U.S. census, Table Rock, Nebraska......55
44. 1870 household census, Nemaha, Nebraska.55
45. Letter to the Provost Marshall...............56
46. North Texas Cattlemen's Association 62
47. Platt showing site of the 7C ranch headquarters..............................63
48. William McClure's letter to his wife 64
49. Receipt for McClure & Cooper..............65
50. Shipping charges..........................66
51. William John, partner in Carson and McClure Real Estate 67
52. Cost of goods.............................67
53. Early ranch home..........................67
54. 1889 Envelope with letter to William J. McClure..................................68
55. Random letter describing land allotment to native tribe families in Oklahoma Territory...69
56. April 22, 1889 Lining up for the Land Run...70
57. Oklahoma City, June 1, 1889...............71
58. Checks written in 1890 and 1891...........72
59. Receipt for payment.......................72
60. Payment and computations.................72
61. First census in Oklahoma Territory, June 1890................................74
62. McClure family census 1890................75
63. One of many William McClure business holdings..................................76
64. Receipt of $2,000.00 for investment in Oklahoma National Bank 76
65. Investment certificate 77
66. Real estate deed..........................78
67. March 7, 1894 Certificate of Stock in Oklahoma National Bank 80
68. Letter dated November 8, 1896 from D.J. Flynn, Guthrie, O.T. to Mr. Wm. McClure, Oklahoma City, O.T..................................80
69. Bureau of Pensions document 81
70. Letter dated Jan. 1, 1897, from Ellsworth, Kansas, to Wm. J. McClure from National Military Home written by Bill's friend, J. W. Dyer.................................81
71. Newspaper notice of William John's death...82
72. Widows pension, 1899.....................83
73. Military pension, 1889 83
74. Notice of William John's funeral 84
75. Widow's application,......................86
76. Newspaper article—no date 88
77. Governor's Proclamation..................88
78. *Chronicles of Oklahoma* article by W. J.'s grandson, William John McClure 90
79. A column in *The Daily Oklahoman* tells location of McClure ranch house in Oklahoma City 90-91
80. Description by grandson of Wm. John's land claim on April 22, 1889 92
81. Description of ranch life, cowboy life, and cattle drives written by grandson, William J. McClure, 1907–1970..........................93
82. News of McClure gravesite vandalism 94
83. Early Oklahoma history mentioning William McClure..................................96
84. Research facts about William John McClure..97
85. Mary Ellen (Kennedy) McClure 99
86. Mary Ellen Kennedy 102
87. Mary Ellen Kennedy's mother, Elizabeth Kennedy 102
88. Mary Ellen Kennedy married William John McClure, July 29, 1869, in Pawnee County, Nebraska................................ 103
89. Marriage certificate, 1869................. 103
90. Mary Ellen wearing her Eastern Star pin ... 110
91. Mary Ellen with friend 113
92. Mary Ellen sitting in carriage.............. 113
93. Oklahoma City house..................... 113
94. Mary Ellen and friend 113
95. Visiting on the porch 114
96. Oklahoma City, 7th and Broadway 114
97. Mary Ellen holding the reins 114
98. Veta driving, Mary standing 114
99. Main Street, Oklahoma City, Oklahoma Territory................................ 115
100. Parade downtown Oklahoma City........ 116
101. Early Oklahoma City streetcar............ 116
102. Eastern Star receipts, 1886 and 1900 116
103. Green Mountain Falls, Colorado.......... 117
104. Hotel, before burning to the ground 117
105. Pond and gazebo at Green Mountain Falls. 118
106. Trail ride with party hats 118
107. Festooned riders and horses on the trail... 118
108. Advertisement for Green Mountain Falls... 119
109. Purchase of China 120
110. Oil painting of Mary Ellen 124
111. Mary Ellen and Veta sailing to Europe for six-month tour 125
112. Mary Ellen and daughter in Europe........ 125
113. Fashionable Veta McClure................ 125
114. Mary Ellen and Veta in Europe............ 125
115. Veta conversing with gentleman.......... 125
116. European trip drama..................... 126
117. Mary Ellen and daughter Veta............ 126
118. San Francisco postcard 127
119. 1900 U.S. census......................... 127
120. Veta Partridge resigns from Eastern Star... 129
121. Mary Ellen with first grandson, William John 132
122. Mary Ellen McClure 133
123. Mary Ellen McClure 133
124. Mary Ellen with first granddaughter, Veta Ann 136
125. Fourteenth census of the United States ... 139
126. Front Page news......................... 143
127. Account of Mary Ellen McClure's death 146
128. Account of court ruling in the death of Mary Ellen McClure 148
129. Mary E. McClure's grave: Fairlawn Cemetery, Oklahoma City, Oklahoma 150
130. Mary Ellen's grave at Fairlawn 150
131. Club directory 155
132. Guy Vincent McClure 157
133. Business card used in Mexico 160
134. Guy McClure's marriage certificate 160
135. Mary Hortense McClure................... 161
136. Mary Hortense McClure................... 161
137. Lake Overholser Dam Plaque: Guy McClure Chief Engineer 162
138. Excavation work—Building Overholser Dam 162
139. Preparing formwork for Overholser Dam .. 162
140. Working concrete stage of Overholser Dam construction 162
141. Order of Service for Guy McClure Funeral.. 164
142. David Victor McClure 171
143. Young David V. McClure.................. 174
144. Dapper David V. McClure 174
145. David V. McClure, Roughrider 174
146. Business card............................ 174
147. Postcard................................. 175
148. Sulphur football team 175
149. Kemper Academy football team.......... 175
150. Kemper school program 176
151. Dave sitting high in the saddle........... 176
152. Cowboy Dave calf-roping 176
153. Sunday afternoon riding party 177
154. Troop D, First Squadron, Roosevelt's Roughriders 177
155. Teddy Roosevelt and aides 178
156. Cutout from Oklahoma newspaper........ 183
157. Roughriders ready for action............. 185
158. A soldier's calling card 186
159. Reception dance card.................... 187
160. Dance card cover: Rough Riders charging up San Juan Hill 187
161. Dapper Dave 187
162. Roman Racing at Frontier Days, Cheyenne, Wyoming 188
163. Dave bulldogging 188
164. Dave calf-roping......................... 188

#	Title	Page
165.	Dave steer-roping	188
166.	Program for Bill Pickett's show	189
167.	Dave bulldogging from automobile	189
168.	Dave and Grace's wedding license	189
169.	Dave and Grace's wedding photograph	189
170.	Dave and William John coming home from hospital	192
171.	Dave arriving by train in Oklahoma City in 1907	192
172.	Dave wearing McClure jockey silks	194
173.	Dave and son William	194
174.	Like father, like son	194
175.	Stationery for Dave's livery stable	194
176.	Dave taking the jumps	195
177.	1910—"The Farm"	195
178.	"The Farm" house	195
179.	Dave in Oklahoma City	195
180.	Dave and Bill at the "Farm"	195
181.	David V. McClure competing in Bromide, Oklahoma, 1916	196
182.	Dave roping a steer	196
183.	Dave and family grouping	197
184.	Dave pays Grace's membership dues	198
185.	Membership card in Cherokee Strip Association	198
186.	Oklahoma City trolley, 1926	199
187.	Racing card at Denver Fair and Racing Grounds	200
188.	Denver Race Association Program, 1927	200
189.	Oklahoma City Saddle and Polo Club	201
190.	Dave with wife, son, and daughter	201
191.	Spanish War Veterans Association dues card	201
192.	Reunion at 101 Ranch	201
193.	Mexican passport	202
194.	David listed as Worthy Patron of Masonic Lodge	202
195.	David Victor McClure	205
196.	Commanding horsemanship	205
197.	Dave looking natural and very much at ease on a beautiful horse	205
198.	Dave and son Guy in front of "The Farm" house	205
199.	Dave McClure portrayed in Detroit, Ohio, comic section	206
200.	Typical grandstand and crowd at a popular track	206
201.	Standing room only on the ground level	206
202.	Dave's horse leading the field	206
203.	Holding a good lead	206
204.	Thundering toward the finish line	207
205.	In the winner's circle	207
206.	Dave taking a bow with jockey	207
207.	Nebraska race card	207
208.	Roster of reunion of original Roughriders	208
209.	Membership card	209
210.	Account of famous roper horse, Skunk	210
211.	Prerace newspaper coverage	213
212.	Feature story about Dave	213
213.	Afternoon nap time for Dave	214
214.	Feature story about Dave and his horses	215
215.	Feature story about Dave's golden filly	216
216.	Philanthropic certificate	216
217.	Grace Anne (Jones) McClure (Lowrance)	223
218.	Grace and her brother performing	226
219.	Young Grace	226
220.	Return address on envelope	226
221.	Grace in height of fashion hats	227
222.	Grace and friend	227
223.	Grace, friend, and Man in the Moon	227
224.	Grace in a "lawn" dress	227
225.	Grace and David's marriage certificate	228
226.	Wedding photograph of Grace and David	228
227.	Dave and Grace on honeymoon	228
228.	Newspaper announcement of funeral	228
229.	Grace and David	229
230.	Lovely Grace	229
231.	Birth of first child, William John	229
232.	Grace with new son, William John	229
233.	Dramatic Grace	230
234.	Grace in repose	230
235.	Grandmother Mary Ellen, baby Veta Ann, William John, and Grace	230
236.	Grace with William John and Veta Ann	230
237.	Grace with Veta Ann and William John	230
238.	Grace's brother, Charles Homer, World War 1	231
239.	Grace	231
240.	Membership in the Women of '89	231
241.	Visiting Sulphur, Oklahoma	232
242.	Grace and William	232
243.	Horse show	233
244.	Horse show program listing Grace	234
245.	Grace could do it all	234
246.	Looking quite at ease	235
247.	Grace's friend wearing fur coat in hog pen	235
248.	Grace looking content and happy	235
249.	Real estate deed	236
250.	Grace Anna McClure	236
251.	Grace and her two boys	237
252.	Grace loved the foals	237
253.	Grace's certificate of marriage to Oscar Lowrance	237
254.	News announcement of McClure-Lowrance wedding	237
255.	Feature news	238
256.	Grace and Oscar in Sulphur, Oklahoma	240
257.	Grace and son, Bill	240
258.	Grace, Bill, and Oscar	240
259.	Family on garden bench	240
260.	Anniversary account	241
261.	Thanksgiving celebration	242
262.	Grace and Oscar Lowrance	243
263.	Grace's death certificate	243
264.	Oscar Lowrance	246
265.	Veta Ellean, McClure	255
266.	Childhood in Indian Territory	258
267.	Veta in Oklahoma City	259
268.	Veta and her mother, Mary Ellen (Kennedy) McClure	259
269.	Veta as a young woman	259
270.	Veta with brother and friends	259
271.	Demur Veta McClure	260
272.	Veta and friend	260
273.	Veta on board walk in early-day Oklahoma City	260
274.	Painting of Veta	260
275.	Charges for one semester at Baird College	261
276.	School girl Veta	261
277.	Expenses at Christian College for Woman	262
278.	Proper young lady's calling card	262
279.	Graduation ceremony at Chrisitan College for Women	263
280.	Veta and mother Mary Ellen boarding ship	263
281.	Dressing for dinner aboard ship	263
282.	Veta and mother Mary Ellen on tour	264
283.	Wedding invitation, 1903	265
284.	Insert in wedding invitation	265
285.	Veta's wedding photograph	266
286.	Festooned wedding car	266
287.	Lieutenant Leon Roscoe Patridge	271
288.	Invitation to wedding to Leon Patridge	271
289.	Wedding photo of Veta in the garden	271
290.	Calling card	272
291.	Veta and mother Mary Ellen in Havana, Cuba	272
292.	Husband number three, C. R. Carhart	273
293.	Swimming in the Great Salt Lake	274
294.	Mary Ellen, Veta, friend in the Great Salt Lake	274
295.	Veta and friends	274
296.	Husband number four, R. M. Smyth	275
297.	Parade Grounds, West Point	275
298.	Beautiful chapel at West Point	275
299.	Getting read for the wolf hunt	276
300.	Riding party	276
301.	Veta and her car	276
302.	Veta with nephew, William John	278
303.	Husband number five, Lieutenant John Herald Muncaster	279
304.	Calling card	279
305.	Picnic	279
306.	Husband number six, George M. Church	280
307.	Mugging camera at Cripple Creek	280
308.	Veta McClure Church in pearls	280
309.	George M. Church on bicycle	282
310.	George M. Church, pilot instructor	282
311.	Veta in front seat	282
312.	George Myers Church at family home	282
313.	Veta portrait by Philippine artist	283
314.	Elegant Veta	283
315.	Veta and nephew William John Mcclure	284
316.	Veta and George Church at Green Mountain Falls	284
317.	Veta's home, Braemar Lodge	284
318.	George and Veta on Colorado trail ride	284
319.	Athens, Greece, at the Acropolis	285
320.	Veta visiting with fellow travelere	285
321.	Cairo, Egypt	286
322.	Pearls and Camels	286
323.	Egypt	286
324.	Dressed for Egyptian desert	286
325.	Veta's bedroom set	294
326.	Veta with hunt trophies	294
327.	Husband number seven, wedding certificate	295
328.	George Scott Findlay	295
329.	Invitations to the White House	299
330.	Veta's Washington, D.C., home	303
331.	Veta's at home	306
332.	In Veta's living room sits the last Steinway played by Paderewski on his final concert tour in the United States	306
333.	Veta and George, Venice	307
334.	Veta's passport photo	308
335.	Newsmakers, Veta and George	308
336.	Sale brochure	318
337.	George Scott Findlay	319
338.	"The Links"	319
339.	George Scott Findlay and his father	319
340.	The Findlays	320
341.	The Findlay clan	320
342.	Saigon Opera House	320
343.	Saigon Cathedral	320
344.	Saigon Harbor	321
345.	Officers, Charter Bank of England	321
346.	Vietnamese river life	321
347.	Vietnamese junk boat	321
348.	George swimming in Saigon	322
349.	"The Old Boys Club"	322
350.	George at social gathering	322
351.	Entry vestibule, Calhoun Mansion	326
352.	South garden on 16 Meeting Street	326
353.	Entry of #16 Meeting Street	326
354.	Calhoun drawing room	327
355.	Calhoun sitting room	327

#	Entry	Page
356.	Calhoun sitting room	327
357.	Library at 16 Meeting Street	327
358.	Calhoun bedroom	327
359.	Veta's obituary	328
360.	William John McClure	331
361.	William John's birth certificate	334
362.	Six-week-old William and his dad	334
363.	William and his mother Grace	335
364.	Baby William	335
365.	William and grandmother, Mary Ellen	335
366.	William John McClure's first birthday	335
367.	Grandmother Mary Ellen and baby William	336
368.	Toddler William on front porch	336
369.	Baby William riding	336
370.	Proud Dave with baby William	336
371.	William, 2 years old	336
372.	William	337
373.	William on donkey	337
374.	Grace, William, and Dave	337
375.	William at ranch	337
376.	William and sister, Veta Ann	337
377.	Veta Ann and William	337
378.	William, age 6	338
379.	William, age 7	338
380.	William, 1913	338
381.	William at train	339
382.	William in uniform of Howe Academy	339
383.	Howe Academy football team	339
384.	William in Howe Academy letter sweater	340
385.	William's first letter sweater	340
386.	William at rest on campus	340
387.	Aunt Veta and William	341
388.	Aunt Veta and William	341
389.	Uncle George Myers Church and William	341
390.	George M. Church and William	342
391.	William growing up	342
392.	Athletic William	344
393.	William's football uniform	344
394.	Gridiron gladiators	344
395.	Gridiron action	344
396.	Sports news	345
397.	Kemper baseball team	345
398.	Kemper's catcher, William	346
399.	William in Kemper togs	346
400.	Kemper track team	346
401.	Kemper swim team	346
402.	Kemper military exercises	348
403.	William at military camp	348
404.	William's commission	348
405.	Buddies	349
406.	Boys being boys	349
407.	Class photograph	349
408.	Graduation photo	350
409.	Football game in Sulphur, Oklahoma	351
410.	Passport photograph	351
411.	William in Venice, Italy	354
412.	William at the Acropolis	354
413.	William in Egypt	354
414.	William at the Pyramids	354
415.	William in Taneytown, Maryland	355
416.	Taneytown, Maryland	356
417.	Driveway view	356
418.	William exercising horse	356
419.	William and Chrys in Winner's Circle	357
420.	William, Chrys, and friends	357
421.	Gusher well	358
422.	Chrystel McClure	363
423.	Birth certificate	365
424.	Family on porch	366
425.	Mary Alice with children	366
426.	Children in the yard	367
427.	Mary Allice and Chrystel	367
428.	Elmo and Chrystel with grandmother	367
429.	Lowell, Arkansas, train depot	367
430.	Elementary school class	368
431.	Junior high school class	368
432.	Chrystel riding bull	368
433.	Graduation from Rogers High School	369
434.	Chrystel's graduation	369
435.	Chrystel and friend	369
436.	Chrystel on date	370
437.	Chrystel and friend	370
438.	Chrystel off to nursing school	370
439.	Chrystel at nursing school	370
440.	Chrystel with friend	370
441.	White dresses, white sidewalls	371
442.	Chrystel, the career woman	371
443.	Christmas card	371
444.	Young career woman	371
445.	Chrystel with colt	372
446.	Chrystel and friends in Dallas	372
447.	Chrystel at Fort Sill	373
448.	Chrystel with cousin Edwin	373
449.	Chrystel with brother, John Samuel	373
450.	Chrystel and family	373
451.	Chrystel with brother and sister	373
452.	Chrystel inspecting artillery	373
453.	War ration book	374
454.	War ration stamps	374
455.	Chrystel in Dallas	374
456.	Fashionable career woman	374
457.	Chrystel in Dallas	375
458.	Chrystel and Bill on date	375
459.	News account of marriage	375
460.	Chrystel and Bill's marriage license	375
461.	Note sent to Chrystel	375
462.	Wedding photograph	376
463.	Chrystel and Bill on their wedding day	376
464.	Wedding day	376
465.	Newly weds	377
466.	Honeymoon	377
467.	Bill on bridge	377
468.	Chrystel at Garden of the Gods	377
469.	Honeymooners	377
470.	Relaxing honeymooners	377
471.	Resignation letter	378
472.	Early married years	378
473.	Chrystel and her mother	378
474.	Chrystel, horse woman	378
475.	1940 fashion	379
476.	Chrystel and family	379
477.	Western Union telegram	379
478.	Newborn Mary Ellen at stables	379
479.	Mary Ellen napping	380
480.	Bill, Chrystel, and Mary Ellen in Detroit, Michigan	380
481.	Chrystel and Mary Ellen at Lincoln Memorial	380
482.	George Findlay, Chrystel, and Mary Ellen at Christmas	381
483.	Chrystel, Mary Ellen, Margaret in Hot Springs, Arkansas	381
484.	Chrystel, Mary Ellen, and friend	381
485.	Chrystel at home	381
486.	Veta Findlay with great niece, Veta Louise	382
487.	Ten-month-old Veta Louise and sister Mary Ellen	382
488.	Mary Ellen and Veta Louise	382
489.	Veta Louise's first birthday	382
490.	Veta Louise gathering blossoms	383
491.	Dressed for church	384
492.	Dressed alike, Manitou Springs, Colorado	384
493.	Chrystel at home with girls	384
494.	Sisters visiting in St Louis, Missouri	384
495.	Admiring the scenery	385
496.	Certificate of honor	385
497.	Installation of Veta Louise as Worthy Advisor	385
498.	Celebration dinner	386
499.	Chrystel playing with grandchildren	386
500.	Chrystel with grandson, Thomas Jason, and Veta Louise	387
501.	Chrystel enjoying gandchildren	387
502.	Chrystel, Veta Louise, and Thomas Jason	387
503.	Chrystel in Amsterdam	387
504.	Chrystel in Lowell, Arkansas	388
505.	Chrystel in Greece	388
506.	Chrystel with friend Helen Granzow	388
507.	Chrystel with her four grandchildren	389
508.	Chrystel with her two daughters	389
509.	Chrystel and Margaret in Saudi Arabia	389
510.	Chrystel with Veta and Rick's house boy	389
511.	Christmas in Manama, Bahrain	390
512.	Chrystel's death certificate	390
513.	Chrystel's obituary	391
514.	Chrystel's grave	391
515.	Veta Ann (McClure) Meals	393
516.	Veta Ann born 1912	395
517.	Baby Veta Ann with grandmother, mother, and brother	395
518.	Veta Ann, mother Grace, and William	395
519.	Pensive Veta Ann	395
520.	Veta Ann in driver's seat	396
521.	Preteen Veta Ann and mother Grace	396
522.	Grace and her two children	396
523.	Veta Ann, school girl	396
524.	Veta Ann with parents	396
525.	Stylish Veta Ann	397
526.	Passport photo	397
527.	Veta Ann traveling with her dog	398
528.	Aboard ship with Chung Lee	399
529.	Very fashionable Veta Ann	399
530.	Robert Meals, born 1936	400
531.	Veta Ann with her two boys	400
532.	Veta Ann, circa 1948	400
533.	Robert Meals with cousin Mary Ellen	402
534.	Guy Victor McClure	405
535.	Guy Victor's birth certificate	407
536.	Two-year-old Guy Victor	407
537.	Guy Victor's Sunday School card	407
538.	The Daily Oklahoman news article	408
539.	Guy Victor's note to her father	409
540.	Guy Victor's certificate of merit	409
541.	Guy Victor's baseball letter	409
542.	Guy Victor's graduation program	409
543.	Newspaper article	410
544.	Army form letter	411
545.	Army letter requesting transfer	412
546.	West Point application approved	413
547.	Guy Victor, young aviator	414
548.	Guy Victor, World War II pilot	414
549.	Guy Victor, military pilot	414
550.	Wolf-hunting prize	415
551.	Coyote hunting from airplane	415
552.	Oklahoma City Times article	415
553.	Edmond newspaper article	416
554.	Guy Victor in motorcycle race	417
555.	Card-carrying member	417
556.	License for motorcycle competition	417

Preface

As a child, I always wanted to hear family stories. I presume you do too. Perhaps your interest in this memoir lies in the fact you are connected to the family tree. If so, this book is written especially for you.

For others—those of you who take delight in family lineage other than your own—I trust you will find the McClure story useful, as well as entertaining. Perhaps it will help you trace your own ancestry. Will it reveal a thread that ties your family history to mine? Stranger things have happened.

The McClure life journey enjoys its share of epic adventures and legendary characters. It is also peopled with ancestors who lived normal, average lives of their time. However, you will discover that each one lived a life of virtue and outstanding character.

In the 1970s I inherited the bulk of what is found in this book. I began organizing the materials, copying what I could (on an old manual typewriter and carbon paper), visiting libraries, and studying microfiche.

I was captivated by what I discovered. The original letters, photographs, and documents speak for themselves. Thus, I have arranged them in this book to tell the story the way it should be told—by the people who lived it.

The book is laid out chronologically by person. This way you can move through the generations as they occurred. I made every attempt to be accurate. However, at times, the old script, the faded ink, and faded paper made the translation difficult. Please accept my apology for any mistakes you may find.

It has been my joy to compile this information. I hope you glean a deeper understanding and love for our family from this book. I hope you will keep the McClure family heritage alive by retelling the tales herein to your children and your grandchildren.

—Mary Ellen (McClure) Randall

Acknowledgments

Thanks to editor Richard M. Crum. His patience and enthusiasm with a first-time author is commendable. Thank you, Richard, it would not have happened without your expertise.

Deep gratitude to Nancy B. Martin, the book's sharp-eyed proofreader.

Of course, my greatest supporter and cheerleader is my husband, George. In addition, the excitement and interest of our family over this project have kept me on task. My heartfelt and grateful thanks to you all.

The American McClures' Stream of Life

Thomas McClure
Mary Jane Young (1st Wife)
Nancy Bailey (2nd Wife)

Jane - Hugh - Marianna - John Wilson - James Belford Sophie
Louise - Daniel Henry Thomas Jr. - Hester Malvena Twin Girls
Ada - William John

William John McClure
married Mary Ellen Kennedy
Guy Vincent - Veta Ellean - David Victor

David Victor McClure
married Grace Anna Jones

William John McClure
married Chrystel McClure

Guy Victor McClure
married Thamar Perkins

Veta Ann McClure Meals
married Robert Wolcott Meals

Mary Ellen McClure
married
George Randall

Veta Louise McClure
married
Thomas R. Roberts

Robert Wolcott Meals
married Martha

David A. Meals

Charles David McClure
married
Judy Mathea

Guy Vincent McClure
married
Wendy Witkowski

Dewey Allen McClure
married
Lisa McMickle

Introduction

Illustration 1. Family Bible

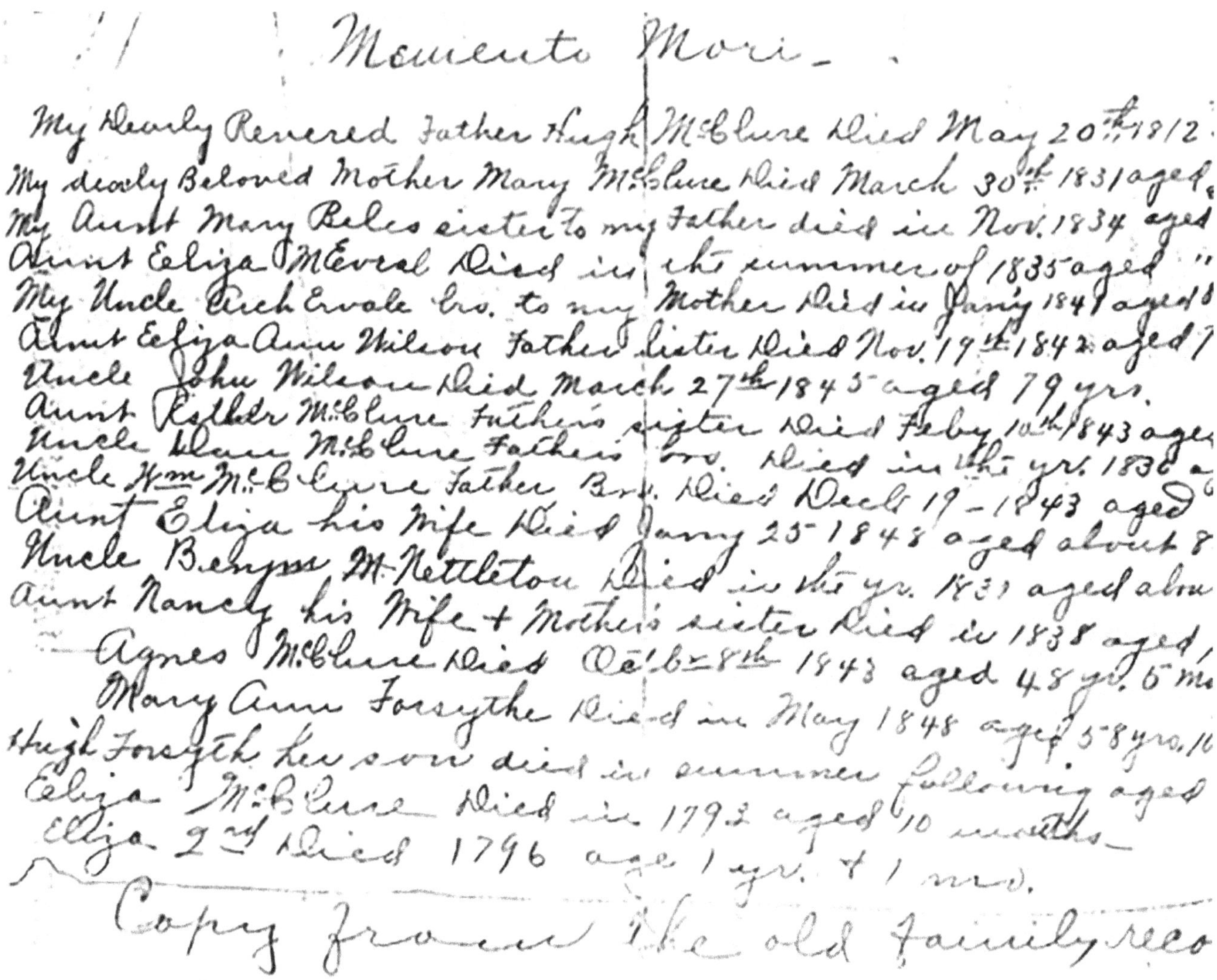

[Handwritten cursive in the family Bible]

Illustration 2. Handwritten cursive in the family Bible

Transcription of handwriting in the old family Bible (see Illustration 2)

Memento Mori

My Dearly Reverend father Hugh McClure Died May 20, 1812 aged 49 yrs.

My dearly Beloved Mother Mary McClure Died March 30th 1831 aged 80 yrs.

My Aunt Mary Beles sister to my father Died in Nov. 1834 aged: almost 82 yrs.

Aunt Eliza M. Ervale Died in the summer of 1835 aged 70 yrs.

My Uncle Arch Ervale bro to my Mother Died in January 1841 aged 84 yrs.

Aunt Eliza Ann Wilson Fathers sister Died Nov. 19, 1842 aged 78 yrs.

Uncle John Wilson Died March 27th 1845 aged 79 yrs.

Aunt Esther McClure Father's sister Died Feb 10, 1843 aged 82 yrs.

Uncle Dave McClure Father's bro Died in the yr. 1830 aged, ?

Uncle Wm. McClure Fathers bro Died Dec. 19, 1843 aged 85 yrs.

Aunt Eliza his wife Died January 25, 1848 aged about 80 yrs.

Uncle Benjm Nettleton Died in the yr. 1847 aged about 90 yrs.
Aunt Nancy his wife & Mother's sister Died in 1838 aged 76 yrs.
Agnes McClure Died October 8, 1843 Aged 48 yr. 5 months
Mary Ann Forsythe Died in May 1848 Aged 58 yr. 10 mo.
Hugh Forsyth her son Died in summer following age 28 yr.
Eliza McClure Died in 1793 Aged 10 months
Eliza 2nd Died 1796 Aged 1 yr. & 1 Mo.

To help any future genealogist who wants to dig deeper into our ancestry, table 1 lists family names left in County Antrim, Ireland, after Thomas McClure Sr. emigrated to America in 1825.

Table 1. Ancestors of Thomas McClure Sr. in Ireland

Name	Role	Born	Died
Thomas McClure	Grandfather	1711	1793
Anne Swan	Grandmother	1727	1770
Rev. Hugh McClure	Father	1763	May 20, 1812
Mary Ervale McClure	Mother	1751 (1752)	March 30, 1832
Father Hugh's Siblings			
Mary Beles	Sister	1755	1834
Eliza Ann Wilson	Sister	1764	1842
Esther McClure	Sister	1761	1843
Dave McClure	Brother	?	1830
William McClure	Brother	1758	1843
Mary Ervale McClure's Siblings			
Arch Ervale	Brother	1757	1841
Nancy Nettleton	Sister	1762	1838

American Branches of the Family Tree

Thomas and Mary Jane were the first McClure generation to come to America. They are the starting point for the purposes of this memoir.

I was tempted to follow rabbit trails leading farther back into our ancestry. However, I resisted and worked only with the bulk of information about the most direct line of our family (see table 2).

Table 2. Five McClure Generations in America

Note: Each number in parenthesis appears as a superscript number throughout the book to identify the McClure generation the named person(s) belongs to.

First McClure American Generation (1)
Thomas McClure

Mary Jane Young	1st Wife
Nancy Bailey	2nd Wife

Second McClure American Generation (2)
Children of Thomas McClure and Mary Jane Young and Nancy, Thomas' second wife

Jane	*Married* Nelson Thurstone
Hugh	*Married* Margaret Gregory
Marianna	
John Wilson	
James Belford	*Married* Hattie Baker, Lillie Harper
Sophie Louise	*Married* Edward J. Gault
Daniel Henry	*Married* Ann Griffin
Thomas Jr.	*Married* Barbara Ellen Ball
Hester Malvena	*Married* Henry G. Gault
Twin Girls	
William John	*Married* Mary Ellen Kennedy
Ada	*Married* Joseph Martin

Third McClure American Generation (3)
Children of William John and Mary Ellen Kennedy McClure

Guy Vincent McClure	*Married* Bernice McAdams
David Victor McClure	*Married* Grace Anna Jones
Veta Ellean Mcclure	*Married* Jones, Partridge, Carhart, Smythe, Muncaster, Church, and Findlay

Fourth McClure American Generation (4)
Children of David Victor and Grace Anna Jones McClure

William John McClure	*Married* Chrystel McClure
Veta Ann McClure Meals	*Married* Robert Wolcott Meals
Guy Victor McCure	*Married* Thamar Perkins

Fifth McClure American Generation (5)

Children of William John and Chrystel McClure

Mary Ellen McClure	*Married* George Randall
Veta Louise McClure	*Married* Thomas R. Roberts

Children of Robert Wolcott and Veta Ann McClure Meals

Robert Wolcott Meals	*Married* Martha
David A. Meals	

Children of Guy Victor and Thamar Perkins McClure

Charles David McClure	*Married* Judy Mathea
Guy Vincent McClure	*Married* Wendy Witkowski
Dewey Allen McClure	*Married* Lisa McMickle

Let us be judged by our actions

Chapter 1
THOMAS McCLURE
1796 - 1878

Illustration 3. Thomas McClure

Thomas was born in Crumlin, County Antrim, Ireland, in 1796. Crumlin is a quaint farming village nestled in the bucolic countryside near Belfast in North Ireland. The village lies just east of Lake Neagh, the largest inland body of water in Great Britain.

Thomas and Mary Jane Young married. Six years later they boarded the brig *Florida* in Belfast and sailed for America. They arrived at the entry port of Philadelphia on July 20, 1825. They remained in Philadelphia for a little over a year. They left after they had purchased land in Monroe, Pennsylvania. This move began their pattern of establishing a homestead and farm, spending three to five years to improve the property, then selling it at a profit. This pattern took Thomas and Mary Jane across the United States.

Thirty-three years later in 1858, Thomas settled in Nebraska—four years after the Nebraska Territory opened in 1854 and four years before the Homestead Act. He lived in Nebraska for the next twenty-four years of his life. He was found dead on the banks of the Nemaha River at age 82. Allegedly, he had been murdered; however, the actual cause of his death was never known.

From the Records
(PLEASE NOTE: The superscript number before a name identifies which generation the name belongs to. For example, [5]Mary Ellen McClure *shows that I am part of the fifth McClure generation in the United States.)*

[1]Thomas McClure, Sr.
   b. August 12, 1796, Crumlin, County Antrim, North Ireland
   d. October 12, 1878, aged 82 years 2 months
   b. Table Rock, Pawnee County, Nebraska; Grave 1; Lot 22; Block 1
     His tombstone reads: *The pains of death are past, Labor and sorrow cease, and life's warfare closed at last, His soul is found in peace.*
  m. [1]Mary Jane Young, Crumlin, North Ireland,
     December 26, 1819, by Rev. Nathaniel Heywood
    b. September. 26, 1798, Crumlin, County Antrim, North Ireland
    d. June 2, 1848, on the Rock River, Lee County, Illinois
      Mary Jane's father:
      William Young b. 1760 d. 1832, Ireland
      Mary Jane's mother:
      Jane Hunter b. 1760 d. unknown
  m. [1]Nancy Bailey, May 28, 1851, McLean County, Illinois
    We have a copy of their marriage license from McClean County.
   b. 1814, Ohio
  f. Presbyterian
   Children of Thomas and [2]Mary Jane Young McClure:
  [2]Jane
    b. September 28, 1820, Crumlin, County Antrim, North Ireland
   m. Nelson Thurston, 1840, Dixon, Lee County, Illinois b. 1813, Canada
     Thurston died on October 4, 1898.
    d. October 12, 1878, Table Rock, Pawnee County, Nebraska
     1856 U.S. Census lists N McClure as wife in Appanoose County, Iowa.
     1860 U.S. Census lists Nancy as Thomas' wife in Nemaha County, Nebraska.

[2]Hugh
- b. May 24, 1822, Crumlin, County Antrim, North Ireland
- m. Margaret Gregory
    - b. January 22, 1822, Glenavy Antrim, North Ireland
    - d. February 1908, Ballendary County, Antrim, North Ireland
    - Children of Hugh and Margaret:
    - [3]Eliza Ann b. 1843, Crumlin, County Antrim
    - [3]William b. 1843, Crumlin, County Antrim
    - [3]Margaret Agnes b. 1846, Crumlin, County Antrim
    - [3]Thomas b. 1849, Crumlin, County Antrim
    - [3]John b. 1850, Crumlin, County Antrim
        - m. Nellie M. Quayle
            - b. 1854, Crumlin, County Antrim
    - [3]Robert Gregory b. 1852, Crumlin, County Antrim
    - [3]Edward Henry b. 1854, Crumlin, County Antrim
        - m. Ada Shaw
            - b. 1858, Crumlin, County Antrim
    - [3]Edmund Harris b. March 7, 1883
        - m. Alice
            - b. June 29, 1856, Aghalee, County Antrim
            - Child of Edmond H. and Alice:
            - Charles Herbert b. February 14, 1891, Crumlin, County Antrim
    - [3]James Belford b. April 15, 1885, Crumlin, County Antrim
        - m. Edna Valantine, Thurber, Utah
        - Children of James and Edna:
        - [4]Norm b. Living [born alive]
        - [4]Nola Mae b. Living
        - [4]Edmund Joseph b. Living
        - [4]Robert Thurber b. Living
        - [4]Ethel May b. September 28, Crumlin, 188(?)
        - [4]Robert Howard b. December 12, 1887, Crumlin, County Antrim
        - [4]John Roscoe b. April 1, 1890, Crumlin, County Antrim
        - [4]Anna Margaretta b. November 9, 1892, Crumlin, County Antrim
        - [4]Winnifred Mary b. June 6, 1895, Crumlin, County Antrim

[2]Mariana
    b. January 24, 1824, Crumlin, County Antrim
    d. Unknown

[2]John Wilson
    b. February 28, 1826, Monroe, Pennsylvania
    d. July 6, 1827

[2]James Belford
    b. February 28/29, 1828, Monroe, Pennsylvania
    In 1839, the family moved to Illinois. At age 20 he settled in Sacramento, October 18, 1849. He worked in the Comstock silver mines for five years in Butte, Plaines, and Sierra Counties. He did merchandising with the Hon. Creed Haymond, an attorney for Southern Pacific Co. He owned several hop farms in the Uriah area. The home farm had 900 acres and the other three several hundred. He became a philanthropist in the Uriah region.
    m. Lillie Harper of Uriah, California, in 1884
        Children of James B. and Lillie Harper:
        [3]Sophia b. 1865 (becomes Mrs. E.H. Smith)
        [3]Nelson b. 1869
        [3]William b. 1872
        [3]Unknown b. 1878 d. December 13, 1892
    d. June 28, 1880

[2]Sophia Louise
    b. December 10, 1830, Huron, Erie, Ohio
    m. Edward J. Gault, December 23, 1853, Appanoose, Iowa
        b. North Ireland, June 1, 1828
        f. Presbyterian
        Edward Gault was an Iowa state senator in 1872, 1874, and again in 1886.
    d. November 27, 1873, Cincinnati, Appanoose City, Iowa
        Children of Edward and Sophia Gault:
        [3]Thomas b. 1855
            m. Laura Sturdivant
        [3]Annie b. 1857
        [3]Frank (Francis Marion Gault) b. 1859
        [3]Mary b. 1863

[3]Alice b. 1865
[3]Richard b. 1867 d. 1935
[3]Jessie b.1869
[3]Sophia b. 1873

[2]Daniel Henry
  b. March 8, 1833, Huron, Erie, Ohio
  m. Ann V. Griffin b. 1822 d. 1873
    Children of Daniel and Ann Griffin:
    [3]Sarah b. 1842
    [3]George b. 1844
    [3]John b. 1846
    [3]Elijah b. 1850
    [3]Rachael b. 1852
    [3]Daniel b. 1855 d. 1873
        Daniel owned a grain business at Elk Creek, Nebraska.
    [3]Nancy b. 1857
    [3]Charles b. 1859

[2]Thomas Jr.
  b. November 1, 1835, Huron, Eric, Ohio
  m. Barbara Ellen Ball, November 28, 1870(?), Monroe City, Ohio b. 1838
  f. Presbyterian
Thomas Jr. became a farmer at Todd Creek Precinct, Nebraska. He owned one farm of 1,185 acres, part of Maple Grove Precinct, and a second farm that contained 685 acres.
  d. September 16, 1921
    Children of Thomas Jr. and Barbara Ellen Ball:
    [3]Hannah
        b. May 3, 1866, Todd Creek Precinct, Nebraska
      m. William C. Wilkinson
        d. April 1944
    [3]Hester
       b.July 10,1868, Indiana
      m. George Edwin Becker, Pawnee City, Nebraska
      b.November 9, 1863, California
      d.May 18, 1939

[3]Ira T.
   b. March 18, 1874, Red Cloud, Nebraska
   m. Nellie Kaley, September 10, 1901
      b. September 11, 1902
         One child: Raymond
   d. Friday, April 3, 1903, Elk Creek, Nebraska

[3]Nina Ellen
   b. December 10, 1877, Elk Creek, Nebraska
   m. Frank George Sevick, 1903, Omaha, Nebraska
      b. January 15, 1881, Czechoslovakia
   d. September 27, 1961

[3]Idella (Della)
   b. 1878, Nebraska
   m. John F. Cramblet
      b. about 1876, Illinois
   d. 1958, Elk Creek, Nebraska

[3]Daisy Margaret
   b. June 6, 1880
   m. Fred E. Bodie

[2]**Hester Malvena S.**
  b. October 17, 1838, Parke, Henry County, Indiana
  m. Henry G. Gault, December 1855
  d. September 14, 1931
  Children of Hester and Henry:
  [3]James R.
  [3]Deborah
  [3]Mary J.
  [3]Harry
  [3]William T.
     (In addition, there were three more children who died. One of them, John, served in the Civil War, October 11, 1862, 18th Infantry, Company F. —*History of Appanoose County*, page 409.)

[2]**Female Twins**
  b. August 7, 1840, Lee County, Illinois
  d. August 7, 1840, Lee County, Illinois

²**William John** (last child born of Mary Jane and Thomas)
- b. December 7, 1842, Lee County, Illinois
- m. Mary Ellen Kennedy from Silver Lake, Kansas, July 27, 1867
    They were married in Pawnee City, Nebraska.
- f. Presbyterian
- d. June 19, 1899, Oklahoma City, Oklahoma Territory
- b. Fairlawn Cemetery, Oklahoma City

    William John served as a private with Company D, 43rd Missouri Volunteer Infantry, a pro-Union regiment. He enlisted at St. Joe, Missouri, September 3, 1864. He was injured and admitted to Jefferson Barracks Post Hospital, St. Louis, Missouri, November 4, 1864, and was released November 27, 1864. Hospital #1006. He was discharged from the service on June 13, 1865, at Burton Barracks, Missouri.

Children of William John and Mary Ellen Kennedy McClure:

³Guy Vincent
- b. December 12, 1877, Silver Lake, Kansas
- m. Bernice McAdam, February 18, 1901, Oklahoma City, Oklahoma, Book 5, Page 92

    Bernice was born in Missouri, her father or brother was J.H. McAdams. Marriage license states that Guy's residence is Mexico City. During that time he was the chief Civil Engineer for the first Mexican railroad.
- b. June 26, 1851, Chattanooga, Tennessee
- d. October 23, 1918
- b. Fairlawn Cemetery, Oklahoma City, Oklahoma
- f. Presbyterian
- d. October 23, 1918
- b. Fairlawn Cemetery, Oklahoma City, Oklahoma

³David Victor
- b. December 10, 1879, Atoka, Indian Territory
- m. Grace Anna Jones, Cincinnati, Ohio
- f. Presbyterian
- d. December 11, 1944
- b. Fairlawn Cemetery, Oklahoma City, Oklahoma

    Children of David and Grace:

    ⁴William John McClure
    - b. July 6, 1907, Covington, Kentucky

   m. Chrystel McClure, January 3, 1943, Oklahoma City, Oklahoma
   (maiden name: McClure; no relation)
   father: Hugh Brown McClure
   mother: Mary Alice Bishop
  f. Presbyterian
  d. February 10, 1970, Aransas Pass, Texas
  b. Fairlawn Cemetery, Oklahoma City, Oklahoma

³Veta Ellean
 b. March 27, 1881, Liberty Hill, Indian Territory
 m. 1903, March 11, Isaac T. Jones, Oklahoma City
 m. 1904, March 2, 1904, Leon Roscoe Partridge
  d. 1908, October, New Hampshire
 m. 1910, E. R. Carhart
 m. 1915, R. M. Smyth
 m. 1918, John Harold Muncaster
 m. 1921, George Myers Church
 m. January 25, 1933, George Scott Findlay, Southampton, England
 f. Presbyterian
 d. August 23, 1963, Oklahoma City, Oklahoma
 b. Fairlawn Cemetery, Oklahoma City, Oklahoma

  ⁴Veta Ann McClure Meals
   b. March 10, 1912
   m. Robert Wolcott Meals, 1933
   f. Presbyterian
   d. March 25, 1945
   b. Memorial Park Cemetery, Edmond, Oklahoma

  ⁴Guy Victor McClure
   b. January 15, 1927
   m. Thamar Perkins
   f. Presbyterian
   d. July 18, 1961
   b. Memorial Park Cemetery, Edmond, Oklahoma

²**Ada** (only child of Thomas McClure Sr. and Nancy Bailey McClure)
 b. February 1857, Sterling Whiteside County, Illinois
 m. Joseph T. Martin, September 21, 1879, Nebraska
 d. February 23, 1907

Thomas McClure's Timeline

1605   1605-1697 Scots/Irish plantations presented to James I, who had been King VI of Scotland before becoming King of England

1640   More than 100,000 Scottish Presbyterians settled in Ulster, Ireland

1711   Thomas' grandfather, Thomas McClure born

1727   Thomas' grandmother, Anne Swan born

1752   Thomas' mother, Mary Ervale born

1763   Thomas' father, Hugh McClure, born in County Antrim, North Ireland

1796   Thomas McClure born in Crumlin, County Antrim, North Ireland

1798   Mary Jane Young born in Crumlin, County Antrim, North Ireland

1800   I have a copy of the Ulster *County Gazette*, dated Saturday, January 4, 1800, published at Kingston, Ulster County, by Samuel Freer & Son. It appears to be kept for sentimental reasons. I could not find any names or persons in our ancestry. The front-page covers the war in Zurich, mentions battles and Bonaparte. The two inside pages of the four-page newspaper cover the death of General George Washington in great detail—even his pallbearers are named. The fourth page is mostly about land, acreages for sale, the possibility of trades of vegetables/fruits for wheat. One posting told of a wench for sale, another of a red bull that had wondered.

1819   [1]Thomas McClure and [1]Mary Jane Young married, December 26, 1819

1825   The Erie Canal opened

1838   Crumlin Presbyterian Church established by 14 families
Listed on church roles:
Thomas McClure, Esq. J.P. Belmont (a township?)
The Misses McClure
Mrs. McClure
Mr. S. McClure

1825 [1]Thomas and [1]Mary Jane
[2]Jane (age 3) and [2]Mariana (Mary Ann) (age 1) McClure
Departed Belfast, Ireland, December 1824 aboard the brig *Florida*.
They landed in Philadelphia, Pennsylvania, July 20, 1825.
They traveled steerage with a passenger list of one hundred eleven souls. They are listed on page 66 of the ship's manifest. *[Mica 333/1/37: Microfilmed by courtesy of The National Archives, Washington, U.S.A. and Public Record Office Belfast, N. Ireland]*

Name:	**Thomas McClure**
Arrival Date:	20 Jul 1825
Age:	24
Port of Arrival:	Philadelphia
Port of Departure:	Belfast, Ireland
Place of Origin:	Ireland
Ship Name:	Florida
Family Number:	194752
National Archives' Series Number:	425
Microfilm Number:	37

Source Information:
Ancestry.com. *Philadelphia, 1800-1850 Passenger and Immigration Lists* [database on-line]. Provo, UT, USA: Ancestry.com Operations Inc, 2003.
Original data: Philadelphia, Pennsylvania. *Passenger Lists of Vessels Arriving at Philadelphia, Pennsylvania, 1800-1882*. Washington, D.C.: National Archives and Records Administration. Micropublication M425, rolls # 1-71.

Description:
This data set contains alphabetical listings of approximately 180,000 individuals who arrived at Philadelphia, Pennsylvania, U.S.A. from foreign ports between 1800 and 1850. The following information may be found in this database: name, gender, birthplace, age, occupation, country of origin, port of departure, port of arrival, date of arrival, destination, ship name, and source information. Learn more...

Illustration 4. Passenger and immigration list

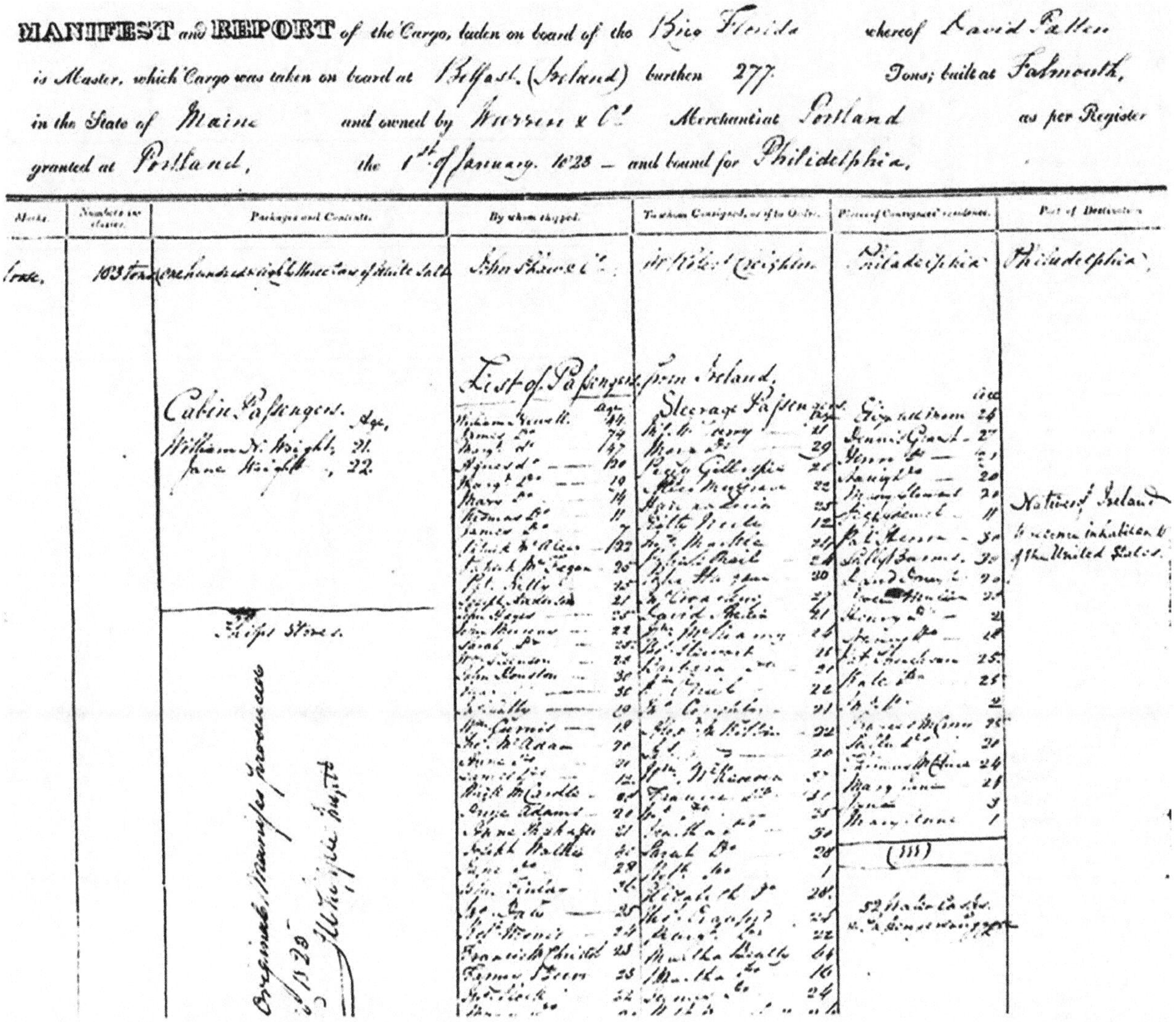
MANIFEST and REPORT of the Cargo, laden on board of the Brig Florida whereof David Patten is Master, which Cargo was taken on board at Belfast (Ireland) burthen 277 Tons; built at Falmouth, in the State of Maine and owned by Warren & Co. Merchants at Portland as per Register granted at Portland, the 1st of January 1823 – and bound for Philidelphia.

Marks	Numbers or Names	Packages and Contents	By whom shipped	To whom Consigned, or if to Order	Place of Consignees' residence	Port of Destination
[illegible]	103 Tons	[illegible] of White Salt	John Shaw & Co.	[illegible]	Philadelphia	Philadelphia

List of Passengers from Ireland.

Cabin Passengers. Age.
William N. Wright 21
Jane Wright 22

Steerage Passengers

Natives of Ireland to become inhabitants of the United States.

Illustration 5. Manifest of brig *Florida*

```
Barbara Stewart        25
Wm. Oneil              22
Jno. Coushly           21
Alexr. McKibbin        22
Jas. Brady             20
Wm. McKeown            37
Francis McKeown        30
Jno. McKeowen          35
Martha McKeown         30
Sarah McKeown          28
Robt. McKeown           1
Elizabeth McKeown      28
Thos. Crawford         24
Margt. Crawford        22
Martha Beatty          64
Martha Beatty          16
James Beatty           24
Robt. Marshall         24
Jno. Hanlon            18
Jno. Taggart           29
Catherine Taggart      22
Patrick Taggart 6 months
Hugh McKeown           30
Mary McKeown           21
Anne Quinn             22
Bernard Mullen         27
Patrick Mullen         25
Hugh Moore             22
Jane Moore             26
Elizabeth Moore        24
Dennis Grant           27
Henry Grant            29
[Naughton?]
[Grant?]               20
Mary Stewart           20    Natives of Ireland
Peggy [Sewel]          11
Pat. Herron            30    to become inhabitants
Sally Barnes           30    of the United States
David Donagh           20
Owen [Henllen?]        28
Henry [Henllen?]        2
Fanny [Henllen?]       28
Pat. Lanpower          25
Kate Lanpower          25
Jno. Lanpower           2
Francis McGrory        25
Sally McGrory          20
✓ Thomas    McClure    24
✓ Mary Jane McClure    24
✓ Jane      McClure     3
✓ Mary Anne McClure     1

     (111)

52 Water Casks
& Passengers Luggage

David Patten

I Certify this to be the Original Manifest produced
to me this 20th of July 1825
          J Whipple Insptr [Inspector?]
```

Illustration 6. Certified copy of brig *Florida's* Manifest

Family Group Record — FamilySearch™ Ancestral File v4.19

Husband's Name
Thomas MC CLURE (AFN:C308-0N)   Pedigree
Born: Abt. 1796   Place: <Crumlin, Antrim, Ireland>
Father: D- Oct 12, 1878 Table Rock, Pawnee, Neb.
Mother:

Wife's Name
Mary Jane YOUNG (AFN:C308-1T)   Pedigree
Born: Abt. 1800   Place: <Crumlin, Antrim, Ireland>
Father: m 26 Dec 1819
Mother:

Children
1. Sex Name
   M Hugh MC CLURE (AFN:34QM-C5)   Pedigree
   Born: 24 May 1822   Place: Crumlin, Antrim, Ireland
   Died: Feb 1908   Place: Ballinderry, Antrim, Ireland

An official Web site of The Church of Jesus Christ of Latter-day Saints
© 2008 Intellectual Reserve, Inc. All rights reserved.

Ref# 160120
Film# 442571

Parish = Camlin   Township = Crumlin   County = Antrim

Presbyterian Marriage Registers contain name of couple and the name of bride's father. P. Church required notice of marriage be given to the Kirk Session. So a record might be found in the Session Minute Book. Or check indexes to Marriage License Bonds (1629-1864). These indexes are deposited in National Archives in Dublin. Also check Registrar General Office in Dublin which are indexed by both bride & grooms name.

Burial Records: many Presbyterians were buried in Church of Ireland Cemeteries. Therefore check burial records of local Established Church. Civil registration didn't begin til 1864 - (no help)

REPRODUCED COURTESY OF THE CHURCH OF JESUS CHRIST OF LATTER-DAY SAINTS

Illustration 7. Family record

Family Group Record — Page 1 of 3

FamilySearch™ International Genealogical Index v5.0 — North America

Family Group Record
Search Results | Download

Husband
Thomas McClure
- Birth: 12 AUG 1796 Crumlin, Antrim, Ireland
- Christening:
- Marriage: 26 DEC 1819
- Death: 12 OCT 1878 Tablerock, Pawnee, Nebraska
- Burial:

Wife
Mary Jane Young
- Birth: 06 SEP 1798 Crumlin, Antrim, Ireland
- Christening:
- Marriage: 26 DEC 1819
- Death: 02 JUN 1848 Rock River, , Lee, Illinois
- Burial:

Children

1. Jane McClure — Female
   - Birth: 28 SEP 1820 Crumlin, Antrim, Ireland
   - Christening:
   - Death: 04 OCT 1898
   - Burial:

2. Hugh McClure — Male
   - Birth: 24 MAY 1822 Crumlin, Antrim, Ireland
   - Christening:
   - Death: FEB 1908
   - Burial:

3. Mariana McClure — Female
   - Birth: 24 JAN 1824 Crumlin, Antrim, Ireland
   - Christening:
   - Death:
   - Burial:

4. John Wilson McClure — Male
   - Birth: 28 FEB 1826 , Monroe, Pennsylvania
   - Christening:
   - Death: 05 JUL 1827
   - Burial:

5. James Belford McClure — Male

Group Record — Page 2 of 3

- Birth: 29 FEB 1828 , Monroe, Pennsylvania
- Christening:
- Death: 13 DEC 1892
- Burial:

6. Sophie Louise McClure — Female
   - Birth: 10 DEC 1830 Huron, Erie, Ohio
   - Christening:
   - Death: 27 NOV 1873
   - Burial:

7. Daniel Henry McClure — Male
   - Birth: 08 MAR 1833 Huron, Erie, Ohio
   - Christening:
   - Death: 1905
   - Burial:

8. Thomas McClure — Male
   - Birth: 01 NOV 1835 Huron, Erie, Ohio
   - Christening:
   - Death: 11 OCT 1906
   - Burial:

9. Hester Malvena McClure — Female
   - Birth: 17 OCT 1837 , Parke, Indiana
   - Christening:
   - Death: 14 SEP 1931
   - Burial:

10. McClure — Female
    - Birth: 07 AUG 1840 , Lee, Illinois
    - Christening:
    - Death: 07 AUG 1840
    - Burial:

11. McClure — Female
    - Birth: 07 AUG 1840 , Lee, Illinois
    - Christening:
    - Death: 07 AUG 1840
    - Burial:

12. William John McClure — Male
    - Birth: 07 DEC 1842 , Lee, Illinois
    - Christening:
    - Death:
    - Burial:

© 1999-2002 by Intellectual Reserve, Inc. All rights reserved. English approval: 3/1999

REPRODUCED COURTESY OF THE CHURCH OF JESUS CHRIST OF LATTER-DAY SAINTS

Illustration 8. Expanded family record

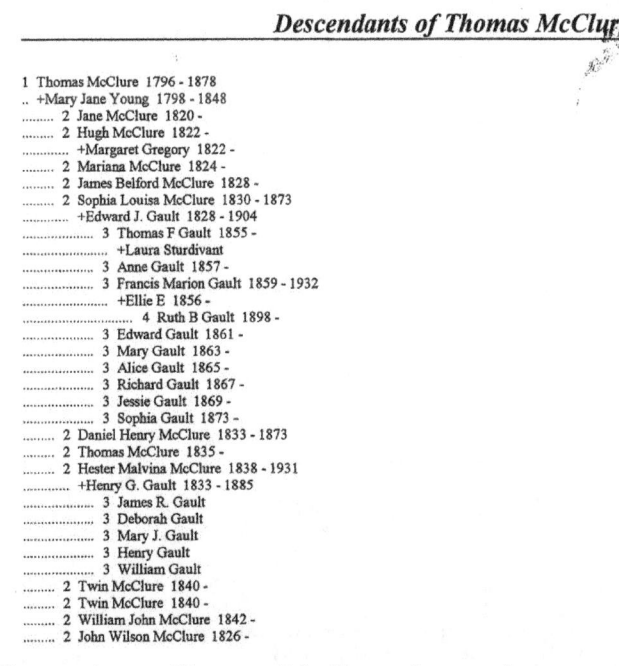

Descendants of Thomas McClure

```
1 Thomas McClure  1796 - 1878
.. +Mary Jane Young  1798 - 1848
........ 2 Jane McClure  1820 -
........ 2 Hugh McClure  1822 -
............ +Margaret Gregory  1822 -
........ 2 Mariana McClure  1824 -
........ 2 James Belford McClure  1828 -
........ 2 Sophia Louisa McClure  1830 - 1873
............ +Edward J. Gault  1828 - 1904
................ 3 Thomas F Gault  1855 -
.................... +Laura Sturdivant
................ 3 Anne Gault  1857 -
................ 3 Francis Marion Gault  1859 - 1932
.................... +Ellie E  1856 -
........................ 4 Ruth B Gault  1898 -
................ 3 Edward Gault  1861 -
................ 3 Mary Gault  1863 -
................ 3 Alice Gault  1865 -
................ 3 Richard Gault  1867 -
................ 3 Jessie Gault  1869 -
................ 3 Sophia Gault  1873 -
........ 2 Daniel Henry McClure  1833 - 1873
........ 2 Thomas McClure  1835 -
........ 2 Hester Malvina McClure  1838 - 1931
............ +Henry G. Gault  1833 - 1885
................ 3 James R. Gault
................ 3 Deborah Gault
................ 3 Mary J. Gault
................ 3 Henry Gault
................ 3 William Gault
........ 2 Twin McClure  1840 -
........ 2 Twin McClure  1840 -
........ 2 William John McClure  1842 -
........ 2 John Wilson McClure  1826 -
```

Illustration 9. Thomas McClure descendants

```
International Genealogical Index (TM) - 1993 Edition - Version 3.02              British Isle
                              INDIVIDUAL RECORD
   MAY 1994                                                                      Pa

NAME: MCCLURE, Jane

SEX:  F

EVENT: Birth
       28 Sep 1820
       Crumlin, Antrim, Ireland
FATHER: Thomas MCCLURE              C308-ON
MOTHER: Mary Jane YOUNG
```

REPRODUCED COURTESY OF THE CHURCH OF JESUS CHRIST OF LATTER-DAY SAINTS

Illustration 10. Birth record of Jane McClure

```
Ancestral File (TM) - ver 4.13         FAMILY GROUP RECORD         19 JUN 1995      Page 1

HUSBAND: Hugh MC CLURE (AFN:34QM-C5)

BORN: 24 May 1822      PLACE: Crumlin, Antrim, Ireland          LDS ORDINANCE DATA
CHR.:                  PLACE:                                   B:  4 Sep 1917
DIED: Feb 1908         PLACE: Ballinderry, Antrim, Ireland      E:  6 Sep 1917
BUR.:                  PLACE:                                   SP:
MAR.: 1842             PLACE:                                   SS: 6 Sep 1917 SL
FATHER: Thomas MC CLURE (AFN:C308-ON)
MOTHER: Mary Jane YOUNG (AFN:C308-1T)
OTHER WIVES: Jesse FERGUSON (AFN:C308-21) and 1 Others

WIFE: Margaret GREGORY (AFN:34QM-D8)

BORN: Jan 1822         PLACE: Glenavy, Antrim, Ireland
CHR.:                  PLACE:                                   B:  4 Sep 1917
DIED: 24 Oct 1868      PLACE: Crumlin, Antrim, Ireland          E:  6 Sep 1917
BUR.:                  PLACE:                                   SP:
FATHER: William GREGORY (AFN:C308-4C)
MOTHER: (Miss) AGNENT (AFN:C308-5J)
OTHER HUSBANDS:

Sex CHILDREN

1. NAME: Eliza Ann MC CLURE (AFN:34QM-J1)
---- BORN: 1843        PLACE: Crumlin, Antrim, Ire.             B:  4 Sep 1917
 F   CHR.:             PLACE:                                   E:  6 Sep 1917
     DIED: 20 Oct 1872 PLACE:                                   SP: 6 Sep 1917 SL
     BUR.:             PLACE:
     SPOUSE:
     MAR.:             PLACE:                                   SS:

2. NAME: William MC CLURE (AFN:34QM-K6)
---- BORN: 1845        PLACE: Crumlin, Antrim, Ire.             B:  7 Jun 1950
 M   CHR.:             PLACE:                                   E: 17 Jul 1951
     DIED:             PLACE:                                   SP: 26 Mar 1953 IF
     BUR.:             PLACE:
     SPOUSE:
     MAR.:             PLACE:                                   SS:

3. NAME: Margaret Agnes MC CLURE (AFN:34QM-LC)
---- BORN: 1846        PLACE: Crumlin, Antrim, Ire.             B:  4 Sep 1917
 F   CHR.:             PLACE:                                   E:  6 Sep 1917
     DIED: 3 Feb 1866  PLACE:                                   SP: 6 Sep 1917 SL
     BUR.:             PLACE:
     SPOUSE:
     MAR.:             PLACE:                                   SS:

4. NAME: Thomas MC CLURE (AFN:34QM-MJ)
---- BORN: 1849        PLACE: Crumlin, Antrim, Ire.             B:  4 Sep 1917
 M   CHR.:             PLACE:                                   E:  6 Sep 1917
     DIED: 6 Jun 1903  PLACE:                                   SP: 6 Sep 1917 SL
     BUR.:             PLACE:
     SPOUSE:
     MAR.:             PLACE:                                   SS:

Codes:  AFN=Ancestral File Number   B=Baptized   E=Endowed   SS=Sealed to Spouse   SP=Sealed to Parents
```

REPRODUCED COURTESY OF THE CHURCH OF JESUS CHRIST OF LATTER-DAY SAINTS

Illustration 11. Family group record

```
                        Ancestral File 4.15              22 JAN 1996
    Esc=Exit  F1=Help  F2=Print/copy  F3=Edit  F4=Search  F9=Sources  F10=Go-back
    ZDDDDDDDDDDDDDDDD? ZDDDDDDDDDDDDDDDD? ZDDDDDDDDDDDDDDDD? ZDDDDDDDDDDDDDDDD?
    3  F5=Index      3 3  F6=Family     3 3  F7=Pedigree   3 3  F8=Descendancy  3
    ZC "DDDDDDDDDDDDDDADADDDDDDDDDDDDDDDAY       Chart     @DADDDDDDDDDDDDDDDDAD?
    3  _ghlight name or arrow (-IMMMMMMMMMMMMMMMMMMMMMMMMMMMMMMMMMMMMMMMMMMMMMM;
    3  press Enter for more.     :              CHILDREN                        :
    3                           _T M:   Use     and press Enter to select child. :
    3                       3    :    ZDBDDDDDDDDDDDDDDDDDDDDDDDDDDDDDDDDDDDDD? :
    3        _Hugh MC CLURE__3  3 3    1. Eliza Ann MC CLURE        1843  3  :
    3        3                    :   CD4   2. William MC CLURE           1845  3  :
    3        3                3_Mar: 3 3    3. Margaret Agnes MC CLURE    1846  3  :
    3        3                    :  3 3    4. Thomas MC CLURE            1849  3  :
    3        3                    :  3 3-   5. John MC CLURE              1850  3  :
    3    Thomas MC CLURE           :  3 3    6. Robert Gregory MC CLURE   1852  3  :
    3        3 Sp:                 :  3 3-   7. Edward Henry MC CLURE     1854  3  :
    3        3                     :  3 3    8. James Belford MC CLURE    1856  3  :
    3        3                  _W G: 3 3-   9. Edmund Harris MC CLURE    1859  3  :
    3        3                3    :   CD4                                       3  :
    3        3_M GREGORY_____3   3 3                                            3  :
    3                           3    :  @DADDDDDDDDDDDDDDDDDDDDDDDDDDDDDDDDDDDDDY :
    3                           3_(Mi:  - Appears as a parent      IMMMMMMMMMMMM; :
    3  IMMMMMMMMMMMMMMM;   IMMMMMMMM:     in another family.         : Esc=Cancel : :
    3  : Enter=Details : : F11=Chi:                                   HMMMMMMMMMM< :
    @DHMMMMMMMMMMMMMMM< DHMMMMMMMMMMMMMMMMMMMMMMMMMMMMMMMMMMMMMMMMMMMMMMMMMMMMMMMM<

    Copyright (c) 1987, August 1993 by The Church of Jesus Christ of Latter-day
    Saints.  All Rights Reserved.
```

REPRODUCED COURTESY OF THE CHURCH OF JESUS CHRIST OF LATTER-DAY SAINTS

Illustration 12. Ancestral file

```
International Genealogical Index (TM) - 1993 Edition - Version 3.02         British Isles

                              INDIVIDUAL RECORD

    MAY 1994                                                               Page 1
    =========================================================================
    NAME: MCCLURE, Mariana
    -------------------------------------------------------------------------
    SEX: F

    EVENT: Birth
           24 Jan 1824
           Crumlin, Antrim, Ireland
    FATHER: Thomas MCCLURE
    MOTHER: Mary Jane YOUNG
    -------------------------------------------------------------------------
```

REPRODUCED COURTESY OF THE CHURCH OF JESUS CHRIST OF LATTER-DAY SAINTS

Illustration 13. Individual birth record of Mariana McClure

1825   July 20 arrived in Philadelphia, Pennsylvania

1826   [2]John Wilson McClure
       b. July 8/28, 1826, Philadelphia, Pennsylvania
       d. July 5, 1827

1828   [2]James Bedford born in Monroe, Pennsylvania

1830   [2]Sophia Louise born in Huron, Erie, Ohio

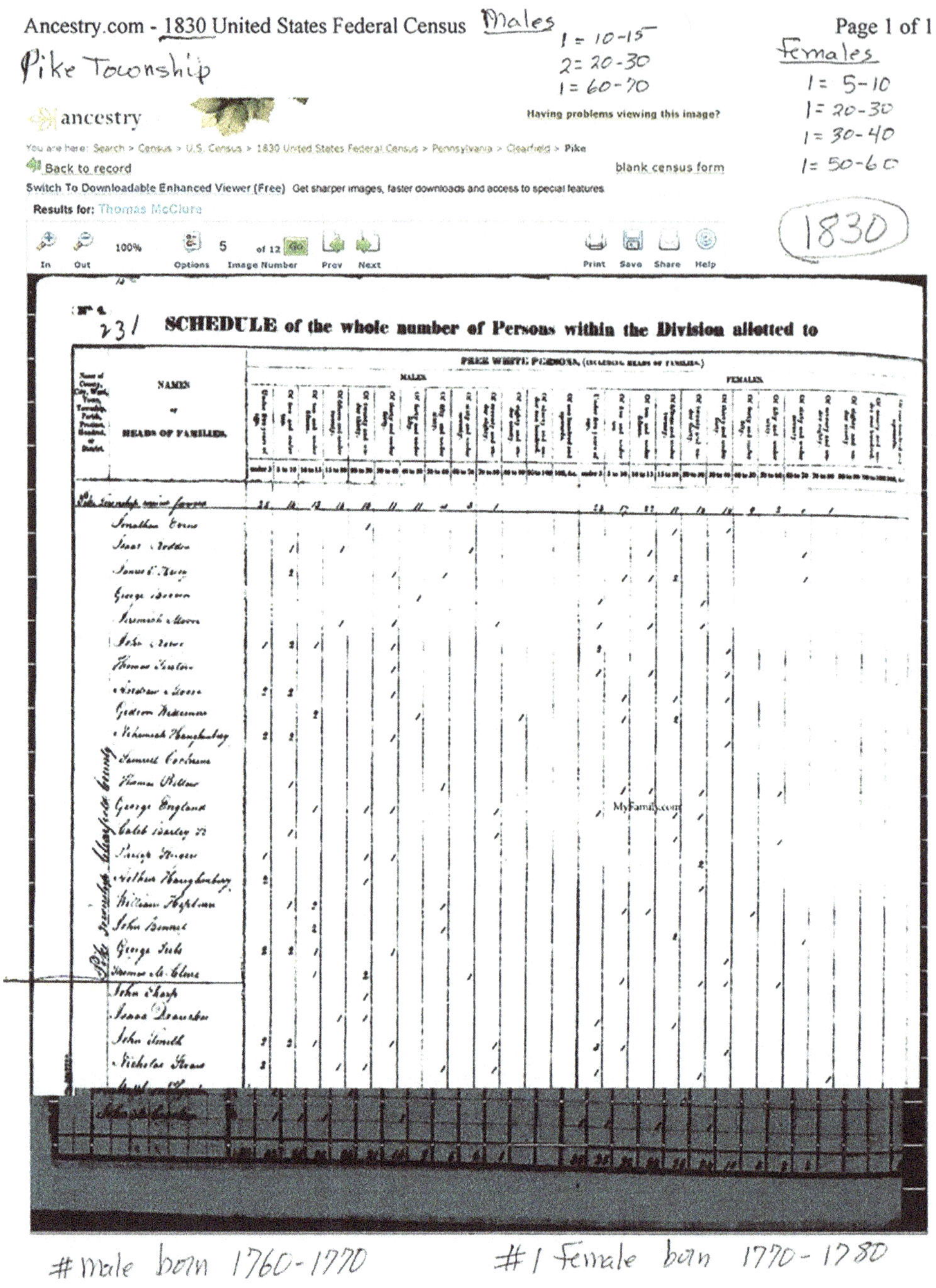

Illustration 14. U.S. 1830 Census

1833 ²Daniel Henry born in Huron, Erie, Ohio

1835 ²Thomas Jr. born in Huron, Erie, Ohio
Moved to Darke County, Ohio, November 1, 1835

1837 ²Hester Malvena S. born in Parke, Indiana
Moved to Henry County, Indiana

1838 Crumlin Presbyterian church was established when 14 families formed a congregation. Church records list Thomas McClure, Esq.; The Misses McClure; Mrs. McClure; Mr. S. McClure.

SALE OF WORK IN CRUMLIN, ON FRIDAY AND SATURDAY LAST
[Glenavy History: copy of newspaper article]

The Market House in Crumlin was the scene of a sale of work, the undertaking being set of foot by the ladies connected with the local Presbyterian Church, probably one of the oldest in connection with the General Assembly. For some past it has been patent to the members of the congregation that the building in which they worship was badly in need of renovation, and they were also aware of the fact that a debt remained on the edifice. A happy idea was broached and it was to the effect that the deft fingers and artistic taste should be utilized in preparing a number of useful and ornamental articles and offering them for sale at a fancy fair. The matter was taken up con amore and (unreadable) commenced their praiseworthy undertaking than (unreadable) and was freely offered. Ladies connected with other churches volunteered their assistance, and this was forthcoming, but only in the form.Of work, but also in money contributions. That was as it should be, and it need not be said that the united effort was crowned with gratifying success. The sympathy and help extended to the enterprise by outsiders indicate the respect felt for the Rev. A. C. Canning, the aged pastor the affections of his own church, but who has been deservedly esteemed by people of all denominations. For more than half a century he laboured in the word and doctrine, and he had the satisfaction of seeing the fifteen families who attended his ministrations augmented to ninety—a congregation thoroughly united and loyal to the pastor, who had gone in and out amongst them for fifty years. This fealty was strikingly illustrated a little more than twelve months ago when the congregation gave a unanimous call to the Rev. J. A. Canning, L.L.B., to be his father's assistant in the pastorate of the congregation, and who is likely to be as much beloved in the future as Mr. Canning, senior, has been in the past. The Market-House was suitably decorated for the occasion, which has been looked forward to with so much interest. Much time was devoted to decorating the stalls and when the doors were thrown open for the admission of the public, the room presented a very attractive appearance. At one o'clock the sale was opened by the Rev. Arthur H. Pakenham, J.P, Langford Lodge, who is deservedly popular with all creeds and classes in the neighbourhood of his ancestral home. Amongst those present during the day were – Rev. Charles Donaldson, Hillsborough; Rev. T.H. Hall, Rev. Thomas Lyle,

Muckamore; Dr. Mussen, Glenavy; Dr. Dunlop, Edenderry; Dr.Alister; Messrs.', Joseph English, W. Mountgarrett, Jonathan Peel, W.A. McKee, D. Jonston, J. Whitield, and T. McConnell. The 100th psalm having been sung. Rev. Mr. West engaged in prayer.

A "Young" buried in the cemetery of Billy Parish Church in N. Antrim

1842 [2]William John born in Lee County, Illinois , December 7, 1842

1843 May 1. Thomas McClure purchased eighty acres in Dixon, Lee County: Certificate #18927 or #18937.

1846 Elias Howe of Massachusetts granted a patent for the world's first practical sewing machine

1848 June 2. Death of Mary Jane Young McClure, Rock River, Lee County, Illinois No record exists of her burial.

1851 Isaac Singer granted Patent No. 8,294 on August 12, 1851 for a commercial sewing machine

1850 U.S. Census: Palmyra Township, Lee County, Illinois
Thomas 52 yr. old	b. Ireland
Mary Ann 23 yr. old	b. Ireland (sometimes spelled Mariane)
Sophiah 19 yr. old	b. Ohio 1831
Daniel H. 16 yr. old	b. Ohio 1833
Thomas 15 yr. old	b. Ohio November 1, 1835, Hudson Cty.
Hester S. 11 yr. old	b. Indiana 1838/9?
William John 7 yr. old	b. Illinois 1843 Dixon, Lee County

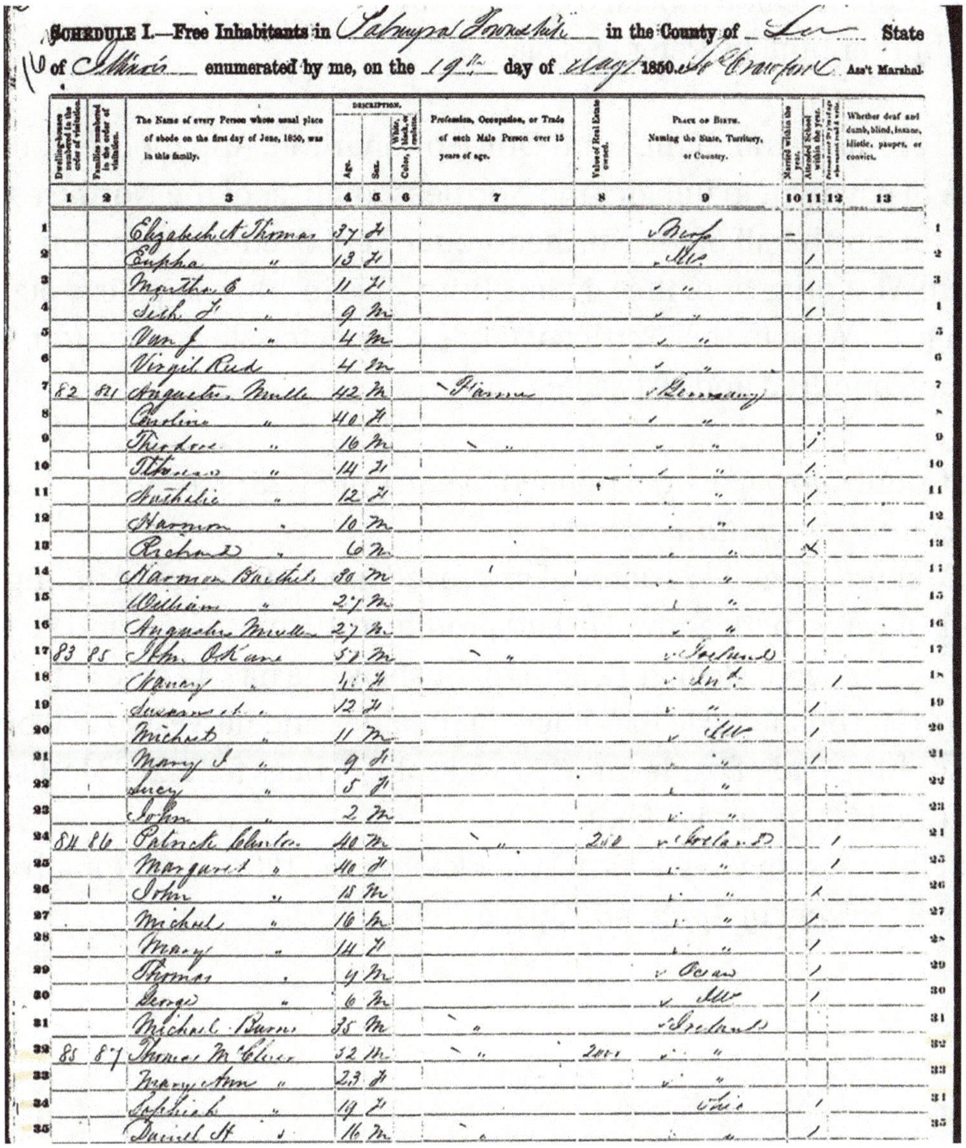

SCHEDULE I.—Free Inhabitants in Palmyra Township in the County of Lee State of Illinois enumerated by me, on the 19th day of Augt 1850. [illegible] Crawford Ass't Marshal.

Dwelling-houses numbered in the order of visitation.	Families numbered in the order of visitation.	The Name of every Person whose usual place of abode on the first day of June, 1850, was in this family.	Age.	Sex.	Color.	Profession, Occupation, or Trade of each Male Person over 15 years of age.	Value of Real Estate owned.	Place of Birth. Naming the State, Territory, or Country.	Married within the year.	Attended School within the year.	Persons over 20 y'rs of age who cannot read & write.	Whether deaf and dumb, blind, insane, idiotic, pauper, or convict.
1	2	3	4	5	6	7	8	9	10	11	12	13
		Elizabeth A Thomas	37	F				Penn				
		Euphia "	13	F				Ill		/		
		Martha E "	11	F				"		/		
		Seth F "	9	M				"		/		
		Van J "	4	M				"				
		Virgil Reed	4	M				"				
82	84	Augustus Muller	42	M		Farmer		Germany				
		Caroline "	40	F				"				
		Theodore "	16	M		"		"		/		
		Ottilia "	14	F				"		/		
		Nathalie "	12	F				"		/		
		Harmon "	10	M				"		/		
		Richard "	6	M				"		X		
		Harmon Barthel	30	M				"				
		William "	27	M				"				
		Augustus Muller	27	M				"				
83	85	John O'Kane	51	M		"		Ireland				
		Nancy "	4[illegible]	F				Ind			/	
		Susan "	12	F				"		/		
		Michael "	11	M				Ill		/		
		Mary J "	9	F				"		/		
		Lucy "	5	F				"				
		John "	2	M				"				
84	86	Patrick Clinton	40	M		"	200	Ireland			/	
		Margaret "	40	F				"			/	
		John "	18	M				"		/		
		Michael "	16	M				"		/		
		Mary "	14	F				"		/		
		Thomas "	9	M				Ocean		/		
		George "	6	M				Ill		/		
		Michael Burns	35	M		"		Ireland				
85	87	Thomas McClure	52	M		"	2000	"				
		Mary Ann "	23	F				"				
		Sophiah "	19	F				Ohio		/		
		Daniel H "	16	M		"		"		/		

Illustration 15. 1850 U. S. Census: Palmyra Township, Lee County, Illinois

[1]Thomas	52 yr. old	b. Ireland	
[2]Mary Ann	23 yr. old	b. Ireland	
(sometimes spelled Mariane)			
[2]Sophiah	19 yr. old	b. Ohio	1831
[2]Daniel H.	16 yr. old	b. Ohio	1833
[2]Thomas	15 yr. old	b. Ohio	November 1, 1835, Hudson Cty.
[2]Hester S.	11 yr. old	b. Indiana	1838/9?
[2]William John	7 yr. old	b. Illinois	1843 Dixon, Lee County

1853 December 1,1855: Thomas McClure purchased one hundred and sixty acres in Chariton, Appanoose County, Iowa Legal Certificate #1411.

1854 Nebraska Territory became official
   The Bunsen burner built by Peter Desaga

1855 Certificate #1411 Registrar of the Land Office of Chariton, Appanoose County, Iowa. Notice of payment in full for: The Northeast quarter of the Northwest quarter and the north half of the Northeast quarter of Section Thirty-four and the NorthWest quarter of the Section Thirty-five in Township Sixty eight North of range (?) West in the District of lands subject to sale at Chariton, Iowa containing one hundred and sixty acres

   Appanoose County, Iowa, district opened to entry at $1.25/acre
   Appanoose county agricultural report:
   Thomas McLure owned 171 acres of improved land, 307 acres of unimproved land, and 15 acres in meadow. He had produced 10 tons of hay and 10 bushels of grass seed. He had 12 acres of bushels. He had 44 acres of corn and harvested 1500 bushels. He had 1 acre of potatoes and harvested 200 bushels. He also sold 10 head of cattle for $350 and sold 24 hogs for $200. He also manufactured 300 pounds of butter.
   Record of John serving in the Civil War, October 11, 1861 - 18th Infantry, Company F (*History of Appanoose*, page 409)

Illustration 16. Thomas McClure

1856 Iowa State Census: Pleasant Township, Cincinnati, Appanoose County, Iowa
[1]Thomas	56 yr. old	b. Ireland	3 yr. in Iowa
[1]M.	49 yr. old	b. Ireland	3 yr. in Iowa
[2]D.H.	23 yr. old	b. Ohio	3 yr. in Iowa
[2]Thomas. Jr.	20 yr. old	b. Illinois	3 yr. in Iowa

1856 Iowa State Census shows M. McClure (49 yr. old) as wife of Thomas McClure Sr. I think this is a *typo*. The probable intent was to write N. McClure.

1858 The first of the seven Lincoln-Douglas debates held

1858 May, the family moves to Nebraska.

[2]Thomas McClure, farmer and stock raiser, Section 23, Elk Creek, P. O., was born and reared in Darke County, Ohio, and came to Nebraska in 1860 and has been actively identified with the agricultural and stock industries of this locality since. In 1860 he was married in Iowa to [2]Miss Ellen Ball, who was born in Ohio. They have a family of one son and five daughters; [3]Hanna F., [3]Hester E., [3]Ira T., [3]Mina, [3]Idella and [3]Daisy E.

Mr. McClure has been actively identified with the growth and development of the social life of his locality. (Thomas McClure, Jr—*History of the State of Nebraska*, page 1013)

[2]D.H. McClure of the firm of Young and McClure, grain and stock dealers Elk Creek, was born in Ohio and reared in Lee County, Illinois. In 1857 he came to Nebraska, where he has very successfully conducted since. In 1881 he entered upon the present business. In 1858 he married Ann V. Griffin who was born in Ohio. (Daniel Henry McClure—*History of the State of Nebraska*, page 1013)

Illustration 17. Extended family
 Front Row: (left to right) Hannah, Mina, Daisy
 Back Row: (left to right) Hester, Edwin, Becks, Will Wilkerson, Nina Ellen

1860 Nebraska Census lists Nancy to be the wife of Thomas McClure Sr. His first wife, Mary Jane Young died June 2, 1848, on the Rock River, Lee County, Illinois. It may have been in or near Dixon, Illinois. The exact location of Mary Jane's burial is unknown.

1860 U.S. Census of Table Rock, Nemaha County, Nebraska
[1]Thomas	b. 1798	62 yr. old	b. Ireland
[(1)]Nancy	b. 1814	46 yr. old	b. Ohio
[2]William	b. 1842	18 yr. old	b. Illinois
[2]Ada	b. 1857	3 yr. old	b. Illinois, February 27, 1857

(Ada married Joseph T. Martin, August 7, 1879; he died February 23, 1907.)

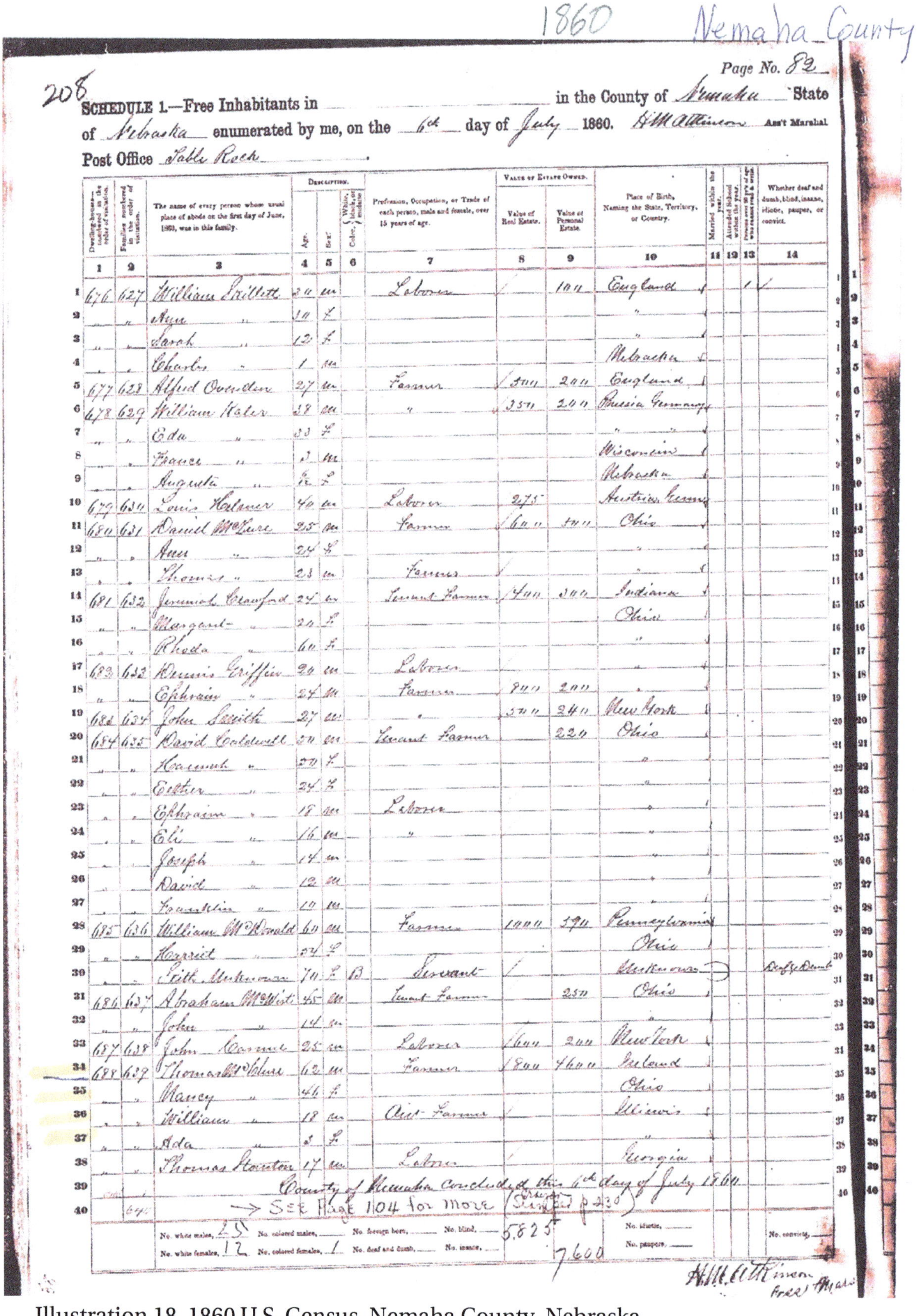

1860 Nemaha County

Page No. 82

208 SCHEDULE 1.—Free Inhabitants in ______ in the County of Nemaha State of Nebraska enumerated by me, on the 6th day of July 1860. H.W. Atkinson Ass't Marshal.

Post Office Table Rock

	Dwelling-houses—numbered in the order of visitation.	Families numbered in the order of visitation.	The name of every person whose usual place of abode on the first day of June, 1860, was in this family.	Age.	Sex.	Color, (White, black, or mulatto.)	Profession, Occupation, or Trade of each person, male and female, over 15 years of age.	Value of Real Estate.	Value of Personal Estate.	Place of Birth, Naming the State, Territory, or Country.	Married within the year.	Attended School within the year.	Persons over 20 y'rs of age who cannot read & write.	Whether deaf and dumb, blind, insane, idiotic, pauper, or convict.
	1	2	3	4	5	6	7	8	9	10	11	12	13	14
1	676	627	William Trillett	30	m		Laborer		100	England			1	
2	"	"	Ann "	30	f					"				
3	"	"	Sarah "	12	f					"				
4	"	"	Charles "	1	m					Nebraska				
5	677	628	Alfred Ovenden	27	m		Farmer	500	200	England				
6	678	629	William Haler	38	m		"	350	200	Prussia Germany				
7	"	"	Eda "	33	f					"				
8	"	"	France "	3	m					Wisconsin				
9	"	"	Augusta "	1/12	f					Nebraska				
10	679	630	Louis Halmer	40	m		Laborer	275		Austria Germ[illegible]				
11	680	631	Daniel McLure	25	m		Farmer	600	300	Ohio				
12	"	"	Ann "	24	f					"				
13	"	"	Thomas "	23	m		Farmer			"				
14	681	632	Jeremiah Crawford	24	m		Tenant Farmer	400	300	Indiana				
15	"	"	Margaret "	20	f					Ohio				
16	"	"	Rhoda "	60	f					"				
17	683	633	Dennis Griffin	20	m		Laborer			"				
18	"	"	Ephraim "	24	m		Farmer	800	200	"				
19	682	634	John Smith	27	m		"	500	200	New York				
20	684	635	David Caldwell	50	m		Tenant Farmer		220	Ohio				
21	"	"	Hannah "	50	f					"				
22	"	"	Esther "	24	f					"				
23	"	"	Ephraim "	18	m		Laborer			"				
24	"	"	Eli "	16	m		"			"				
25	"	"	Joseph "	14	m					"				
26	"	"	David "	12	m					"				
27	"	"	Franklin "	10	m					"				
28	685	636	William McDonald	60	m		Farmer	1000	590	Pennsylvania				
29	"	"	Harriet "	54	f					Ohio				
30	"	"	Faith Unknown	70	f	B	Servant			Unknown				Deaf & Dumb
31	686	637	Abraham McWhit[illegible]	45	m		Tenant Farmer		250	Ohio				
32	"	"	John "	14	m					"				
33	687	638	John Cannel	25	m		Laborer	600	200	New York				
34	688	639	Thomas McClure	62	m		Farmer	800	4600	Ireland				
35	"	"	Nancy "	41	f					Ohio				
36	"	"	William "	18	m		Ass't Farmer			Illinois				
37	"	"	Ada "	3	f					"				
38	"	"	Thomas Stanton	17	m		Laborer			Georgia				
39			County of Nemaha concluded this 6th day of July 1860											
40		640	→ See Page 104 for more (Stiffed p 230)											

No. white males, 25 No. colored males, ___ No. foreign born, ___ No. blind, ___ 5825

No. white females, 12 No. colored females, 1 No. deaf and dumb, ___ No. insane, ___ 7600

No. idiotic, ___ No. paupers, ___ No. convicts, ___

H.W. Atkinson Ass't Marshal

Illustration 18. 1860 U.S. Census, Nemaha County, Nebraska

1850-1860 CENSUS OF THE UNITED STATES

Year 1860
Date of Search 3-9-88
Legibility of Record: [X] Good [ ] Poor
[ ] Original Copy
[ ] Extract Copy
[X] Microfilm Copy
[ ] Printed Copy

(For those who use the Calendar Method of keeping research notes)
Search No. ___
Enclosure No. ___
Call No. ___

Notes: Nebraska settled 30 May 1854
Statehood 1-May-1867
Territory 12 yrs.

Place of Enumeration: Nemaha County NEMA C82 ASPINWAL

Page	Dwelling No.	Family No.	Names	Age	Sex	Color	Occupation, etc.	Value-Real Estate	Value-Personal Property	Birthplace	Married in yr.	School in year	Can't Read or Write	Enumeration Date	Remarks
82	688	631	Thomas McClure	62	M		Farmer	800	4,600	Ireland					
			Nancy McClure	46	F					Ohio					
			William McClure	15	M		(ow) Farmer			Illinois					
			Ada McClure	3	F					Illinois					
			Thomas Staunton	17	M		Laborer			Georgia					
			(See pg 104 for more)												

Illustration 19. 1860 U.S. Census, showing McClure family

1860 U.S. Census of Table Rock, Nemaha County, Nebraska
   [2]Daniel 25 yr. old b. Ohio (son of Thomas Sr., now married)
     m. Ann 24 yr. old b. Ohio
      Children:
   [2]Thomas 23 yr. old b. Ohio
   (son of Thomas Sr., now living with his brother Daniel)

1862 Homestead Act

1867 Nebraska statehood, May 1, 1867

1870 U.S. Census of Table Rock, Pawnee County, Nebraska
   [1]Thomas   70 yr. old   b. Ireland
   Julia D.   60 yr. old   b. New York (listed as housekeeper)
   [2]Ada   13 yr. old   b. Illinois

1870 U.S. Census of Benton Precinct, Nemaha County, Nebraska, Post Office, Brownville Enumeration date: 7 July, 1870, page 6
   ²Wm. McClure age 25, Farmer, Value of Real estate $500; Value of Personal Property $600 b. Illinois
   ²Ellen McClure age 19, Keeping House, b. Kansas
   Barney Cooper age 9, at home b. Michigan

Illustration 20. Thomas McClure at home in Nebraska

1873 Application patent for barbed wire

1873 November 27, death of Sophia

1875 February 1875. The death date of "Mother McClure" in either Table Rock or Pawnee City

1876 Mark Twain's *The Adventures of Tom Sawyer* published

1878 ¹Thomas McClure Sr. found dead on the banks of the Nemaha River at age 82 (within 6 to 8 months of 83 years old)

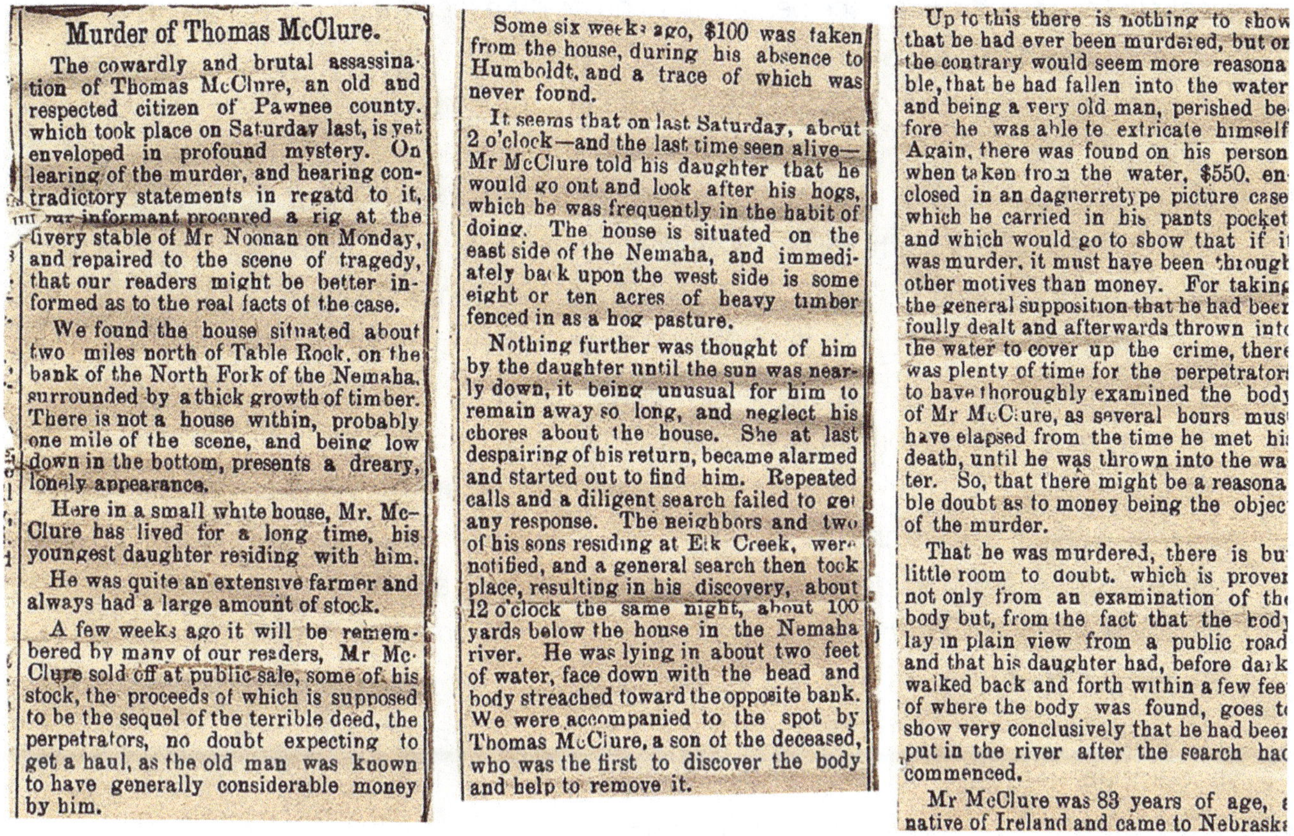

Illustration 21. Newspaper report of Thomas McClure's murder

MURDER OF THOMAS MCCLURE
[newspaper headline]

The cowardly and brutal assassination of Thomas McClure, an old and respected citizen of Pawnee County which took place on Saturday last, is yet enveloped in profound mystery. On learning of the murder, and hearing contradictory statements in regard to it, your informant procured a rig at the livery stable of Mr. Noonan on Monday and repaired to the scene of the tragedy, that our readers might be better informed as to the real facts of the case.

We found the house situated about two miles north of Table Rock, on the bank of the North Fork of the Nemaha, surrounded by a thick growth of timber. There is not a house within, probably one mile of the scene, and being low down in the bottom, presents a dreary, lonely appearance.

Here in a small white house, Mr. McClure lived for a long time, his youngest daughter residing with him.

He was quite an extensive farmer and always had a large amount of stock.

A few weeks ago it will be remembered by many of our readers, Mr. McClure sold off at public sale, some of his stock, the proceeds of which is supposed to be the sequel of the terrible deed, the perpetrators no doubt expecting to get a haul, as the old man was known to have generally considerable money by him.

Some six weeks ago, $100.00 was taken from the house, during his absence to Humboldt, and a trace of which was never found. It seems that on last Saturday, about 2 o'clock---and the last time seen alive---Mr. McClure told his daughter that he would go out and look after his hogs, which he was frequently in the habit of doing. The house is situated on east side of the Nemaha, and immediately back upon the west side is some eight or ten acres of heavy timber fenced in as a hog pasture.

Nothing further was thought of him by the daughter until the sun was nearly down, it being unusual for him to remain away so long, and neglect his chores about the house. She at last despairing of his return, became alarmed and started out to find him. Repeated calls and diligent search failed to get any response. The neighbors and two of his sons residing at Elk Creek, were notified, and a general search then took place, resulting in his discovery, about `1 o'clock the same night, about 100 yards below the house in the Nemaha river. He was lying in about two feet of water, face down with the head and body stretched toward the opposite bank. We were accompanied to the spot by Thomas McClure, a son of the deceased, who was the first to discover the body and help to remove it.

Up to this there is nothing to show that he had ever been murdered, but on contrary would seem more reasonable that he had fallen into the water, and being a very old man, perished before he was able to extricate himself. Again, there was found on his person, when taken from the water, $550, enclosed in a daguerreotype picture case, which he carried in his pants pocket, and which would go to show that if it was murder, it must have been for motives other than money. For taking the general supposition that he had been foully dealt and afterwards thrown into the water to cover up the crime, there was plenty of time for the perpetrators to have thoroughly examined the body of Mr. McClure, as several hours must have elapsed from the time he met his death, until he was thrown into the water. So, that there might be a reasonable doubt as to the money being the object of the murder. That he was murdered, there is but little room to doubt, which is proven not only from an examination of the body but, from the fact that the body lay in plain view from a public road, and that his daughter had, before dark walked back and forth within a few feet of where the body was found, go to show very conclusively that he had been put in the river after the search had commenced.

Mr. McClure was 83 years of age, a native of Ireland and came to Nebraska in the year 1860, just 18 years ago. He was a successful farmer, and although raised in a large family of children had accumulated considerable wealth.

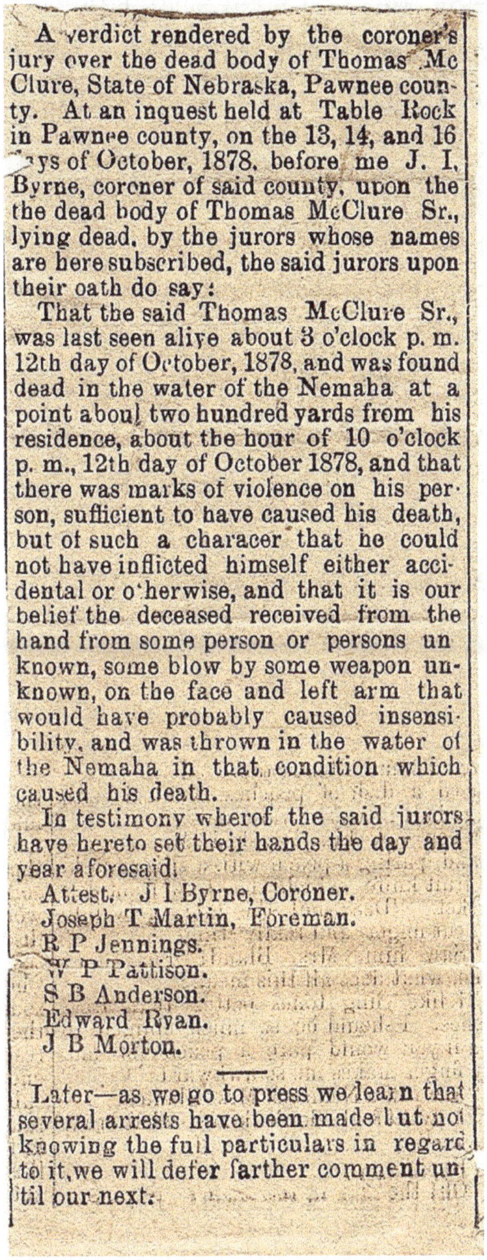

Illustration 22. Newspaper report of Thomas McClure's murder

THE VERDICT

[newspaper report of Thomas McClure's Murder - see illustration 22]

A verdict rendered by the coroner's jury over the dead body of Thomas McClure, State of Nebraska, Pawnee County. At an inquest held at Table Rock in Pawnee county, on the 13, 14, and 16 days of October, 1878, before me J.I. Byrne, coroner of the said county, upon the dead body of Thomas McClure, Sr., lying dead, by the jurors whose names are here subscribed, the said jurors upon their oath do say: That the said Thomas McClure Sr., was last seen alive about 3 o'clock p.m. 12th day of October, 1878, and was found dead in the water of the Nemaha at a point about two hundred yards from his residence, about the hour of 10 o'clock p.m., 12th day of October, 1878, and that there were marks of violence on his person, sufficient to have caused his death, but of such a character that he could not have inflicted himself either accidental or otherwise, and that it is our belief the deceased received from the hand of some person or persons unknown, some blow by some weapon unknown, on the face and left arm that would have probably caused insensibility, and was thrown in the water of the Nemaha in that condition which caused his death. In testimony whereof the said jurors have hereto set their hands the day and year aforesaid. Attest, J.I. Byrne, Coroner, Joseph T. Martin, Foreman; R.P. Pattison, S.B. Anderson, Edward Ryan, J.B. Morton

Later—as we go to press we learn that several arrests have been made but not knowing the full particulars in regard to it, we will defer further comment until our next.

TRAGEDY IN PAWNEE COUNTY
[Nebraska State Journal, Lincoln, Nebraska, October 16, 1878]

Last Saturday about 8pm Mr. Thomas McClure, one of the oldest residents of Table Rock precinct in Pawnee County was missed by his family and a search was instituted for him. At nine o'clock in the evening his body was found a few rods from his residence in the Nemaha River. He was lying in a shallow place near a log crossing. A coroner's inquest was held on Monday which adjourned over until evening. Upon the person of Mr. McClure was found over five hundred dollars in a daguerreotype case. It was variously conjectured that he had been foully dealt with since lately he had received a considerable sum of money and had been robbed not long since by some unknown person of about fifty dollars and that he had fallen into the water in a fainting fit or that he had committed suicide. Mr. McClure has been a successful farmer and stock raiser in Pawnee for many years and had quite aged having passed his eighty sixth birthday. He leaves a large family of grown-up sons and daughters, several of whom live in the neighborhood.—Table Rock, Nebraska

Letter mailed to William McClure Esq., Johnson P. O., Indian Territory
From: Linn & Cooper, dealers in Stock, Grain, Coal, Lumber. Table Rock, Neb.
To: Mr. William McClure, October 13, 1878

Dear Friend,

The painful duty has delved upon us of communicating to you the sad intelligence of the death of your Father at the request of Thomas and Daniel. The facts and circumstances near as we can learn about as follows. Your Father left home about 3 o'clock on the afternoon of yesterday (12). No one being at home but Ada and past returning at his usual time she became alarmed and spent some time in searching for him herself and being unsuccessful alarmed the neighbors who ____ into the number of 40-50 and continued the search, and about 12 o'clock found him in the River about 20 rods below the house and on the opposite side of the river with his face downward, his clothes and his hat drawn down close on his head. He had the appearance of having been struck in the face with some blunt instrument as there were bruised spots on his checks nose and over one eye. Also, one on his left arm just below the elbow, none of them appearing to have been severe enough to cause death. He laid almost on ____ of the water and was not bloated in the least, which indicates that he was not drowned. We were up to see him this afternoon and he looked very natural. The supposition is that he went over on the west side of the River to look after some hogs that went missing and that he hurt himself accidentally and then became bewildered and wandered which he had in his pocket. $670.00 in an old daguerreotype case in his pocket. No one would ever have thought of looking in it for money and the money was still on his person and apparently nothing about him had been disturbed. He had a sale on the 11th of this month and sold off all _____ except the gray ponies and the light spring wagon and intended going to live with Daniel in a few days. The Coroner was notified of the circumstance as soon as the body was found and impaneled. A jury to hold an inquest which is still in session. We will send your copy of the verdict as soon as rendered. The funeral takes place tomorrow at 1 o'clock at the house. The whole community sympathizes with you in your bereavement, but none more than your Friends, Linn & Cooper

Letter dated October 14, 1878

Friend William,

The jurors sat till 12 o'clock last night and found no verdict and adjourned till this morning. So now cannot send you their verdict by ____ mail namely every man has a different view about how ____ by his death we have given you the particulars as well *as we could & you can draw your own conclusions. It seems to me it must a been an accident if we got any more light on the subject we will write you at once. Trusting this will find your & yours with Family all well. We remain your sympathetic Friends Linn & Cooper*

Illustration 23. Monument for Thomas in Table Rock, Nebraska, 1878

Illustration 24. Close-up view of McClure Monument

Individual Record

1880 United States Census

Search results | Download — Next Individual

Daniel MCCLURE — Household

Male

Other Information:

Birth Year	<1847>
Birthplace	IN
Age	33
Occupation	Farmer
Marital Status	M
Race	W
Head of Household	Daniel MCCLURE
Relation	Self
Father's Birthplace	OH
Mother's Birthplace	OH

Source Information:

Census Place	Mead, Merrick, Nebraska
Family History Library Film	1254752
NA Film Number	T9-0752
Page Number	35A

Illustration 25. Individual record of Daniel McClure

1880 U.S. Census of Table Rock, Pawnee County, Nebraska

[2]Daniel	47 yr. old	b. Ohio F/Ireland M/Ireland	
Ann	43 yr. old	b. Ohio F/Vermont	
	m. Vadah Cremner		b. Connecticut, age 72

Let us be judged by our actions

Chapter 2
WILLIAM JOHN McCLURE
1842 - 1899

Illustration 26. William John McClure

[2]William John was the last child born to Thomas and Mary Jane. He served in the Civil War as a Union soldier. Two years after the close of the Civil War, he moved to Indian Territory and later purchased the Jesse Chisholm family ranch, the famous 7C. He became one of the earliest ranchers in Indian Territory. At the time of the Great Land Run he was the first legal settler to arrive in Oklahoma City, Oklahoma Territory. He became the largest property owner in Oklahoma City.

From the Records
[2]William John McClure
b. December 7, 1842, Palmyra Township, Lee County, Illinois
m. Mary Ellen Kennedy, August 27, 1867
   (Widow's Application for Pension states that the marriage was held, July 29, 1869, in Pawnee City, Nebraska, in the home of the minister, Rev. McGolphin, Presbyterian Church.)
b. December 24, 1855, Silver Lake, Shawnee County, Kansas
d. April 20, 1923, Oklahoma City, Oklahoma
f. Presbyterian
d. June 19, 1899, Oklahoma City, Oklahoma Territory, age 57 years
b. Fairlawn Cemetery, Oklahoma City, Oklahoma Territory
   (Fairlawn has no records prior to 1907.)
    Father: [1]Thomas McClure
        b. August 12, 1796, Crumlin, County Antrim, Ireland
        d. October 12, 1878, Table Rock, Pawnee County, Nebraska
    Mother: [1]Mary Jane Young McClure
        b. September 6, 1798, Crumlin, County Antrim, Ireland
        d. June 2, 1848, Rock River, Lee County, Illinois

Siblings:
[2]Jane
   b. September 28, 1820, Crumlin, County Antrim, Ireland
   d. October 4, 1898
[2]Hugh
   b. May 24, 1822, Crumlin, County Antrim, Ireland
   d. February 1908, Ballendary, County Antrim, Ireland
[2]Mariana
   b. January 24, 1824, Crumlin, County Antrim, Ireland
   d. unknown
[2]John Wilson
   b. February 28, 1826, Philadelphia, Pennsylvania
   d. July 6, 1827
[2]James Belford
   b. February 29, 1828, Monroe, Pennsylvania
   d. December 13, 1891
[2]Sophia Louise

    b. December 10, 1830, Huron, Eric, Ohio
²Daniel Henry
    b. March 8, 1833, Huron, Eric, Ohio
    d. 1905
²Thomas Jr.
    b. November 1, 1835, Huron, Eric, Ohio
    d. October 11, 1906
²Hester Malvina S.
    b. October 17, 1837, Parke, Indiana
    d. September 14, 1931
²Twins
    b. August 7, 1840, Lee County, Illinois
    d. August 7, 1840
²William John
    b. December 7, 1843
    d. June 19, 1899

Children of William John and Mary Ellen
³Guy Vincent
    b. Dec. 12, 1877, Silver Lake, Kansas
    m. Bernice McAdams
    b. August 6, 1881, Missouri
    d. 1951
    d. Oct. 23, 1918, in the Spanish Flu Epidemic at age 41
        Guy was 12 years old at the time of the Land Run in 1889. He became the engineer who planned and built the Oklahoma City water supply, Lake Overholser. Guy's widow lived in Galveston at the time of William John's death in 1899.
    b. Fairlawn Cemetery, Oklahoma City, Oklahoma
³David Victor
    b. December 10, 1879, Atoka, Indian Territory
        He graduated from Kemper Military Academy in Booneville, Missouri, with classmate Will Rogers. David was one of Teddy Roosevelt's original Rough Riders with Company "D" in the Spanish-American War.
    m. Grace Anna Jones, June 20, 1905, Cincinnati, Ohio
    d. December 11, 1944, Oklahoma City, Oklahoma
    b. Fairlawn Cemetery, Oklahoma City, Oklahoma

[3]Veta Ellean
- b. March 27, 1882, Liberty Hill, Atoka, Indian Territory
  She attended Baird School for Ladies when she was 13 years old. She graduated from Christian College for Women in Columbia, Missouri.
- m. She was married seven times.
  No Children were born from her marriages.
- d. August 23, 1963, Oklahoma City, Oklahoma
- b. Fairlawn Cemetery, Oklahoma City

William John McClure's Timeline

1842 [2]William John born in Lee County, Illinois

1851 One letter said, "Mother McClure passed away."

1853 His father, [1]Thomas McClure, purchased 160 acres in Chariton, Appanoose County, Iowa, Legal Certificate #1411. Family moved to Iowa. W. J. was 11 years old at the time of the move.

1854 May 30. The Kansas-Nebraska Act of 1854 (10 Stat. 277) created the territories of Kansas and Nebraska and was drafted by Senator Stephen A. Douglas of Illinois and President Franklin Pierce. The initial purpose was to open thousands of new farms and make feasible a Midwestern Transcontinental Railroad. The Kansas-Nebraska Act allowed people in the territories of Kansas and Nebraska to decide for themselves whether or not to allow slavery within their borders. The Act served to repeal the Missouri Compromise of 1820, which prohibited slavery north of latitude 36"30'.

1856 Census Schedule of Pleasant Township, Appanoose County, Iowa

Dwelling #		Names of Persons	Family # 1	Age 2	Sex 3	Married 4	Widowed 5	Years Resident in the State 6	Where Born 7	Profession or Trade 8	Native Voter 9	Militia 10	Naturalized Voter 11	Owners of Land 12
28	1	Tho. McLure	30	56	M			3	Ireland	Farmer			✓	✓
28	2	M McLure	30	49	F	✓		3	Ireland					
28	3	D. H. McLure	30	23	M			3	Ohio		✓	✓		✓
28	4	Tho. McLure	30	20	M			3	Ohio			✓		
28	5	W. J. McLure	30	13	M			3	Ohio					
	6													
29	7	H. B. Fox	31		M			1	Ohio	Farmer				
29	8	M. A. Fox	31	19	F			1	Ohio					
	9													
30	10	E. Gault	32	28	M			3	Ireland	Farmer				
30	11	S. Gault	32	25	F			3	Ohio					
30	12	T. F. Gault	32	1	M			1	Iowa					
	13													
	14													
	15													
	16													
	17													
	18													
	19													
	20													
	21													
	22													
	23													
	24													
	25													
	26													
	27													
	28													
	29													
	30													
	31													

Illustration 27. 1856 Census, Appanoose County, Iowa

1858 First news over the Atlantic Telegraph Cable

May 1858 the family moved to Nebraska. After the family settled in Nebraska and in the years prior to the Civil War, William John accompanied his father into Texas and northern Mexico to buy longhorn cattle and range cattle to cross breed with their stock. The goal was to produce a stronger strain of cattle to withstand the brutal winters. It was during these trips that William John saw and learned to appreciate the lush rangeland in Oklahoma. It was here they found milder winters and a longer grazing season for cattle.

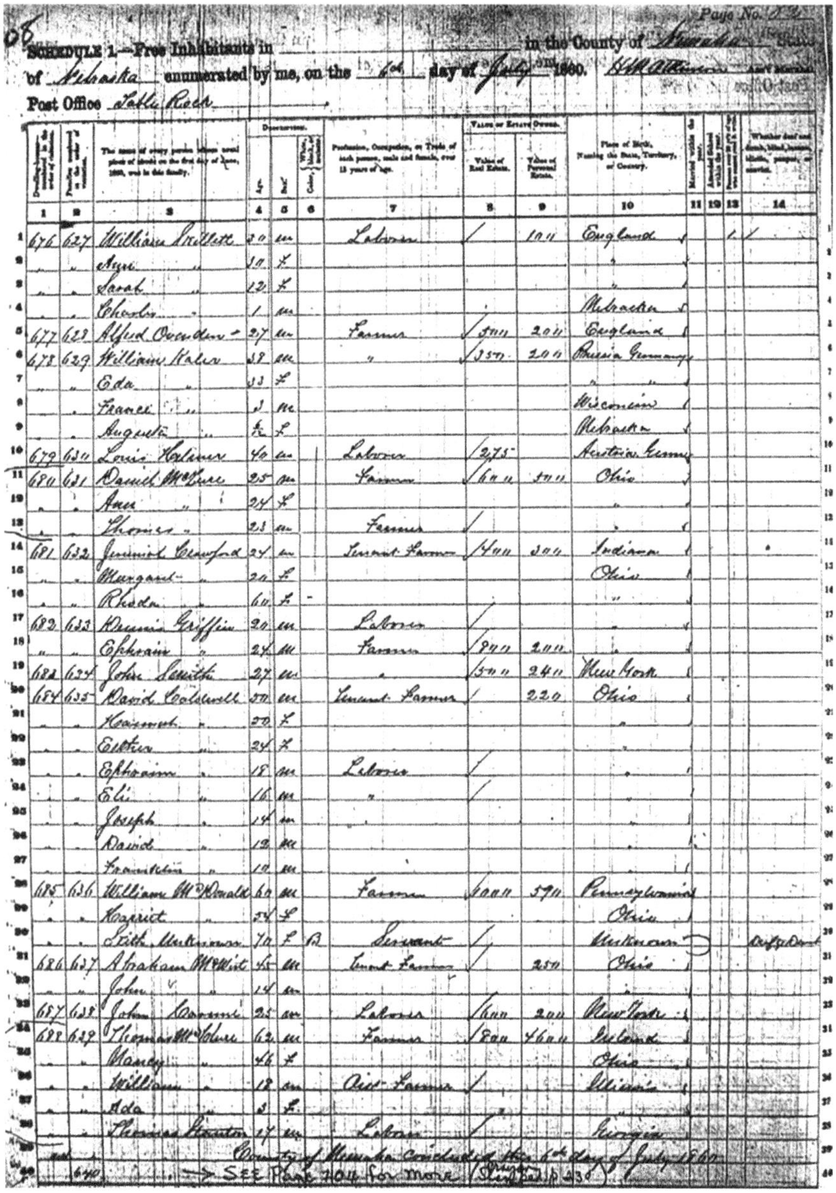
Page No. 82

SCHEDULE 1.—Free Inhabitants in ______ in the County of Nemaha State of Nebraska enumerated by me, on the 6th day of July 1860. H.W. Atkinson Ass't Marshal.

Post Office Table Rock

Dwelling-houses numbered in the order of visitation	Families numbered in the order of visitation	The name of every person whose usual place of abode on the first day of June, 1860, was in this family	Age	Sex	Color	Profession, Occupation, or Trade of each person, male and female, over 15 years of age	Value of Real Estate	Value of Personal Estate	Place of Birth, Naming the State, Territory, or Country	Married within the year	Attended School within the year	Persons over 20 y'rs of age who cannot read & write	Whether deaf and dumb, blind, insane, idiotic, pauper, or convict
1	2	3	4	5	6	7	8	9	10	11	12	13	14
676	627	William Willett	30	m		Laborer		100	England			1	
"	"	Ann "	30	f					"				
"	"	Sarah "	12	f					"				
"	"	Charles "	1	m					Nebraska				
677	628	Alfred Ovenden	27	m		Farmer	500	200	England				
678	629	William Kaler	38	m		"	350	200	Prussia Germany				
	"	Eda "	33	f					" "				
	"	France "	3	m					Wisconsin				
	"	Augusta "	1/12	f					Nebraska				
679	630	Louis Holmer	40	m		Laborer	275		Austria Germany				
680	631	Daniel McClure	25	m		Farmer	600	500	Ohio				
"	"	Ann "	24	f					"				
"	"	Thomas "	23	m		Farmer			"				
681	632	Jeremiah Crawford	24	m		Tenant Farmer	400	300	Indiana				
"	"	Margaret "	20	f					Ohio				
"	"	Rhoda "	60	f					"				
682	633	Dennis Griffin	20	m		Laborer			"				
"	"	Ephraim "	24	m		Farmer	900	200	"				
683	634	John Smith	27	m		"	500	240	New York				
684	635	David Caldwell	50	m		Tenant Farmer		220	Ohio				
"	"	Hannah "	50	f					"				
"	"	Esther "	24	f					"				
"	"	Ephraim "	18	m		Laborer			"				
"	"	Eli "	16	m		"			"				
"	"	Joseph "	14	m					"				
"	"	David "	12	m					"				
	"	Franklin "	10	m					"				
685	636	William McDonald	60	m		Farmer	1000	590	Pennsylvania				
"	"	Harriet "	54	f					Ohio				
"	"	Stith Unknown	70	f	B	Servant			Unknown				Deaf & Dumb
686	637	Abraham McWhit	45	m		Tenant Farmer		250	Ohio				
	"	John "	14	m					"				
687	638	John Cornie	25	m		Laborer	600	200	New York				
688	639	Thomas McClure	62	m		Farmer	800	460	Ireland				
"	"	Nancy "	46	f					Ohio				
"	"	William "	18	m		Ass't Farmer			Illinois				
"	"	Ada "	2	f									
"	"	Thomas Stanton	17	m		Laborer			Georgia				

County of Nemaha concluded the 6th day of July 1860

640 → SEE Page 404 for more

Illustration 28. 1860 U.S. Census

1860 U. S. Federal Census, Page 82, Nemaha County, U. S. Post Office, Table Rock, Nebraska

[1]Thomas McClure	age 62, Farmer	Place of Birth, Ireland
[1]Nancy (second wife)	age 48	Place of Birth, Ohio
[2]William	age 18	Place of Birth, Illinois
[2]Ada	age 2	child of Thomas and Nancy
[2]Daniel McClure	age 25, Farmer,	b. Ohio
[2]Ann	age 24	b. Ohio (incorrect)

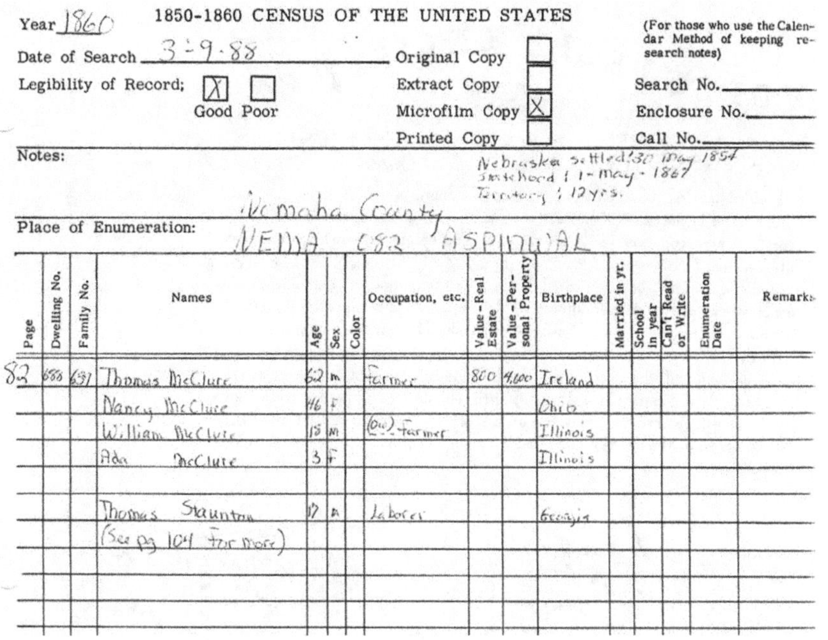

Year 1860 1850-1860 CENSUS OF THE UNITED STATES

(For those who use the Calendar Method of keeping research notes)

Date of Search 3-9-88 Original Copy ☐

Legibility of Record; ☒ Good ☐ Poor Extract Copy ☐ Search No.

Microfilm Copy ☒ Enclosure No.

Printed Copy ☐ Call No.

Notes: Nebraska settled 30 May 1854 Statehood 1-May-1867 Territory 12 yrs.

Place of Enumeration: Nemaha County NEMA ASPINWAL

Page	Dwelling No.	Family No.	Names	Age	Sex	Color	Occupation, etc.	Value - Real Estate	Value - Personal Property	Birthplace	Married in yr.	School in year	Can't Read or Write	Enumeration Date	Remarks
82	686	691	Thomas McClure	62	M		Farmer	800	4,000	Ireland					
			Nancy McClure	46	F					Ohio					
			William McClure	15	M		(Own) Farmer			Illinois					
			Ada McClure	3	F					Illinois					
			Thomas Staunton	17	M		Laborer			Georgia					
			(See pg 104 for more)												

Illustration 29. 1860 family census

1861 Civil War begins when the Confederates bombard Union soldiers at Fort Sumter, South Carolina, on April 12, 1861.

1862 Homestead Act: Signed into law by President Abraham Lincoln on May 20, 1862. The Homestead Act encouraged Western migration by providing settlers 160 acres of public land. In exchange, the homesteaders were charged a small filing fee and were required to complete five years of continuous residence before receiving ownership of the land.

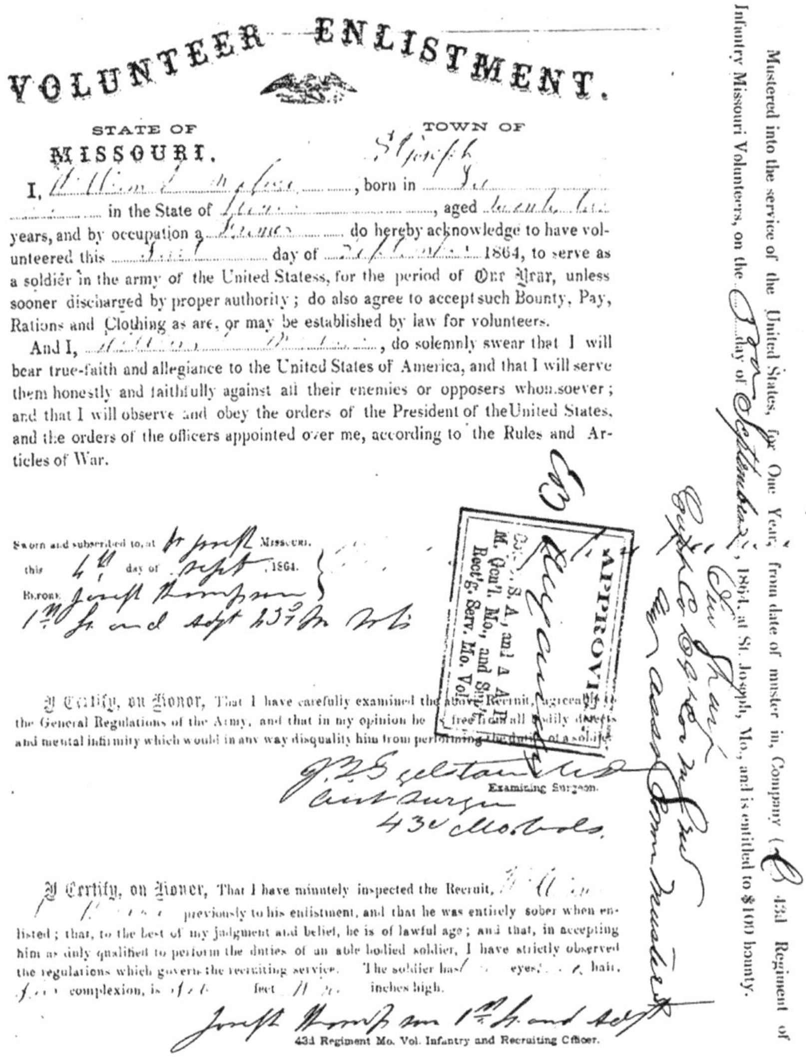

Illustration 30. William John's Civil War enlistment paper

U.S. Civil War Soldiers, 1861-1865

Name:	**William I. McClure**
Side:	Union
Regiment State/Origin:	Missouri
Regiment Name:	43 Missouri Infantry.
Regiment Name Expanded:	43rd Regiment, Missouri Infantry
Company:	D
Rank In:	Private
Rank In Expanded:	Private
Rank Out:	Private
Rank Out Expanded:	Private
Film Number:	M390 roll 31

Source Information:
National Park Service. *U.S. Civil War Soldiers, 1861-1865* [database on-line]. Provo, UT, USA: Ancestry.com Operations Inc, 2007.
Original data: National Park Service, Civil War Soldiers and Sailors System, online <>. acquired 2007.

Description:
This database contains the names of approximately 6.3 million soldiers who served in the American Civil War. In addition to their names, information that may be listed for each soldier includes regiment, company, and rank.

Illustration 31. William John's Civil War enlistment paper

682
McClure, William J
Co D, 43 Missouri Inf.
Prints | Prints
CARD NUMBERS.
1 8605054
2 8605144
3 8605227
4 8605319
5 8605406
6 8605489
Book Mark:

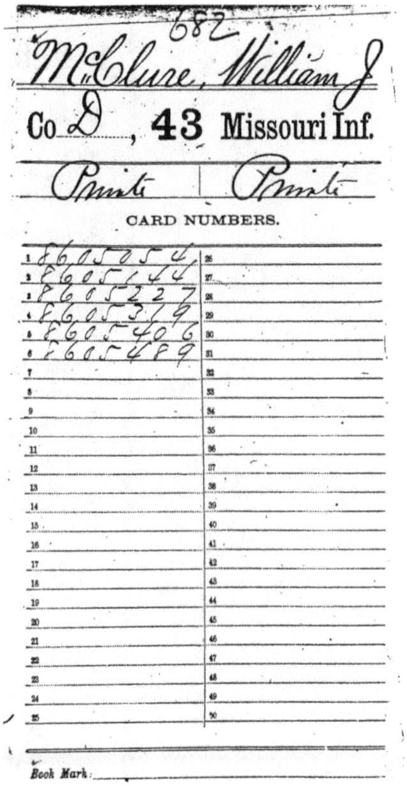

Illustration 32. William John's Civil War card

M | 43 | Mo.
William J. McClure
Pvt, Co. D, 43 Reg't Missouri Infantry.
Appears on
Company Muster Roll
for dated Oct. 31, 1864.
Present or absent: Present
Remarks: Absent sick since Oct. 21/64 at Brownsville, Mo. Returned Oct. 31 in time for muster.

M | 43 | Mo.
William J. McClure
Pvt, Co. D, 43 Reg't Missouri Infantry.
Appears on
Company Muster-in and Descriptive Roll
of the organization named above. Roll dated St. Joseph, Mo., Sept. 2, 1864.
Where born: Lee Co., Ill.
Age 22 y'rs; occupation Farmer
When enlisted: Sept. 1, 1864.
Where enlisted: St. Joseph, Mo.
For what period enlisted: 1 years.
Eyes: Grey; hair: Dk
Complexion: Fair; height 5 ft. 7 in.
When mustered in: Sept. 2, 1864.
Where mustered in: St. Joseph
Bounty paid $100; due $100
Where credited
Company to which assigned
Remarks: Rec'd 1st Inst. Gov't Bounty. Credited to St. Joseph, Buchanan Co. Mo. 7th Cong. Dist.

M | 43 | Mo.
William J. McClure
Pvt, Co. D, 43 Reg't Missouri Infantry.
Appears on
Company Muster Roll
for Nov. & Dec., 1864.
Present or absent: Absent
Remarks: Absent with leave since Nov. 22/64 in Nebraska Ter.

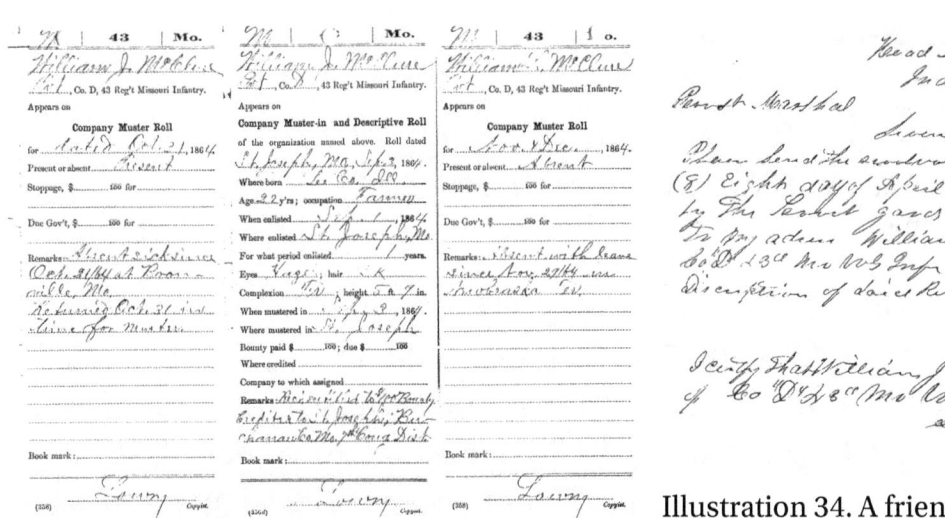

Illustration 33. William John's Civil War muster record

Head Qrs Co "D" 43rd Mo Vol Inf
Independence Mo April 15-65
Provost Marshal
Leavenworth City Kansas
Please send the revolver taken from me on the (8) Eight day of April 1865 in the City of Leavenworth by the Provost Guard Express it to Independence Mo To my adress William J McClure Private of Co "D" 43rd Mo Vol Inf
Discription of said Revolver Colts Navy
W J McClure
I certify that William J McClure is a member of Co "D" 43rd Mo Vol Inf
Lt Charles S Pickett
Comdg Co "D" 43rd Mo Inf

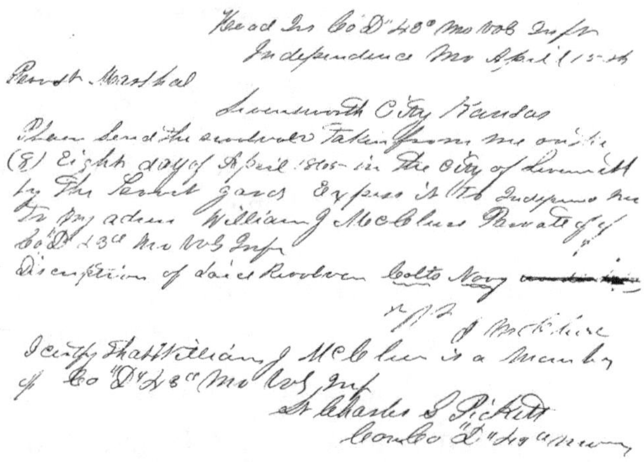

Illustration 34. A friend's voucher of William John

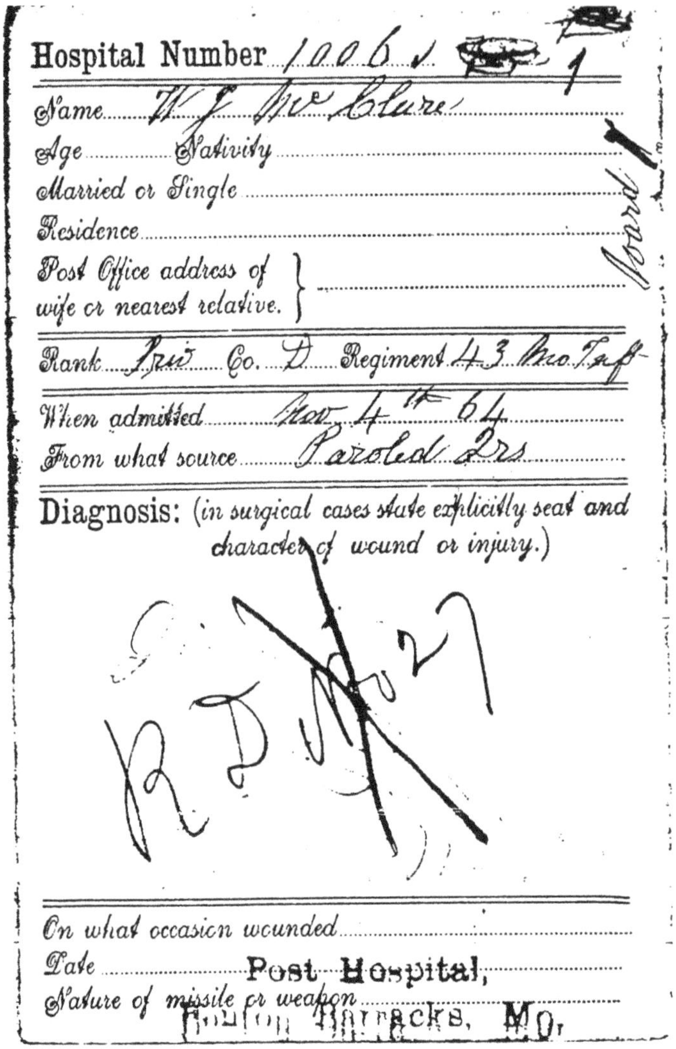

Illustration 35. Jefferson Barracks Army Hospital, St. Louis

1864 ²William John enlists as a 21-year-old private at St. Joseph, Missouri, September 1, 1864, with Company D. 43rd Missouri Volunteer Infantry. (Film #M390, Roll 31). He is discharged June 13, 1865, at Burton Barracks, Missouri. He had been injured and admitted to Jefferson Barracks Post Hospital, November 4, 1864, and discharged June 30, 1865. The Hospital Number was #1006. Papers tell that his injury was: "injury to his left leg: the knee of his left leg being broken; his left leg being broken below the knee of his said left leg, and the hip of his said left leg being fractured, also suffers from the effects of measles; chronic diarrhea, caused by said measles"—stated by the Department of the Interior's Declaration for Invalid Pension Act of June 27, 1890

He received a Notification of Allowance Form 21. G.V.B. 100 Settlement #265356 for: William J. McClure Service, Pvt Co. "D" 43 Mo Vol. The Regiment saw action at Booneville, Missouri, October 9 and 12, 1864; Brunswick, October 11, 1864; 11th Battle of Glasgow, October 15, 1864.

1865 Company D, operates against guerrillas in Central Missouri, June. Company D fought Little Blue River March 11, 1865. Company D, 43rd Missouri Volunteers had a skirmish at Star House near Lexington, May 4, 1864.

Casualties of the Regiment:

11 enlisted men killed

53 enlisted men by disease

Total lost: 64

D. F. MacMartin, Attorney at Law, Oklahoma City, Okla.

To all whom it may Concern.

Know ye, That ____ of Captain ____ Company, ( ) ____ Regiment of ____ VOLUNTEERS who was enrolled on the ____ day of ____ one thousand eight hundred and ____ to serve ____ years or during the war, is hereby Discharged from the service of the United States, this Thirtieth day of June, 1865, at Benton Barracks Mo by reason of ____ (No objection to his being re-enlisted is known to exist.)

Said ____ was born in ____ in the State of ____, is ____ years of age, ____ feet ____ inches high, ____ complexion, ____ eyes, ____ hair, and by occupation, when enrolled, a ____.

Given at Benton Barracks Mo this Thirtieth day of June 1865.

Commanding the Regt.

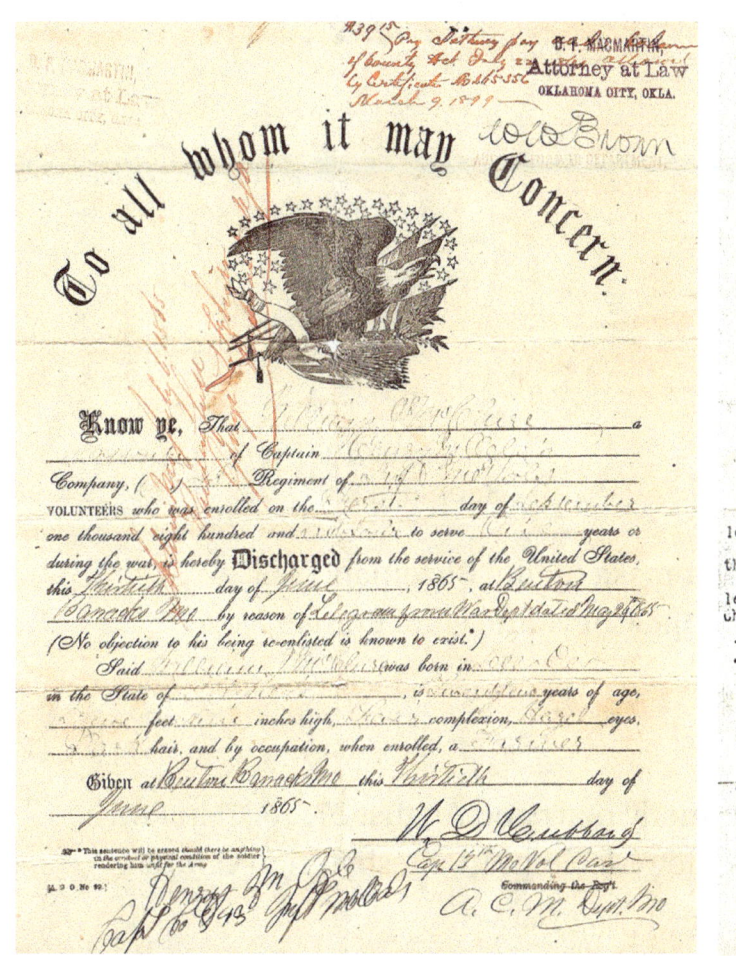

Illustration 36. William John's Civil War discharge papers

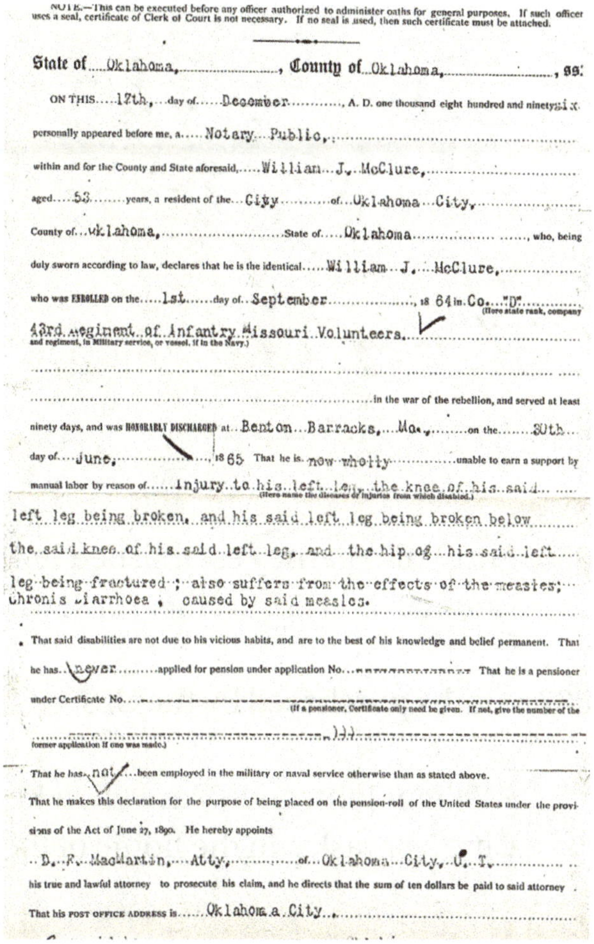
NOTE.—This can be executed before any officer authorized to administer oaths for general purposes. If such officer uses a seal, certificate of Clerk of Court is not necessary. If no seal is used, then such certificate must be attached.

State of Oklahoma, County of Oklahoma, ss:

ON THIS 17th, day of December, A. D. one thousand eight hundred and ninety six, personally appeared before me, a Notary Public, within and for the County and State aforesaid, William J. McClure, aged 53 years, a resident of the City of Oklahoma City, County of Oklahoma, State of Oklahoma, who, being duly sworn according to law, declares that he is the identical William J. McClure, who was ENROLLED on the 1st day of September, 18 64 in Co. "D" 43rd Regiment of Infantry Missouri Volunteers, in the war of the rebellion, and served at least ninety days, and was HONORABLY DISCHARGED at Benton Barracks, Mo., on the 30th day of June, 1865. That he is now wholly unable to earn a support by manual labor by reason of injury to his left leg, the knee of his said left leg being broken, and his said left leg being broken below the said knee of his said left leg, and the hip of his said left leg being fractured; also suffers from the effects of the measles; chronic diarrhoea, caused by said measles.

That said disabilities are not due to his vicious habits, and are to the best of his knowledge and belief permanent. That he has never applied for pension under application No. ____ That he is a pensioner under Certificate No. ____

That he has not been employed in the military or naval service otherwise than as stated above.

That he makes this declaration for the purpose of being placed on the pension-roll of the United States under the provisions of the Act of June 27, 1890. He hereby appoints D. F. MacMartin, Atty, of Oklahoma City, O. T. his true and lawful attorney to prosecute his claim, and he directs that the sum of ten dollars be paid to said attorney.

That his POST OFFICE ADDRESS is Oklahoma City.

Illustration 37. Application for pension

1865 The Civil War officially ends on April 9, 1865, when Robert E. Lee surrenders to Ulysses S. Grant at the Appomattox Courthouse.

1865   ²William John goes back to the family ranch in Pawnee City, Nebraska, from 1865–1867.

Little Arkansas Treaty was a set of treaties signed in Kansas in October 1865. Harney-Sanborn Treaty gave emigrants the right to travel through the Sioux and North Cheyenne lands.

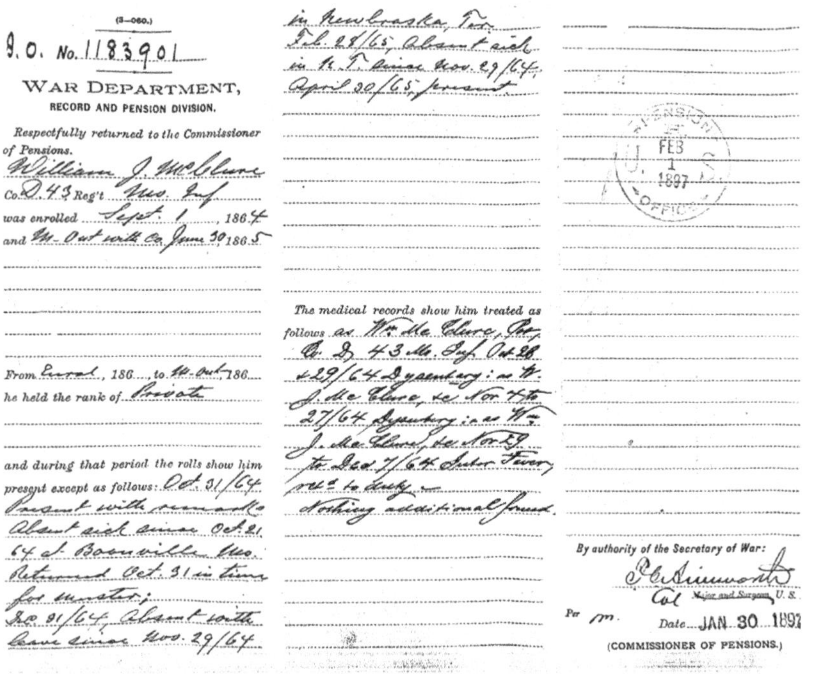

Illustration 38. Civil War pension

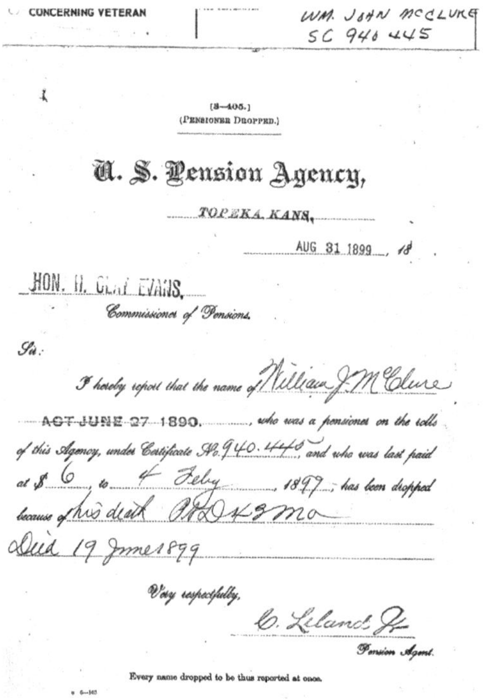

Illustration 39. Notice of pension termination

1866   Fort Phil Kearney established in Nebraska on the Bozeman Trail
       Council held at Fort Ellsworth with the Cheyenne chief Roman Nose

1867   Alaska purchased by the U. S.

²William John and ²Mary Ellen Kennedy marry on August 27, 1867, in Pawnee City, Nebraska, in the home of the Rev. McGolphin, Presbyterian Church.

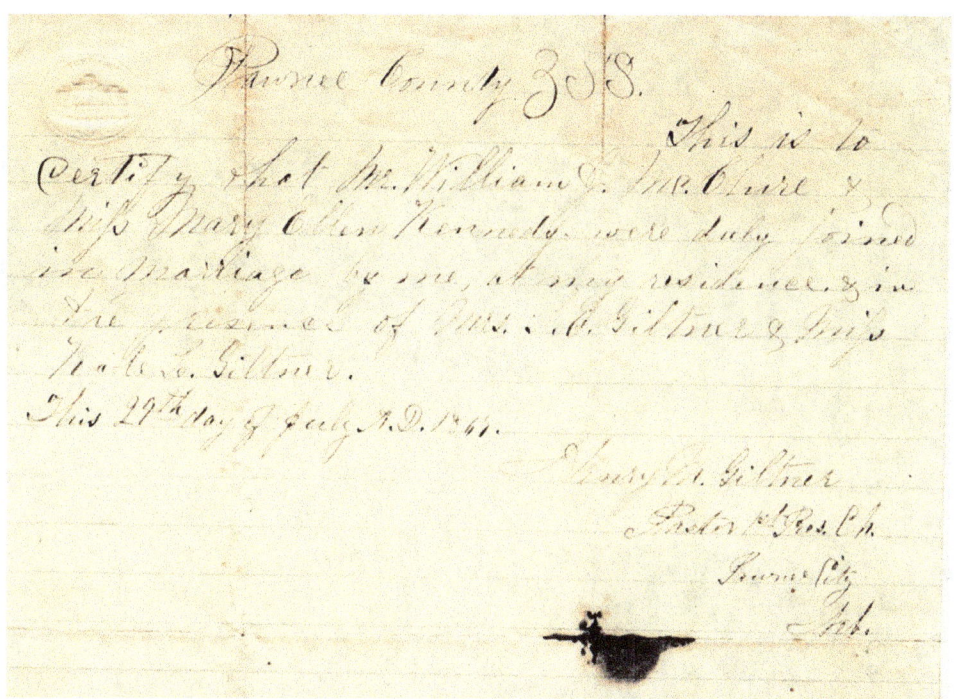

Illustration 40. Marriage certificate: William John and Mary Ellen Kennedy

1867 [2]William John arrives at Muskogee, the capital of Indian Territory

1868 At the time William John is settling in Indian Territory, the U. S. government is battling Native American tribes in a conflict known as the Plains Wars. At stake was who would control the western region of the Great Plains. One government fighting outfit was called the Rough Riders, a name later picked up and made famous by Theodore Roosevelt in the Spanish-American War.

1869 [2]William John purchases the 7C Ranch from the Chisholm family. The ranch consisted of a lease of the Kickapoo and the Pottawatomie Indian lands. The Pottawatomie lands extended from the Canadian River to the North Canadian between the western boundary of the Seminole Nation and the Indian Meridian. The Kickapoo lands extended west from the Sac and Fox reservation line to the Indian Meridian between Deep Fork and the North Canadian rivers. This ranch was established in 1865 or 1866. It was one of the first in this section of the country. The ranch house was located one mile north and a quarter of a mile northeast of Choctaw City, Indian Territory.[1]

---

[1]Albert McRill, *And Satan Came Also*, revised and annotated by Larry Johnson (Oklahoma City: Full Circle Press, 2013) 58-59, 80, 86).

Illustration 41. Bill McClure's 7C Ranch cowboys

Illustration 42. McClure's 7C Ranch cowboys

1869 The first transcontinental railroad completed

The Choctaw Nation cattle paper/flier showed:

W. McClure; PO Atoka Ranch, North Fork Canadian, Shawnee country. None (no cattle) sold except for Shipment. $100 REWARD for information leading to the conviction of any person stealing stock in the above brand.

Ft. Sill established January 8, 1869, by General Philip H. Sheridan

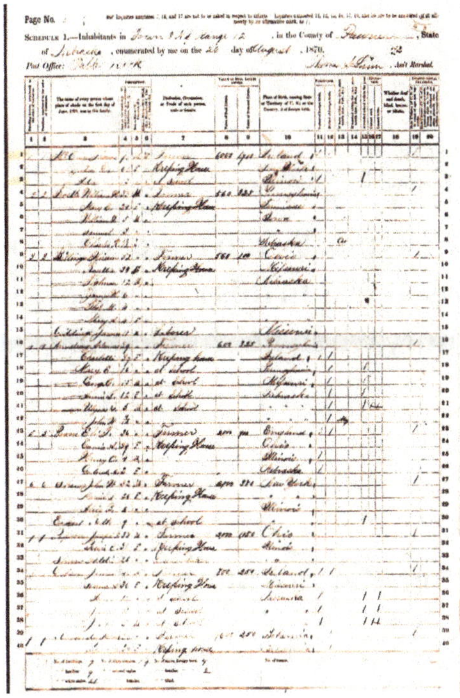

Illustration 43. 1870 U.S. Census
Table Rock, Nebraska

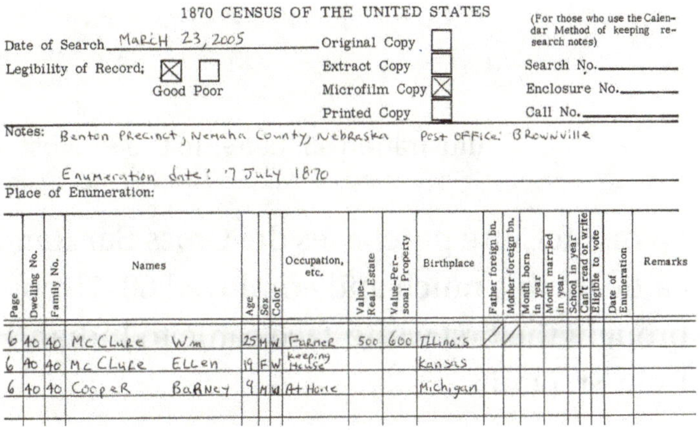

1870 CENSUS OF THE UNITED STATES

(For those who use the Calendar Method of keeping research notes)

Date of Search MARCH 23, 2005 — Original Copy — Search No.
Legibility of Record: [X] Good [ ] Poor — Extract Copy — Enclosure No.
Microfilm Copy [X] — Call No.
Printed Copy

Notes: Benton Precinct, Nemaha County, Nebraska Post Office: Brownville

Enumeration date: 7 July 1870

Place of Enumeration:

Page	Dwelling No.	Family No.	Names		Age	Sex	Color	Occupation, etc.	Value-Real Estate	Value-Personal Property	Birthplace	Father foreign bn.	Mother foreign bn.	Month born in year	Month married in year	School in year	Can't read or write	Eligible to vote	Date of Enumeration	Remarks
6	40	40	McCLURE	Wm	25	M	W	Farmer	500	600	Illinois	/	/							
6	40	40	McCLURE	ELLEN	19	F	W	Keeping House			Kansas									
6	40	40	COOPER	BARNEY	9	M	W	At Home			Michigan									

Illustration 44. 1870 Household Census, Nemaha County, Nebraska

1870 Census of United States: Benton Precinct, Nemaha County, Nebraska, Post Office: Brownville, Page 6

1. [2]Wm. McClure, age 25, Farmer, Value Real Estate 500/ Value Personal Property 600, b. Illinois; Mother and Father both foreign born
2. [2]Ellen McClure, age 19, Keeping House, born Kansas
3. Barney Cooper, age 9, At Home, born Michigan

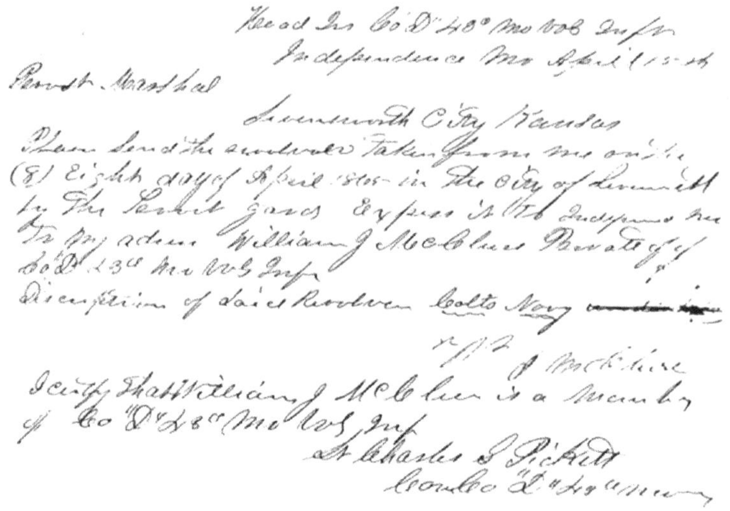

Illustration 45. Letter to the Provost Marshall

1870 ²Wm. McClure purchases the Cross Bar Ranch. He typically ran large herds of cattle on this ranch and employed 60–70 cowboys. It was to this ranch that he brought the first white-face cattle to Indian Territory when he shipped 400 cattle from St. Louis.

1874 Ft. Reno established in July in Indian Territory

1874 Letter from ²Wm. J. McClure mailed from Fort Scott, Kansas, March 14, to ²Mary Ellen McClure in Table Rock, Nebraska

Dearest Ellen,

Letter off to you at Topeka but – did not mail the letter but will do better in the future. We arrived here today and we are all well. We have traveled slowly on account of the roads being bad in places. The horses look well. We have a northern ___. He is a brother mason. And is a very nice man. We have had a very good time. We stopped at ___ one day and at Topeka one day and had a ___ on Jo and won it by 7 feet. The best horse in Topeka. I sold him for 200 dollars, but I am going to take him ___. We won about 100 dollars. I saw uncle ___ and he wants you to come down and stay with ___ while he goes south. ___told he would come after you if you would come and I said that you might. ___ And if you want to go it is all right . . . (remainder of letter missing).

1874 A partial letter with no date

getting green and so are the prairies. One more week and we will have grass for our horses. I intend to go ___ in Texas if I ___my time off for ___ before now. Ellen, I want

56

you to write to me as soon as you get directions where to write to. I will drop you a few lines when we get to Baxter Springs and tell you ____ to ___ We will get there in about two days. I sent you pictures as I told you I would. Give ____ to his mother. We could not get ____ for we lost him at (Norwell?) and had to send back for him. We are ____ then this afternoon and am going to have swim. The boys are all fishing and we are going to have fish for supper. I wish you could have a swim. Now my dearest, I must close. Give my love to father and mother and all the rest ____ and tell Dan that ____ for him to do what he wants with his fall wheat, but don't let the "old Dutchman" have it, unless he pays well for it. Now dearest Ellen, I will bid you good-bye hoping this will find you well and all the ____ W. J. McClure

Letter from [2]William John (Muskogee) to [2]Mary Ellen, April 1874

Dear and most beloved Wife,

Today finds me well and I hope it may find you all in the same good health. I have not received an answer to my last, yet, but hope that I will shortly. We have not had more than four days of dry weather since ____ but today is very fine. I am in hopes that our wet season is over. I have no news of any importance tonight. ___ has been very high ___ was about on the Grand River a few days ago. And four mules drowned everything ___ here at present but if the weather stays ___ cattle will soon be fat and then times will liven up. Since the grass has got up so that cattle can fill themselves they don't trouble me much and I have got considerable spare time to loaf, but it is a dull place for that business. I go to town every day and spend a few hours and that way I manage to get along without getting the blues too bad. Now my dearest, I want you to write soon. Now a pleasant goodbye to you all, W. J. McClure

1874 Letter from Wm. John McClure in Muskogee to Mary Ellen McClure, April 11, 1874

Dearest Ellen,

I will commence that long letter that I promised you. Well, you wanted me to let you know what I do every day. I do the same thing every day. Eat my breakfast and saddle my pony and herd cattle. Sometimes all day and sometimes half a day. The weather has cleared off and it is very ___ and everything looks very promising. Wesley is mixing bread for dinner. Maybe you will remember what we will have for our dinner. I can't tell you. Sometimes bread and meat, ___ fried eggs, peaches and currents too. I guess it will be bread and meat today. Well, you can tell Wesses folks that he is about gone. He has fallen in love with a very beautiful but a little dar ____. Well for the want of time I had to stop until this afternoon the 13th. We have been out cow hunting   and I just returned. ___ got after me and wanted to give up my ___ but did not. They thought that I was at Cherokee. Tell ____ that I have not found a location yet. I went to see what the ___ is going to do. They are trying to form _____ (Granges?) here but cannot tell yet how they will come out. Well goodbye my dearest—and everybody

1874 The 14th

Dear Ellen,

 I received yours today and it was good to hear that you were all well. I have just gotten in and it is raining. You can tell Father that he need not worry about what I ___ William that I told him before I left that I would pay him and he never ___ to me. So now I___ get an order from his father for the money and I will pay him. I will ___ him as a stranger for I don't know as I owe him anything, but I owe his father one hundred dollars. So goodbye to you all for the present Wm McClure"

1874

 About 15 days I want you to let me know in your next post if ___ (Dan?) has seen any geldings and what he said about them? ___year old for I have a chance to get them delivered here. So, I will close till tomorrow.

1874 The 13th

Dearest Ellen,

 When I wrote the last I ___ one day ahead. I have just returned from hunting cattle and an ___ what ___ my cattle ranges on a check about five miles ___ and I go over every day and round them up and count them and that takes me about all my time. Next week I will bring them over here and then I will have more time to loaf. I can go by town every day and stop at the post office. But I don't often get a letter. I have received one since I got back one from Lynn and one from Robinson. I have no news at present as I came through town today the little ___end of... (rest of letter lost).

Letter June 22

Dearest Ellen,

 I suppose you think I am ___, but we are safe and sound in the ___Nation. ___ when we started and one at Red River but did not meet with a chance to make it and it got ___. We have had a very wet time. It ___ ___ I have fifty head of beef carted to ship as soon as they get a little fatter. And the ___ heads ___ gets so I can drive. Tell Dan I want him to borrow one hundred dollars and send it to me. I will ship my cattle in six weeks and will come home then. I had bad luck on the trip. I lost a horse that cost me 55 dollars and when ___ him I lost 53 dollars in the cold and did not get Eastern bank. This is a very fine country and good stock country. I am going to ___ stock ___ this winter. Stock does not need feed in the winter. West Nesbit is going to take care of them. I will ship to Saint Louis. I can ship for 70 dollars a car and I will be home in two months at the outside. Well, I must close for Frank Danburg is waiting to take my letter to the office. It is 25 miles to the office we are staying with him at present.

My love to all,
W. McClure

1875 Mary Ellen moved to Johnstonville, Indian Territory
Letter dated February 6, 1875, to Mary Ellen McClure

Dear Sister,

I am at home and thought I would write to you for I commenced work and intend to write my letter diary fashion. Beginning with the hour you left me at the rustic __ stone house. The Gaults recommended so highly. Well the lady you saw there was going my road so far as Cameron and was very sociable and seemed pleased to have company to start with and was in favor of sitting up until train time. Said if she went to bed she would not close her eyes and I knew it would be the same with me and concluded to wait in the sitting room. I rested some on the lounge and at midnight the word came that the train was four hours behind. You can better imagine my feeling than understand the description I would give. Suffice it to say my heart almost sank within me. Then I told the waiter I would retire and was shown to a dingy room with a hard bed and there with my mind traveling. I tried to sleep but did not succeed and just as the bed began to feel warm was called to prepare for starting. Then as a natural consequence I was behind time in getting to Atchison which gave me a very pleasant visit at Mr. Egelstons. Time flies much faster than it would at the Hotel. Wednesday was a stormy day and I didn't go out in town until it was train time and was met by Dan Tucker at Table Rock. He was glad and I was glad and we were both glad and haven't got over it yet. Then we had one of Nebraska's worst storms to go home in. The wind blew and the snow flew, but I tell you we were not long driving home. We didn't drive a blind horse without shoes like the Honorable E. J. Gault. And since I have been home I have heard Dan say he must have the horses shoes taken off and sharpened. I didn't say a word but thought to myself ah poor fellow you don't know how to save the dollar. No. no. I will leave you to guess how bad I felt. John and Dan had a good time batching. Went so far as to have an oyster supper and dance. Had all of our same set except Miss Kate. For which she has forgiven them yet. Dan told her it was John's fault, she said he ought to have known better than to have trusted John. Well I got home just in time for a party at Mr. Howe, which comes off tonight. I have been resting myself for it. You will think so when I tell you this is Friday evening and I have cooked but one meal and washed dishes but once. Have never stepped off the porch, been upstairs or swept the floor. The bachelors were willing to do it and I was willing to let them as I have not got over my jolting yet.

Letter dated February 7 to Mary Ellen McClure

Well, Ellen the party as ever, had a very, very good time and I feel better today than I did yesterday. After I got there I heard Mother was very sick and they had sent for Geo. And Ada had gave up coming for which I was very sorry, for I had not seen her. But she finally came saying Mother was better and Lydia was with her. Lt. Cooper came with her, also O. A. Cooper with a lady from Table Rock. Mother has been sick some time, about as she was last winter. George says it is just ____ and father's back is bad again. We are going there this evening. I expect mother is feeling abused already but I was not able to go until yesterday, and then couldn't go there and to the party too. I suppose it could be hard to make mother understand how I could feel better after the party, but it is even so and you can see how it is when I tell you we ate breakfast at 12 today.

Letter—no date

Have been to my fathers, found mother so sick that I think she will never get well. We stayed a day and night, just came home this evening and thought I would write while Dan read the news. The woman they have had was that dreadful woman Mrs. Gool, has left her husband again, and her and her baby made more work than she did and now when they are needing help so bad, she is away. ____fashion, but has her thing there expecting to come back when she pleases. Will bid you good night as I am very sleepy.

1875 Letter dated February 20, 1875, to Mary Ellen and William John

Dear Brother and Sister,

It is my duty to inform you of the death of Mother McClure. We left her on Sunday night very sick. We did not think of her dying so soon. We were sent for before day. Went as soon as we could get there but found her a corpse. George says her disease was inflammation of the kidney and dropsy, but I think George didn't know. Dan will write to you in a few days. With love to you both, I close hoping to hear from you soon. . . . .A. V. McClure

1875 Letter dated April 12, 1875, to Mary Ellen McClure

Dear Ellen,

Received your last a few days since. Was very happy to hear from Will and that he had been well and safe for I did feel uneasy. I am also thankful that you find ways of passing your time pleasantly during his long stay. One thing I presume you are blessed with, that is something like summer weather while we are having perfect winter. It has been blowing and snowing for the last twenty-four hours, which looks dull for my little chickens and pale looking tomato plants. But it is clearing off now and we expect spring weather just as we have been doing for the last month. Went to Table Rock Saturday. Mrs. Norris came to the store and invited me home with her and as I was tired staying at the store and didn't expect Dan to be ready to come home until late, I went, and as you might suppose was caught there for supper, had a short grace. I am not prepared to say whether it was good, bad or indifferent, as I paid no attention. I was taking that opportunity to observe the pious actions of the rest of the company. While there the hack drove down to Murfries and stopped, but stood in such a way I could not see whether anyone got out. I thought it might be your arrival, would have gone down to see, but Mrs. Norris sent her little boy and arranged everything for keeping me there. Told the boy to ask if Mrs. Will McClure had come, if so, to tell her Mrs. Dan McClure was there. My business was to see Mary about the weaving so, stopped a few minutes at Mr. Perishes. It is one of the prettiest places I know of, but the house was full of women. Need I tell you who they were? Sometimes I feel very lonely indeed but would rather be alone always than in such company. Mrs. Chamber is moving into Lon Cooper's house. He tried hard to get Dan to move in his house and board him. The idea didn't suit me one bit. Dan hardly knows what he will do yet sometimes talks of having his cattle herder at house. I know just how pleasant that would be for me. While he would be running around, I would stay here to see to the wants of the herder. I feel like I would rather do the herding myself even if I had to stay out in the rain and get thunder stroked. Charley Norris is hired to Mr. Gidding to work on the farm. They don't know what to do with him, he has no notion of being a gentleman or merchant wants to run around something like Will. They say when he talks to them about it he always holds up Will for an example. I believe he will be a smart and good man. How many boys raised like him, would think of working on a farm. Lyde is in Kansas City staying with a man by the name of Thomas, so he can prove his citizenship and thereby get employment. I believe I have never told you that John Ball was married last New Years to Maggie Liby. To me it is clear out of the notion of buying the mill. Thinks he can make more in some other way. The surest way for him is to put the money in the bank in land. French Benidozz is in a bad situation. Sold his ___ to go to California and now can't sell his place. says he had a tract of land rented in California. Mr. Bell is as bad off as ever, and would like to sell his rented house in California. He would also like to sell his farm. He tried hard to get the money to pay the debts that Dan was security on, but failed. So he let Dan have a team and Dan is to pay the debts. Jim is just able to go about – sometimes his feet and legs are very much swollen and sometimes he has no power of them. Nancy Brocks man is still at Pikes Peak. Will not be home this summer. She says he writes for her to come to him but she won't go. I told her I should think she would go with half an invitation. When you come to Atchison, if you have time to go to see Eglestones, you will find them clever and she told me to be sure to tell you and Will to come and see them when you are passing through. Mary Allen can play croquet and I think you and her and Kate can learn too. You will find in one of the investigators I sent Col lecture. I will send a couple more. Hope you will write as soon as you get this. I suppose Dan would send some love or speak if he was here. My love to yourself and Will and Ann.

1876   The U.S. government issues a ruling that all Indians must live on reservations.

        June 25: The Battle of Little BigHorn

Illustration 46. Photo roster of the members of North Texas Cattlemen's Association. William John appears in second row from bottom, fourth photo from left.

1877 [2]Mary Ellen goes back to Silver Lake, Kansas, for the birth of first child, [3]Guy Vincent.

[2]William John partners with D.N. Robb in Mercantile & Cattle Company in Atoka, Indian Territory.

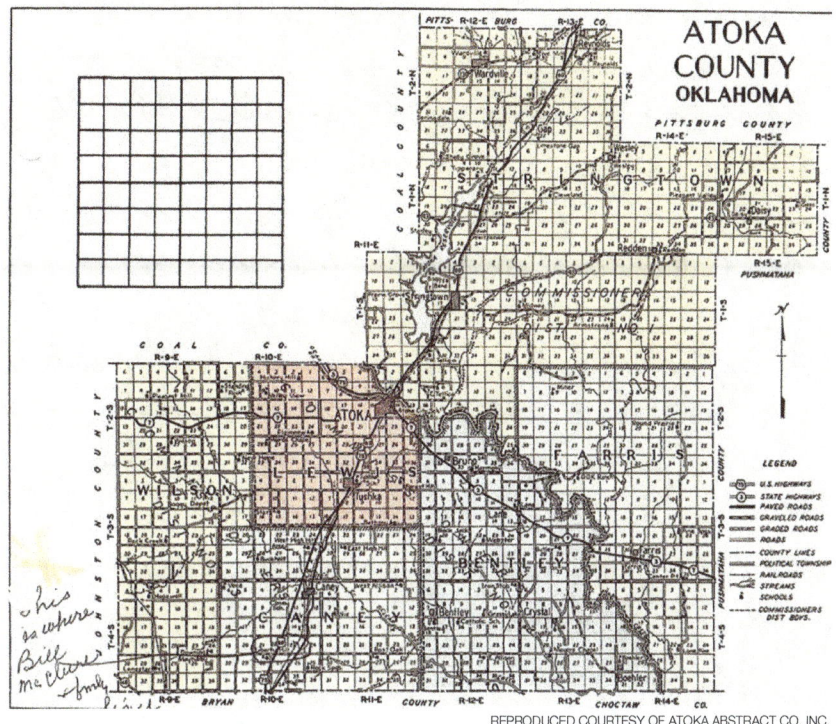
Illustration 47. Platt showing site of the 7C Ranch headquarters

1877 Letter dated October 4, 1877, from W.J. McClure in Atoka, Indian Territory, to Mary Ellen McClure in Silver Lake, Kansas (Shawnee County)

Dearest Ellen,

I received yours of the 29 yesterday and you cannot imagine how much pleasure it gave me to hear that your good health still continued. I have been here 4 days, have been buying cattle here, will ship tomorrow, will go to Nebraska first for I expect Sister Mary is wanting to see me. I will only go as far as Sedalia, Mo. You can write to me at Nebraska. I will be down to see you as soon as I can get off. As I have no news to write I will close hoping to see you soon. Yours ever, W. McClure

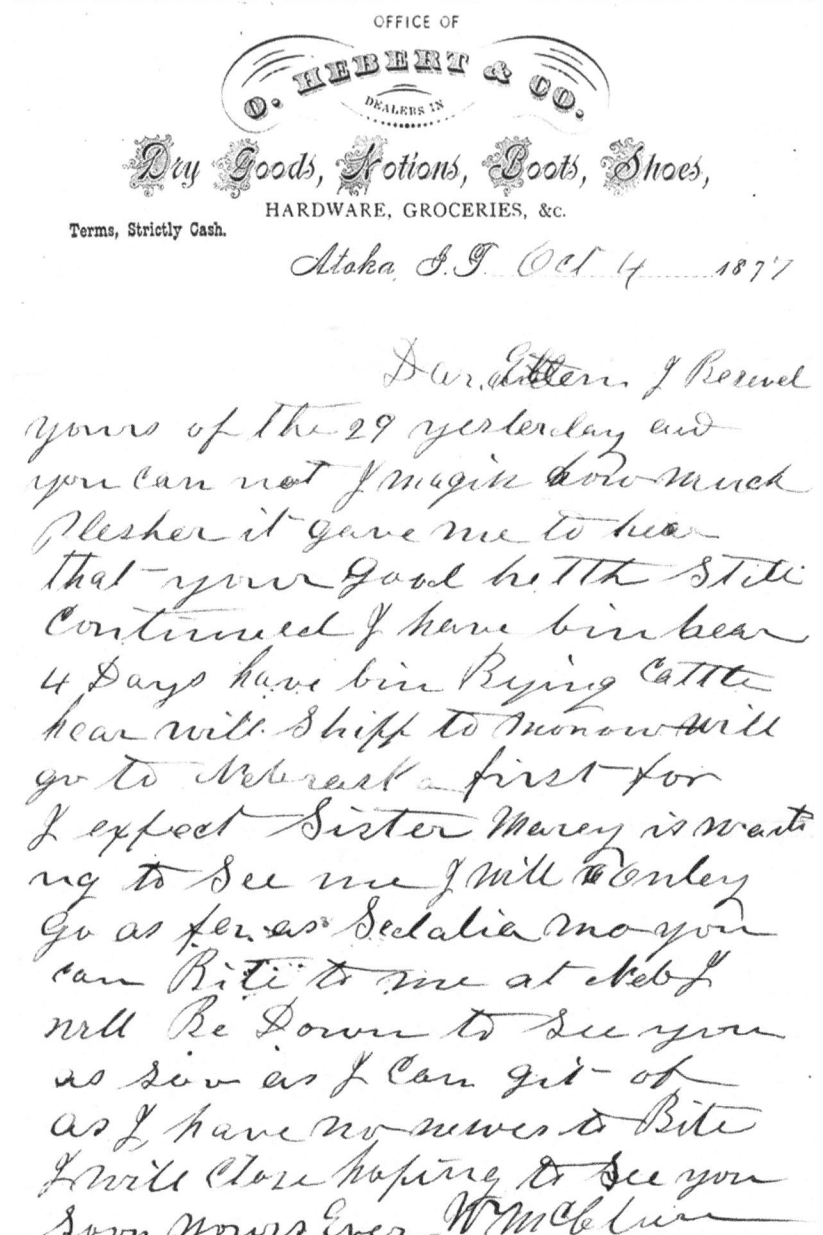

Illustration 48. ²William McClure's letter to his wife

May 19 – July 2, 1877. Notification about overcharge on cars for shipping cattle. Tonnage overcharge of $445.00 July, 1877, M.K. & T. Railroad—to McClure & Cooper at Atoka I. T.

1877   Sioux chief Crazy Horse dies.

Letter to Mary Ellen from William John

Dearest Ellen,

    I got back here today and went to the offices and found a letter from earlier to you and saw that Mary _____ is in Nebraska and wants to return in eight weeks to cut and hay. Brysun is so that I cannot go without going west. I have written to others to have our story . . . (rest of letter lost).

Letter written to Mary Ellen from W. J. McClure. No date given

Dear and Most Beloved Wife,

    Today finds me well and I hope it may find you well in the same good health. I have not received an answer to my last, yet but hope that I will shortly. We have not had more than four days of dry weather since ____ but today is very fine. I am in hopes that our wet season is over. I have no news of any importance tonight. ____ has been very high ____ was about on the Grand River a few days ago. And four mules drowned everything lost here at present but if the weather stays the cattle will soon be fat and then times will liven up. Since grass has got up so that cattle can fill themselves they don't trouble me much and I have got considerable spare time to loaf, but it is a dull place for that business. I go to town every day and spend a few hours and that way I manage to get along without getting the blues too bad. Now my dearest, I want you to write soon. Now a pleasant goodbye to you all — W. J. McClure

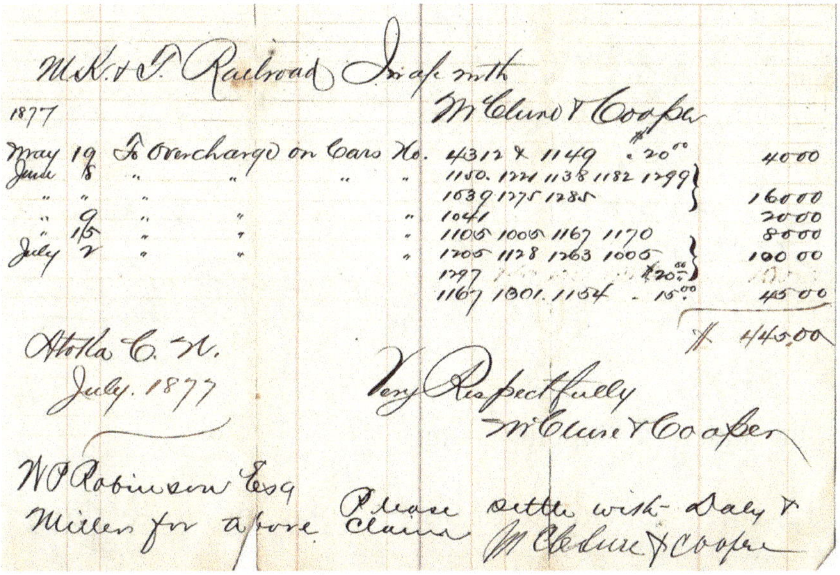

Illustration 49. Receipt for McClure & Cooper

1878 By this date the McClures had moved to Atoka, Indian Territory. We have a letter from Missouri, Kansas & Texas Railway addressed to Wm. McClure Esq. dated February 8, 1878, postmarked St. Louis. Sent to Johnson PO, Indian Territory.

Dear Sir,

In answer to your favor of the 24th _____. Will name you the following rates on cattle. ____good for the present, Stringtown to St. Louis. $90.00 per car; Atoka to St. Louis good for the present. Stringtown to St. Louis, $90.00 per car; Atoka to St. Louis $90.00 per car; McAllister to St. Louis, $90.00 per car; Caddo to St. Louis, $90.00 per car. ____rates are accepted please advise me. Yours truly, W.F. Robinson

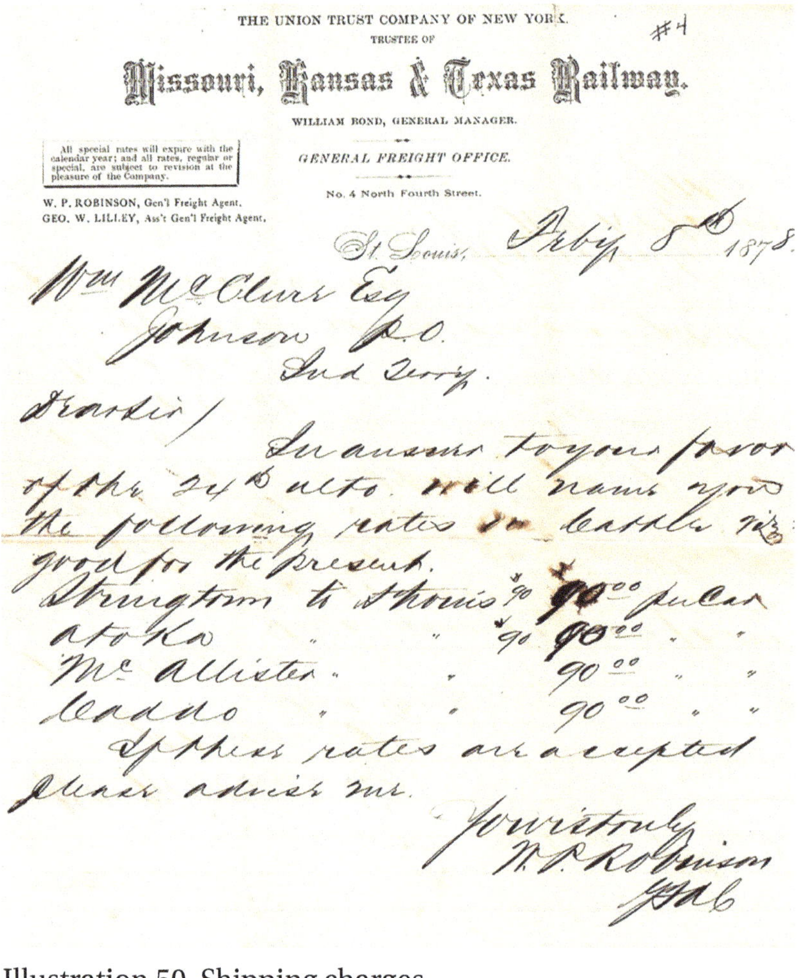

THE UNION TRUST COMPANY OF NEW YORK.
TRUSTEE OF
Missouri, Kansas & Texas Railway.
WILLIAM BOND, GENERAL MANAGER.

All special rates will expire with the calendar year; and all rates, regular or special, are subject to revision at the pleasure of the Company.

GENERAL FREIGHT OFFICE.
No. 4 North Fourth Street.

W. P. ROBINSON, Gen'l Freight Agent.
GEO. W. LILLEY, Ass't Gen'l Freight Agent.

#4

St. Louis, Feby 8th 1878.

Wm McClure Esq
Johnson P.O.
Ind Terry.

Dear Sir/
In answer to your favor of the 24th ulto. will name you the following rates on cattle viz: good for the present.
Stringtown to St. Louis 90 90.00 per car
Atoka " " 90 90.00 " "
McAllister " " 90.00 " "
Caddo " " 90.00 " "
If these rates are accepted please advise me.

Yours truly
W. P. Robinson
G.F.A.

Illustration 50. Shipping charges

1879 December 12, 1879. [3]David Victor born, Atoka, Indian Territory

1880 U. S. Federal Census
[2]W. J.'s brother [2]Thomas Jr. and family located in Johnson County Nebraska, Thomas Jr., Ellen, Hannah, Hester, Ira, Nina, Idella

1882 March 27, [3]Veta Ellen born in Liberty Hill, Atoka, Indian Territory

1882 William John buys the M. H. Ranch when Mage Hodge dies.
He ran cattle here.

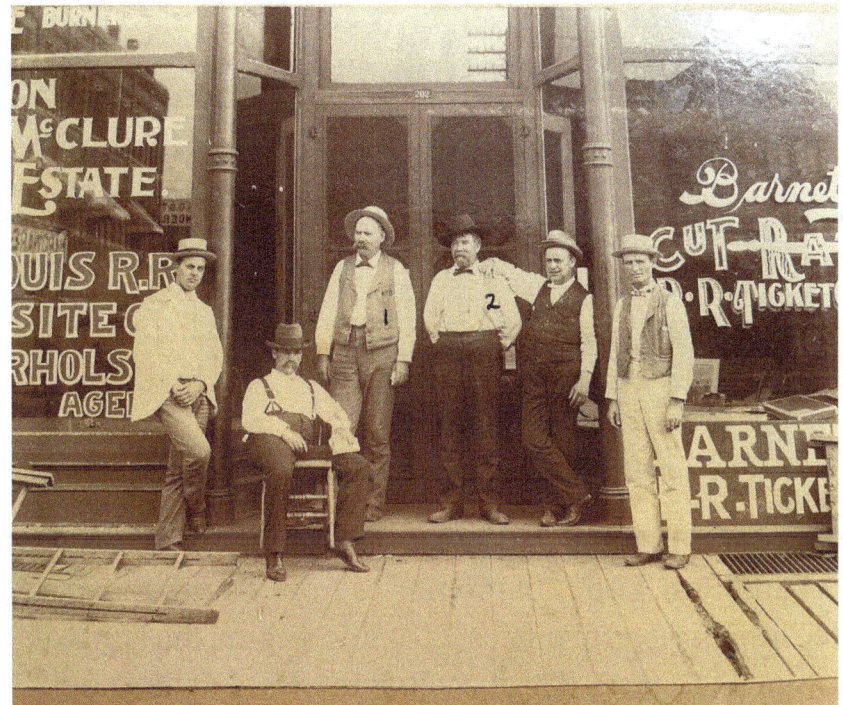

Illustration 51. William John as a partner in Carson and McClure Real Estate

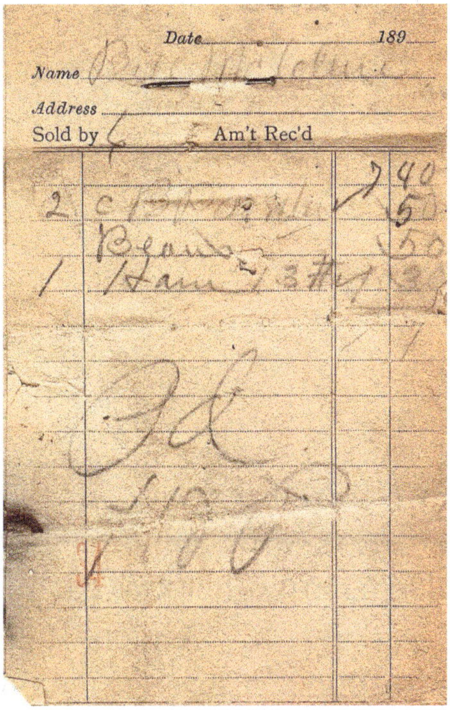
Date 189
Name
Address
Sold by Am't Rec'd
Beans
Ham

Illustration 52. Cost of goods

1883 Member in good standing of Oklahoma Lodge No. 4, Atoka, Indian Territory
Affiliated March 17, 1883

1884 William John buys out the Griffinstein Ranch, called the Turkey Track Ranch.

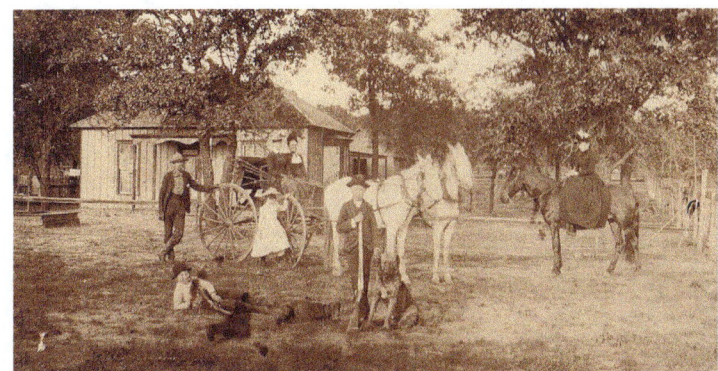

Illustration 53. (1886) Early ranch home
(left to right: Dave, #2; Veta, #3; Guy, #4)

1884   Glass milk bottles introduced

1889   The Oklahoma land run on April 22, 1889, opens settlement in Oklahoma Territory

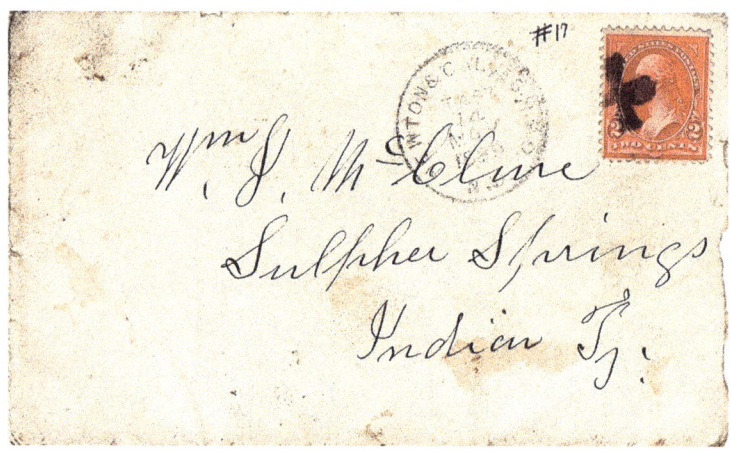

Illustration 54. 1889 Envelope with letter to William J. McClure

1889   Shortly after the Oklahoma Land Run. Letter of memories from an unknown lady who mentions ²Bill McClure in several places. Last line begins the story of ²Bill McClure. He rented about 75 horses for homesteaders to make the Land Run of 1889.

> The heads of the family and all the children over twenty-one years and older could allot 160 acres. All under twenty-one years old only got 80 acres.
>
> My mother died when I was fifteen years old. My baby sister was three weeks old. Grandmother took the baby and raised her. Our cousin, Mary Hardin, came to live with us and assist me in taking care of my younger brothers and sisters. There were nine children of us.
>
> Indian - Pioneer History
> Vol. 7, page 272-274

Illustration 55. Random letter outside the McClure Family describing Land Allotment to Native Tribe Families in Oklahoma Territory

1887 The Santa Fe Railroad comes through Indian Territory. William John was the first to ship a trainload of cattle on this new line. His cowboys built the loading corrals near the present site of the Santa Fe Station in Oklahoma City. The tally of cattle with the 7C brand was in the thousands.

One of the best known of the old cattlemen whose operations were extended to Indian Territory shortly after the close of the Civil war was the late William J. McClure, who died at his home in Oklahoma City in 1899. The extent of his early operations can be judged from the fact that at one time he had under lease the entire Kickapoo and Pottawatomie Indian reservations, comprising what are now Pottawatomie and Lincoln Counties of the state of Oklahoma. He was a typical pioneer— courageous, energetic, and resourceful. He belonged to a pioneer family of the state of Nebraska, having been born near Nebraska City, and in 1869 came with other members of his family to the Indian Territory, where he quickly became one of the most prominent stockmen. Twenty years before the original Oklahoma was opened for settlement, he established what became the famous Seven C ranch, on the Canadian river, about sixteen miles east of the present site of Oklahoma City. (The Seven C flats take their name from this ranch.) The Seven C was Mr. McClure's head ranch, although his family had their home at Johnsonville, farther down the Canadian, in the Chickasaw Nation. In 1878 the family moved to Atoka in the Choctaw Nation. At the opening of Oklahoma, on April 22, 1889, Mr. McClure and his son, Guy V., made the run. The homestead selected by the elder McClure is best known in Oklahoma as the famous Maywood addition, adjoining the city on the northeast, which is now the aristocratic residence section of Oklahoma City. In 1896 he was the largest individual property holder in Oklahoma City and furnished more money toward getting the Frisco Railway into the city from Sapulpa than any other man. He was a charter member of the Oklahoma Consistory and the India Temple, A.A.O.N.M.S.— *A History of the State of Oklahoma–1908*

Illustration 56. April 22, 1889. Lining up for the Land Run

1889 Oklahoma Territory is part of the 7C Ranch, when William John is ordered to move his cattle out prior to the opening/land run. He decided to leave several of his cowboys posted along the route with fresh horses. He started from the ranch house at Choctaw and with the advantage of fresh horses he made it into Oklahoma Station—present day Oklahoma City—before anyone else. He was the first to stake a claim—the Maywood Addition. Later, Mr. Morris Lowenstein—the next man to stake a claim after William John—contested William John's claim. But, when it was brought to trial, Judge Roy Hoffman, who tried the case, said they "could find no law prohibiting these cowboys from using their own cowboy's horses to form a relay-type race into the territory." Others from William John's ranch, including his nephew and ranch foreman,

Frank Gault, also used the relay method and staked early claims. The case was ultimately taken to federal district court. William John McClure's claim was upheld.

Separate trial of William John's nephew and ranch manager—Frank Gault. Secretary Hoke Smith found that Gault did not *personally take* relay horses to be used in the race on April 22, 1899 (Fuller v. Gault et al., 21 L. D. 176 (1895). Witness Dan W. Perry said that Gault, Bill McClure, and Frank Cook "sent horses ahead by some Indian boys who were holding them beside the trail and they changed horses twice before they reached their respective homesteads."

Illustration 57. Oklahoma City June 1, 1889. Forty days after the Land Run on April 22: Is it possible to put up so many nearly completed structures in 39 days?

$53.00 Oklahoma, O. T. Oct 30 1891
On or before December 11, 1891 days after date, waiving grace or protest, we, or either of us, jointly and severally, promise to pay the order of at First National Bank in Oklahoma City,
Fifty-three DOLLARS
value received, with 12 per cent. interest per annum thereon, from maturity until paid, and in case of legal proceedings to collect this note we agree to pay 10 per cent additional to the amount as attorneys' fees.
No. 1737
Due Dec 11/91
Edgar M. Smeet
Wm McClure

Sherman, Texas, 1890 No.
THE MERCHANTS & PLANTERS NATIONAL BANK OF SHERMAN
Pay to the order of $2100.00
Two thousand Dollars
PAID APR 24 1890 Merchants & Planters Nat. Bank SHERMAN, TEXAS
Wm McClure

Sherman, Texas, Sept 1 1890 No.
THE MERCHANTS & PLANTERS NATIONAL BANK OF SHERMAN
Pay to the order of J H & E H Brand $8940.00
Eight thousand nine hundred forty Dollars
PAID
Wm McClure

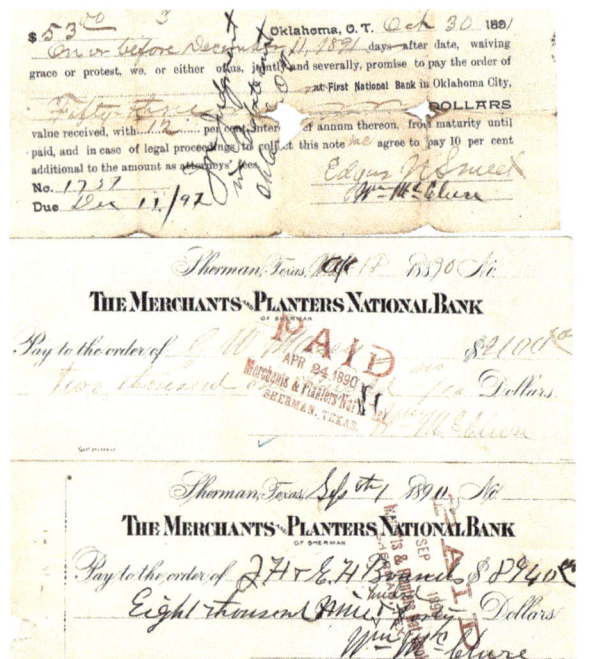

Illustration 58. Checks written in 1890 and 1891

JAMES GEARY, PREST. L. A. GILBERT, CASH. A. L. WELSH, ASST. CASH.
Citizens Bank
CAPITAL $50,000.
Oklahoma City, I. T. June 1892
Recd of Wm McClure ~~note~~ Two Thousand dollars as first payt of 50% on 40 shares stock in Oklahoma Natl Bank
L A Gilbert

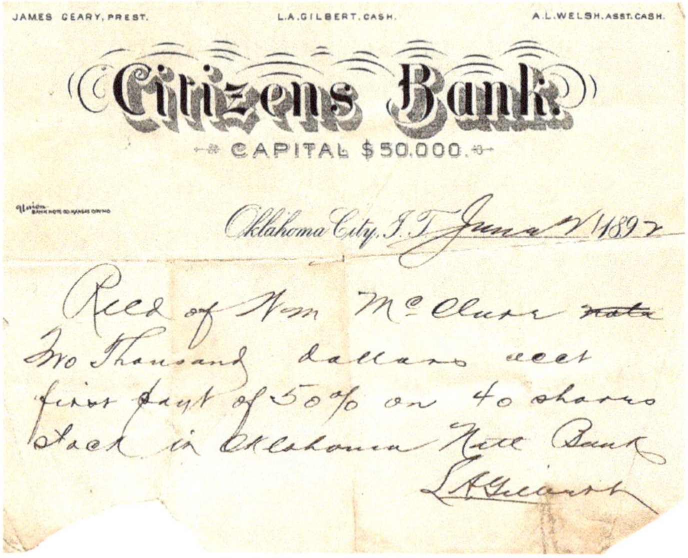

Illustration 59. Receipt for payment

JAMES GEARY, PREST. L. A. WELSH, ASST. CASH.
Citizens Bank #15
CAPITAL $50,000.
Oklahoma City, I. T. 1893
Received of Stiles and Geary on their note of August 6 due Feb 1st 94 $9194.00 Endorsed this date
W J McClure
Oct 13 '93 Received of Stiles and Geary to be credited on their note given to Womans $338.00
W J McClure

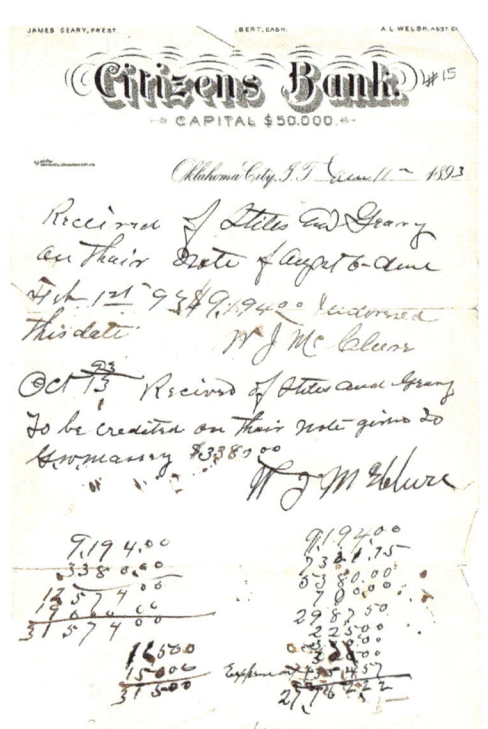

Illustration 60. Payment and computations

1890 NA, GLO, "G" Letter Book vol. 12, pp. 115-120; Sec. Hoke Smith to Com. Gen. Land Office, April 8(?), 1895. NA, Int. Dept., Lands and R. R. Div., Rec. Letters Sent. Vol. 171, p. 114-115; Garner v Brooks, 94 Pac. 694 (1908), 97 Pac. 995

(1908); BLM, Oklahoma City Tract Book, page 2 — *The Chronicles of Oklahoma, Spring, 1959*[2]

The Oklahoma City claim staked was east of the Santa Fe tracks on what was known as the Maywood Addition. Later the McClures purchased property on the west side, and at one time had large property holdings there. McClure's Addition was named after the McClures. The addition includes the area around NW 11th and North Hudson.

He had a house at 7th & Broadway.
He gave the land for St. Anthony Hospital.
He gave the land for the railroad tracks.
He sold the land where the Skirvin Hotel currently stands.
He gave 200 horses for the construction of the railroad into Oklahoma City.
He built the first grandstand and rodeo grounds on his property.

An Oklahoma City newspaper article from 1950

"THE SMOKING ROOM" BY R. G. M.
From The Daily Oklahoman

The McClure ranch house was at the present NW 7th and North Broadway, and St. Anthony's hospital occupies a part of that ranch land.

OKLAHOMA CITY TIMES
Old stories in new type: from the Times files —

Under Thirty Years Ago— [2]William McClure, the well-known stockman of this City, was riding his horse "Comanche" a few days ago when the animal reared up and fell over backward and before McClure, who was an expert horseman, could get his feet from the stirrups, the horse fell on him, breaking one of his legs. McClure was rounding up cattle when the accident occurred.

We have a hand-written sheet listing the lots owned in Maywood:
    Lots 1 to 11 inclusive in in B4
    Lots 12 to 22 inclusive in B3
    Lots 12 to 22 inclusive
    In B/2 north half of B Lots 1 to 16 9
    Lots 27 to B9

---
[2] *The Chronicles of Oklahoma*, Spring 1959, XXXVII (no.1). Reproduced courtesy of the Oklahoma Historical Society

Lots 17 to 26 inclusive
In B16; Lots 5 to 12 inclusive
B28. McClure Addition
all of B2; D5
Lots 1 and 4 in B3
Lots 4 and 5 in B4
Lot 1 in B9
Lots 1 and 2 in B8
In Johnson and Gault Additions
Lots 1 and 2 and 3 in B2; also 13, 14, 15, 16,
Lots 1,2,3 in E44 Oklahoma City

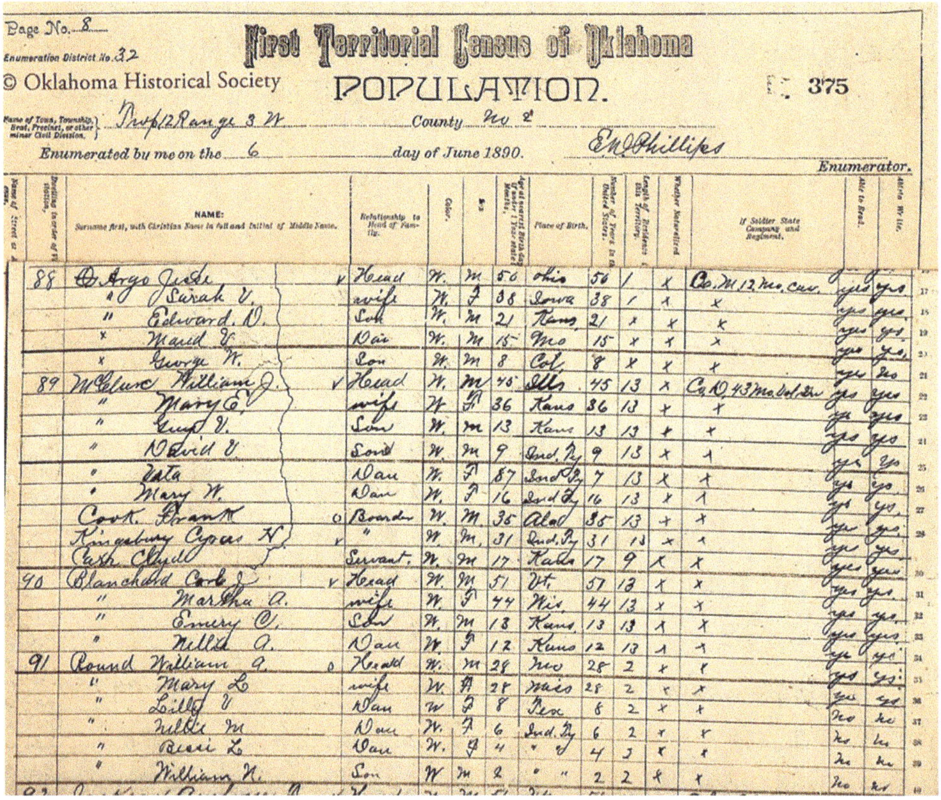
Page No. 8
Enumeration District No. 32
© Oklahoma Historical Society

First Territorial Census of Oklahoma
POPULATION.
375

Name of Town, Township, Precinct, or other minor Civil Division. Twp 12 Range 3 W County No 2
Enumerated by me on the 6 day of June 1890. E. W. Phillips Enumerator.

Dwelling in order of visitation	NAME: Surname first, with Christian Name in full and Initial of Middle Name.	Relationship to Head of Family.	Color.	Sex	Age	Place of Birth.	Number of Years in the United States.	Length of Residence in this Territory.	Whether Naturalized	If Soldier State Company and Regiment.	Able to Read.	Able to Write.
88	Argo Jesse	Head	W.	M	56	Ohio	56	1	x	Co. M 12 Mo. Cav.	yes	yes
	" Sarah V.	wife	W.	F	38	Iowa	38	1	x	x	yes	yes
	" Edward D.	Son	W.	M	21	Kans.	21	x	x	x	yes	yes
	" Maud V.	Dau	W.	M	15	Mo	15	x	x	x	yes	yes
	" George W.	Son	W.	M	8	Col.	8	x	x	x	yes	yes
89	McClure William J.	Head	W.	M	45	Ills	45	13	x	Co. D 43 Mo. Vol. Inf	yes	no
	" Mary E.	wife	W.	F	36	Kans	36	13	x	x	yes	yes
	" Guy V.	Son	W.	M	13	Kans	13	13	x	x	yes	yes
	" David V.	Son	W.	M	9	Ind. Ty	9	13	x	x	yes	yes
	" Veta	Dau	W.	F	87	Ind. Ty	7	13	x	x	yes	yes
	" Mary M.	Dau	W.	F	16	Ind. Ty	16	13	x	x	yes	yes
	Cook Frank	Boarder	W.	M	35	Ala	35	13	x	x	yes	yes
	Kingsbury Cyrus H.	"	W.	M	31	Ind. Ty	31	13	x	x	yes	yes
	Cash Clyde	Servant.	W.	M	17	Kans	17	9	x	x	yes	yes
90	Blanchard Cook J.	Head	W.	M	51	Vt.	57	13	x	x	yes	yes
	" Martha A.	wife	W.	F	44	Wis.	44	13	x	x	yes	yes
	" Emery C.	Son	W.	M	13	Kans.	13	13	x	x	yes	yes
	" Nellie A.	Dau	W.	F	12	Kans	12	13	x	x	yes	yes
91	Round William A.	Head	W.	M	28	Mo	28	2	x	x	yes	yes
	" Mary L.	wife	W.	F	28	Miss	28	2	x	x	yes	yes
	" Lilly V.	Dau	W	F	8	Tex	8	2	x	x	yes	yes
	" Nellie M	Dau	W.	F	6	Ind. Ty	6	2	x	x	no	no
	" Bessie L.	Dau	W.	F	4	" "	4	2	x	x	no	no
	" William H.	Son	W	M	2	" "	2	2	x	x	no	no

Illustration 61. First Census in Oklahoma Territory–June 1890

1890 First Territorial Census of Oklahoma. Page No. 8 Enumeration District No. 32; Twp. Range 3W; County No. 2; June 6, 1890. Position #89: William J. McClure; Mary E. McClure; Guy V.; David V.; Veta; Mary M

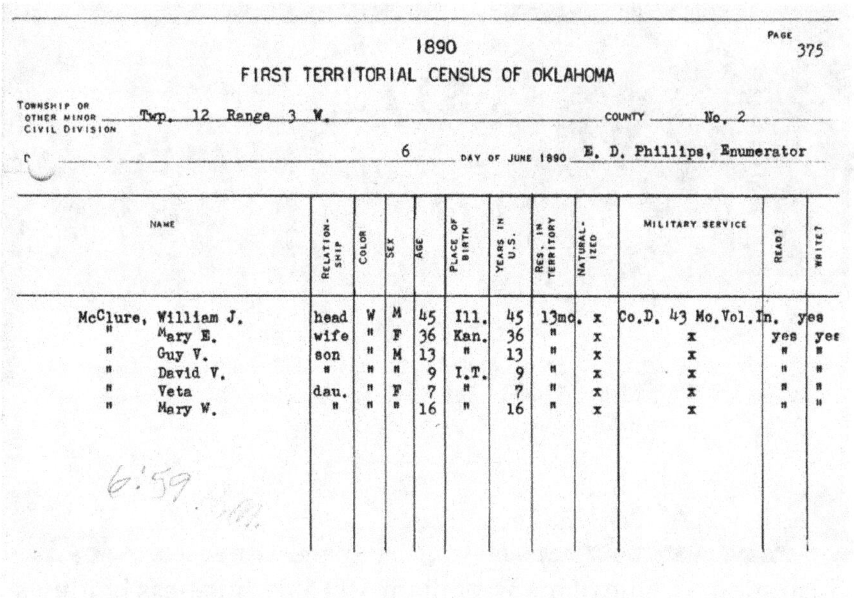

	1890 FIRST TERRITORIAL CENSUS OF OKLAHOMA	PAGE 375

Township or other minor Civil Division: Twp. 12 Range 3 W.   County No. 2

6 day of June 1890   E. D. Phillips, Enumerator

Name	Relationship	Color	Sex	Age	Place of Birth	Years in U.S.	Res. in Territory	Naturalized	Military Service	Read?	Write?
McClure, William J.	head	W	M	45	Ill.	45	13mo.	x	Co.D. 43 Mo.Vol.In.	yes	yes
" Mary E.	wife	"	F	36	Kan.	36	"	x	x	yes	yes
" Guy V.	son	"	M	13	"	13	"	x	x	"	"
" David V.	"	"	"	9	I.T.	9	"	x	x	"	"
" Veta	dau.	"	F	7	"	7	"	x	x	"	"
" Mary W.	"	"	"	16	"	16	"	x	x	"	"

Illustration 62. McClure family census–1890

1890 Bank Checks

    Sept. 8, The Merchants and Planters National Bank, Sherman, Texas—
      Pay to the order of J. H. & E.H. Bounds, $8,327.50 by Wm. McClure.

    September 18, The Merchants and Planters National Bank, Sherman, Texas—
      Pay to the order of G.W. Masey, $2,100.00 by Wm. McClure.

    September 24, The Merchants and Planters National Bank, Sherman Texas—
      Pay to the order of J. H. and E. H. Bounds, $8,940.00 by Wm McClure.

Receipt from Mason Temple for dues December 12, 1890, for $3.50

August 1, 1890. Certificate showing one share at $100.00 in the Masonic Hall

18?? The Battle of Wounded Knee with the Sioux-Ghost Dancers

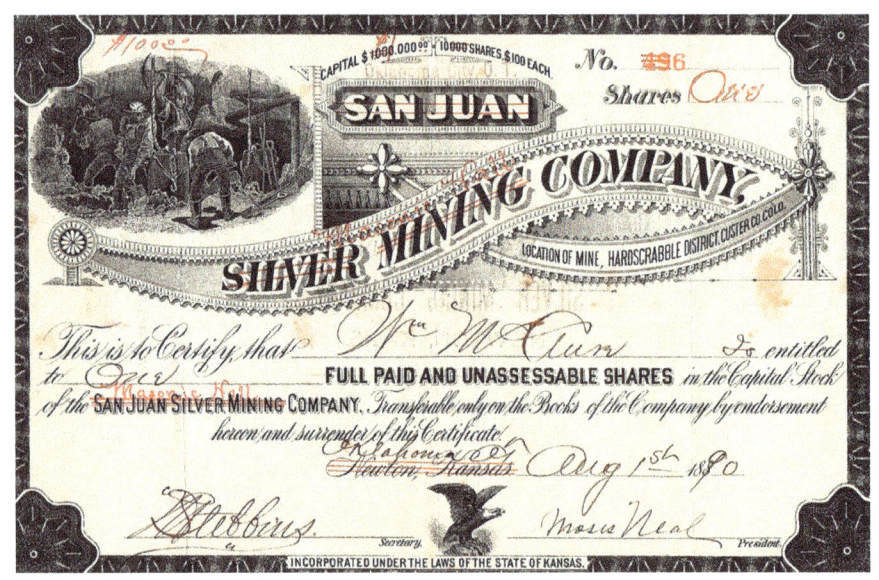

Illustration 63. One of many William McClure business holdings

1891 $53.00 Oklahoma, O. T., Oct. 30, 1891: On or before December 11, 1891, after date, waiving grace or protest, we, or either of us, jointly and severally, promise to pay to the order of the First National Bank in Oklahoma City, $53.00 value received, with 12% interest per annum thereon, from maturity until paid, and in case of legal proceedings to collect this note we agree to pay 10% additional to the amount as attorney's fees. Edgar N. Sweet & Wm McClure: No 1757. Due Dec. 13, 1891

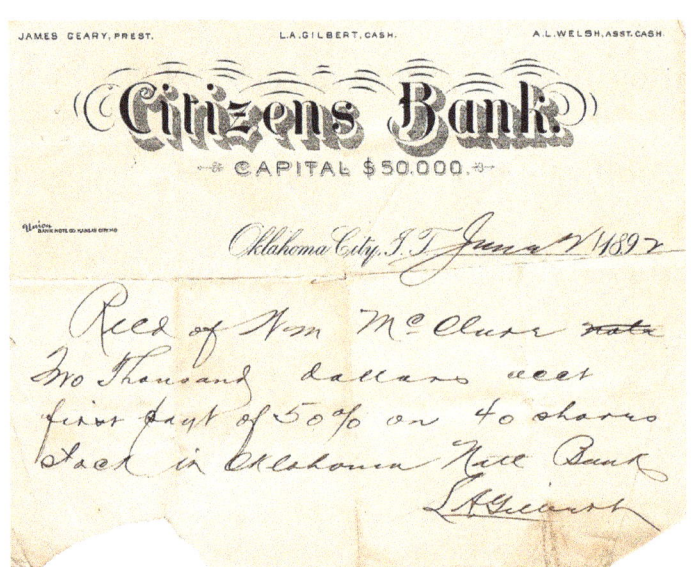

Illustration 64. Receipt of $2,000.00 for investment in Oklahoma National Bank

1893 January 11. Citizens Bank Oklahoma City, I. T. Received of Stiles and Geary on their note of deposit—due Feb. 1, 1893. $89,194.900 enclosed to date to W. J. McClure

October 13. Received of Stiles and Gray to be credited on their note given for $3,380.00 to W. J. McClure

May 22. Certificate of Noble Shrine India Temple

July 21. Certificate of Scottish Rite

1894

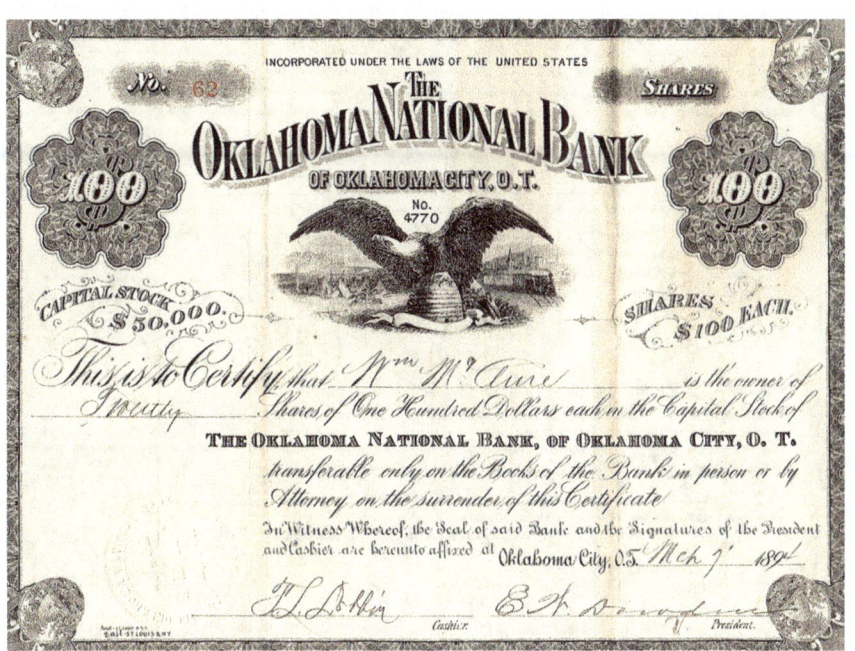

Illustration 65. Investment certificate

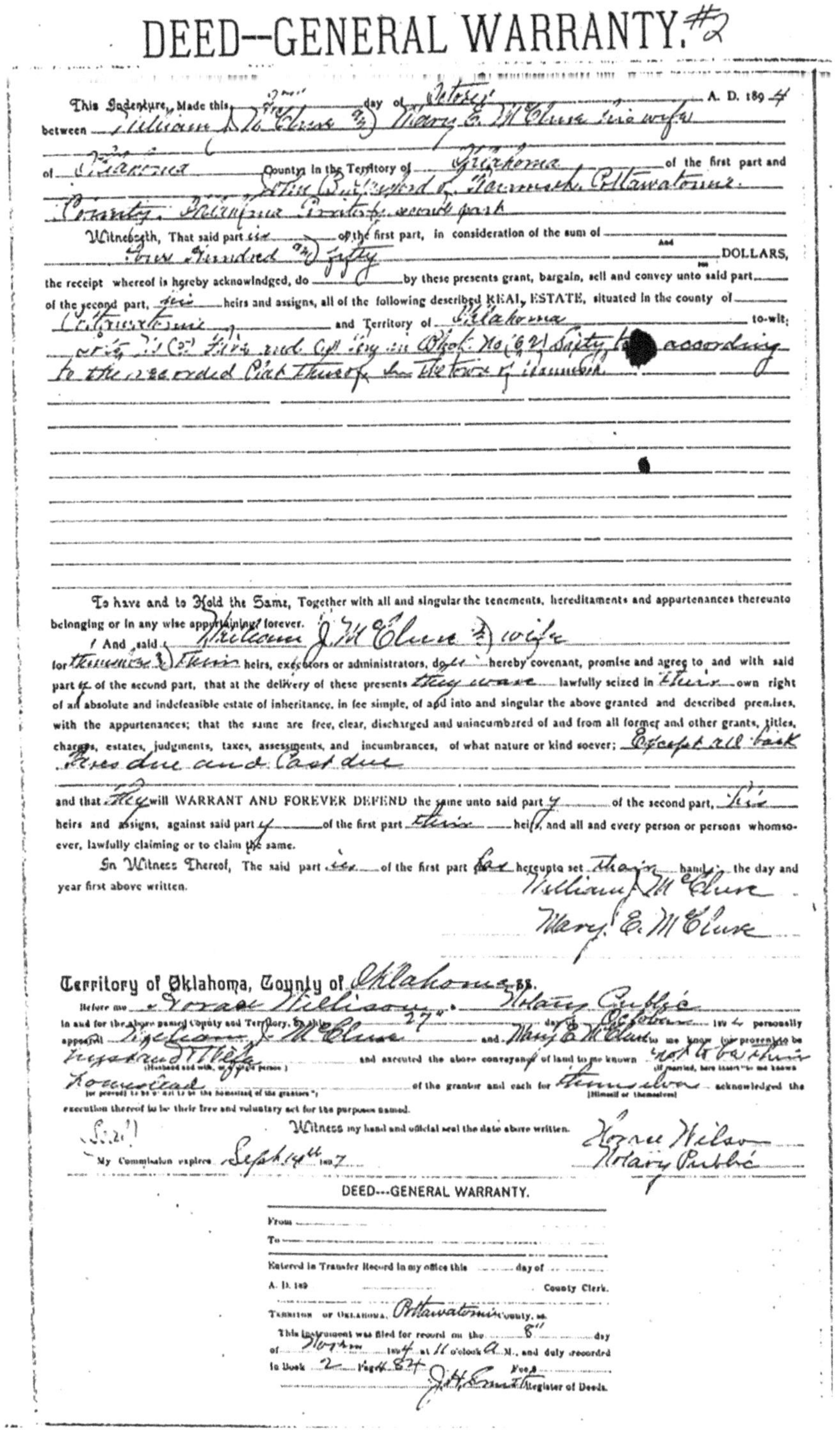

DEED--GENERAL WARRANTY. #2

This Indenture, Made this 2nd day of October A. D. 1894 between William J. McClure and Mary E. McClure his wife of Pottawatomie County in the Territory of Oklahoma of the first part and John Butterford of Tecumseh, Pottawatomie County, Oklahoma Territory, second part

Witnesseth, That said parties of the first part, in consideration of the sum of Four Hundred and Fifty DOLLARS, the receipt whereof is hereby acknowledged, do by these presents grant, bargain, sell and convey unto said part of the second part, his heirs and assigns, all of the following described REAL ESTATE, situated in the county of Pottawatomie and Territory of Oklahoma to-wit: Lots Three (3) Five and Six in Block No. (62) Sixty two according to the recorded Plat thereof in the town of Tecumseh

To have and to Hold the Same, Together with all and singular the tenements, hereditaments and appurtenances thereunto belonging or in any wise appertaining forever. And said William J. McClure and wife for themselves and their heirs, executors or administrators, do hereby covenant, promise and agree to and with said part of the second part, that at the delivery of these presents they were lawfully seized in their own right of an absolute and indefeasible estate of inheritance, in fee simple, of and into and singular the above granted and described premises, with the appurtenances; that the same are free, clear, discharged and unincumbered of and from all former and other grants, titles, charges, estates, judgments, taxes, assessments, and incumbrances, of what nature or kind soever; Except all back taxes due and past due

and that they will WARRANT AND FOREVER DEFEND the same unto said part y of the second part, his heirs and assigns, against said part y of the first part their heirs, and all and every person or persons whomsoever, lawfully claiming or to claim the same.

In Witness Thereof, The said parties of the first part has hereunto set their hands the day and year first above written.

William J. McClure
Mary E. McClure

Territory of Oklahoma, County of Oklahoma ss.

Before me Horace Williams, Notary Public in and for the above named County and Territory, on this 27 day of October 1894 personally appeared William J. McClure and Mary E. McClure to me known (or proven) to be husband and wife and executed the above conveyance of land to me known not to be their homestead of the grantor and each for themselves acknowledged the execution thereof to be their free and voluntary act for the purposes named.

Witness my hand and official seal the date above written.

(Seal) Horace Wilson
Notary Public

My Commission expires Sept 14th 1897

DEED---GENERAL WARRANTY.

From
To
Entered in Transfer Record in my office this day of
A. D. 189 County Clerk.
Territory of Oklahoma, Pottawatomie County, ss.
This instrument was filed for record on the 8th day of Nov 1894 at 11 o'clock A. M., and duly recorded in Book 2 Page 824 Fees
J. H. Smith Register of Deeds.

Illustration 66. Real estate deed

1894 March 26

DAILY TIMES JOURNAL
page 1, column 5:

Oklahoma City, March 26–Bill McClure, a widely known capitalist and stockman, yesterday morning shot and instantly killed Hank Cunningham, a well-known character of this county. The difficulty grew out of some testimony regarding claim contests and has been brewing for years. Early in the night Cunningham threatened to kill McClure and went and got his Winchester. McClure was armed with a revolver. They met in the Turf Saloon yesterday morning about 6 o'clock. McClure's first shot broke Cunningham's shoulder and before he could fire a shot McClure emptied his six-shooter, putting two bullets through Cunningham's breast. The affair has been long expected, but still excites very strong comments.

A KILLING
The Norman Transcript *on Friday, March 30, 1894, pg. 1, Column 4:*

Hank Cunningham, a man with a record, was killed in Oklahoma City last Sunday morning by Bill McClure, a stock man of the place. The killing happened in the Turf Saloon at 6 o'clock in the morning. The parties had been quarreling during the day before. Cunningham made for McClure with a Winchester and McClure defended himself with a six shooter. At the preliminary trial McClure was released as it was proven that he did the deed in self-defense.

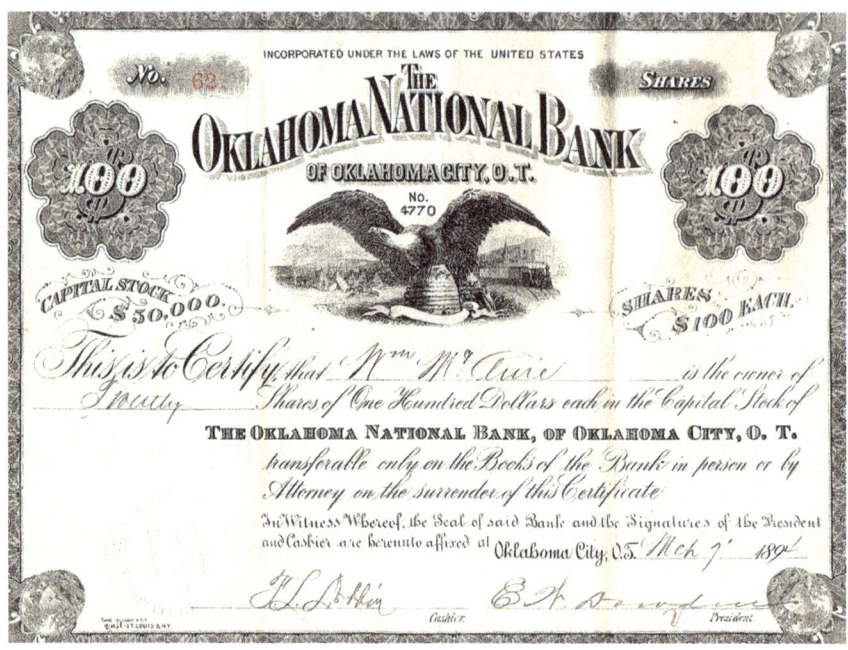

Illustration 67. March 7, 1894, Certificate of Stock in Oklahoma National Bank. 20 shares @ $100.00 each.

1895 October 3, Clinton, Missouri: Received from [2]W.J. McClure, Esqr. One Hundred and Five Dollars on Account at Baird College—Session 1895-1896, H. J. Baird. This was for [3]Veta Ellean's tuition.

1896

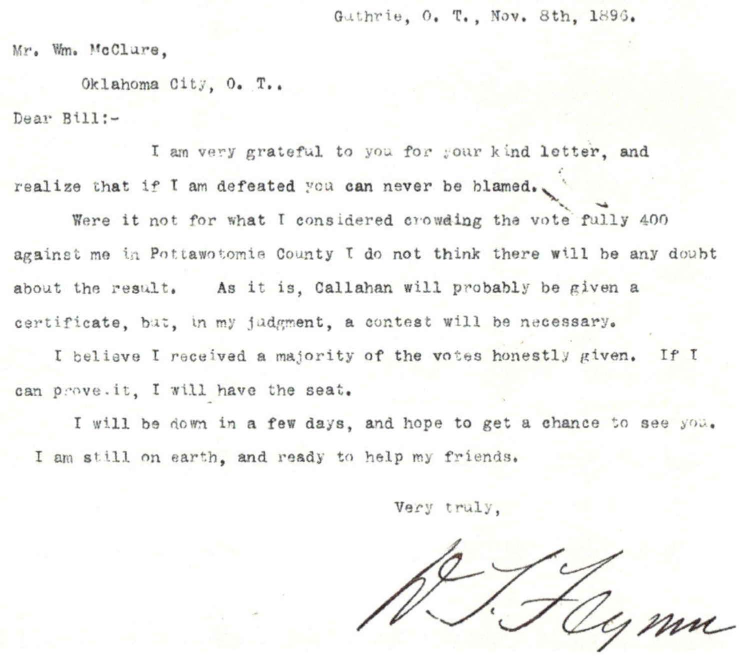

```
                                    Guthrie, O. T., Nov. 8th, 1896.

Mr. Wm. McClure,
      Oklahoma City, O. T..
Dear Bill:-
              I am very grateful to you for your kind letter, and
realize that if I am defeated you can never be blamed.
     Were it not for what I considered crowding the vote fully 400
against me in Pottawotomie County I do not think there will be any doubt
about the result.    As it is, Callahan will probably be given a
certificate, but, in my judgment, a contest will be necessary.
     I believe I received a majority of the votes honestly given.  If I
can prove it, I will have the seat.
     I will be down in a few days, and hope to get a chance to see you.
I am still on earth, and ready to help my friends.

                                         Very truly,
```

Illustration 68. Letter dated November 8, 1896 from D.J. Flynn, Guthrie, O.T. to Mr. Wm. McClure, Oklahoma City, O.T.

May 12, Gainesville, Texas: At sight pay to the order of Gainesville National Bank $57.55. Value received and charge to account of Porter & Porter to William McClure, Oklahoma City, Oklahoma Territory.

1897

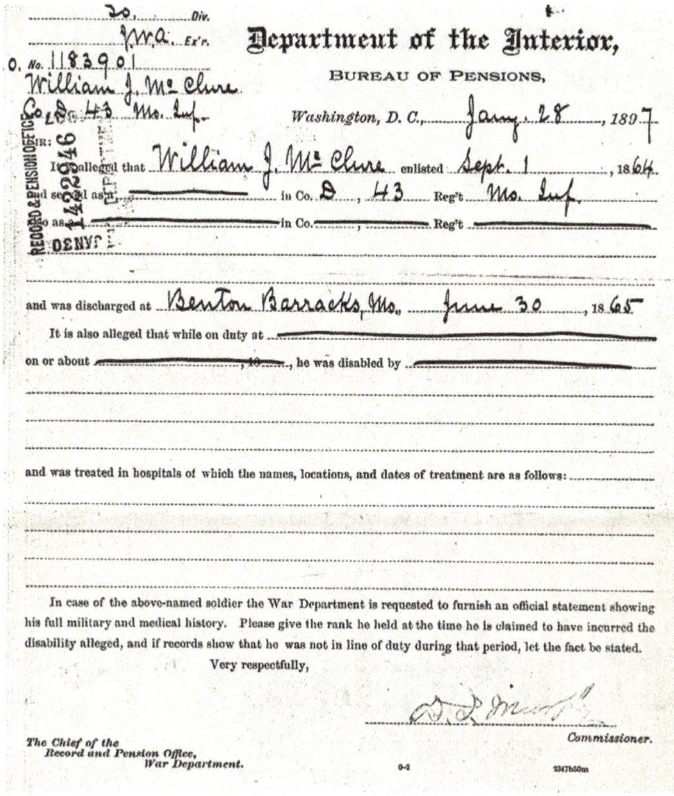

20 Div.
W.A. Ex'r.
O. No. 1183901
William J. McClure
Co. D, 43 Mo. Inf.

Department of the Interior,
BUREAU OF PENSIONS,
Washington, D. C., Jany. 28, 1897

SIR: It is alleged that William J. McClure enlisted Sept. 1, 1864, and served as ——— in Co. D, 43 Reg't Mo. Inf. also as ——— in Co. ———, Reg't ———, and was discharged at Benton Barracks, Mo. June 30, 1865.

It is also alleged that while on duty at ——— on or about ———, 18—, he was disabled by ———

and was treated in hospitals of which the names, locations, and dates of treatment are as follows:

In case of the above-named soldier the War Department is requested to furnish an official statement showing his full military and medical history. Please give the rank he held at the time he is claimed to have incurred the disability alleged, and if records show that he was not in line of duty during that period, let the fact be stated.

Very respectfully,

Commissioner.

The Chief of the Record and Pension Office, War Department.

Illustration 69. Bureau of Pensions document

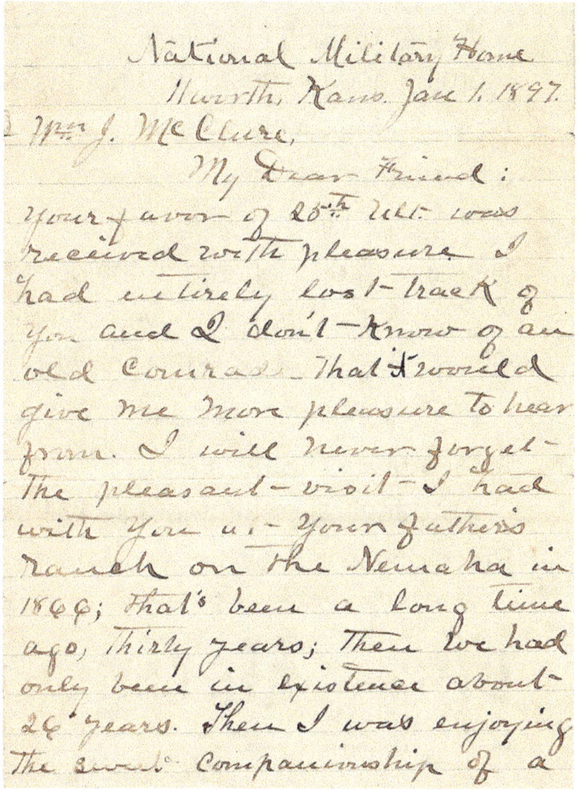

National Military Home
llworth, Kans. Jan 1. 1897.

Mr J. McClure,

My Dear Friend:

Your favor of 25th ult. was received with pleasure. I had entirely lost track of you and I don't know of an old comrade that I would give me more pleasure to hear from. I will never forget the pleasant visit I had with you at your father's ranch on the Nemaha in 1866; that's been a long time ago, thirty years; then we had only been in existence about 26 years. Then I was enjoying the sweet companionship of a

Illustration 70. Letter dated Jan. 1, 1897, from Ellsworth, Kansas to Wm. J. McClure from National Military Home written by Bill's friend, J. W. Dyer

1898 Spanish American War in Cuba. William John's son, David Victor serves as one of Teddy Roosevelt's original Roughriders.

1899 June 19. [2]William John dies at age 54. The newspaper called his death, "acute brain fever". Given today's medical knowledge, William John's death was probably caused by an abscessed tooth. He died at home with his family at his bedside. His son, [3]Guy, was in Mexico working as a civil engineer building the first major railroad in Mexico, at the time of his father's death. [3]Guy did not attend the funeral.

The Daily Times-Journal, June 20

WILLIAM MCCLURE DEAD
Died at 8 o'clock Last Night, After Several Months Illness

Last night at 8 o'clock the long expected death of William McClure occurred. Mr. McClure, who had been feeble for several months, took suddenly worse yesterday morning and his death was hourly expected all day. His children were telegraphed for when Miss Veta and Dave arrived, but Guy who was down in Mexico, could not arrive in time.

Mr. McClure has been in this and the Indian Territory for more than thirty years. He came into Oklahoma at the opening in '89. He has amassed a handsome home on Sixth street, where he lived several years and where he died.

He was 53 years old. He had been a man of remarkably strong constitution. He was a union soldier and a Mason of high standing. He has many friends who deeply sympathize with the bereaved family.

The funeral of Mr. McClure will take place tomorrow evening at 4 o'clock in the Presbyterian church.

Illustration 71. Newspaper notice of William John's Death

PASSED AWAY

Wm. J. McClure Expired Surrounded by His Family and Friends

At eight o'clock last evening Wm. J. McClure died of an acute brain trouble at his residence on the corner of 4th and Harvey streets. For several months he has been quite feeble and for a number of weeks was in an alarming condition while for several days just past his most intimate friends have despaired of his life.

About his bedside were his wife and son Dave and daughter Miss Veta. His older son Guy being unavoidably absent. His family and a large circle of friends did what they could to stay the ravages of death and without avail and he quietly passed away just as the sun was setting in the west.

Mr. McClure came to Oklahoma City at the opening day in 1889 and settled at the Maywood a present a part of Oklahoma City, later he erected his house on sixth street where he died, and where he lived for many years with his family.

He was 57 years of age. He acquired large real estate interests in various additions as well as the city proper, and left a considerable estate.

No one had more friends, and his (remainder of article lost).

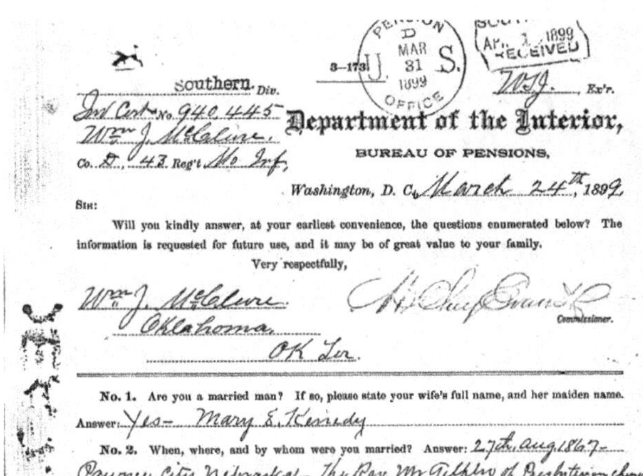

Southern Div. 3–1731 W.J.J. Ex'r.
Inv Cert No. 940.445
Wm J. McClure,
Co. D, 43 Reg't Mo Inf
Department of the Interior,
BUREAU OF PENSIONS,
Washington, D. C., March 24th, 1899.

SIR:

Will you kindly answer, at your earliest convenience, the questions enumerated below? The information is requested for future use, and it may be of great value to your family.

Very respectfully,
Commissioner.

Wm J. McClure
Oklahoma
OK Ter.

No. 1. Are you a married man? If so, please state your wife's full name, and her maiden name.
Answer: Yes – Mary E. Kennedy

No. 2. When, where, and by whom were you married? Answer: 27th Aug 1867 – Pawnee City Nebraska – The Rev. Mr Gilpin of Presbyterian church

No. 3. What record of marriage exists? Answer: The Certificate which is recorded in the clerks office Pawnee City Neb.

No. 4. Were you previously married? If so, please state the name of your former wife and the date and place of her death or divorce. Answer: No

No. 5. Have you any children living? If so, please state their names and the dates of their birth. Answer: Yes
Guy V. McClure Dec. 12th 1877 –
David V. McClure " 10th 1879 –
Veta E. McClure Mch 27th 1882

Date of reply, March 28th, 1899. Wm J. McClure (Signature.)

Illustration 72. Widow's pension, 1899

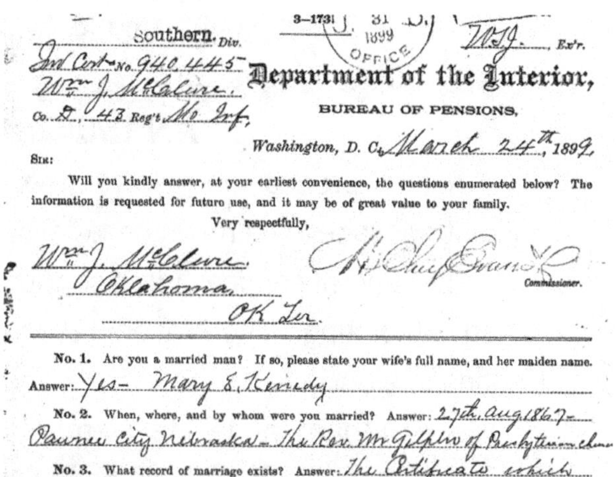

Southern Div. 3–1731 W.J.J. Ex'r.
Inv Cert No. 940.445
Wm J. McClure,
Co. D, 43 Reg't Mo Inf
Department of the Interior,
BUREAU OF PENSIONS,
Washington, D. C., March 24th, 1899.

SIR:

Will you kindly answer, at your earliest convenience, the questions enumerated below? The information is requested for future use, and it may be of great value to your family.

Very respectfully,
Commissioner.

Wm J. McClure
Oklahoma
OK Ter.

No. 1. Are you a married man? If so, please state your wife's full name, and her maiden name.
Answer: Yes – Mary E. Kennedy

No. 2. When, where, and by whom were you married? Answer: 27th Aug 1867 – Pawnee City Nebraska – The Rev. Mr Gilpin of Presbyterian church

No. 3. What record of marriage exists? Answer: The Certificate which is recorded in the clerks office Pawnee City Neb.

No. 4. Were you previously married? If so, please state the name of your former wife and the date and place of her death or divorce. Answer: No

No. 5. Have you any children living? If so, please state their names and the dates of their birth. Answer: Yes
Guy V. McClure Dec. 12th 1877 –
David V. McClure " 10th 1879 –
Veta E. McClure Mch 27th 1882

Date of reply, March 28th, 1899. Wm J. McClure (Signature.)

Illustration 73. Military pension, 1889

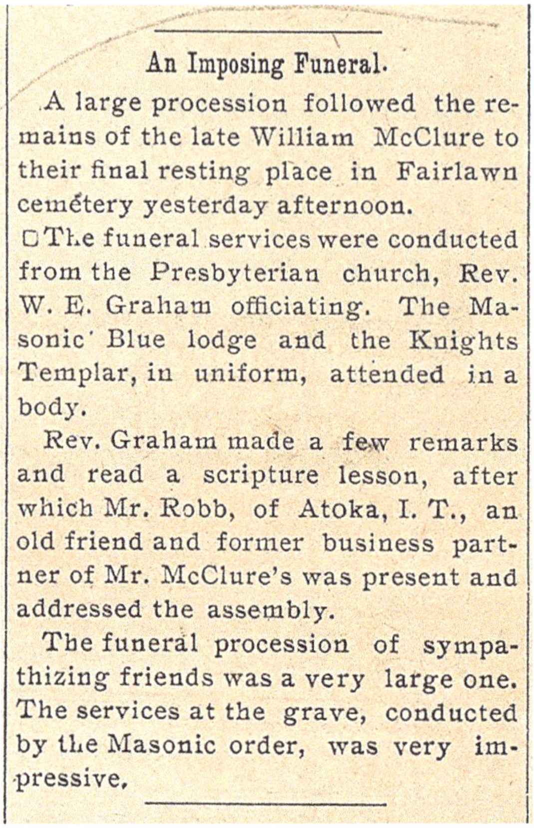

Illustration 74. Newspaper notice of William John's funeral

AN IMPOSING FUNERAL

A large procession followed the remains of the late William McClure to their final resting place in Fairlawn cemetery yesterday afternoon.

The funeral services were conducted from the Presbyterian church, Rev. W.E. Graham officiating. The Masonic Blue Lodge and the Knights Templar, in uniform, attended in a body.

Rev. Graham made a few remarks and read a scripture lesson, after which Mr. Robb, of Atoka, I. T. An old friend and former business partner of Mr. McClure's, was present and addressed the assembly.

The funeral procession of sympathizing friends was a very large one. The services at the grave, conducted by the Masonic order, was very impressive.

1899 June 20. Perry Oklahoma Territory letter to [2]Mary Ellen

My dear Sister,

I was pained to see on opening the evening paper the death of Mr. McClure. I felt when I last saw Mr. McClure that his days on Earth were short. Let me express in this

your hour of grief my sincerest sympathy, not simply moral expression, but sorrow. I have lost a friend for such, Mr. Mac has always shown himself to me to be. He has ever been to you a devoted and loving husband to his children. He was an exceptionally kind and tender father. The loss to you and them is irreparable and one which only time alone can heal. You can have no regrets as you have so faithfully and self sacrificing attended to his every want. While circumstances are such that it will be impossible for me to be with you, My dear Sister, I am with you in thought and my prayer is that you will trust on "Him" who has promised to be a husband to the widow and a father to the fatherless. Lovingly yours, Mrs. C. P. Walker

June 21. Letter to Mary Ellen from a friend at The Waverly Hotel, Eureka Springs, Arkansas

My Dear Mrs. McClure,

    I have just received the sad news of Mr. McC's death. Words fail to express my sympathy for you and the family. I know how sad and lonely you feel Dear Friend ____ I ____ to reconcile. I am so sorry I am away. I have not forgotten your comforting and say _____. Words when I was called upon to ____with my dear companion. Will come to see you on my return . Again you have my heart-felt sympathy. Yours devotedly,

    E. W. Massey

June 22, 1899. Letter to Mary Ellen on Bank of Minco stationary

My Dear Friend Mrs. McC,

    Feeble words will not express my regret of hearing the sad intelligence of the death of your noble and ever loving companion and my warm friend, Mr. McClure. But this is a debt we all have to pay and those who are living by Faith and God's promises have every assurance this departure is only temporary. And what a glorious meeting there will be in the celestial temple above. Please do not try to bear this affliction all alone, but _____ will share a part of it if we will only ask him. Rec'd the intelligence too late for me to attend the funeral exercises, which I will always regret. If _____ come down and spend a few days with _____ us any day and come meet you at the train. With God's blessings and my best wishes, I am Your Loving adopted Boy Ed B. Johnson

June 30. Letter to Mrs. McClure on office stationery of the Indian Citizen Publishing Company, Atoka, Indian Territory

Dear Mrs. McClure,

    Yours inclosing the $12.00 to place to your credit for Indian Citizen recd. Many thanks for the same, I am glad you enjoy the paper. I felt much sympathy for you in your *recent sorrow, but loneliness will be your great source of pain. Grown children bring grown and you provided for in this _____ good will somewhat lighten your troubles that must now come upon you single handed and alone. I have thought of you many, many times. I wish you all the success and pleasure that life can _____ hold for you. Love to Veta and the boys, and yourself. Sincerely, Thomas E. Smiser*

1900 U.S. Federal Census; Oklahoma Territory, Oklahoma City
#1340, Vol. 12, District Number 167, Sheet #16, Page B:

1. [2]Mary E. McClure b. Dec. 1854; age 45
   Mother. Widow; Mother of 3; b. Kansas
   Father b. Ohio;
   Mother b. Ohio;
   Occupation, LandLady
2. [3]Veta E. b. March 1882, age 18, single; b. Indian Territory
3. [3]Guy V. b. 1877, age 22, single; b. Kansas; civil engineer

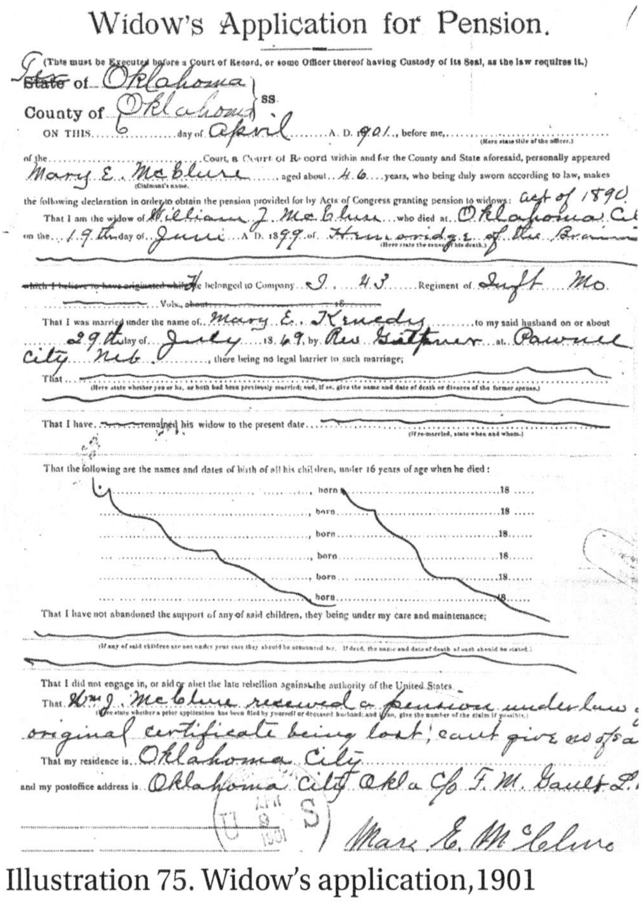

Widow's Application for Pension.

(This must be Executed before a Court of Record, or some Officer thereof having Custody of its Seal, as the law requires it.)

Ter State of Oklahoma }
County of Oklahoma } ss

ON THIS 6 day of April A. D. 1901, before me, (Here state title of the officer.) of the Court, a Court of Record within and for the County and State aforesaid, personally appeared Mary E. McClure (Claimant's name.), aged about 46 years, who being duly sworn according to law, makes the following declaration in order to obtain the pension provided for by Acts of Congress granting pension to widows: act of 1890

That I am the widow of William J. McClure who died at Oklahoma City on the 19th day of June A. D. 1899, of Hemoridge of the Brain (Here state the cause of his death.)

~~which I believe to have originated while~~ He belonged to Company I, 43 Regiment of Inft Mo Vols., ~~about 16~~

That I was married under the name of Mary E. Kenedy to my said husband on or about 29th day of July 1869, by Rev Gatpner at Pawnee City Neb, there being no legal barrier to such marriage;

That (Here state whether you or he, or both had been previously married; and, if so, give the name and date of death or divorce of the former spouse.)

That I have remained his widow to the present date (If re-married, state when and whom.)

That the following are the names and dates of birth of all his children, under 16 years of age when he died:

born 18
born 18
born 18
born 18
born 18
born 18

That I have not abandoned the support of any of said children, they being under my care and maintenance;

(If any of said children are not under your care they should be accounted for. If dead, the name and date of death of each should be stated.)

That I did not engage in, or aid or abet the late rebellion against the authority of the United States.

That Wm J. McClure received a pension under law; original certificate being lost; cant give no of sa (Here state whether a prior application has been filed by yourself or deceased husband; and if so, give the number of the claim if possible.)

That my residence is Oklahoma City

and my postoffice address is Oklahoma City Okla C/o F. M. Gault L.

U. S. APR 9 1901

Mary E. McClure

Illustration 75. Widow's application, 1901

1908 From *A History of Oklahoma*

One of the best known of the old cattlemen whose operations were extended to Indian Territory shortly after the close of the Civil war was the late William J. McClure, who died at his house in Oklahoma City in 1899. The extent of his early operations can be judged from the fact that at one time he had under lease the entire Kickapoo and Pottawatomie Indian reservations, comprising what are now Pottawatomie and Lincoln counties of the state of Oklahoma. He was a typical pioneer—courageous, energetic and resourceful. He belonged to a pioneer family of the state of Nebraska and in 1867 came with other members of his family to the Indian Territory, where he quickly became one of the most prominent stockmen. Twenty years before the original Oklahoma was opened to settlement, he established what became the famous Seven C ranch, on the Canadian river, about sixteen miles east of the present site of Oklahoma City. (The Seven C Flats take their name from this ranch.) The Seven C was Mr. McClure's head ranch, although his family had their home at Johnsonville, further down the Canadian, in the Chickasaw Nation. In 1878 the family moved to Atoka in the Choctaw Nation. At the opening of Oklahoma, on April 22, 1889, Mr. McClure and his son, Guy V., made the run. The homestead selected by the elder McClure is best known in modern Oklahoma as the famous Maywood addition, adjoining the city on the northeast, which is now the aristocratic residence section of Oklahoma City. In 1899 he was the largest individual property holder in Oklahoma City and furnished more money toward getting the Frisco Railway into the city from Sapulpa than any other man. He was a charter member of the Oklahoma Consistory and the India Temple, A.A.O.N.M.S. Guy V. McClure, son of the pioneer Oklahoman above mentioned, has the rare distinction (for a man of adult age) of having been born in the old Indian Territory before it was opened to settlement. His birthplace was Johnsonville, in what is now McClain county, Oklahoma, but at that time in the Chickasaw Nation of Indian Territory. He was born in 1871. His mother, Mary E. (Kennedy) McClure, is still living, her home being in Oklahoma City. Along with his active outdoor life and early experiences in the great cattle industry during the range era, he obtained an excellent education. He was a student at St. Mary's College in Kansas, later at Add-Ran College at Thorp Springs, Texas, and finally graduated from Kemper College of Boonville, Missouri. In the latter school he made a specialty of mathematical studies and civil engineering, and has since followed the profession for which he prepared himself in college. Mr. McClure is one of the best known engineers of Oklahoma, and since March 1907, has been chief engineer for the Oklahoma City Railway Company, which operates the street railway lines of Oklahoma City and also the interurban lines

extending north toward Guthrie . . . member of the engineering firm of Moore and McClure, who do general engineering. For several years Mr. McClure was engaged in railroad engineering for the Rock Island System and the Frisco and other roads in Missouri, Arkansas and Colorado, and for three and a half years was engaged in work for the Mexican Central in old Mexico. Mr. McClure has been through all the high Masonic degrees, and is a Knight Templar and a Shriner. He married, in Oklahoma City, Miss Bernice H. McAdams, a member of a family who came to Oklahoma at the first opening. They have one daughter, Mary Hortense (later Mary Willingham of Lookout Mountain, Georgia).
—[www.usgennet.org/usa/topic/historical/1908ok_2_8htm]

* * *
Does the corner of Seventh and Broadway in the city have any historical interest? Only that on that corner the McClure ranch house was located in early days; it was too far out for downtown stores to make deliveries.
* * *

Illustration 76. Newspaper article—no date

1915

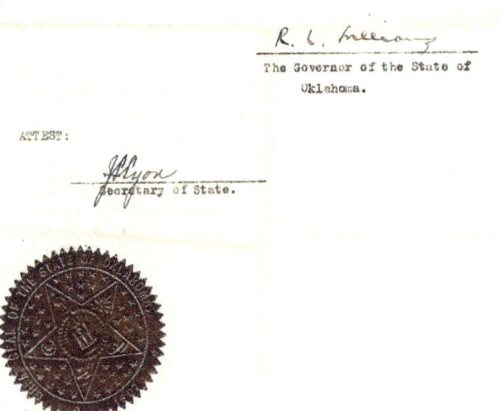

Illustration 77. Governor's proclamation

WHEREAS, Thursday, April 22nd, 1915, is the twenty-sixth anniversary of the opening of Oklahoma Territory to settlement, an event dear to the heart of every citizen of the state, and a reminder of those pioneer days and events that made possible the manifest blessings of statehood so much enjoyed by our people today.

Now Therefore, in order to show due recognition of the day and for the purpose of creating in the minds of our citizenship a proper sentiment in its observance, I do hereby request that in our homes, schools and places of business we suitably commemorate this event, and as a further evidence of same that all state offices be closed at the noon hour, April 22nd, 1915, and to remain closed for the balance of the day.

Given under my hand and the Great Seal of the State of Oklahoma, this the 19th day of April, 1915.

R.L. Williams
The Governor of the State of Oklahoma

1920 U.S. Federal Census, Oklahoma City, Okla. Series T625; Roll 1473, Page 229
1. [3]David V., age 40;   Father b. Illinois; Mother b. Kansas
2. [3]Grace A., age 30;   Father b. Ohio;   Mother b. Ohio
3. [4]William J., age 12; b. Kentucky;   Father b. Illinois; Mother b. Ohio
4. [4]Margarett, age 7;   b. Oklahoma
5. [2]Mary E., age 63;   b. Kansas;   Father b. Indiana; Mother b. Virginia

1923 April 21. Mary Ellen was crossing the street when she was struck and killed by a car going 23 mph and driven by a friend of her grandson, William John (b. 1907). Pallbearers: Judge George W. Clark, William J. Pettee, John K. Wright, Leslie Swan, W.I. Overholser,, and Newton Avey

1955 November 3, newspaper article

STREET SIGNS ECHO PIONEER LIVES
McClure Avenue was named for the homesteader and prominent cattleman here in the early days.

1960

THE FIRST LEGAL SETTLER IN OKLAHOMA CITY

By WILLIAM J. McCLURE

MY GRANDFATHER, William J. McClure, came to Muskogee in 1867 and went into the cattle business. In 1869 he bought the 7 C ranch from Bill Chisholm, of Chisholm Trail fame.

The ranch was established in 1865 or 1866 and was about the first ranch established in this section of the country. Before this period it was impossible to graze cattle on the ranges because there were so many wolves. During the Civil War the buffalo hunters had killed many of the buffalo and driven the rest to the northwest, thus taking away most of the wolves' food. The hunters had killed many wolves, too.

The ranch consisted of the Kickapoo and Pottawatomie Indian Nations holdings and the eastern half of Oklahoma proper. The ranch house was located a mile north, and a quarter of a mile northeast of Choctaw City.

Grandfather used to catch large numbers of wild horses. He had several runs, but the only run I know about had the pens located on the south side of the Canadian river bank three miles west of Reno. The horses were started from the range around Pocassett and chased into the blind pens, which were high log corrals.

In 1882 Grandfather bought 400 white-face bulls in St. Louis, shipped them to Atoka, which was the closest shipping point, and

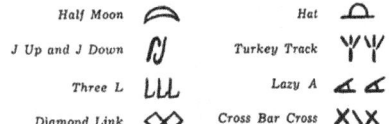

drove them to the 7 C range. These were the first white-face cattle to be crossed with the range cattle.

When the Santa Fe Railroad came through the country in 1887 Grandfather shipped the first trainload of cattle to be shipped over the road. The cowboys had to build the loading corrals, close to where the Santa Fe station now stands, to load the cattle they had gathered. The round-up that year tallied, or counted, 47,000 head of cattle with the 7 C brand.

Uncle Jimmy, (J. B.) Bond, established the 4 B ranch about the same time; his range was around Minco.

Frank Bird, a half-Indian, had the F. B. ranch at what was called Bird's Mill, near Stratford. He established the ranch in the early 70's and ran about 8,000 to 10,000 head. Grandfather used to buy his cattle to feed.

Caddo Bill Williams established the Half Moon ranch in about 1870. His range was the Kiowa and Comanche nations' territories.

W. B. Ror, a half-Indian, was another to establish about this time near Stonewall. He ran about 10,000 head.

Snap White had the 3 L (LLL) ranch close to Coalgate. It was also established in the early 70's.

Mage Hodge established the M. H. ranch in the early 70's; the ranch was west of Lehigh. After his death in 1882 Grandfather bought his cattle and gathered 35,000 head.

Jimmy Allen started the J up and J down ranch about the same time. It was east of Claretta on what was known as the McGee Prairie.

Booker James, a full-blood Indian, established a ranch southeast of Claretta about '69. He ran from 20,000 to 25,000 head of cattle.

Sy Delaney, a quarter-blood Indian, established the Z Y ranch, south of Lehigh, in the early 70's. He ran around 15,000 head.

Joel Nail, a three-quarter-blood Indian, established the 85 ranch west of Caddo in the late 60's.

Charley LeFlore, a half-blood Indian, started the C H ranch between Stringtown and Kiowa in the early 70's. Before the opening of Oklahoma proper he was a U. S. marshal. LeFlore County was named for him.

D. N. Robb married an Indian. He established the DR ranch northeast of Atoka in the early 70's.

Dave Pollack, a half-blood Indian, started the PPP ranch west of Kiowa in the early 70's.

Mumford Johnson established the Diamond Link ranch in the early 70's close to Minco. He ran 15,000 to 20,000 head.

Ed Johnson had the Hat ranch west of Norman on the Chickasaw side. It was started in the early 80's and ran about 10,000 head.

The G M ranch was started in about '85, close to Purcell, by a

Illustration 78. *Chronicles of Oklahoma* article by W. J.'s grandson, William John McClure

part Indian by the name of Garvan. He ran about 4,000 or 5,000 head.

The Turkey Track ranch was started in '82 by Griffinstein about 14 miles west of Choctaw City. He brought 12,000 steers from Texas; the steers had the Texas fever and started the fever in this country. In 1884 Grandfather bought the ranch out.

Pete Anderson established the lazy A ranch in about '66. It was about 7 miles east of Choctaw. He had only about 600 or 700 head, and the year after he started, John Bly, a cattle rustler, killed him.

The Pottawatomie Indian court was held just a short distance from the 7 C ranch corrals. When an Indian was tried and if he was convicted and sentenced to be whipped, his hands were tied together, then tied to a limb of the tree they always used as the court, and he was given the number of lashes sentenced. If he was sentenced to death, the time was set for his execution and the prisoner went free in the intervening time, making all his arrangements and also preparing for his burial. On the appointed day and hour the tribe would gather, the prisoner would give away his few last possessions, then pick out the person he wished to shoot him, usually some relative. Then the prisoner would kneel in front of the court tree, an X was marked over his heart and the appointed one would shoot him. After the execution everyone would proceed with his business as though nothing had happened. It was unheard of or unthought of for a condemned person to escape.

Grandfather had a store south and east of Choctaw, where he kept provisions for the cow outfits. The Indians used to trade there and the "Pots" were paid their allotment there. The man who ran the store bought some silk top hats that had been damaged, and once while Dad was down there an Indian buck came in to get all dressed up. He had had an argument with his girl friend, so he wanted to fix up and go see her. He got a silk hat, cut the brim and top off and put a feather in the band; then he bought a pair of pants, cut the seat out and laced the trouser legs to fit his legs tight, and cut the remainder of the trouser legs sticking out into fringe. He was then dressed to go and make amends with the girl friend.

The Indians used to come into the store and sit on the counters with their blankets around them, never moving. Dad and Uncle Guy decided to get the Indians off the counters once. Talking and pleading would do no good, so they fixed a number of darning needles on levers operated by pulling a string to each needle from in back of a partition. The Indians would come in and sit down as usual, then Dad and Uncle Guy would jerk a string and up would go the Indian who had been affected. The ones sitting on each side of the speared Indian would never change expressions; soon another would take the vacated seat and someone else down the line would let out a yell. It finally got to the point that the Indians wouldn't even take anything off the counter.

Three years before the country opened, a pack of about fifteen wolves attacked a herd of about five hundred head of cattle on the Kickapoo flat, which was only a few miles from the ranch. As soon as the first cow smelled or saw the wolves that cow gave an alarm. When the wolves attacked, the cattle had begun to mill. The bulls and steers formed a circle on the outside; the cows then formed an inner circle with the calves huddled in the center. The cattle continued to mill in this formation. When a wolf attempted to attack a steer by tearing his hamstring, the steer behind the attacked one would charge and gore the wolf. These fights usually lasted from three to five hours, and where once thick grass two feet high grew, the ground would be bare and ground to dust. Horses fight wolves in the same manner, only they strike with their front feet.

There were two round-ups each year — Spring and Fall. An outfit would have at least one chuck-wagon which had a water-tight bed so that when it was necessary to cross a swollen creek or river the cowboys would tie logs on each side of the wagon box to make it float. Then cowboys would tie ropes to the wagon and ride upstream to keep the wagon from turning over. The chuck-wagon carried the cowboy's blanket rolls and what clothing he needed, which wasn't much. The wagon also carried all the food supplies, which usually consisted of salt pork, navy beans, canned tomatoes, flour, coffee, sugar, salt, and sometimes dried fruit. For meat they had prairie chicken, deer, turkey, and often they would kill a beef.

An outfit would have as many as sixty men sometimes. Each man had six to eight horses of his own. The horses not in use were herded in a bunch by a horse wrangler and permitted to graze along slowly. At night each cowboy would hobble his own horses. First, all the horses were driven into a corral formed by tying two ropes to a tree or to the chuck-wagon, and holding the ropes tight and at right angles. Then the cowboy would carry his hobble ropes and crawl around among the horses, tying the two front feet together, after which the horses were permitted to graze at will for the night. The next morning the procedure was reversed.

The reason each man had so many horses was that the horses, having only grass to eat, required rest between each ride and were usually ridden only half a day at a time. When the work was hard a horse would only be ridden a quarter of a day.

A cowboy's working day started at daylight and ended at nightfall. The cook would have breakfast ready at daybreak. It usually consisted of bacon, sourdough biscuits, gravy, potatoes, coffee, and sometimes a fruit or molasses. The other two meals were about the same. At night each man had a tarpaulin to sleep under, and when it rained they dug a trench around their beds, if they were not lucky enough to get under the chuck-wagon. The men were divided into three shifts at night to ride "night watch" on the herd, and if there was a large bunch of cattle in the herd being held or if the cattle were restless, the men would be divided

Illustration 78 (continued)

Illustration 78 (continued)[3]

The Smoking Room
By R. G. M.

EVIDENTLY many young fellers, about Cub Scout age, have been assigned the task of assembling some points about Oklahoma City's very earliest history. The Smoking Room has received several calls from youngn's asking about first buildings, first automobiles, first circus grounds, first play park, etc. Their school libraries should have the information but we are always glad to help people know their city and state. Perhaps these points will be of value to them. Capt. David Payne's Boomers camped in the creekbed on the present Lincoln school grounds. The oldest brick building, still standing as it was built, is at the northeast corner of Main and Broadway. The first bath tub was in the T. M. Richardson home where the Home State Life building stands now. The first automobile in the city was owned by J. H. Everest. The first paved streets were three blocks each on Grand and Broadway. The first carnival and circus site was across the Santa Fe tracks between NE 1 and NE 3. The first amusement park was near the present Exchange and Western. The first livery stable was near where the Petroleum building is now. The McClure ranch house was at the present NW 7 and N Broadway, and St. Anthony's hospital occupies a part of that ranch land. The first church service was on open ground near the present NW 3 and Broadway.

* * *

Illustration 79. A column in *The Daily Oklahoman* citing location of McClure ranch house in Oklahoma City

---

[3] Petricia Lester, *The Chronicles of Oklahoma,* Summer 1980, LVII (no.2): 296-307. Reproduced courtesy of the Oklahoma Historical Society

THE SMOKING ROOM
A column in The Daily Oklahoman *tells location of McClure ranch house in Oklahoma City.*

Evidently many young fellers, about Cub Scout age, have been assigned the task of assembling some points about Oklahoma City's very earliest history. The Smoking Room has received several calls from youngn's asking about first buildings, first automobiles, first circus grounds, first play park, etc. Their school libraries should have the information but we are always glad to help people know their city and state. Perhaps these points will be of value to them. Capt. David Payne's Boomers camped in the creekbed on the present Lincoln school grounds. The oldest brick building still standing as it was built, is at the northeast corner of Main and Broadway. The first bathtub was in the T. M. Richardson home where the Home State Life building stands now. The first automobile in the city was owned by J. H. Everest. The first paved streets were three blocks each on Grand and Broadway. The first carnival and circus site was across the Santa Fe tracks between NE 1 and NE 3. The first amusement park was near the present Exchange and Western. The first livery stable was near where the Petroleum building is now. The McClure ranch house was at the present NW 7 and Broadway, and St. Anthony's hospital occupies a part of that ranch land. The first church service was on open ground near the present NW 3 and Broadway.

> A man by the name of Lowenstein contested his claim on the two lots and it was proved in court that Grandfather was in Oklahoma City at least thirty minutes or more ahead of anyone else. The case was carried to the Supreme Court and there found that the cowboys were legally in the territory and no law could be cited prohibiting Grandfather from changing horses with the cowboys.
>
> Grandfather established a home on the Maywood farm, the house being located at about what is now Tenth Street and Central. Grandmother didn't like to leave the home at Atoka because of her flowers, so Grandfather had five hundred rose bushes sent from Kansas City and planted them before Grandmother ever came to Oklahoma City.

Illustration 80. Description by grandson of [2]Wm. John's land claim on April 22, 1889. The letter says the case was heard in the Supreme Court, but it was probably tried in federal district court.

- 7 -

not lucky enough to get under the chuck-wagon. The men were divided into three shifts at night to ride night watch on the herd, and if there was a large bunch of cattle in the herd being held or if the cattle were restless, the men would be divided into two shifts. Each ranch would send several men with their own horses to other ranch's outfits.

Cattle would range together over a large area. Each area would be rounded up and the calves branded and earmarked with the same brand as their mothers. The cattle from other ranches would be separated and the cowboys from those ranches would drive the cattle back to their own ranges. The round-up would work in a large circle, taking in each range of cattle.

When a trail herd passed a ranch some rider from the ranch would always bring the word in a day or two ahead of the trail herd and the ranch would prepare a big meal for all the trail cowboys and its own hands would take turns riding herd on the cattle at night, letting the trail hands get a good night's sleep. It was the same on round-ups. When an outfit came close to a ranch the ranch would do the same thing, and of course there was never a charge for this.

Cowboys going through the country would stop at a ranch and remain maybe several weeks. Their horses would be fed and taken care of as well, and no charge was ever thought of. If there was work to be done, the traveler would pitch in and make a hand.

Some ranches when they had finished up in the fall and didn't have much work would let part of the cowboys go. The cowboy would go to town and spend what money he had made, then go back to the ranch and just move in without ever saying a word. They would stay around several months until the spring round-up. These men and their horses would re-

- 8 -

ceive the same treatment as the other cowboys and they would work just as hard as those on the payroll if there was work to be done.

Grandfather married my Grandmother, Mary Ellen Kennedy, in 1875 and brought her to Johnstonville, close to Stratford. Guy McClure was born at Johnstonville in 1877. The town consisted of a general store with the post office. There were four families in the town, Mumford Johnston, a cowman, Harwood and Rainey, who had the store, and Bill McClure, cowman. Grandfather had the Cross Bar Cross +\+ ranch down there and ran about 7,000 or 8,000 head. In 1878 the McClures moved to Atoka, where my father, Dave, was born.

When the proclamation was first issued for Oklahoma proper to be opened for settlement, soldiers were sent into the territory to keep people off the land to be opened. The Government issued permits to some of Grandfather's cowboys, who did not wish to stake land or who had Indian blood and could not stake land, to enter Oklahoma proper and drive Grandfather's cattle back onto his (Kickapoo and Pottawatomie) ranges.

Grandfather did not cross the line into Oklahoma proper after the proclamation was issued until the territory was officially opened for settlement, twelve o'clock noon, April 22, 1889.

Grandfather started from the 7 C ranchhouse, which was just across the line. He rode to the sand hills about 5 or 6 miles from the house; there he met by appointment one of the cowboys driving the cattle out of Oklahoma proper and changed to his fresh horse. Grandfather then rode to Lightning Creek and changed to another fresh horse of one of his cowboys, then rode into Oklahoma City about thirty minutes ahead of anyone else. He staked the 160 acres in what is nown known as Maywood and two lots at First and Harvey streets.

Illustration 81. Description of ranch life, cowboy life, and cattle drives written by grandson, [4]William J. McClure, 1907–1970

- 15 -

been a small grandstand built on Grandfather's farm, at about what is now Sixth Street and Central. The first thing on the program was some horse races and my Father, Dave, won the first race, which was for a purse of five dollars. The grandstand was packed with about two hundred people, and during the races it collapsed injuring a number of people and killing one child.

When the Rock Island Railroad was building into Oklahoma City the Railroad refused to build the road into the city limits, so the town floated bonds to complete the work. The bonds were paid off by taxing each bottle of liquor. Most of the lots required for the right-of-way were donated by the owners. Grandfather gave the use of two hundred work horses for this purpose.

Grandfather was a charter member of the first Masonic Lodge, the Consistory, and the Knights Templar. Grandmother was a charter member of the first Eastern Star Chapter and was the first Worthy Grand Matron of the State of Oklahoma.

In about 1883 some cattle rustlers stole about five hundred head of steers from my Grandfather, driving the cattle southeast. Grandfather, Frank Gault, Pete Anderson, and a couple of the cowboys trailed the cattle and did not catch up with them until they crossed the line, in the southeastern part of the state, into Arkansas. They waited until the rustlers were all together eating breakfast, then they closed in on them and not a shot was fired. Grandfather and the others tied the rustlers' hands behind them, then put them on their horses and tied their feet together under their horses. They then pulled off the bridles and turned the horses loose, driving

- 14 -

them with the cattle back to the ranch. There they took the rustlers to Fort Smith, which was the closest Federal court.

―――――――

Shorts

The main pastime of the boys was riding the dray wagons around on their deliveries.

―――――――

When the Santa Fe came through this country in 1887, Grandfather shipped the first train load of cattle over this road. The road had just come through, but wasn't completed. The cowboys had to build loading pens to load the cattle they had gathered.

The first celebration Oklahoma City ever had was on the fourth of July. There had

Illustration 81 (continued)

Illustration 81 (continued)

93

Illustration 82. News of McClure gravesite vandalism

1981 July 30. *Oklahoma City Times*, page 1 N

∞∞∞

HEIRLOOM TAKEN FROM GRAVE
Pioneer's tribute stolen

He went to the U. S. Supreme Court to defend his status as the first legal white settler in Oklahoma City. He loaded the first Santa Fe railway car through this territory with his cattle, and he reportedly fathered the first child born here to a pioneer family.

He was William J. McClure, son of an Irish immigrant and one of few white men to penetrate Muskogee, Indian Territory, as early as 1867. He built a ranch and a family with two hands, sweat, and backbone.

He died in 1899. One year later, his daughter, Veta Ellean, traveled to Paris, France, where she found what she considered the ideal decoration for his monument: a hand made, glass bead, Parisian wreath. She brought it back to Oklahoma and placed it on his grave in Oklahoma Cities' Fairlawn cemetery.

The wreath laid on McClure's monument for 81 years until earlier this month, when a thief decided to claim the heirloom for his own. Members of the McClure family are hurt and angry.

"He gave so much to the city," said Mrs. W.J. McClure, Edmond, wife of the elder McClure's grandson." "And on our diamond jubilee year. To me that was infuriating.

This is to desecrate his grave. This is the way I see it."

Mrs. McClure said she has spoken with a number of antique dealers who agreed the wreath is valuable.

"One of them even sent word about a month ago that I shouldn't leave it out there, that it would be taken. And within a week or two they called from the (Fairlawn) office that it was gone."

Mary Ellen Randall, Wichita, Kan, McClure's great-granddaughter, has painstakingly put together a personal history detailing the McClure family heritage. She, too, was angry when she learned the wreath had been stolen.

"What a sad commentary on today's times", she said. "People all around the countryside who are familiar with Oklahoma heritage know the story of the wreath."

Most local historians know of McClure, too. And if there was ever doubt he was Oklahoma City's first white settler, the U.S. Supreme court put it to rest.

Morris Lowenstein challenged McClure's claim, and the lawsuit eventually ended up in the nations highest court, where it was officially declared that McClure was indeed the holder of the honor.

McClure staked out two claims near First and Harvey streets in what is now downtown Oklahoma City. He also took ownership of a 160-acre tract, which later became the Maywood Addition, one of Oklahoma City's original residential districts.

Mrs. McClure said that Fairlawn cemetery officials had allowed the wreath to rest undisturbed on McClure's headstone since 1900, not even removing it during the summers as they do most artificial ornaments in the warm weather months.

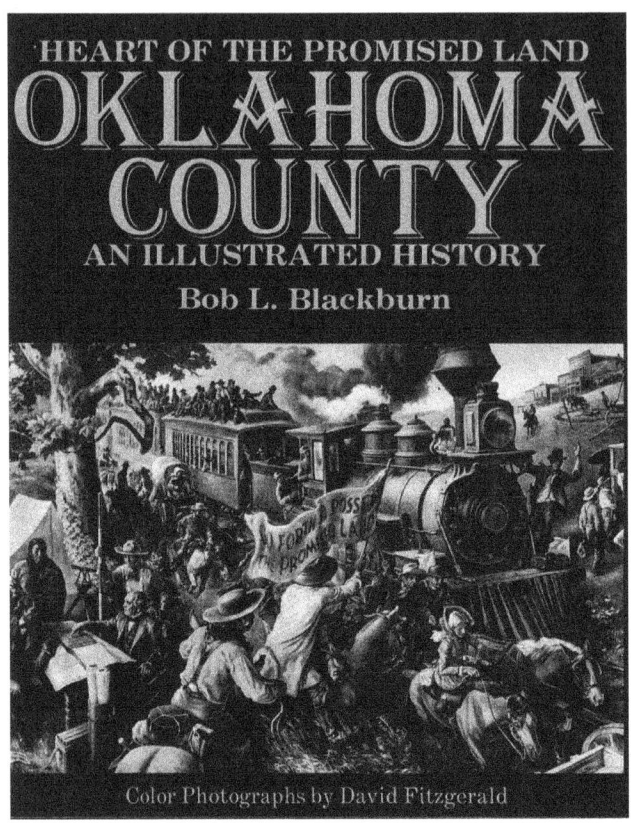

Illustration 83. Early Oklahoma history mentioning William McClure

Illustration 83 (continued)

From 1866 to 1874 troopers and federal lawmen fought Plains Indians who sporadically entered the future Oklahoma County. At the same time, these agents of law and order faced another, more elusive enemy—the Western outlaw.

To combat the growing surge of outlawry after the Civil War, by 1866 all of the Five Civilized Tribes employed their own lawmen. The only law enforcement agency with the interjurisdictional authority to combat outlaws in Indian Territory, however, was the federal court at Fort Smith. In 1875 this court entered a new era with the arrival of Isaac "Hanging Judge" Parker, who brought "law and order" to the frontier court. He appointed an army of 200 deputy marshals, and for the next 20 years he ruled the region with an iron fist.

One of the most common crimes committed by both outlaws and raiding Indians in the crosstimbers region was cattle rustling. Robert Lake, who operated the Circle Bar Ranch along the North Canadian River in the future Oklahoma County, suffered these depredations countless times before 1889. Although he was in the Unassigned Lands illegally, Lake had a ranchhouse on the future site of Oklahoma City, a cattle pen on a small tributary to the west, and a pond where Belle Isle amusement park later would be located. Another rancher running cattle in the future Oklahoma County was William McClure, whose 7C Ranch headquarters were located farther east on the North Canadian in the lands of the Potawatomi.

Rustlers also struck herds moving north on cattle trails. Two major trails skirted the boundaries of Oklahoma County: the West Shawnee Trail and the famous Chisholm Trail. Established in 1867, after more easterly trails aroused opposition among settlers, the West Shawnee Trail diverged from the old Texas Road at Boggy Depot, veered northwest to the South Canadian, and then crossed the North Canadian near present-day Shawnee. The preferred route, however, was the Chisholm Trail.

Rancher William McClure ran cattle in the future Oklahoma County after 1867. Twenty years later he drove cattle to Oklahoma Station for loading onto railroad cars. Courtesy, Veta McClure.

Western artist Frederic Remington sketched cattle on the long treks from southern Texas. Cattle rustlers often preyed upon cattle driven along the various northward trails. From Harper's Weekly.

FIGHT FOR THE PROMISED LAND   31

REPRODUCED COURTESY OF BOB L. BLACKBURN

Illustration 83 (continued)

IGI Individual Record

FamilySearch™ International Genealogical Index v5.0

North America

Search Results | Download | Pedigree

William John McClure
Male

Event(s):
Birth: 07 DEC 1842 , Lee, Illinois
Christening:
Death:
Burial:

Parents:
Father: Thomas McClure   Family
Mother: Mary Jane Young

Messages:
Record submitted by a member of the LDS Church. The record often shows the name of the individual and his or her relationship to a descendant, shown as the heir, family representative, or relative. The original records are not indexed, and you may have to look at the film frame-by-frame to find the information you want. A family group record for this couple may be in the Family Group Record Collection; Archive Section. (See the Family History Library Catalog for the film number.) These records are alphabetical by name of the father or husband.

Source Information:
Film Number: 458870
Page Number:
Reference number:

© 1999-2002 by Intellectual Reserve, Inc. All rights reserved. English approval: 3/1999
Use of this site constitutes your acceptance of these Conditions of Use (last updated: 3/22/1999).
Privacy Policy (last updated: 11/24/2004).   28   http://www.familysearch.org v.2.5.0

REPRODUCED COURTESY OF THE CHURCH OF JESUS CHRIST OF LATTER-DAY SAINTS

Illustration 84. Research facts about William John McClure

Let us be judged by our actions

Chapter 3
MARY ELLEN (KENNEDY) MCCLURE
1852 - 1923

Illustration 85. Mary Ellen (Kennedy) McClure

[2]Mary Ellen Kennedy McClure was born in the Silver Lake Kansas area. She had three brothers and two sisters. Her father, Joseph, died when she was three years old. She lived part of her childhood with an uncle and then went to boarding school at St. Mary's.

While visiting an older sister in Pawnee, Nebraska, she met her future husband, William John McClure. Mary Ellen stayed in Nebraska and Kansas the first years of her marriage while her husband started his cattle operations in Indian Territory. In 1875 she moved permanently to Indian Territory. She became the First Worthy Grand Matron of Indian Territory. After the Land Run of April 22, 1889, she moved her family into Oklahoma City. It was there that she became the First Worthy Grand Matron of Oklahoma Territory. For many years her oil portrait hung in the Oklahoma Historical Museum alongside a painting of her husband. Her death was caused by a young man who struck her while he was driving a car 23 miles an hour. The driver was a friend of her grandson. She died instantly.

From the Records
[2]**Mary Ellen Kennedy McClure**
 b. December 24, 1852
m. July 29, 1869, to William John McClure
　married in Pawnee City, Pawnee County, Nebraska
 f. Presbyterian
d. April 20, 1923, Oklahoma City, Oklahoma, 72 years old
b. April 24, 1923, Fairlawn Cemetery, Oklahoma City, Oklahoma
　(Fairlawn has no records prior to 1907.)
　Ed. L. Hahn Funeral Home

Education: St. Mary's Convent and College in St. Mary's, Kansas

Children
[3]Guy Vincent
　　b. December 12, 1877, Silver Lake, Kansas
　m. Bernice McAdams
　　　Children, [4]Mary Hortense (m. Willingham)
　d. October 23, 1918; Flu epidemic
　b. Fairlawn Cemetery, Oklahoma City, Oklahoma

[3]David Victor
　　b. December 12, 1879, Atoka, Indian Territory
　m. Grace Anna (Armsey) Jones; June 20, 1905, Cincinnati, Ohio
　　Children of David Victor and Grace Anna
　　　[4]William John b. July 6, 1907　d. February 10, 1970
　　　[4]Veta Ann b. March 10, 1912　d. March 25, 1948
　　　[4]Guy Victor b. January 15, 1925　d. July 18, 1961
　d. December 11, 1944; 65 years old
　b. Fairlawn Cemetery, Oklahoma City, Oklahoma

³Veta Ellean
- b. March 27, 1882, Atoka, Indian Territory
- m. seven husbands, no children
- m. 903, March 11, Isaac T. Jones, Oklahoma City
- m. 1904, March 2, Leon Roscoe Partridge d. 1908, October, New Hampshire
- m. 1910, E. R. Carhart
- m. 1915, R. M. Smyth
- m. 1918, John Harold Muncaster
- m. 1921, George Myers Church
- m. 1933, January 25, George Scott Findlay, Southampton, England
- d. August 23, 1963, Oklahoma City, Oklahoma
- b. Fairlawn Cemetery, Oklahoma City, Oklahoma

Parents
Father: Joseph Kennedy b. About 1835 in Indiana or Ohio d. 1855
Mother: Elizabeth b. Before 1835 in Illinois or Ohio
   Both parents may have been born in Ohio—possibly they were in Darke County, Ohio, with the McClure family (not verified). One record said that her father, Joseph, died when she was 3 years old. She lived with an uncle until she went to St. Mary's Convent/School at St. Mary's Kansas.

Siblings
William Henry Kennedy; brother living in Santa Cruz, California, 1901
 b. May, 1852, Silver Lake, Kansas
m. unknown
m. Maria Louisa Francis, second wife
 b. 1832/1838, England d. January 5, 1913
 d. January 23, 1938 Santa Cruz, California; Funeral held by
   Wessendorf Funeral Home
   son: George Warren Kennedy b. Kansas, 1898
[Possible Siblings]
   Eliza Kennedy (these two girls' names might be the same person?)
   Elizabeth (Maggie) Kennedy
   My record said that there were three sons and three daughters in this family.

Mary Ellen's mother was still living after 1901.

One source said her parents may have run a trading post (not verified).

The Silver Lake Township Cemetery listed the Kennedys buried at Silver Lake: George Kennedy 1880-1952; Maude Kennedy 1896-1946; Eunice Kennedy—no dates; James Kennedy 1883-1970

Clubs

First Families of Oklahoma

The Women of '89

Eastern Star–both in Indian Territory and Oklahoma Territory

Eastern Star

Right Worthy Grand Marshall of the General Grand Chapter O. E. S.

Past Matrons club, Matron of Chapter No. 10 (first organized in Oklahoma City. Mary Ellen was made a life member.)

Eastern Star (in) Indian Territory, First Worthy Grand Matron, first time in 1886

Eastern Star (in) Oklahoma Territory, first time in 1890 Grand Matron

Illustration 86. Mary Ellen Kennedy

Illustration 87. Mary Ellen Kennedy's mother, Elizabeth Kennedy

Mary Ellen (Kennedy) McClure's Timeline

1869 The periodic table invented by Dmitri Mendeleev, a Russian chemist

Illustration 88. Mary Ellen Kennedy married William John McClure, July 29, 1869, in Pawnee County, Nebraska

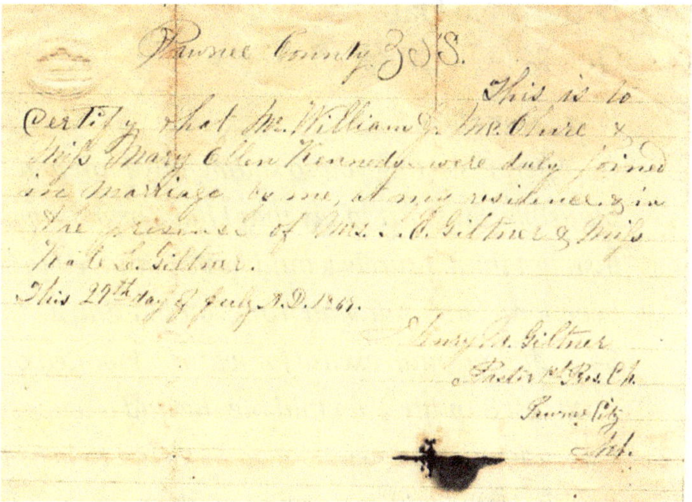

Illustration 89. Marriage certificate, 1869

1870 Census, William Kennedy, Benton Precinct, Pawnee City, Nebraska (mil 867)
Elizabeth Kennedy, page 287
William Kennedy, page 291

1871 City of Silver Lake, Kansas, incorporated

1874 Letter Dated December 21

Dear Sister Ellen,

I will send your ___ to you at last. I would have sent those before this but have neglected it. But forgive me this time. I will do better in the future ___ ___ ___, not all well. Hoping it will find you in the same health. We are having the finest weather this winter that I ever saw. There has been no snow hardly this winter. Dans folks are coming down Christmas and I guess I will go to the party at Table Rock Christmas night. Pa had a letter from Ned Gault the other day, he said they were all well when he wrote. I thank you so much for your long letter and hope that you will write another one like it. How soon are you coming up? Will said you were coming soon when he was up and I ___ has been quite a while and I have begun to think you are not coming at all. Well, I will have to close for this time as I am in a hurry to get to town. I wish you a Merry Christmas. My love to all, yourself included, Ada McClure

1870s Letter – No Date

Oct. 27, Elk Creek

Ever Dear Ellen,

After neglecting you so shamefully I am at a loss to know but an apology would seem plausible. Suffice it to say that I have been drove perfectly drove ever since I received your last, but think I surely would have managed to send you a few lines ere this had it not been for a letter Ada had from you bidding her not write until she heard from you again. So with that small excuse for waiting I waited on, with my conscience slightly relieved, until last Sunday. Ada told me she had a letter saying you were at your mothers, which I considered good news. I was very glad to hear that you were enjoying tolerable good health. Now I will try to give you the news as it happened since I last wrote. The first of importance is Mother, Ned Norris and old Nic made their appearance on the fifth of Sept. right in the midst of haying; well all would have been delightful but for the disappointment at the last minute in getting good help. After depending all summer on Mrs. Harrold on that especial occasion. When Dan went after her she was fixing to attend the camp meeting, and said if she had known sooner just when I wanted her so as to have her sewing done she could have helped me until the meeting commenced. So I dabbled along with Carrie Bell one week, then got a girl that was four times worse than Carrie, let her dally a week, and then Sis and I had to do the work ourselves. Had no work hands except Joe and Jeff. We got two meals a day and got along tolerably well, done what we pleased, and as we please and called it having a good time to be sure we had to work too much but we crowded in considerable visiting as we went along. I guess mother and Ted were not a little surprised at my careless way of keeping house, if we wanted to go play where the breakfast table was not cleared, and a large ironing to be done, we went. Sis would remonstrate and if we could not persuade her, we took her by force. one on each side. We would walk her down to the croquet ground and when we came back it would seem as if a ghost had been around the house for the dishes would be washed and all the wash done up. (I guess that makes your eyes.). Then when night came if the ironing was not done Sis would scold me, say if we hadn't wound up going to play we would have been done. I told her I had found that if I never stopped until the work was all done I would never have one minute of recreation and didn't care what folks thought of my housekeeping. Well, Mrs. Heeren managed to get to the C meeting one day and was so good just asked me if I still wanted her, I told her no, but what do you care for all this when you're having no housekeeping trouble. Well, the next on the docket is the fair. Dan went to the Pawnee fair and pronounced it good, we all went to the Johnson County fair. I thought it was tolerable. Tom thought it was wonderful, but Dan of course contended that the Pawnee was the best. Then we all went to the state *fair held at Lincoln. It was very good, why I almost imagined I was at the Centennial. Then we attended the opera at night, and had a general good time, came home perfectly satisfied with the trip and all the pleasures connected there with. A few days after Dan took our folks down to the river where they have had a tolerable good _____ now. And all my canning and pickling and preserving is done. And everything washed up. So what is to hinder? Now the next news of importance is, we have had a flying visit from Margaret Thurston, who started home day before yesterday, came partly to look at fathers place once more for her health, which is very poor. The doctor told Thurston if she wanted she could live a year she must have a change of air, the mountain air was too light, so he was going to send her to the springs and she asked the doctor if a trip to the sister would do. He said it would be the thing, so in three days she was on her way. When the train stopped at Elk there were a number of men standing there and she thought she would look if she could see any of her folks there. Dan and Tom were both there she didn't know them. Says she remembers Tom's face among them and thought there was something familiar looking about him but didn't think of him being her brother. She did it seems as I had pictured her but I like her. Doctor Cochean happened at fathers a few days after she came, and father set him right to doctoring her. She objected strongly at first but the doctor and father over persuaded her, and after the doctor examined her he told her that if she had perfect faith that he could cure her, and told her if she would take the medicine according to directions she would be the best friend he had in California. She did, and the medicine or the charmer did her a great deal of good. She feels encouraged and says she could give him a good trial. She is dreadfully afflicted with dropsy, pneumonia, lung disease, and heart disease. I never saw anyone have such a distressing cough as when she came here and when she went away her cough was only light. I am very sorry you and Will did not get to see her, and to think William so near. Charlie says he left him at _____. Charlie hadn't got a boarding place when I saw him. Smaltz is Professor at T Rock this winter and Ada does want to go to school. Kate Cooper said she would board her just to have her go with Gayla, says Mr. Cooper would take them in bad weather, but what is the use of her taking the place she feels now is one of her own choosing. A man by the name of Tim is waiting on her, not Tom, a very good man. Father seems to think more of him than any beau she ever had, and sometimes, I see signs in Ada, or I think I do, that she's thinking of getting married. But if she is I don't see why she wants to go to school. That may be for a fling, she is in the quilt and carpet business and says she won't want to keep house for father another year. Ada Bell boards at O A. Cooper's and goes to school. We had a visit from Tom and wife this fall. Oh well here I have run on and made a long letter out of little. I will promise to answer the next letter immediately then perhaps I won't have so much to say. But for that matter I feel like it would take me a week to say all I have to say, besides there are things I would say that I don't want to* *write. Wish you could have a visit with mother and Ned. I expect to have a good time when they come back, which may be this very day. For I have a girl now that is willing to do the work. Dan has been suffering since yesterday morning with a severe toothache and neuralgia in the head. With good wishes for the health and enjoyment of yourself and Will. I close hoping to hear from you soon. Ann*

1875 Moved to Johnstonville, Indian Territory

The First Kentucky Derby run in Louisville

April 12

Dear Ellen,

I received your last a few days since and was very happy to hear from Will and that he had been well and safe for I did feel uneasy. Am also thankful that you find ways of passing your time pleasantly during his long stay. One thing presume you are blessed with, that is something like summer weather while we are having perfect winter. It has been snowing and blowing for the last twenty-four hours which looks dull for my little chickens and pale looking tomato plants, but it is clearing off now and we expect spring weather just as we have been doing for the last month. Went to Table Rock Saturday. Mrs. Morris came to the store and invited me home with her, and as I was tired staying at the store, and didn't expect Dan to be ready to come home until late I went. And as you might suppose was caught there for supper, had a short grace. I am not prepared to say whether it was good, bad or indifferent as I paid no attention, taking that opportunity to observe the pious activities of the rest of the company. While there the hack drove down Murfree's and stopped. I could not see whether anyone got out and I thought it might be your arrival. We would have gone down to see, but Mrs. Morris sent her little boy and arranged everything for keeping me there. Told the boys to ask if Mrs. Will McClure had come. If so, to tell her, Mrs. Dan McClure was there. My business was to see Mary about the weaving so stopped a few minutes at Mr. Parish. It is one of the prettiest places I know of, but the house was full of women. Need to tell you who they were, sometimes I feel very lonely indeed but would rather be alone than always been in such company. Mrs. Chambers is moving in Lynn Cooper's house. I tried hard to get Dan to move in his house and board him. The idea didn't suit me one bit. Dan hardly knows what he will do get sometimes talks of having his cattle herded at house. I know just how pleasant that would be for me while he would be running around. I could stay here to see to the wants of the herder. I feel like I would rather do the hurting myself even if I had to stay out in the rain and get thunder stroked. Charlie Morris is hired to Mr.

Giddings to work on his farm. They don't know what to do with him he has no notion of being a gentleman or merchant. Wants to run around something like Will. They say when he talks to them about it he always holds up Will for an example. I believe he will be a smart and good man. How many boys raised like him would think of working on a farm. Lydia is in Kansas City staying with a man by the name of Thomas, so he can prove his citizenship and thereby get employment. I believe I have never told you that John Bell was married last New Year's to Marge's Libby. Tom is clear out of the notion of buying the mill. Thanks he can make more some other way, the surest way for him is to put the money In the bank or in land. French Benidozz is in a bad situation, sold his team to get to California and now can't sell his place. Says he had a tractive land rented in California. Mr. Bill is as bad off as ever and would like to sell his farm. He tried hard to get the money to pay the debts that Dan was security on, but failed to do so. He let Dan have a team and Dan is to pay the debts. Jim is just able to go about sometime his feet and legs are so very much swollen and sometimes he has no power of them. Nancy Croc's man is still in Pikes Peak and will not be home this summer. She says he writes for her to come to him, but she won't go. I told her I should think she would go with half an invitation. When you come to Atchison, if you have time to go see Eggleston's, you will find them so clever and she told me to be sure and tell you and Will to come and see them when you were passing through. Mary Allen can play croquet and I think you and her and Kate can learn me. You will find in one of the investigators I sent Colonel Pyresols' lecture. I will send a couple more. Hope you will write soon as you get this. I suppose Dan would send some love or speech if he was here. My love to yourself and Will, Ann don't write anything in your letters to me that you would not want father to see, they show me all their letters and I know they expect the same of me, anything about the place for instance. Father knew you had any notion of it he might be harder to trade with.

1870s Letter addressed to: Mrs. Mary E. McClure Pawnee City Nebraska

Muskogee
April the 13th
Dear and most beloved Wife,

I received your very long, kind and loving letter yesterday. And was very glad to hear that you are well yourself. You said you had the ____. You must not get thin for if you don't ____ to town down here you would not for I will come home in a jiffy and then I will not leave you anymore. You must keep in good spirits for a little while. I got a letter from George Kennedy and he likes California very well and wants me to come out there this fall. Everything looks very beautiful here at present and my cattle are getting fat. I *don't have to ride after them much now, only go out every day and look after them. You how ____ gives men getting lonely ___. Came by Wichita Kansas and buy some cattle bred well not to drive them myself for I can get them delivered as cheap as if I came and drove them myself. I want to get home as soon as possible but you must not think the time long for it will soon come. Tell ____that I will come and pay them a long visit. When I come back to ____ for not coming when I was up in the winter. I will go up to the Pottawatomie Country and then I will be ready to come home. I say home, we have no home, but we will have a home somewhat before long, I am tired of living apart from you. A good bye, give my love to all and write soon, Love, W. J. McClure*

1870s Letter addressed to Mrs. Mary McClure, Table Rock, Nebraska (no date, place or person given and first of the letter missing)

____have been to see the dentist, he was very pleasant and I told him about your filling. He said for you to come to see him as soon as you come back and he thought likely your tooth was not perfectly dry and added you had ____ saliva (and I believed him). Have not been to fathers only once since you left. Thought then that there was some dissatisfaction on the side of ____ of that household. Ada had a hired girl and was in the process of the house cleaning yet, for it was raining ____ and twice or someday you know ____tried to persuade her to wait until the rainy weather was over, but she has a head of her own. Rain poured down in the dining room ____ could see in from her, but let us excuse her, as she is a new beginner and did not know anything about that house. The folks belonging to it, (herself not excepted). She thinks still that she is going to make that carpet ____ not to put down there. Hadn't better make another bet of six or eight yards so as to have a fall dress when it does come, according to Ada's say father and William have their outs and ____ time father was coming over ____, William had said about ____, and Ada went for him. She says you think William is the ____, ____ in this country, yet you will take his word against any ____ you have. I thought that ____ in about ____ if it was Ada ____. Ada says William is trying to make disturbances between father and Roscoe. Roscoe said if he caught William telling father he's one of them ____ a whipping. I told her if Roscoe would be as good as his word I wouldn't care if William did tell one more lie. You ____ would tell me when you wrote what to do about your things, but didn't. When I was there your birds were the raggedest worse looking fowls I ever saw, but Ada seemed to take as good of care of them as she could and ____ trying to get a calf. I told her you said feed the 34 little turkeys and about 200 ground chickens. The mother of the baby chicks is about ready to come off with another flock that is nothing remarkable as her first is ready to fry. Old ____ has been rather lazy but has a nice flock now of half a hundred. Of course you could not show this awful letter, but please don't

read or tell any of this chicken hearted ____ to your city friends. I took it for granted you would like to know ____ and Whitie and Speaky, and spotty were doing. Dan Baker proves to be a good herder and him and Joe do the milking and we get milk enough to make all the butter we can eat. I had Carrie liking me for a while after you went away and Ada is helping me now so you see how I am doing without a girl this summer. I don't get lonesome this summer, we have a very nice ____ around and between the ____ play and company I have no time to get lonesome. Last Sunday morning as soon as breakfast was over ____ insisted on my going to ____. We played until about ____. Dan was going to gather maple up before we get some ____ that there was to....."

(Remainder of letter lost; either another page; possibly a different letter—but written by the same person)

_____to keep house for father in other years. We were up to see Tom's two weeks ago for the first time since their baby came to town. They sent to Montgomery early in the spring for a large bill of goods, lace curtains and carpets and carpets and carpets, but have none of them in use yet. Oh I will take that back, they put down one of the hemp carpets in the parlor and fixed it up for a sick room, but that same old rag carpet adorns their sitting room yet. Now perhaps you think I had better look at home. You know I have never got my new carpet for I would have been to proud to keep it and you have never felt interest enough in us to ask. I predict you see us looking so shabby as when you left, so I must enlighten you. Well, I work faithfully for a while after you ____ on the old carpet rags and could have had my carpet at the weavers in two weeks or less time, but I was neglecting everything else to do it, and you know we were in too shabby a state to do that, so I thought I would shove all the rags to one side, clean up the house do up my sewing and take my own time for making the carpet. Thinking it would all be done before the fourth, but the fourth has come and been and gone and I have never got round to that carpet yet. Now let me tell you how I did manage to make the house neat. Took the sitting room carpet had it cleaned good and put down in the kitchen. I took the carpet from my room upstairs for the sitting room and took the sitting room, and took the new kitchen carpet for my room upstairs. I made the house quite neat without a dollar of expense. We are all wired in from the flies and skeeters and never lived more cozey. I have made but small additions to my wardrobe, but it was all I needed. Got one lite calico saque and one white one for afternoon fire up, got a pretty slip, hat and a linen suit. I think your dreams very pretty looks so cool. I had a letter from Sis lately. She says they still intend visiting us this fall, they were all well and Ann has a little boy. You were right we did spend our fourth at Pawnee, but if you think I smiled once more than I felt like, you are mistaken. It was uncommon cool for the fourth and I just gave *up to perfect lazy contentment. Got under a big tree and heard the Declaration read, heard professor Durerbery make a few remarks and try to look wise. Saw Governor Butlers go into fits and almost choke to death, then he dismissed us and we went and clambered into our wagon and ate heartily of the good things we found there and for a great wonder, I was hungry. Mrs. Harron ate dinner with us. I expect to get her for my help when mother and Sis comes. Dear Ellen, now I have run at a headlong rate and the teams are coming in and I must hurry up the supper and tomorrow is washday and I feel like I was not half alone talking to you.*

Illustration 90. Mary Ellen wearing her Eastern Star pin

1877 Traveled to Silver Lake, Kansas, for the birth of first child, Guy Vincent, December 12

1877 Letter addressed to Mary E. McClure, Silver Lake, Kansas from Johnson, Indian Territory, October 25, 1877. Ink is too faded to read.

1877 Table Rock, Nebraska, November 1st, 1877

Dear Sister Ellen,

I will now try to answer your most welcome letter which I received some time ago and should have written sooner. But when I just got your letter, Sister Mary Ann was here so I thought as we have had no hand for some time till this evening. We have Jessie Morton's stepson. I do wish you could have seen Mary Ann, she is one of the best women I ever saw. She was at our house four weeks. Jane and James her sons are coming out in the spring to live with Pa. I was in hopes they would come this fall so I could go to school this winter. Mrs. Somntry is teaching again this winter but I can't go this winter and I suppose I will not get to go any more. For I think I will____ a school off one scholar ____all if nothing happens, but please don't write anything about it to anyone as I don't want Pa to find it out yet for he would write it to everyone of the family. But he likes my fellow for wonder, and Mary Ann liked him. He is a ____but it is not Hon. He lives five miles and a half east of Pawnee City. I had a note from your Sister the other asking where you was. She said they were all well and that the ____could sit alone. I have not had a chance to send your water profile to her yet but will the first chance I get. I was sorry to hear that you had so much trouble about your trunk, but was glad that you got it without having to go back for it, well, Ellen. Old Mr. Brett is dead. He dropped dead on his wagon in Humboldt. They said he was as well as usual when he left home and Trina Frank is dead, she died of typhoid fever and Mrs. Miller died this morning. She has been sick for a long time. I was up to Dan's last Wednesday, they were all well then and were expecting their folks back from the river. Oh yes, Ellen, Tom, told me to tell you she wanted you to write to her. They are all well. I had a letter from Joan Kate last Monday. She is living with Nettie now. Rodney is in Arkansas looking for a place and if he finds one to suit him they will move there. Kate wants me to come and live with her if they do. But I don't think I will, but I think I will go see them any way. Well was you aware that Hattie Gile & Arnold Palmer was married and also Martha Meadin is married. Charlie Campbell got back last Saturday. He is boarding at Mrs. Loanes. He said Will was coming home in July for five weeks. If he does won't you come with him. I think you might. I will close hoping to hear from you soon. Now please don't wait so long this time. Ever your loving Sister Ada McClure- good bye.

1877 Table Rock Nebraska, August 4th

I thought I would try and answer your most welcome letter which was received day before yesterday. I was very glad that you were so punctual for you don't know how much pleasure your Dear letters give me for I get so lonesome sometimes thinking how I would like to see you and when your letters come they seem like messengers of joy. I *could forgive you for writing short letters if you would only write often. Dear Ellen, Will has not come yet, and I have looked for him every time the train comes in, but so far only to be disappointed. How I do wish he would come for it seems like ages since I seen either one of you. Indeed I should be glad to get the baby Victor and Dear Sister, I should be very glad to get your and Wills Vincent. Tell Will that I wish he would please send me his picture if he does not come up as I have not any of His and I want one so bad. I am going up to Dans sometime this week to stay for three weeks. Ann has such a time with the thrashers. They have had them for over a week. It has rained so much they could not thrash. Oh, I must tell you the news. Clarence Barnard has got a boy at their house and they have only been married six months and not hardly that. It weighs 11 pounds. Mrs. Barnard feels very bad but I do not feel very sorry for her. That is his Mother for you know how she talked about Charley Campbell the last winter he went to school here she thought he was not fit for you boys as social. I guess this affair has taken her down a little. Her boys are not quite so near perfection. I suppose Ann has written you that Old Mrs. Morton was dead. She died about two months ago. You said you thought Charley ____ in very much little Ada's death. They did increase lake in yard. She was such a bright sweet child no one that knew her could help but love her. I was up at the old home place one day last week. ____ and I went after ____ and Dear Sister you don't know how everything has changed. It hardly looks like the same place. The hedge is all cut down low around the house and the weeds so high. You don't know how deserted and lonesome everything looks. Everything recalls vividly to mind the sad past and it seems sometimes as though if we could only know what did happen it would be some consolation. I dreamed of seeing Father last night, and Ellen, if that dream could only be realized what would I not give. There has none of us had any letters from California yet. I suppose Will told you about that miserable Postal Card that Victor sent last winter. I think that is the only word that we have had from them yet. I must close for this time hoping to hear from you soon, From your loving Sister. Please give my love to Will and kiss the baby for me. How I should love to see Guy. Please write soon, Ada McClure.*

1878 Moved back to Atoka, Indian Territory

1879 [3]David Victor born in 1879, Atoka, Indian Territory

1881 [3]Veta Ellen born at Liberty Hill, Atoka, Indian Territory

1887 The first contact lens developed by Adolf Fick

1889 April 21. Oklahoma Land Run. The McClure family moves to Oklahoma City. They had a home at 7th and Broadway.

Illustration 91. Mary Ellen (left) with friend

Illustration 92. Mary Ellen (middle) sitting in carriage

Illustration 93. Oklahoma City house

Illustration 94. Mary Ellen (left) and friend

Illustration 95. Visiting on the porch

Illustration 96. Oklahoma City, 7th and Broadway

Illustration 97. Mary Ellen holding the reins

Illustration 98. Veta driving; Mary Ellen standing at pony's shoulder

1890 March 12. Letter from Fairmont, West Virginia

My Dear Mrs. McClure,

I was very glad indeed to hear from you and certainly surprised to know you were in Oklahoma. I supposed you had not received my letter at the time of the opening up of the Oklahoma country. We all were very much interested in the accounts and the way people were "getting there" but we did not think of anyone we know being in the race. I told the boys my brother –of Mr. McClure's side and the thought it must have been a very hard one – were you not scared? From what I have heard of the country it must be delightful. Do you like it better than Atoka? I certainly do hope you will like it and that Mr. McClure may realize his fondest expectations. My we have had an ugly winter. Just now we have had a real nice sleighing snow and the only ice of the season. They are putting up ice about three or four inches thick. When the snow fell the peach and pear trees and early apples were in bloom. So our prospect for fruit is slightly "nipped.: Father is real well this winter, has not even had "La Grppe". Soon as I told him I had had a letter from you. He wanted to know what you said about Veta. We often speak of her. Lawrence is well except for a cold. We went to an adjoining county yesterday to attend to some oil leases he has been leasing oil territory. We have had big oil excitement in our county, that is about all it has amounted to so far. Lots of people think there "Millions in it", though but I am not one of them I spent the Christmas Holidays in Chicago. We have an Uncle living there. Gypsy Fleming my niece went with me and we certainly enjoyed the trip. We were there three weeks and I did not lost much time. We went to hear Patti & ? of course that was quite a treat to country girls as indeed our whole trip was. We had some place to go, or something to go see every day. Do you really like Oklahoma? Tell me what kind of a City it is. I've not heard anything since last winter from Eureka. Wonder if the old town is still there. I'd like to spend a few weeks there again very much. I think if Father had felt as if he could leave his business he would have gone back last fall. He thinks he was very much beautiful and he certainly has had a great deal better health since he was there. Now I'll be glad to hear from you whenever you have time to write. Remember me to Mr. McClure and love to Veta— Your friend, Lucy W-----

Illustration 99. Main Street, Oklahoma City, Oklahoma Territory

Illustration 100. Parade downtown Oklahoma City

Illustration 101. Early Oklahoma City streetcar

Illustration 102. Eastern Star receipts 1886 and 1890

1891 Pyotr Ilyich Tchaikovsky serves as first conductor at Carnegie Hall.

1899 Letter dated May 14, 1899, Oklahoma City; Envelope addressed to W. J. McClure, Sulphur, Indian Territory

Dear Will,

Yes I am ready for church and it is not yet time to go so I thought I would put in my time writing to you. I went over to see Mr. Barlow's last evening. He is bad. But I think his family has given up too quick. I met him as I was leaving his house. I don't think he

looks badly but he has to have two or three gallons of water taken from him every two weeks. Mr. McCormick the grain buyer, says he is coming down there most Saturdays and spends Sundays with you. He says if you don't want the spring block he will take it, just from my description of it, for I want to do it myself. Have you decided on anything yet? Mr. Douglas has not made the estimate, says it is very easy to make the house with a north front and get the South breeze too. He will go to work on it tomorrow. I could just as well have spent today with you, for Veta has not come home yet. Last night when she did not come I thought I would telegraph and find out what was the matter and ____ ____ they have no telegraph connections there. I am getting very uneasy about her. I don't see why she wrote that she was coming and then not do so. I am glad David was so well pleased with his trip. Will, what are the lots worth on Maywood? Two parties are wanting to buy. I priced those up in the timber at 85 per lot. Thought I would get them high enough ____ ____, lovingly yours, Ellen

1899   June 19. William John dies at age 57. Apparent heart attack

Sometime in the late 1800s, Mary Ellen and William John built the House of Seven Gables in Green Mountain Falls, Colorado—just north of Colorado Springs. There was a large hotel built to be a destination spot for vacationers. Their House of Seven Gables was the first house built near the hotel. The hotel never opened because it burned two weeks prior to the opening. The House of Seven Gables is still standing today. After enjoying the summer house in the cool of the mountains for more than 40 years, the McClures sold it.

Illustration 103. Green Mountain Falls, Colorado

Illustration 104. Hotel before burning to the ground

Illustration 105. Pond and gazebo still at Green Mountain Falls

Illustration 106. Trail ride with party hats

Illustration 107. Festooned riders and horses on the trail

August 9, *Pike's Peak Daily News*:
> A Grand and Historic Mountain and a Remarkable Railroad: This document lists people who traveled to the top of Pikes Peak by rail; listing on page 3: Third Section: Mrs. [2]M. E. McClure, Miss [3]Veta McClure— among the passengers. Passengers were from all over the U.S.A., including Massachusetts, Kentucky, New York, Texas, Iowa, Pennsylvania, Missouri, Oklahoma, Mississippi, as well as Cuba and Argentina.

Illustration 108. Advertisement for Green Mountain Falls

Letter to Mrs. Mary E. McClure, Oklahoma City, Oklahoma Territory from A. V. McClure, Elk Creek, Nebraska

Dear Sister Ellen,

Accept our deepest sympathy for yourself and family in this your great bereavement. I hope you will be able to look at what may seem a calamity, in its best light. That he didn't ____ a great sufferer, that his disease was incurable and that although you cannot help mourning the loss of one so near and dear – he is at rest. I regret so much that I could not see him and we will never be done feeling sorry we did not get your letter on time. If you had only put a delivery _____ or it. Am sorry Guy could not get there in time. Think it could have been some comfort to have seen his father even in the embrace of death. For as he looked upon him with his breaking heart he would find consolation. He thought that the sufferer was at rest. I still mourn you. You are blessed with true friends, I do hope to hear from you soon, I can assure you would find an ____ for my not writing sooner if you knew all that I had realization I should not explain. I wrote you yesterday but was quite sick, With much love and sympathy for yourself and family. From Dan and myself, I Close, A.V.

October 16, Order of Select Friends, Friendship, Hope of Protection, Parsons, Kansas

Dear Sister McClure, I am sick with disappointment in not getting to attend the Texas G Chapter had all arrangements made to go but find I am not going to get to go. I am most down sick over it, but will try to make the best of it. Now I wish you would write and by return mail if you can be in Parsons on Friday. October 24 by leaving Dennison,

Thursday night at 11:00 o'clock you can arrive here Friday at 10 ½ a.m. My reason for ____Saturday night is Blue Lodge night and we would have to wait as will you come here the first of the following week, if so you can let me know just what day you can be here and how long you will remain with us and then I can arrange things. Our regular meeting comes on the first and third Monday and we want to give you as nice a visit as we can so I feel more anxious. So if you can let me know the exact time we will do our best to make your visit pleasant and profitable. We will be very much disappointed if we are to loose the honor of your visit. I am in a hurry writing from the Dr. office. I expect you can hardly read this. It is so hurried for train is due now. I hope to hear from you soon. With love, Gabriel (Envelope postmarked received, Oklahoma, Indian Territory.)

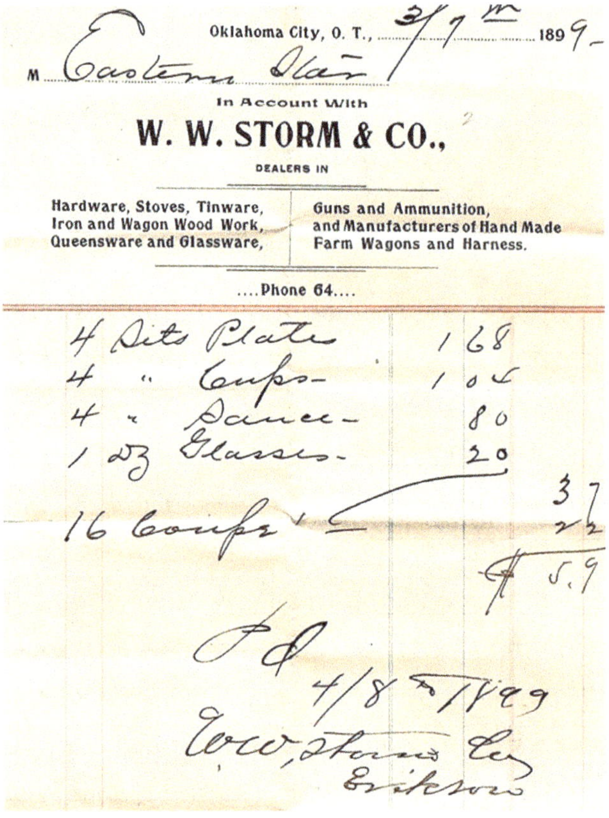

Illustration 109. Purchase of china

November 11, from Parsons, Kansas

Dear Sister McClure,

I can't tell you how much we as a Chapter are disappointed we had counted so much on your making us a visit. It seems I am doomed to disappointment lately, everything I set my heart on goes wrong. I have had more than my share. I do hope my luck will change soon. I want you to make us a visit when you come over this way on official visits. We will try to make your visit pleasant. Now I am somewhat surprised at Texas being behind in their OES work. (I thank you for the nice compliment you paid me on instructions.) I would only be but glad if my means would allow me to make the rounds of Official visits with you and visit every Chapter in your jurisdiction and give you the benefit of some new instructions. I would assist you in many new ideas that beautifies and perfects OES work. Now my dear don't think this is boasting on my part- it is not- so intended, but I mean it in a business sense. There are many Chapters in Kansas that needs so much as some of yours, but it is not my business to say anything while our Grand Matron is able to work. I have done considerable work with new Chapters near me and am surprised at some of the older ones not know more than they do. Tomorrow night is our regular meeting. We will take in five, making in all when in this year 44 not a bad years work is it. We now have 150 members and it likes thinking it keeps them in good working order, but indeed we do have a nice Chapter, good attendance every meeting. I have only three more meetings to serve as Worthy Matron after tomorrow night. I will feel relieved somewhat after five years service, but I will work just as hard out of the-chair as in it. I have invitations from two Chapters to install their new officers for the ensuing year. I am conducting the ceremony but don't make much headway have so much company and talk so much. I have just written a letter to W. Grand Matron of Texas Sister Hadley asking her to make herself known to cousin who has gone to San Antonio for his health. He has consumption. He will not live long, his wife is a sweet little woman and I feel so sorry for her away so far from friends among strangers and a sick husband who she will not have with her long. I hope Sister Hadley will go see them. It was on their account I did not get to go to Denison. Oh how bad I did want to go too. Now Sister ME how does it come that Bro. Doyle did the work at Guthrie, one of our own members was out there and it seems to me he does some strange work. Forgive my saying this, but I mean it in the true spirit – for good only. Now the way he did or at least the way I hear he did would be illegal in this state and a Charter would not be granted them after his work. Is he still working as deputy of G.G.C. If so, why? You have a grand Chapter of your own now, and a G. Patron, so more work from the G.G.C. for you. Your G. Patron deputized his worker. Now I mention this to you not to make trouble but to save trouble indeed I want to help you not find trouble. I have no right to say anything but I am interested in your _____. I know you have material and can work right and for your sake I am interested. I have written so much now I must close it is midnight. Hoping to hear from you soon. I am as ever your fraternal Sister, Gabriel

No date given, but approximately this time period (1899). It appears the following is a speech that Mary E. McClure gave:

> To the W. M. W. T. Officers and Members of Guthrie's Chapter No. 12 O.E.S. On behalf of the sub Chapters of O.T. We thank you for your cordial

welcome and kindly words of greeting. We are truly grateful that we are among the numbers of this representatives of this glorious territory who have the honor of sharing the hospitality and ____ So beauteously and graciously bestowed. for ____ by the Sisters and Brothers of our beautiful Capital city. This is not our first visit to your city. We know where of we speak. When we say a more hospitable city, is not built on these red sands of Oklahoma Territory. We are more than pleased to see so many of our Sisters from others further than us. It encourages us greatly. Uncle Sam is reaching out as fast becoming a prominent factor in the commercial interests and centers of the world. Russia, Germany and other nations look askance at the inroads our ____ are making in their countries. Mrs. F. Vanderbilt, recently assistant Secretary of the Treasury a thorough ____ gives the following picture and observation, American locomotives running on American rails, move whistles past the pyramids of Egypt. And across to the long Siberian Steppes. They carry the timber from all parts of the empire and to the sacred waters of the Ganges. Three years ago there was but one American locomotive in the United Kingdom. And today there is not a road of importance there on which trains are not being pulled by American engines. American bridges span rivers on every continent. American Cranes are swinging over many foreign miles. Wherever they are extensive harvest there may be found American machinery to gather the grain. In every great market of the world tools can have no better recommendation than the mark made in America. Our cotton can be found in Manchester as well as on the shores of Africa and in the native shops of the Orient. Bread is baked in Palestine from flour made in Minneapolis. One might get on without enumerating the progress of America. Oklahoma has her share in this expansion. She has sent her Rough Riders to Cuba. Many of our soldier Laddies to the Philippines. Our teachers are helping set the pace in the educational world of our new possessions. One of Oklahoma Ex US Attorney now holds a trusted position in ____, one of our own dear sisters, Sister Novia Golbrith, has the honor to be the first of the W.M. of the first O.E.S. Chapter organized in ____ then is it not meant that the sisters of the O.E.S. of this ____ rise in their might and become bright and shining lights in the fraternal world. We have the natural right here in our order, let us not fail to send it out into the highway and hedges but looking about us, due what our hands find to do and do it with our might for the hospitality courtesy extended I again thank you in the name of all visitors, sisters and brothers.

Years ago when Oklahoma City was in her infancy, when our beloved Chapter was not as flourishing as it now is, when our quarters were small, our members few. I doubt if there be a half dozen present tonight who were with us then – one night there came knocking for admittance at the door of our Chapter room. Three candidates, seeking for the light, shed by the star which was sent to the wise men of the east ages ago, to lead them across the divide stretches of sand to the spot where the Christ Child lay – the star which has continued to shine with undiminished luster down through the ages to our present day. One of that trio, the quiet timid one, who scarce permitted the sound of her voice to be heard above a whisper is with us tonight, but so grows in strength, so ever ready in her quiet way to respond to the call of the needy, to extend the hand of aid to the helpless, she has filled many of the leading offices in our chapter, and now is closing a most successful year as W. M. It is with great reluctance that we see her lay down her gavel of authority; but we know that whenever she duly demands, as the call of the needy is heard – she will be ever ready to assume her share of responsibility. It is with great pleasure that, on behalf of the chapter I present you, my dear sister, this small token of esteem and hope that in future, as in the past – the good deeds will shine with undiminished luster but outweighing scintillations of this glass. To our good Sister who came to us later who has nobly placed his shoulder to the wheel and aided us in every possible way. Also wish to present a small token of esteem, not that we think that in any way the brush is symbolical for we do not think he needs it to brush any cobwebs from his eyes.

1900 Census Microfilm Roll No. 1340 Series, T623, Oklahoma Territory, Oklahoma County; Oklahoma Township, Ward One; Dist. 219, Sheet 16. Enum. Dist. No. 167

[2]Mary E. McClure, b. Dec. 1854; age 45; widow; b. Kansas
   Father b. Ohio; Mother b. unknown

[3]Veta E. McClure, b. March 1882; age 18; b. Indian Territory
   Mother b. Kansas; Father, b. Virginia—(This is incorrect on census.)

[3]Guy V. McClure, b. December 1877; age 22; b. Kansas
   Mother, b. Kansas; Father, b. Virginia—(This is also incorrect.)

Illustration 110. 6' x 9' oil painting of Mary Ellen. It hung in the Guthrie Consistory for many years before the Atoka Eastern Star Chapter asked to have it in their lodge. Mary Ellen was the First Worthy Grand Matron of Indian Territory in Atoka. In early 2000 the building and the painting burned in a fire set by arsonists.

Illustration 111. Mary Ellen and Veta sailing to Europe for a six-month tour

Illustration 112. Mary Ellen and daughter Veta in Europe

Illustration 113. Fashionable Veta McClure

Illustration 114. Mary Ellen and Veta in Europe

Illustration 115. Veta conversing with gentleman

Illustration 116. European trip drama

Illustration 117. Mary Ellen and daughter Veta

1900 September 2. A letter written from San Francisco—Presidio, California

My dear Auntie Clure,

Oh, how often I have tried to answer that nice newsy letter written by my lovely auntie Clure. Tomorrow is Labor Day and we have a holiday and I am not a bit sorry either. How is Veta just as sure as ever I guess. Papa gave me a very agreeable surprise the other day. It was a bicycle and a nice one too. Midge is too fat for anything he can hardly get in the shafts. Mama made herself a present of a banner phantom, it is just lovely. Roy has not come back yet from the park but he will, about October 20. I am just convalescing from a delightful case of mumps. My head was ever so large that everyone said that I had a swell head. There is going to be big-time here tonight because it is the native sons celebration. How is Veta? Has she gone back to school yet? I have been absent for a week. I suppose you are having such a lovely time but California isn't. Will tell you it all right. And how is that swell David I do hope he remembers who I am when you mention my name. Mama is just washing our little angora cat. My what a time she has it scratches her and bites her and everything else. I had a surprise the other day and it was a ____ now I am happy. Hoping this reaches you all well with love from us all to both Veta and you I remain your loving niece, Ethel

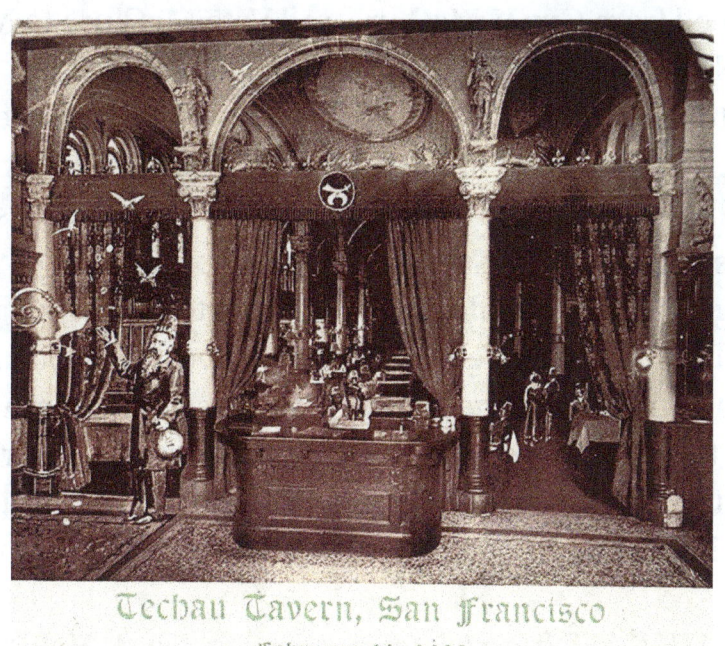

Illustration 118. San Francisco postcard

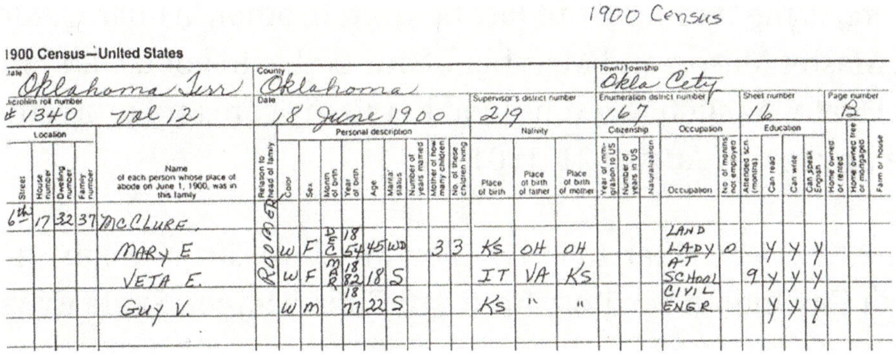

1900 Census

1900 Census—United States

State: Oklahoma Terr | County: Oklahoma | Town/Township: Okla City
Microfilm roll number: # 1340 Vol 12 | Date: 18 June 1900 | Supervisor's district number: 219 | Enumeration district number: 167 | Sheet number: 16 | Page number: B

Street	House number	Dwelling number	Family number	Name of each person whose place of abode on June 1, 1900, was in this family	Relation to head of family	Color	Sex	Month of birth	Year of birth	Age	Marital status	Number of years married	Mother of how many children	No. of these children living	Place of birth	Place of birth of father	Place of birth of mother	Year of immigration to US	Number of years in US	Naturalization	Occupation	No. of months not employed	Attended sch. (months)	Can read	Can write	Can speak English	Home owned or rented	Home owned free or mortgaged	Farm or house
6th	17	32	37	McCLURE.	ROOMER																								
				MARY E		W	F	DEC	1854	45	WD		3	3	KS	OH	OH				LAND LADY	0		Y	Y	Y			
				VETA E.		W	F	MAR	1882	18	S				IT	VA	KS				AT SCHOOL		9	Y	Y	Y			
				GUY V.		W	M		1877	22	S				KS	"	"				CIVIL ENGR			Y	Y	Y			

Illustration 119. 1900 U.S. Census

1900 Census United States Microfilm #1340, Vol. 12, Sheet 16, Page B
Oklahoma Territory; Oklahoma County, Oklahoma City Township, House #17, 6th Street, Oklahoma City

[2]Mary E. b. December, 1854; age 45; widow; LandLady, b. Kansas
Father b. Ohio,
Mother b. Ohio

[3]Veta E. b. March 1882, single; age 18; b. Indian Territory, at school
Father b. Virginia(incorrect)
Mother b. Kansas

[3]Guy V. b. 1877, single; age 22; b. Kansas, Civil Engineer

1901 Quit-Claim Deed from Guy V. McClure and Veta McClure to Mary E. McClure
Feb. 28, 1901; Book 17, page 334; ____ 100; Register of Deeds

> This indenture, made this 4th day of February 1901 between Guy V. McClure and Veta E. McClure, Two of the heirs of William J. McClure, deceased, parties of the first part, and Mary E. McClure, party of the second part. That said parties of the first part in consideration of the sum of $One Dollar and other good and valuable considerations to them duly paid, the receipt whereof is hereby acknowledged have remised, released and quit-claimed for themselves or their heirs the said part of the second part and to her heirs all their right, title, interest in and to all of the following described property and lying in Oklahoma City to wit: Lots numbered One, Two, and Three in Block No. 44 in Oklahoma City, according to the recorded plat thereof.

WIDOWS CERTIFICATE from Oklahoma Lodge, No. 4, Held at Atoka in State of: Indian Territory, County of Atoka

> To all Whom it may Concern, Greeting, Know Ye, that Mrs. Mary Ellen McClure, is the Widow of our late beloved Brother, William J. McClure who was a Master Mason and Member of our Lodge in good standing at the time of his Death. As such we commend her to the care and protection of the whole Fraternity. August 21, 1901

February 23, Letter written to Mary Ellen McClure, 301 N. Sixth Street, Oklahoma City Indian Territory from #10 Cherry Street, Santa Cruz, California

> *Well Dear Sister, I have written you a good long letter but it is not a hundred percent of what I could tell you if I could see you personally. There is lots of things that I want I can't think of to write but could tell you if that has transpired since I last saw you. Dear sister I will close by asking you to not wait so many years before you answer this letter because I do want to hear from you and your family. It being so long to me. To think that I had some relatives that did not care something for me. But probably you have not thought much about it - that I am your only brother that is living and one that has always loved you forever from the bottom of my heart and always will though we may never meet on earth but t hope to be with you in heaven because we are both getting along in years as well as the rest of our family. Dear sister, forgive me for not writing to you in years that has gone by but I have written several letters to you but never got answered. So goodbye, forever your most loving brother WH Kennedy oh yes dear sister*

there is one more question that I will ask, do you know anything about sister July's child, where they are, and what any of them are doing, where their PO address is. Do you know where Maggie Kennedy is and what is her address and Wilkins and his family is and their address is. In fact all of the ____ Kansas in general. I am your loving brother WH Kennedy answer by return mail.

Grand Lodge of Indian Territory; Sept 24, 1901

Mrs. M.E. McClure
Dear Sister,

The enclosed was handed to me yesterday. It has been a wary time getting ready but I am glad that I can send it to you now. It is a shame that it has been delayed so long. You'll be glad to hear that our little town is commencing to prosper. Six or eight new homes have been built recently and others are to be built. The celebrated Methodist evangelist, Abe Miley, has been here the past week and some of the hard cases in town have professed conversion and joined the Methodist and Presbyterian churches. Among a whole lot of others are Mike Conlin, Carmen Williams and John Harrison, John Harkins and Mr. Braine. We pray that God may be sincere and prove steadfast. May God bless you and your dear children I pray Sincerely JS Morrow

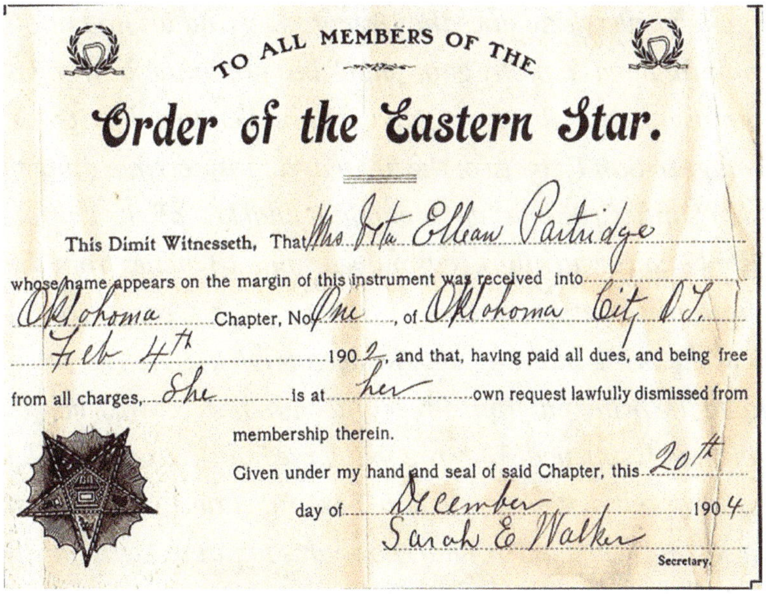

TO ALL MEMBERS OF THE

Order of the Eastern Star.

This Dimit Witnesseth, That Mrs Veta Ellean Patridge whose name appears on the margin of this instrument was received into Oklahoma Chapter, No One, of Oklahoma City O.T. Feb 4th 1902, and that, having paid all dues, and being free from all charges, She is at her own request lawfully dismissed from membership therein.

Given under my hand and seal of said Chapter, this 20th day of December 1904

Sarah E Walker
Secretary.

Illustration 120. Veta Partridge resigns from Eastern Star.

1903 January 27. Grand Chapter of Indian Territory O.E.S.

Dear Sister McClure,

It is the wish of our Grand Matron and I need not say of many others also, that you represent the Grand Chapter of Indian Territory near the Grand Chapter of Oklahoma

Territory. It is with great pleasure that I encase you this commission and should there ever arise any necessity for a peacemaker, I am sure your gracious tact and dignity should dispel at once any feeling of rivalry or jealousy, the relations between the two Grand Bodies at present is very cordial and has____ and I sincerely trust it may ever be. Old No. 1 is still plodding along— we are not very____ but we are united and faithful, which may end better. With much love for yourself and Veta, Faithfully, ____

1906 Letter to Mary Ellen from her brother in San Francisco describing the earthquake of 1906

61 Park Street, Santa Cruz, California
May 29, 1906
My Dear Sister Ellen,

Your dear letter of May 14th was received a few days ago; we were very glad to hear from you once more; I have written several letters to you also Postal cards, but I did not receive any answers to any of them. I suppose you must not have received any of them or we would have heard from you. Will says that you must have been with Veta and did not get them; we do not mind now that we have had a letter from you and we would be glad to see you again. I have been expecting to hear from Sister Eliza but I suppose she is busy just now on the farm. Yes Dear Sister that was a terrible earthquake and we have been having them every day since the 18th of April and we had another one on the 17th of this month. It was a pretty good shock but not quite so strong it did not do so much damage. I must say that the earthquake was bad enough but it was the fire that did the most damage in San Francisco; the fire was a most terrible thing to happen; the earthquake here in Santa Cruz was bad enough. It knocked all the chimneys down both of ours were twisted and my furniture was moved some 18 inches from the wall; the new library the fire house, the courthouse the ____ block, the St. George Hotel, the Leonard Block, in fact all of the Brink Building, Pacific ocean house, hotel, all were damaged here. To walk down the principal front street and church street you would think that something terrible had happened. They are fixing the houses up that – I left after the quake. I am glad I was out of it and now I am in a little house of four rooms. I had to sell the bedroom set that you left. For I had no rooms to put it. I can hardly turn around so I do not know how long we will stay in it. I have no back yard and that makes it bad; and I have been feeling very bad since the quake, but I have got some medicines now that I think is going to help me. Dear Sister, I am so sorry about your left eye. It must be awfully bad for you and I do hope and trust that you will be able to see out of it – before long you must be very careful and not take cold in it or you will lose it altogether and that would be very bad. I do hope and trust to God that you will come out all right when *you undertake to have it operated on. We have had quite a lot of rain this spring. I am afraid that the quakes are not over with yet. The mail man has just brought me a letter from London England from one of my nieces. Oh she felt so bad about the quake here in Santa Cruz. She says that the papers are full of it and says that so many are homeless in Santa Cruz. But that is not so, there is not one here in Santa Cruz that is homeless. No not here but in San Francisco there they are homeless. But they are being cared for and a great many are a good deal better off than they were before. Buildings that have been put up since you were here. Will has got to finish this after his supper. Ever your loving Sister Louise Kennedy". "Dear Sister, as I have finished my supper I will try and write you a few lines. We are getting along pretty well. My wife is a little better of her Rheumatism. She has been pretty bad all winter. She has been helpless for several months, but can help herself some now. But she has to have crutches. We have tried all kinds of medicines and nothing seems to do any good. I have had a hard time of it this winter, but hope that the worst is over now. She is liking some medicines that is called the Standard Medical Society Baltimore Maryland. She has not taken enough of it to know whether it will help her or not. We are glad that Guy has got a Baby Girl and that she is so sweet. We would like to see her in fact we would like to see you all very much. You did not tell us what you have named her and you must. Be sure and send us her picture, also tell Guy to send us his and her picture. And tell them to write to us. We expect a letter from Sister Eliza but have not got any yet. We wrote to her when we wrote to you last but have not got any answer from her. We want you to send yours. Give to Veta and _____ and tell them to write to us also to David and Wife. We would like to have all of your pictures. Tell them to be sure and send them to us. I will tell you of Warren. He is married and is living in Oakland. He is head typesetter in the Oakland Tribune office. He is getting three and a half per day. They are getting along nice. They rent furnished rooms. He pays several dollars per month. I have been in to see them. He had the ____ and I went to see him. He is all right now. I thought that he was a going to die. He has got a nice wife. They have been married over a year. Well Dear Sister I will close for this time hoping to hear from you and family. So good night. We both send our love to you from Brother and Sister W__ Kennedy"*

1907   First grandson, William John born, July 6, 1907

Illustration 121. Mary Ellen with first grandson, William John

November 25, Tax Certificate City of Oklahoma City, Oklahoma Territory: Paid $159.71 for property, East Tenth (10th) Street from the East line of Broadway to the West line of Phillips Avenue.

January 18, Mary Ellen paid taxes in Topeka, Kansas, for Lot 3 in Silver Lake City

1907   Oklahoma admitted as the 46th state into the Union

State Fair Association of Oklahoma, Mary Ellen purchased ten shares stock at $10.00 each.

Illustration 122. Mary Ellen McClure   Illustration 123. Mary Ellen McClure

1909 A postcard dated December 20 to Mary E. McClure

Dear Sister Ellen,

Why don't you write to me. My wife thinks it is strange that you don't do so. We are all getting old and will not last much longer. I shall and I am looking for a letter from my dear sister Ellen, from your ever loving brother, William H Kennedy

Women of '89, Organized July 17, 1909, in Oklahoma City. Original certificate

1910 Letter dated January 17, to Mary E. McClure from Santa Cruz, California

My dear sister Ellen,

I was taken sick the next day after sending you the PO card is the reason we did not write. I sent sister Elizabeth also a PO card. On it I told her that you were talking of coming out here soon. Said about one month or six weeks and that we must not be surprised if we saw you both come trudging along and I told her that we should only be so pleased to see you both. So I shall hope to see you both for I have never seen sister and Eliza and I do hope she will come with you. I hope you will let me know about what time or about the date you think we may look for you so that I will be at home. Willie is so pleased to think to see you so soon, so am I. Oh my what dreadful weather you are having back there but I do hope that you both are all right, hoping to hear from you soon and that you will excuse a short letter for this time as I do not feel well, but I thought a short one is better than none. With the best of our love from us both, we remain your loving brother and sister William H. And Louise Kennedy.

Letter dated February 22, no year listed but appears to be about this time (1909)

My dear darling sister,

I received your kind and most welcome letter on the 16th and was so glad to hear from you. It has been years and years since I last heard from you or any of your family. It has been so long since I have had a letter from you I hardly know how to write. I have been in California for 12 years. I have been alone for six years and have been divorced for four years and I am____ And alone in the state not a relative in the state that I know of and I have not seen a relative since 1885. Don't know anything about our people still. Dear sister I sometimes feel very lonely and lonesome and sit down and think of the past and what I might have done if I had had the right companion. But as it was my lot I had to do the best I could to get along in the world that was the reason I left all of you. I know that I did not get the right kind of a wife to live with. Nor listen to my own mother or sister or any of the family. That is the reason that I never stayed around any of my folks when I married her. I thought that I got the finest girl in all the world, but my judgment was not good and when I found out that I was deceived by her, I made the best of it I could and the plan I took was to keep her away from you all. Dear sister I can't tell you all by letter but if the Lord spares our lives until we meet again I will tell you all that has been the trouble in my married life. I have spent my life, time and money with her and no benefit to me or anyone else. Since we came to California she went blind and I took her to San Francisco to see the best Onulist in the city. I spent every dollar that I had to get her cured. I had over $800 in cash and a good home that I paid $600 for and it all went to Dr. And as good luck would have it she was brought to her site once more and she has as good eyes as she ever had. But the balance I will tell you if ever I live to see you again and I hope that time will be soon. Dear sister, I have been in Santa Cruz for the last three years. I have been working for the union ice company for nearly 3 years delivering ice for them here and will still work for them this year. We run the business the year-round. I am driving the ice wagon at the present time and will all next summer if I am well and keep my health. I am well and hearty and never felt better in my life. This is one of the finest climates that anyone ever lived in. We don't have any cold weather here in winter. No lightning or thunderstorms, perfectly dry weather in summer with some fog once in a while and rain and winter and sunshine. We have flowers year-round of all description and vegetables too year-round and the finest water that flows out of the mountains. There's three ranges of mountains here. The Santa Cruz, the Ben Lomond and the Santiago mountains. Santa Cruz is a beautiful little city situated on *the Monterey Bay. It is just eight miles from San Francisco. There is two railroads run into Santa Cruz, the Broad gauge and the Narrow gauge Road. They both run from San Francisco. There is all kind of fruit trees here, also orange and lemons grow here, all kinds of berries too. Well sister you asked me about property here. Property is very high but if anyone wanted a home on this coast I don't think that it can be bettered anywhere but for speculation it is too high. It is really a summer resort, there is a great many just come here in summers and people from San Joaquin and Sacramento Valley to spend a few months in summer. Those valleys are very hot, the temperatures run from 120 to 160 there and they come here to get the sea breeze. They stay here from 2 to 3 months in hot area. . . . (Remainder lost)*

1910 U.S. Census, Series T624; Roll 1265, Page 248; Sheet 9
[2]Mary E. McClure, age 52, b. Kansas
    Father b. Indiana
    Mother, b. Illinois
Owns home at 801 N. Broadway, Oklahoma City, Oklahoma

NEWSPAPER ARTICLE
(no date)

March 1st, anniversary of the birth of Mrs. Jane Kennedy, one of the old landmarks of this section, was duly celebrated, with a successful surprise on this, her 66 year. Her many friends took possession of her house in her absence, prepared a sumptuous feast, and on her return to find the tables loaded with good things, and the rooms full of close friends, surprised her greatly and warmed up her heart with the thought that her friends had not forgotten her old and declining years.

1912 July 2. Receipt from County Treasurer's Office: Received of Mary E. McClure $432.07 for last ½ of the Following Taxes for the Year 1912

Illustration 124. Mary Ellen with first granddaughter, Veta Ann

November 6, Lease: Mary E. McClure leased a Dwelling on Lot One, McClure's Addition to Oklahoma City, Oklahoma, being 303 W. Twelfth Street. J. T. Garrett paid her $357.50. Payable in $32.50 on the 6th day of each month thereafter during the life of this contract. Mr. Garrett was responsible for all charges for water, gas, electric lights, garbage service, and responsible for all repairs to said property.

Lots 1,2,3, Twp. or Block 8, Receipt from County Treasurer's Office Received of Mary E. McClure, $222.10 for ½ of the taxes for this year. Taxes on McClure Subdivision Lot 2, B8, Lot Valuation estimates: $6,500; $5,500; $4,850

1915 December 24, Letter from Oklahoma City Treasurer office
 I hereby certify that there is nothing due in this office at the present time on lots (2) of lot (2), block 8, McClure Addition to Oklahoma City Oklahoma.

1917 April 24, 1917, Quit Claim Deed from Mrs. Mary E. McClure, 311 W. 12th to George N. Frise, Sale of Lot three (3), block twelve (12) in Oklahoma City, Oklahoma County, State of Oklahoma, as same appears from supplemental plat and survey of said city.

1918 Letter from the YMCA headquarters in Paris, France
Written by her son-in-law, Major R. W. Smyth, 4th Infantry, France, July 4, 1918

My Dear Mrs. McClure,

I've been intending to write to you for some time and let you know a little about conditions over here, but first I must tell you the good news that I've been fortunate enough to receive my promotion as a Major. I certainly consider myself a lucky person to have received my majority after only four years service with troops. We left our training area a little over a month ago and were sent by rail to one of the front line sectors. I was still supply officer when we left and I had my hands full for a while, but after we reached this area things straightened out pretty well and now are going pretty smoothly. I got my majority a few days ago and am now merely hanging around awaiting an assignment. I'd like to stay with the 4th but am afraid that my chances are very small. I wish that you could have the opportunity to see conditions as they really are over here. At times out in the country one can hardly realize that there is any war because everything is so quiet and peaceful and the fields are all under cultivation. But when one goes into a town the war is brought home to you with a vengeance. Up here near the front all of the villages are vacated with the possible exception of two or three people. One sees where the shells have dropped onto the buildings and torn large holes there and everything is in a state of devastation and you can almost constantly hear the sound of the guns either near or at a distance but most of the firing is done at night. As a rule it is very quiet during the day. I don't know where all the people go when they move out and I can't see how they exist because apparently they just pick up and leave practically everything behind. After going into one of the towns and seeing the interior of some of the businesses are readily see the origin of the expressions "Taking French leave". To my mind the most pitiful sight I have seen is to pass a family, which is on the road leaving their house. The party generally consists of one elderly man or couple, women and two or three children; all loaded down with as much as they can carry. And each and all of them with the most forelorn and unhappy expression on their faces imaginable. We saw quite a bit of that when we first came to this section because it is one in which the Germans had recently made a drive. Our regiment has been under fire a little and everyone has done himself credit. Our casualties have been comparatively small not any more than one could measurably expect. I was fortunate enough to get to Paris last week. I left in the morning, got there about noon and stayed until noon of the next day. I was on business and didn't get much of an opportunity to see the city as I would have liked to have seen it. The night before I went there the city had been attacked by an air raid. A couple of bombs had dropped near the Louvre. I don't imagine the place is much like it was when you saw it. At night all the lights on the street are extinguished with the exception of one occasional light and it certainly is a weird sight. The night I was there the alarm was given that an air attack was coming but nothing materialized. Veta has written me that she has been on a visit in Oklahoma. I bet you enjoyed her stay and I hope that she didn't make all of her fleeting calls on you and leave before you had become accustomed to having her with you. I wish I could make myself believe that we would be back to the U.S. before long but I can't see where there is much hope of that. Sincerely, R. W. Smyth

1918 Spanish Influenza epidemic

Receipt for Special Assessment for year 1918, $35,177.39, Maywood Addition

1919 January 1. First Mortgage Bond, United States Bond and Mortgage Company
Mary E. McClure paid $1,700.00, Paid 6 ½% paid semi-annually

Owned 311 W. 12th St. Registration Certificate #403, Precinct 9, Ward 1
February 26, 1919, 60 years of age, 5'6" height, 150 lb. weight

Receipt: CHARTER MEMBERSHIP RECEIPT No. 528, Oklahoma City, Okla. May 26, Received of Mrs. Mary McClure the sum of $1.50 for charter membership in the Oklahoma County Roosevelt Club and the statewide Republican Club to be organized on September 15, 1919, said sum to include one year's subscription to the National Republican, a weekly newspaper published at Washington, D. C.

1920 Census: Oklahoma County, Oklahoma; Precinct, Oklahoma City
Series, T625; Roll, 1473, Page 229 Surname: McClure
[3]David McClure, b. Oklahoma, age: 40
   Occupation— Buyer/Seller Mule Business
    Father b. Illinois
    Mother b. Kansas
[3]Grace A. McClure, Wife, b. Ohio, age 30
    Father b. Ohio;
    Mother b. Ohio
[4]William J. McClure, Son, b. Kentucky, age 12

Father b. Oklahoma;
Mother b. Ohio

⁴Margarite McClure, Daughter

(Margarite is our mystery child. No records are available, only a roll call for Sunday School. Those are found in the Grace McClure chapter in this book. My [the author] guess is that she was the second child born to Guy and Bernice.)

²Mary E. McClure, "Head", Owner/ Free Mortgage. age 63, b. Kansas
Father b. Indiana
Mother b. Virginia

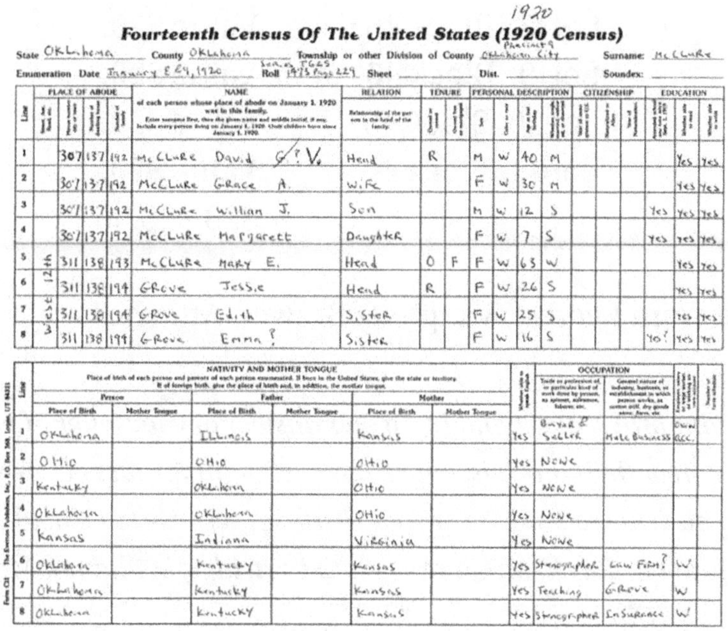

Illustration 125. Fourteenth Census of the United States

1921 U. S. purchases the territory of Florida from Spain.

December 9, 1921, County Treasurer's Office, Murray County, Sulphur, Oklahoma, Received of Mary E. McClure of Sulphur the sum of $8.07, real estate tax

Sec. or Lot 1, Block 137, Value $1,250
Lot 2, Block 150, Value $150
Pd $9.40 Lots 1 & 2, Block 157 Value $400

1921 Real Estate Assessment List 1921 Mary E. McClure 311 W. 12th Street
Original Platt   Lot 22, Block 35   Value $14,000.

	Lot 23, Block 35	Value $14,000.
McClure Addition	Lot 2, Block 8	Value $5,300.
	Lot 3, Block 8	Value $4,900.
Maywood Addition	Lot 1, Block 9	Value $2,210.
	Lot 2, Block	Value $2,000.
	Lot 3, Block 9	Value $850.
	Lot 4, Block 9	Value $850.
Britton Heights	Lot 24, Block 9	Value $35.
	Lot 30, Block 9	Value $35.
	Lot 31, Block 9	Value $35.
	Lot 32, Block 9	Value $35.
	Lot 8, Block 46	Value $20.
	Lot 9, Block 46,	Value $20.
	Lot 10, Block 46	Value $20.
	Lot 11, Block 46	Value $20.
		$43,920.00

1921 April 16. Letter from Everest, Vaught & Brewer, Attorneys

Dear Mrs. McClure,

Pursuant to your oral request and in further answer of your letter of July 7, 1919 I am enclose your herewith four deeds, which were left with me just before you made your trip to Europe, to be delivered in case of your death, otherwise to be held subject to your order. These deeds are to Guy V. McClure, Veta E. Partridge, William J. McClure, son of David, and David McClure.

1922 May 27. New York Life Insurance Company: Policy No. 3281 28

Dear Madam,

In accordance with the terms of the above numbered policy a dividend of $967.32 will be apportioned to the policy. This dividend may be taken in cash or it may be applied to purchase Non-participating Paid-up Insurance of $1,380.00,

Mary E. McClure, "Head", Owner/ Free Mortgage. Age 63, b. Kansas
Father b. Indiana; Mother b. Virginia

1923 February 1. Receipt for Mortgage Tax, Received of Mary E. McClure, $80.00 in payment of real estate mortgage tax.
Mortgagor, Alexander Drug Co. Mortgagee: Mary E. McClure.

April 20, She [Mary E. McClure] was run down and killed instantly at Thirteenth Street and Harvey Avenue about 9:45. She lived at 301 West 12th Street.

Death Certificate: Place of Death, 13th Street and Harvey St., Oklahoma City, Car Accident
Registration No. #317

Oklahoma City Times, April 21, front page

AUTO KILLS AGED CLUBWOMAN PIONEER
Oklahoman Dies Under Wheels

Mrs. Mary E. McClure, 72 years old a prominent Oklahoma City clubwoman and settler of Oklahoma before the territory was opened, was run down and instantly killed at Thirteenth street and Harvey Avenue Friday night at 9:45 o'clock by an automobile traveling east, driven by Don McCafferty, 18 years old. Mrs. McClure lived at 301 West Twelfth street. The only witness in the accident were Don McCafferty and the occupants of his automobile. Mrs. McClure was living alone, and evidently was returning from an entertainment in the city, according to her neighbors who said they noticed a light in her home during the evening. She turned on the lights always when she left home, they said. Her home was locked. According to the story told by J.K. Wright, county attorney, by McCafferty, he and a party of friends were on their way to a Sunday school social at the home of a church member when the accident occurred. McCafferty said he did not see Mrs. McClure and that the first intimation he had of the accident was when he heard the car strike her. He was going at a moderate speed, he said, and stopped as quickly as possible. Police officers declared Mrs. McClure probably had been dragged twenty feet. No charges have been filed against Don McCaferty. He was exonerated.

Oklahoma City Times, Monday, April 23, page 2, Col 2

MRS. MCCLURE'S FUNERAL
Fixed Service To Be Held At Masonic Auditorium.

The Women of '89 will meet Tuesday at 1:45 o'clock in the parlor on the second floor of the Masonic temple to attend in a body, the Masonic auditorium. Members of all departments of the Sorosis club also will meet in a body at the temple at 1:45 o'clock to attend the services. Mrs. McClure was killed Friday night by an automobile accident. Burial will take place in Fairlawn cemetery. No charges will be filed on Don McCafferty, driver of the car, according to J.R. Wright, county attorney. With her husband, the late William J. McClure, and their three children she lived on a cattle ranch near Atoka before Oklahoma was opened to settlement. She has lived in Oklahoma City many years and made her home at 301 West Twelfth street. Mrs. McClure was Right Worthy Grand Marshal of the General Grand Chapter O.E.S. Past Matron of Chapter No. 10 and a member of the Past Matron's Club. She was also a member of the First Presbyterian church, the Women of '89, the First Families of Oklahoma and several social clubs. Mrs. McClure leaves a daughter, Mrs. George M. Church of New York and a son Dave McClure, who lives on a farm west of Britton. The eldest son, Guy V. McClure, died several years ago.

Oklahoma City Times, Saturday, April 21, page 3, Col 6

MRS. MCCLURE PAID TRIBUTE AT '89ER MEET
Visitors From All Sections Of State To Attend

Memorial services for Mrs. Mary E. McClure, prominent '89er who was killed by an automobile Friday night, will feature the annual banquet and reunion of the Eighty Niners at the First Presbyterian church Saturday night. Rev. I.T. Riley, one of the city's first pastors will make the memorial address for Mrs. McClure. Dr. J. A. Ryan, president of the association will preside. The program will consist of five talks from various members to be called on extemporaneously, Dr. Ryan stated. All those who have interesting anecdotes to tell of the early days will be welcomed as speakers, talks to be limited to five minutes. Because of the large number of out of town men and women present for the banquet it was not postponed, as was at first suggested when Mrs. McClure's death was announced. Dr. Ryan said. There will be visitors from practically all sections of the state and from a number of neighboring states. Three hundred reservations have been made.

Illustration 126. Front page news

PIONEER OKLAHOMAN
Dies Under Wheels

Mrs. Mary E. McClure, 71 years old, a prominent Oklahoma City clubwoman and settler of Oklahoma before the territory was opened, was run down and instantly killed at Thirteenth street and Harvey avenue Friday night at 9:45 o'clock by an automobile traveling east, driven by Don McCafferty, 18 years old.

Mrs. McClure lived at 307 West Twelfth street. McCafferty is the son of Charles McCafferty, 210 East Twelfth street. The only witnesses to the accident were Don McCafferty and the occupants of his automobile.

She Was Living Alone

Mrs. McClure was living alone, and evidently was returning from an entertainment in the city, according to her neighbors, who said they noticed a light in her home during the evening. She turned on the lights always when she left home, they said. Her home was locked.

According to the story told to J. K. Wright, county attorney by McCafferty, he and a party of friends were on their way to a Sunday school social at the home of a church member when the accident occurred. McCafferty said he did not see Mrs. McClure and that the first intimation he had of the accident was when he heard the car strike her. He was going at a moderate speed, he said, and stopped as quickly as possible.

Police officers declared Mrs. McClure probably had been dragged twenty feet.

No Charges Are Filed

No charges have been filed against McCafferty, but county and city officers will continue their investigation Saturday.

McCafferty carried Mrs. McClure to the home of Mrs. E. Lund, 229 West Thirteenth street, and notified police immediately. The woman was dead when the Lund home was reached.

Then McCafferty, accompanied by his parents, went to the police station and surrendered to Briggs Chumley, captain on duty, and Chumley sent him to the county attorney. McCafferty said he had stopped to permit a street car to pass just before the accident.

Mrs. McClure's purse was found in the street after she had been taken to the Lund home. One of her shoes, also was found there.

She Was Pioneer In State

Mrs. McClure was one of the best known of Oklahoma's pioneer women. With her husband, the late William J. McClure, and their three children, she lived on a cattle ranch near Atoka in the old Indian Territory before Oklahoma was opened to settlement.

At the time of the run, Mr. and Mrs. McClure staked their claim east of the Santa Fe tracks on what was known as the Maywood addition. Later, they purchased property on the west side, and at one time had large property holdings there. McClure addition was named after them.

Mrs. McClure was the first Grand Matron of the Order of the Eastern Star in the Indian Territory. She was the last of the charter members of the Oklahoma chapter No. 10, the first organized in Oklahoma City. She was made a life member.

Member of Many Lodges

She was Right Worthy Grand Marshall of the General Grand Chapter O.E.S., Past

Matron of Chapter No. 10, and a member of the Past Matron's club.

Mrs. McClure was a member of the First Presbyterian church, of the Women of '89, the First Families of Oklahoma, and several social clubs. She leaves a daughter, Mrs. George M. Church of New York, and a son, Dave McClure, who lives on a farm west of Britton. The eldest son, Guy V. McClure, died several years ago in Oklahoma City. At one time he was city engineer, Mrs. Guy V. McClure, who has made her home in Galveston since her husband's death, was expected to arrive in Oklahoma City Saturday to attend the annual banquet of the Eighty-niners.

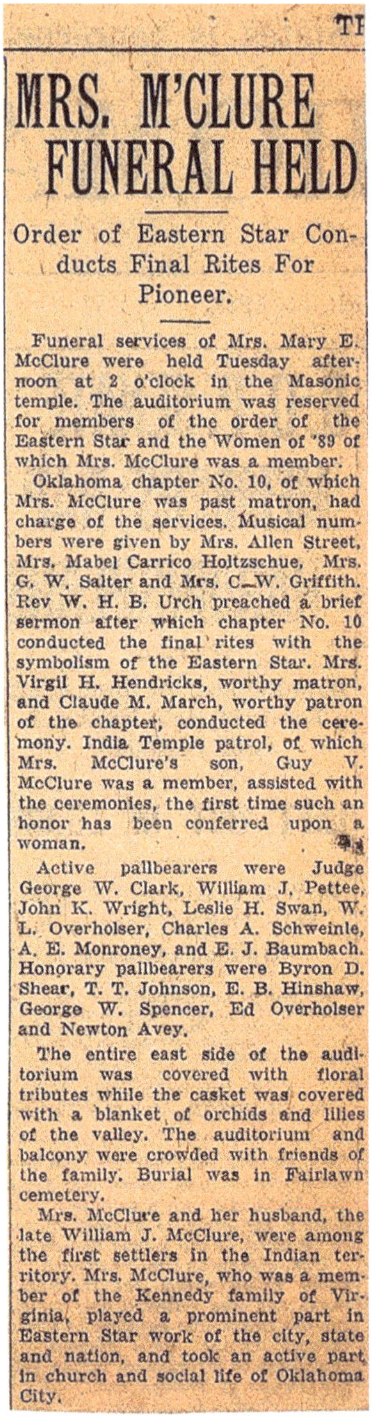

MRS. M'CLURE FUNERAL HELD

Order of Eastern Star Conducts Final Rites For Pioneer.

Funeral services of Mrs. Mary E. McClure were held Tuesday afternoon at 2 o'clock in the Masonic temple. The auditorium was reserved for members of the order of the Eastern Star and the Women of '89 of which Mrs. McClure was a member.

Oklahoma chapter No. 10, of which Mrs. McClure was past matron, had charge of the services. Musical numbers were given by Mrs. Allen Street, Mrs. Mabel Carrico Holtzschue, Mrs. G. W. Salter and Mrs. C. W. Griffith. Rev W. H. B. Urch preached a brief sermon after which chapter No. 10 conducted the final rites with the symbolism of the Eastern Star. Mrs. Virgil H. Hendricks, worthy matron, and Claude M. March, worthy patron of the chapter, conducted the ceremony. India Temple patrol, of which Mrs. McClure's son, Guy V. McClure was a member, assisted with the ceremonies, the first time such an honor has been conferred upon a woman.

Active pallbearers were Judge George W. Clark, William J. Pettee, John K. Wright, Leslie H. Swan, W. L. Overholser, Charles A. Schweinle, A. E. Monroney, and E. J. Baumbach. Honorary pallbearers were Byron D. Shear, T. T. Johnson, E. B. Hinshaw, George W. Spencer, Ed Overholser and Newton Avey.

The entire east side of the auditorium was covered with floral tributes while the casket was covered with a blanket of orchids and lilies of the valley. The auditorium and balcony were crowded with friends of the family. Burial was in Fairlawn cemetery.

Mrs. McClure and her husband, the late William J. McClure, were among the first settlers in the Indian territory. Mrs. McClure, who was a member of the Kennedy family of Virginia, played a prominent part in Eastern Star work of the city, state and nation, and took an active part in church and social life of Oklahoma City.

Illustration 127. Account of Mary Ellen McClure's death

MRS. M'CCLURE FUNERAL HELD
Order of Eastern Star Conducts Final Rites For Pioneer.

Funeral services of Mrs. Mary E. McClure were held Tuesday afternoon at 2 o'clock in the Masonic temple. The auditorium was reserved for members of the order of the Eastern Star and the Women of '89 of which Mrs. McClure was a member.

Oklahoma chapter No. 10, of which Mrs. McClure was past matron, had charge of the services. Musical numbers were given by Mrs. Allen Street, Mrs. Mabel Carrico Holtzchue, Mrs. G. W. Salter and Mrs. C. W. Griffity. Rev. W. H. B. Urch preached a brief sermon after which chapter No. 10 conducted the final rites with the symbolism of the Eastern Star. Mrs. Virgil H. Hendricks, worthy matron, and Calude M. March, worthy patron of the chapter, conducted the ceremony. India Temple patrol, of which Mrs. McClure's son, Guy V. McClure was a member, assisted with the ceremonies, the first time such an honor has been conferred upon a woman.

Active pallbearers were Judge George W. Clark, William J. Pettee, John K. Wright, Leslie H. Swan, W. L. Overholser, Charles A. Schweinle, A. E. Monroney, and E. J. Baumbach. Honorary pallbearers were Byron D. Shear, T. T. Johnson, E. H. Hinshaw, George W. Spencer, Ed Overholser and Newton Avey.

The entire east side of the auditorium was covered with floral tributes while the casket was covered with a blanket of orchids and lilies of the valley. The auditorium and balcony were crowded with friends of the family. Burial was in Fairlawn cemetery.

Mrs. McClure and her husband, the late William J. McClure were among the first settlers in the Indian territory. Mrs. McClure, who was a member of the Kennedy family of Virginia, played a prominent part in Eastern Star work of the city, state and nation, and took an active part in church and social life of Oklahoma City

DON McCAFFERTY

DEATH DRIVER EXONERATED

Wright Indicates Boy Not to Blame for Tragedy

PIONEER WOMAN KILLED

Autoist Tells His Story— Memorial for Victim

Exoneration of Don McCafferty, 18, 210 E. 12th-st, of criminal blame for the death of Mrs. Mary E. McClure, 72, of 311 W. 12th-st, was announced Saturday by County Attorney J. K. Wright.

Mrs. McClure was struck and almost instantly killed by the heavy Cadillac driven by young McCafferty at 13th-st and Harvey-av about 9:30 p. m. Friday night.

Warned by Companions

"Don, you have hit somebody," was the cry of youthful passengers in the rear seat of the car and with exception of a slight thud as the aged body was crushed by the machine, was the first intimation to the youth of the tragedy.

McCafferty, son of Charles McCafferty, deputy court clerk, was too excited to halt his car instantly and became almost hysterical as he viewed the crushed form of the pioneer woman.

The youth reported to police while his father with Attorney Ross N. Lillard saw County Attorney J. K. Wright.

Mrs. McClure and the McCafferty family had been close friends for years.

His Own Story

The boy's own story was:

"I was going to a church social at A. B. Jones' home in the 500 block on W. 13th-st. I had stopped at Robinson-av, and when I crossed Harvey I was going at a moderate speed. The street lights were bad and I didn't see Mrs. McClure—I didn't know that I had hit anything until I felt a jar."

"Someone in the back seat said: "'You have killed someone.' I went completely to pieces. I lost control of the car for a minute but finally stopped."

The boy estimated his speed at 12 to 15 miles an hour.

"Women of '89" to which Mrs. McClure belonged will hold memorial services, Mrs. E. S. Malone announced Saturday. No date has yet been set.

Pioneer Woman

Mrs. McClure was a pioneer. Her husband the late William J. McClure lived in the old Indian territory on a cattle ranch near Atoka. He and his wife made the run here and staked out claims east of the Santa Fe tracks.

Plans were being perfected Saturday for a joint memorial between the various lodges. They will

Illustration 128. Account of driver's story and court ruling in Mary E. McClure's death

Autoist Tells His Story— Memorial for Victim

Exoneration of Don McCafferty, 18, 210 E. 12th-st of criminal blame for the death of Mrs. Mary E. McClure, 72, of 311 W. 12th st was announced Saturday by County Attorney J.N. Wright.

Mrs. McClure was struck and almost instantly killed by the heavy Cadillac driven by young McCafferty at 13th st. and Harvey st about 9:30 p.m. Friday night.

Warned by Companions

"Don, you have hit somebody," was the cry of youthful passengers in the rear seat of the car and with exception of a sight thud as the aged body was crushed by the machine was the first intimation in the youth of the tragedy.

McCafferty, son of Charles McCafferty, court clerk, was too excited to halt his car instantly and became almost hysterical as he viewed the form of the pioneer woman.

The youth reported to police while his father with attorney Ross N. Lillard, saw County Attorney J.K. Wright.

Mrs. McClure and the McCafferty family had been close friends for years.

His Own Story

The boy's own story was: "I was going to a church social at A.B. Jones' home in the 500 block of west 13th. I had stopped at Robinson avenue, and when I crossed Harvey I was going at a moderate speed. The street lights were bad and I didn't see Mrs. McClure—I didn't even know I had hit anything until I felt a jar.

"Someone in the back seat said: 'You have killed someone.' I went completely to pieces. I lost control of the car for a minute but finally stopped."

The boy estimated his speed at 12 to 15 miles an hour.

"Women of 89" to which Mrs. McClure belonged will hold memorial services, Mrs. E.S. Malone announced Saturday. No date has been set yet.

Pioneer Woman

Mrs. McClure was a pioneer, her husband the late William J. McClure lived in the old Indian Territory on a cattle ranch near Atoka.

He and his wife made the run here and staked out claims east of the Santa Fe tracks.

Plans were being perfected Saturday for a joint memorial between the various lodges. They will announce late Saturday, it was said.

Mrs. McClure is survived by a daughter, Mrs. G. M. Church of New York, and a son, Dave, who lives near Britton. Another son, Guy, died in 1918 while a city engineer.

Illustration 129. Mary E. McClure's gravesite: Fairlawn Cemetery, Oklahoma City, Oklahoma

Illustration 130. Mary Ellen's grave at Fairlawn

Notice of Application for Appointment of Administration, No. 5,508 in Oklahoma County of the State of Oklahoma. In the Matter of the Estate of Mary E. McClure, Deceased. You are hereby notified that David V. McClure has applied for letters of administration on said estate to be granted to said David V. McClure and that said application will be heard on May 8, 1923.

June 7th, Letter from Order of the Eastern Star to Mr. and Mrs. George Church

When you were here on your recent sad mission, we know you did not have the opportunity of going through our magnificent Temple, which will not only be a monument to Masonry, but a pride to our citizenship of this state.

Unlike most Masonic Temples, this one is to be used by the public. We are to have two large auditoriums to be used for grand opera and similar high entertainment. We are to have a beautiful O.E.S. Chapter room in this temple and we as a committee have been appointed to select the furnishings for this room.

We are desirous of paying a lasting tribute to your mother, who as you know was dear to us all and whose life was an inspiration to every Eastern Star member.

As you know she was the first Grand Matron of this state and was the best beloved counselor of Oklahoma Chapter #10 up to the very last meeting she attended. Words are inadequate to express the love and admiration the members of our chapter had for her. With this thought uppermost in our minds, "to pay tribute where it justly belongs " we are writing this letter to tell you of our plans, which we feel sure will meet with your approval and cooperation. The plan which has been carried out by the Consistory at Guthrie in placing memorials with bronze tablets, we believe would be the best plan for us to use, yet up to this time no memorials have been excepted.

This committee is about to place the order for furnishing and equipment of our O. E. S. Chapter room, which we find will not be so elaborate and complete as we had hoped for, owing to the fact that the cost of the Temple as a whole has far exceeded the contemplated cost of $1,300,000.00.

The extent of our finances amounts to only about $5000 and the entire furnishings for this room alone will cost about $15,000 including the pipe organ which is $4000.

Now we thought perhaps you might like to have the privilege of furnishing this room as a memorial to your mother, which would be known as the "Mary E. McClure Chapter Room" a bronze tablet with its inscription would be placed on the door. Knowing her as we did and having heard her express herself as wishing to have some part when the time came, in helping to furnish this room, we feel that nothing could please her more and no greater or more lasting monument could be erected to her memory. It would be a lasting memorial to your Mother and her family.

Hoping this may meet with your approval and that we may hear from you at an early date. We are, Sincerely and Fraternally ....

November 19, 10-page Final Settlement and Distribution of the Estate of Mary Ellen McClure

Dec. 19, from Wright & Blinn, Lawyers; Mr. David V. McClure:
Dear Mr. McClure,

Mary Hortense McClure delivered her receipt to us today, and we immediately procured the order of discharge in the estate of Mary Ellen McClure, deceased, and we are herewith enclosing a certified copy of the Journal Entry of Final Settlement and Distribution and Order of Discharge in said estate. This certified copy should be filed in the office of the county clerk, register of deeds division, and the cost of filing should be borne by each of the three heirs equally. After it has been recorded in the office of the county clerk of this county, it should be likewise filed and recorded in the office of the county clerk of Murray County, although it could be filed there at any time Mrs. Church should sell the Sulfur property. In the event it is not filed in Murray County at once, still we suggest that it be filed in the office of the county clerk of this county. And making the final statement of the estate, we omitted to procure your check for $19.45 representing fees paid by us, although in settlement of the accounts and then preparing a statement for the errors, which charged up the item. We simply overlooked asking you for your check for the amount. Thanking you for having favored us with this business and with very best wishes for the Christmas season and the coming year we remain sincerely yours

MEMORIAM: Whereas: — the fact that life is a queer mixture of hopes, fears, happiness and uncertainties, was forcibly brought to the Women of '89 on the evening of April 20, 1923. In the tragic transition of our greatly beloved sister, Mrs. Mary E McClure, from this life to the life eternal. Therefore, the Women of '89 now assemble do sincerely deplore the loss of this precious woman, whose life as a citizen of a new country was ideal, and who had the strength of character, forbearance and love to tide the years of pioneering and who throughout the following years stood for all that was best for the community. #1—Mrs. McClure was a charter member of the Women of '89, assisted in its organization, and served as president during 1914 through 1915 and throughout past years her life has been intimately linked with its existence and usefulness. #2—As a parliamentarian, her kindly words of advice and decision in the meetings of the Women of '89 gave courage and confidence to their aspirations. #3—In the future whatever be the accomplishments and pleasures of this organization there will be a void, they will ever miss her gracious presence. #4—The intense bereavement of the Women of '89 is only alleviated by the hope that Mrs. McClure's going means- "Passing I'll add the shadows, getting a clear light, stepping behind the curtain, getting a clear sight laying aside the burden, the weary mortal soul done with the world's vexations, done with the tears and toil." #5—Therefore be it received, that the Women of '89 extend loving sympathy to the members of Mrs. McClure's family, and that a copy of this resolution be placed on the records of the Women of '89 and copies be sent to the family. Respectfully submitted Mrs. WM Bottoms, Chairman Mrs. Charlie Schweinle, Mrs. J. E. Harrall

Part of Eastern Star Honors Program for Mary E. McClure. No date
Mary E. McClure, Grand Matron of the Eastern Star 1889 – 1891. Mary E McClure was born December 24, 1852, near Topeka Kansas. She was the daughter of Joseph and Elizabeth Kennedy. She was one of six children, there being three sons and three daughters. Her father died when she was three years old. She was taken to live with an uncle until she was sent to Saint Mary's convent at Saint Mary's Kansas, where she remained five years, receiving the highest honors. While visiting an old sister in Pawnee City, Nebraska she met William J McClure and they were married July 29, 1869. They lived in Nebraska two years then moved to a ranch in Indian Territory, near Atoka. In 1879 they moved to Atoka where Sister McClure at once became a favorite and in the summer of 1881 she received the

degree of the O.E.S. Conductress, Associate Matron and Worthy Matron. In July 1889 she was one of a group to organize the Indian Territory Grand Chapter and was elected the first Grand Matron. This organization took place in Atoka, Brother John Tennie of Lehigh served as Grand Patron. In June 1890 the second annual session was held in McAlester, when she was re-elected Grand Matron, serving until June 1891. Brother J.S. Murrow being elected Grand Patron. Clara A. McBride was the next Grand Matron and soon after taking office commissioned brother JB Morrow to present sister McClure with a past grand matron schedule. She held the office of Grand Treasurer in 1897, served as District Deputy Grand Matron in 1893 and in 1896. She had the honor of being Grand Representative to Indiana, Alabama and Vermont. In 1892 she attended the General Grand Chapter in Columbus, Ohio and was honored by being appointed Right Worthy Grand Martha. She attended the last session of the General Grand Chapter held in Washington DC last November. Sister McClure was well known all over the state as one of the pioneer workers in the Order of O. E. S. We find in the proceedings of the fifth annual communication of the Grand Chapter of the O. E. S. of Indian Territory, 1894, distribute "as a loving wife, kind and tender mother, hospitable neighbor, always having a kind word for everyone she met, nursing the sick, feeding the hungry and clothing the poor, she stood without peer, whom to know was to love and revere." In 1889 the family moved to Oklahoma City and in November she assisted in the organization of Oklahoma Chapter Number 10 and served as the first Worthy Matron after the chapter was constituted and was reelected and served a second term, also filled the office of Conductress in 1894. She received a life certificate for this chapter in 1914 signed by Sarah Morris Worthy Matron; Lesli Swan, Patron; Sarah Walker secretary. On April 17th Oklahoma chapter No. 10 gave a farewell reception in honor of sister Sarah Morris before her departure for California. It was on this evening Sister McClure did her last O.E.S. service, giving an original toast to Sister Morris. Just three days later, April 23 Sister McClure was struck by an automobile and almost instantly killed. The funeral services were held from the Masonic Temple, Tuesday afternoon April 24. Reverend W.H. Burch, pastor of the First Presbyterian Church of which Sister McClure had been a member for many years, preached a brief service after which Chapter number 10 conducted the Eastern Star funeral service with Mrs. Virgil H Hendrix, Worthy Matron and Claude M March, Worthy Patron. India Temple Patrol, of which the late Guy V. McClure was a member, assisted with the services, the first time such an honor has been conferred upon a woman. Musical numbers were given by Mrs. Mable Garrison Mrs. G. W. Salter, Mrs. C. Griffith and a solo of "Face to Face" by Mrs. Allen Street, a special request of Sister McClure's. The entire east side of the auditorium was covered with floral tributes while the casket was covered with a blanket of orchids and lilies of the valley. Sister McClure's husband the late William John McClure died June 19, 1899. She leaves a son, David McClure of Oklahoma City and a daughter Mrs. George M. Church of New York City and three grandchildren; her body was laid to rest in Fairlawn cemetery.

1928 *The Daily Oklahoman,* April 22, 1928

FLASHBACK OF OKLAHOMA CITY,
Twenty- five years ago:

Few women were better known or better loved in Oklahoma City than the late Mrs. Mary McClure and it is fitting that this old time picture of her and her daughter, Veta should be shown today, on the anniversary of the opening of Oklahoma to white settlement.

Mrs. McClure came with her husband, W.J. McClure in '89 and they took a claim on land which later became Maywood addition to Oklahoma City. The old house stood for years across the end of Central Avenue on Tenth street. Later a beautiful residence was built at Seventh street and Broadway and very dear associations marked that spot. It was ever a rendezvous for the boys and girls who flooded to Veta's happy parties.

Mrs. McClure, through all the years, was prominent in Eastern Star work. She was the Grand Worthy Matron of Oklahoma Territory and filled other offices in the order. She was a member too, of the First Families of Oklahoma, the '89ers, the Sorosis club and the First Presbyterian church and its societies. Veta McClure Church of later years has become a globetrotter. She has spent the winter in India and will be here about May 1. No girl in Oklahoma City ever enjoyed her youth time more than she. Her magnetic personality and vivacious ways and background of her home life made her a social favorite.

1938 Two oil portraits, one of Mary Ellen McClure and one of William John McClure hung in the Oklahoma Historical Museum in Oklahoma City until the new museum was built in 2005.

Illustration 131. Club directory

McClure Elementary School, USD #501 Topeka, Kansas, may have been named after our McClure family.

Kennedy Clan
    Parents: Joseph and Elizabeth Kennedy
    Siblings: William H. Kennedy (divorced), 2nd wife Louise,
                   has a son George Warren
              Elizabeth (Eliza) Kennedy
              July (Jane or Julia) Kennedy, b. March 1, 1918,
                   lived in Silver Lake, Kansas
              Maggie (Margaret) Kennedy
              Wilkins Kennedy
              Mary Ellen Kennedy McClure

Let us be judged by our actions

Chapter 4
GUY VINCENT MCCLURE
1877 - 1918

Illustration 132. Guy Vincent McClure

[3]Guy Vincent McClure was the first child of William John and Mary Ellen. His mother traveled home to Silver Lake, Kansas, for his birth while his father continued the ranching business in Indian Territory.

Guy lived his early years on the open ranges of cattle country. He was twelve years old at the time of the land opening, April 22, 1889. Family legend has it that in school he was an outstanding mathematician. He went on to become a civil engineer, domestically and internationally.

As chief engineer, he oversaw the construction of the National Railroad of Mexico (Ferrocarril Nacional de Mexico). This was a pre-nationalization railway that went from Mexico City to Nuevo Laredo.

He and his partner laid out the plat plans for Oklahoma City, as well as the interurban system. He was the Chief Engineer on the construction of the Lake Overholser dam project, which assured Oklahoma City of water. He was working on that project when he contracted the Spanish Flu and died.

From the Records
[3]Guy Vincent McClure
b. December 12, 1877, Silver Lake, Kansas

m. Bernice M. McAdams, February 18, 1901, Oklahoma City, Oklahoma,
Book 5, Page 92
(Bernice b. Missouri; her father or brother was J. H. McAdams.)
(Marriage license states that Guy's residence is Mexico City— at the time he was the chief civil engineer for the first Mexican railroad.)

f. Presbyterian

d. October 23, 1918, age 41 years; Cause—Spanish Influenza

b. October 25, 1918, Fairlawn Cemetery, Oklahoma City, Oklahoma

Parents
[2]Father: William John McClure, b. 1842, Lee County, Illinois
Mother: Mary Ellen (Kennedy) McClure, b. 1855, Kansas

Children
[4]Mary Hortense
b. June 2, 1905, b. at home
m. Jay Willingham, Chattanooga, Tennessee
Children: Mickey (married Mary, nicknamed Julie)
Children: Guy

Siblings
[3]David Victor McClure
b. December 10, 1879, Atoka, Indian Territory
d. December 11, 1944, Oklahoma City, Oklahoma
[3]Veta Ellean McClure
b. March 27, 1881, Liberty Hill, Indian Territory
d. August 23, 1963, Oklahoma City, Oklahoma

Education
St. Mary's College, Kansas
Add-Ran College, Thorp Springs, Texas,
Kemper College, Booneville, Missouri

Guy Vincent McClure's Timeline

1892 Balance Sheet from School of Expenses for Guy McClure, ledger of his school account

September Cash Deposit on account	$55.00
Baseball	$25.00
Stamps	$10.00
Lock Box	$1.35
Uniform Cap	$1.15
Book Bill	$9.65
Library Fund	$1.00
Theater	$.50
October	
Drawing Book & Pencils	$.30
Hair Cut	$.25
Repairing Shoes	$1.25
November	
Stamps, Cap, Paper	$3.00
Two Pair Pants	$15.00
5 Pr Gloves, Dress Coat	$16.90
Locker Key	$.30
Cough Syrup	$.50
Medicine	$.85

Social club listing committee chairmen of an organization he belonged to: Guy McClure—Entertainment

1900 Letter from Guy to his mother, May 12. Stationery Heading reads: Compania Limitada del Ferrocarril, Central Mexicano Camp Rio Tarecuato, to Mrs. Mary McClure, Oklahoma City

Dear Mammia!

I received your letter yesterday and was so glad to hear from you. I also noted what you say in regard to the Government position and I am glad things have turned out as

they have for I have come to the conclusion that I must remain here until I finish this job, for I have the most important job in Mexico. I will pay out here around $1,000,000.00 and besides it will make my reputation that will last for as long as establishing me to membership to the American Society of Civil Engineers and when this is done I will be able to secure a position any place in the states if I do not want to remain here. I moved camp the other day and now I am living clear out in the woods by myself and loving the Mexican cooking. But I expect the hard grater camp at the last of the month. I now have about 30 kilometers and four more bridges the same size as the one Mr. Corrica raised so much fuss about. No there is no sense for me to get back home before next June 1901. Give Veta my love and tell her the first chance I have I will send her a belt. I now have $1,500 saved up so you can expect me to return with around $2,000.00 gold. With all my love, I remain as ever, Your loving boy, Guy

Illustration 133. Business card used in Mexico

1901

Marriage License.

THE TERRITORY OF OKLAHOMA, Oklahoma County, ss. IN THE PROBATE COURT.

To any person authorized to perform the Marriage Ceremony, Greeting:

You are hereby authorized to join in marriage Mr. Guy V. McClure and Miss Bernice M. McAdams, of the County, aforesaid, whose ages, residence, etc., are as follows:

NAMES OF PARTIES.		AGE.	COLOR.	PLACE OF BIRTH.	RESIDENCE.
Guy V. McClure	Groom	24	white	Kansas	City Mexico
Bernice M. McAdams	Bride	21	white	Mo	Oklahoma City O.T.

And of this license you will make due return to my office within thirty days from this date.

SEAL.

In Testimony Whereof, I have hereunto set my hand and affixed the seal of said Court, at my office in Oklahoma City, in said County, this 18th day of February A. D. 1901.

J. P. Allen
Judge of the Probate Court.

Certificate of Marriage.

TERRITORY OF OKLAHOMA, SS.

I, Wm E. Graham (Name of Official or Minister), Clergyman (Official or Clerical Designation), Presbyterian Church (Name of Court or Congregation) of Oklahoma City (Name of Place Where Located) in Oklahoma County, Oklahoma Territory, do hereby certify that I joined in marriage, the persons named in and authorized by this license to be married, on the 18th day of February A. D. 1901, at Oklahoma City in Oklahoma County, O. T., in the presence of J.H. McAdams of Oklahoma City, and James Geary of

J. H. McAdams
James Geary
Witnesses.

Wm E. Graham

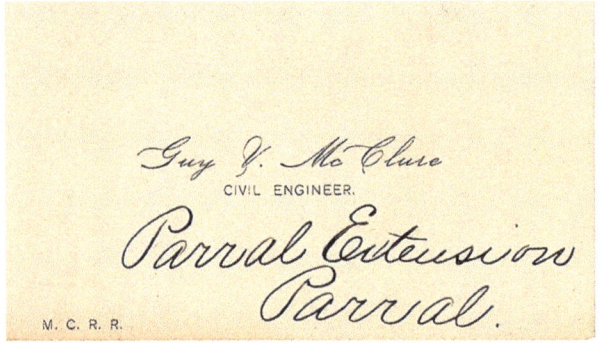

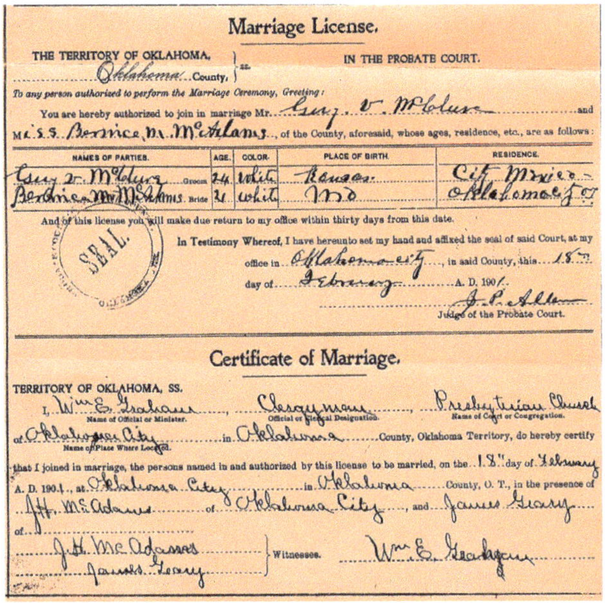

Illustration 134. Guy McClure's marriage certificate

1904 St. Louis World's Fair

Dues Receipt Dec. 6, 1904, to Mrs. Bernice McClure of Oklahoma Chapter Eastern Star Chapter No. 1.

1905 June 3. [4]Mary Hortense born, 8 pounds

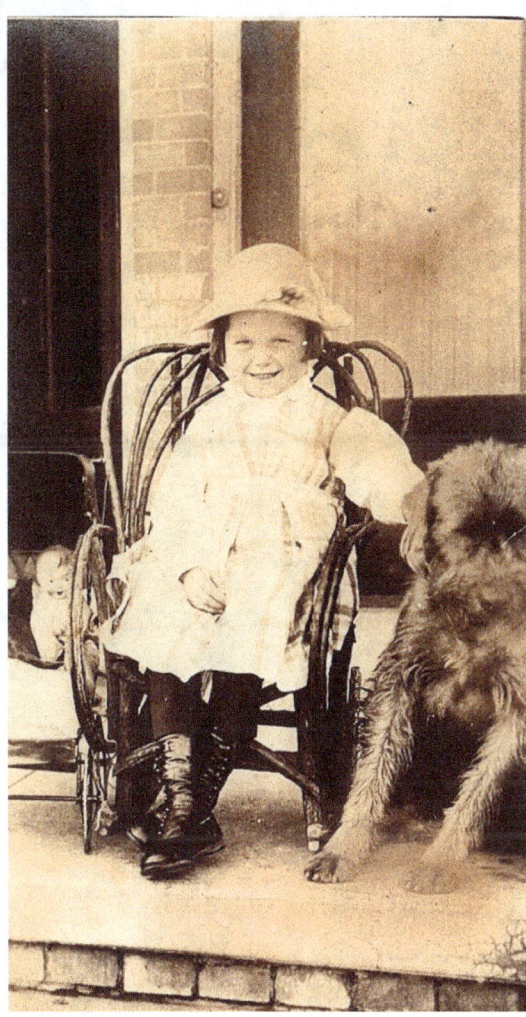

Illustration 135. Mary Hortense, daughter of Guy and Bernice McClure

Illustration 136. Mary Hortense, daughter of Guy and Bernice McClure

Illustration 137. Plaque on dam at Lake Overholser—Guy McClure Chief Engineer

Illustration 138. Excavation work–Building Overholser Dam

Illustration 139. Preparing formwork for Overholser Dam

Illustration 140. Working the concrete stage of Overholser Dam construction

1918 *The Daily Oklahoman* newspaper article: Oklahoma City, Oklahoma

GUY V. MCCLURE, CITY ENGINEER, FALLS VICTIM TO INFLUENZA
Builder of Waterworks Dam Succumbs After Week's Illness

After an illness of a little over a week, Guy V. McClure, Chief Construction Engineer of the Oklahoma City waterworks dam, died at 9 o'clock this forenoon of influenza pneumonia at his home, 307 West Twelfth street. Born in the old Indian Territory, Dec. 10, 1876 [not true— he was born Dec. 12, 1877, in Silver Lake, Kansas.] Mr. McClure was prominently identified in the "up building" of Oklahoma. He received his early education in engineering at the Kemper Military school in Missouri; he followed that profession through life and the waterworks dam in this city was his crowning engineering achievement.

The Daily Oklahoman newspaper article

HE CAME HERE IN '89

He came to Oklahoma City with his father, William J. McClure in 1889. He was chief engineer in building the Frisco railway to Quanah, Texas, and was also chief engineer in the construction of the Clinton & Oklahoma Western railway. For a number of years he was in charge, as Chief Engineer, of an engineering crew connected with the construction work of the Mexican National railway. Later he was in partnership with Warren E. Moore, that firm laid out and platted the majority of the additions to Oklahoma City. For six years he was city chief engineer and for one year and eight months he was chief engineer in building the city waterworks dam. Mr. McClure was prominent in Masonic circles. He was made a Mason while in Mexico, but on account of Masonic nonaffiliation—between that country and American Masons—it was necessary for him to take his degrees a second time in Oklahoma City. He passed to the Royal Arch chapter, thence to the Knights Templar and Shrine degrees. He was a thirty-second degree Mason. Mr. McClure was ___[sic] of India Temple in 1916, captain of the Arab patrol for five years, and held other high offices in the order.

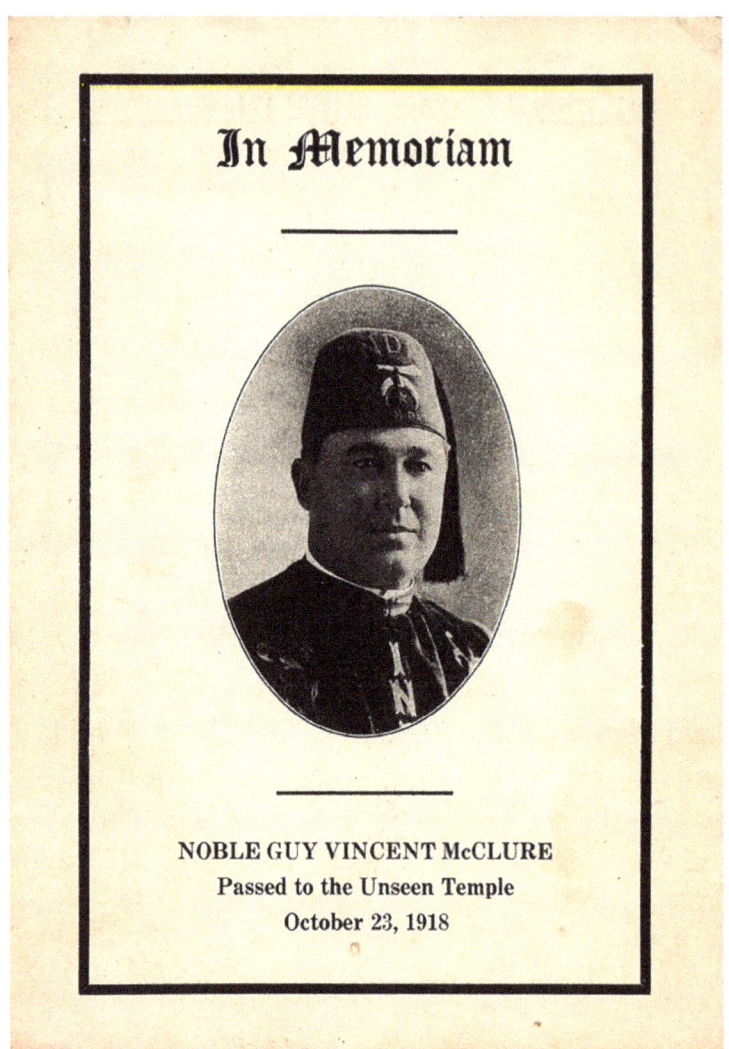

Illustration 141. Order of Service for the funeral of Guy McClure

Oklahoma City Times newspaper article

FUNERAL NOT SET

Mr. McClure leaves a wife and one daughter, 13 years old. His mother, Mrs. Mary E. McClure, 311 West Twelfth street, a brother, David of this city, and a sister, Mrs. Veta Muncaster of New York, also survive him. Mrs. Muncaster was sent for this morning and is expected to arrive for the funeral. Until she is heard from, no definite arrangements will be made for the funeral service, other than that the Masons will be in charge. The unfinished work left by Mr. McClure on the waterworks dam will be given in charge of H.A. Pressey, consulting engineer, who has been with his chief on this work since it started. Mr. Pressey will remain in charge.

The Daily Oklahoman newspaper article

CITY LAKE MAY BE NAMED FOR MCCLURE

Friends of the late Guy V. McClure, construction engineer in charge of the building of Oklahoma City's waterworks dam, who succumbed Tuesday to Spanish Influenza, have suggested that the big lake which is a part of the project be named "McClure Lake," as an honor to the man who had supervised virtually every detail in the construction of the great waterworks system. For almost two years McClure directed the construction work and those who are behind the movement to name the lake in his honor declare that, should it be done, it will remain a monument to his engineering ability.

A *History of the State of Oklahoma—1908*

Guy V. McClure, son of the pioneer Oklahoman above mentioned, has the rare distinction (for a man of adult age) of having been born in the old Indian Territory before it was opened to settlement. His birthplace was Johnsonville, in what is now McClain County, Oklahoma, but at that time in the Chickasaw Nation of Indian Territory [Incorrect, he was born in Silver Lake, Kansas] He was born in 1877. His mother, Mary E. (Kennedy) McClure, is still living in her home being in Oklahoma City. Along with the active outdoor life, and early experiences in the great cattle industry during the range era, he obtained an excellent education. He was a student at St. Mary's College in Kansas, later at Add-Ran College at Thorp Springs, Texas, and finally graduated from Kemper College of Boonville, Missouri. In the latter school he made a specialty of mathematical studies and civil engineering, and has since followed the profession for which he prepared himself in college. Mr. McClure is one of the best known engineers of Oklahoma, and since March, 1907, has been chief engineer for the Oklahoma City Railway Company, which operates the street railway lines of Oklahoma City and also the interurban lines extending north toward Guthrie, and has charge of the construction work on all these lines. He is also a member of the engineering firm of Moore and McClure, who do general engineering. For several years Mr. McClure was engaged in railroad engineering for the Rock Island System and the Frisco and other roads in Missouri, Arkansas, and Colorado, and for three and a half years was engaged in work for the Mexican Central in old Mexico. Mr. McClure has been through all the higher Masonic degrees and is a Knight Templar and a Shriner. He married in Oklahoma City, Miss

Bernice H. McAdams, a member of a family who came to Oklahoma at the first opening. They have one daughter, Mary Hortense.

(www.usgennet.org/usa/topic/historical/1908ok_2_8.htm pg. 2 of 26.)

The Daily Oklahoman newspaper article

GUY V. MCCLURE

One of the best known of the old cattlemen whose operations were extended to Indian Territory shortly after the close of the Civil war was the late William J. McClure, who died at his home in Oklahoma City in 1899. The extent of his early operation can be judged from the fact that at one time he had under lease the entire Kickapoo and Pottawatomie Indian reservations, comprising who are now Pottawatomie and Lincoln counties of the state of Oklahoma. He was a typical pioneer---courageous, energetic and resourceful. He belonged to a pioneer family of the state of Nebraska, having been born near Nebraska City (not true- born Lee County Illinois) and in 1869 came with other members of his family to the Indian Territory, where he quickly became one of the most prominent stockmen. Twenty years before the original Oklahoma was opened to settlement, he established what became the famous Seven C ranch, on the Canadian river, about sixteen miles east of the present site of Oklahoma City. (The Seven C flats take their name from this ranch. The Seven C was Mr. McClure's head ranch, although his family had their home at Johnsonville, further down the Canadian, in the Chickasaw Nation. In 1878 the family moved to Atoka in the Choctaw Nation. At the opening of Oklahoma, on April 22, 1889, Mr. McClure and his son, Guy V., made the run. The homestead selected by the elder McClure is best known in modern Oklahoma as the famous Maywood Addition, adjoining the city on the northeast, which is now the aristocratic residence section of Oklahoma City. In 1896 he was the largest individual property holder in Oklahoma City and furnished more money toward getting the Frisco Railway into the city from Sapulpa than any other man. He was a charter member of the Oklahoma Consistory and the India Temple A.A.O.N.M.S. Guy McClure, son of the pioneer Oklahoman above mentioned, has the rare distinction (for a man of adult age) of having been born in the old Indian Territory (incorrect, he was born at Silver Lake, Kansas) before it was opened to settlement. His birthplace was Johnsonville, in what is now McClain County, Oklahoma, but at that time in the Chickasaw Nation of Indian Territory. He was born in 1877. His mother, Mary E. (Kennedy) McClure, is still living, her home being in Oklahoma City. Along with the active outdoor life and early experiences in the great cattle industry during the range era, he obtained an excellent education. He was a student at St. Mary's College in Kansas, later at Ad-Ran College in Thorpe Texas, and Kemper Military Academy, Booneville, Missouri.

October 16, 1918. *The Daily Oklahoman* newspaper article

Friends of the late Guy V. McClure, construction engineer in charge of the building of Oklahoma City's waterworks dam, who succumbed Tuesday to Spanish influenza, have suggested that the big lake which is part of the project be named "McClure Lake" as an honor to the man who had supervised virtually every detail in the construction of the great waterworks system.

The Daily Oklahoman newspaper article

BUILDER OF WATERWORKS DAM SUCCUMBS AFTER WEEK'S ILLNESS.

After an illness of a little over a week, Guy V. McClure, chief construction engineer of the Oklahoma City water works dam, died at 9 o'clock this forenoon of influenza pneumonia, at his home, 307 West Twelfth street. Born in the old Indian Territory, Dec. 10, 1876, Mr. McClure was prominently identified in the "up building" of Oklahoma. Receiving his early education in engineering at the Kemper Military school in Missouri, he followed that profession through life and the waterworks dam in this city was his crowning engineering achievement. He came to Oklahoma City with his father, William J. McClure in 1889. He was the chief engineer in building the Frisco railway to Quanah, Texas, and was also chief engineer in the construction of the Clinton & Oklahoma Western railway. For a number of years he was in charge of an engineering crew connected with construction work of the Mexican National railways. In partnership with Warren E. Moore, that firm laid out and platted a majority of the additions to Oklahoma City. For six years he was chief city engineer and for one year and eight months he was chief engineer in building the city waterworks dam. The plans for the Lincoln Park Lake were his. Mr. McClure was prominent in Masonic circles. He was made a Mason while in Mexico, but on account of Masonic non—affiliation – between that country and American Masons it was necessary for him to take his degrees a second time in Oklahoma City. He passed in the Royal Arch chapter, thence to the Knights Templar and Shrine degrees. He was also a thirty-second degree Mason. Mr. McClure was potentate of India Temple, in 1916, captain of the Arab patrol for five years, and held other high offices in the order. Mr. McClure leaves a wife and one daughter, 13 years old. His mother, Mrs. Mary E. McClure, 311 West Twelfth street, a brother, David of this city, and a sister, Mrs. Veta Muncaster of New York, also survive him. Mrs. Muncaster was sent for this morning and is expected to arrive for the funeral. Until she is heard from, no definite arrangements will be made for the funeral service, other than that the Masons will be in charge. The unfinished work left by Mr. McClure on the water works dam will be given in charge of H.A. Pressey, consulting engineer, who has been with his chief on this work since it started. Mr. Pressey will remain in charge until other arrangements are made by the city commissioners.

Funeral Notice, *The Daily Oklahoman* newspaper article

All Masons, you are invited to meet with us at Siloam Masonic temple, 124 West Fifth street, today (Friday), at 3:30 o'clock pm preparatory to conducting the last sad rites over the body of our deceased brother Guy Vincent McClure. The lodge, assisted by India Temple patrol and band, will escort the body from Masonic Temple, Third and Broadway, to Fairlawn cemetery, where the services will be conducted by Past Master Judge George W. Clark.

The Daily Oklahoman newspaper article

MASONS PAY HONOR TO GUY MCCLURE

Funeral services for the late Guy V. McClure who died of influenza last Wednesday morning will be held at the Masonic Temple late this afternoon the Reverend P.C. Baird, pastor of the First Presbyterian church, officiating. The body was taken to the Temple at 10 o'clock this morning and lay in state in the assembly rooms the remainder of the day. Siloam lodge A.F. and A.M. had charge of the funeral, with escorts from the Arab patrol of India Temple. Knights Templar, and other degrees in Masonry of which Mr. McClure had been a member. The Shrine band will lead the procession to Fairlawn Cemetery, where the last rites will be performed. All city offices were closed at 3 o'clock this afternoon in honor of the dead. Activity at the city waterworks dam, of which Mr. McClure was chief construction engineer, will cease during the funeral, and all employees were requested to attend the ceremonies in a body.

The Daily Oklahoman newspaper article

MCCLURE FUNERAL VERY IMPRESSIVE

Impressive funeral services for the late Guy V. McClure, construction engineer at the city waterworks dam, who died Tuesday of influenza, were held yesterday afternoon. The service began at 4 o'clock in the Masonic Temple and a public ceremony in charge of the Masonic bodies of which Mr. McClure was affiliated was held at 5 o'clock at Fairlawn Cemetery, where burial was made following a short service at the temple to which only members of the family were permitted, the procession formed on Broadway and led by the India Temple band, marched slowly north on Broadway. The Shrine Patrol, of which Mr. McClure had been captain for five years, came next. The Knights Templar in dress uniform were next and members of Siloam Lodge for the last section of the procession.

Let us be judged by our actions

Chapter 5
DAVID VICTOR MCCLURE
1879 - 1944

Illustration 142. David Victor McClure

³David Victor McClure was the second child of Wm. J. and Mary Ellen. He was born in Indian Territory at the Atoka ranch. He was ten years old at the time of the land run of 1889. He was quite a horseman his entire life, at one time being named one of the five best rodeo cowboys. He attended Kemper Military Academy. He was an avid sportsman playing on the school football, baseball, and swim teams. It was here that he made a lifelong friendship with Will Rogers. He served in the Spanish-American War as one of Teddy Roosevelt's original Rough Riders and made the charge up San Juan Hill – a famous decisive battle. He was a rancher, and he owned a thoroughbred horse racing stable, with his

horses competing on the big tracks in the east. Magazine articles were written about him and his horses in trade magazines.

From the Records
[3]**David Victor McClure**
>b. December 12, 1879, Atoka, Indian Territory
>>m. Grace Anna Jones, May 20, 1905, Covington, Kentucky
>>>b. 1889
>>>d. 1974, Sulphur, Oklahoma
>>>Her parents: Rebecca Armsey and Homer Jones married July 4, 1871, in Ross County, Ohio
>
>f. Presbyterian
>d. December 15, 1944, Oklahoma City, Oklahoma; age 65; Cause—Apoplexy
>b. Fairlawn Cemetery, Oklahoma City, Oklahoma

>**Parents**
>>Father   [2]William John McClure 1842-1899
>>Mother   [2]Mary Ellen Kennedy McClure 1855-1923

>**Siblings**
>>[3]Guy Vincent McClure 1877-1918
>>[3]Veta Ellean McClure 1882-1963

>**Children**
>>[4]William John McClure
>>>b. July 6, 1907, Latonia, Covington, Kentucky
>>>m. Chrystel McClure, January 3, 1944, Oklahoma City, Oklahoma
>>>d. Feb. 10, 1970, Aransas Pass, Texas
>>>b. Fairlawn Cemetery, Oklahoma City, Oklahoma
>>
>>[4]Veta Ann McClure
>>>b. March 10, 1912, Oklahoma City, Oklahoma
>>>m. Colonel Robert Wolcott Meals, West Point
>>>d. March 25,1948, Ankara, Turkey
>>>b. Memorial Park, Edmond, Oklahoma, Sec. 4, NW corner near pond
>>
>>[4]Guy Victor McClure
>>>b. January 15, 1925, Oklahoma City, Oklahoma
>>>m. Thamer Perkins

d. March 25, 1948
b. Memorial Park, Edmond, Oklahoma; Sec. 41, SE corner of tower
Military Service: Pvt. 4168 Base Unit AAF, World War II

Politics
Registered Republican

Education
Kemper Military School, Boonville, Missouri, 1890s, where he was friends with classmate Will Rogers

Organizations
'89er Association
Cherokee Strip Organization
Masons and Shriners, Member of the Blue Lodge and Consistory
Patron of the Eastern Star six times and associate Patron four times
Last Man's Club of the Rough Riders
Oklahoma City, Oklahoma Saddle and Polo Club

Young Dave's youth was spent on the 7C Ranch. It must have been special to be able to ride with cowboys on the open range. It has been told to family members that he spoke Choctaw before English. He was ten years old when the "run of '89" occurred and the family moved into Oklahoma City.

Dave won the first horse race ever run for a purse in the Oklahoma Territory. This race was at the first July 4th celebration in 1889 held on his father's ranch. His father, Bill McClure, had paid for a grandstand to be constructed for the contests. Just as Dave finished the race, the grandstand collapsed, killing one person.

He was a jockey until 1908. He was named one of the five best rodeo cowboys of all time. He owned a ranch and thoroughbred horse stables. He also owned the Ninth Street Barn, Livery, Boarding and Sale Stables at 2nd and W. 9th St., Oklahoma City, and the Cigar and Billiards Club in Sulphur.

Illustration 143. Young David V. McClure

Illustration 144. Dapper David V. McClure

Illustration 145. David V. McClure, Roughrider

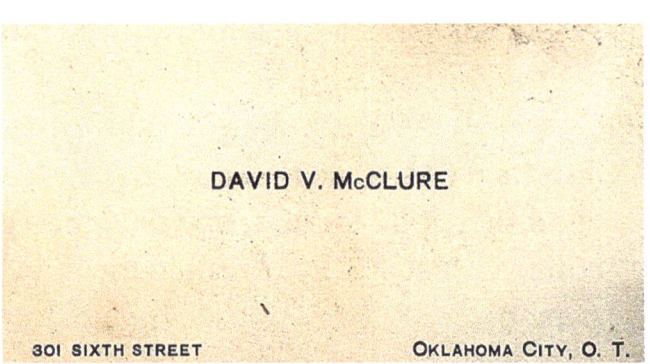
Illustration 146. Business card

Illustration 147. Postcard

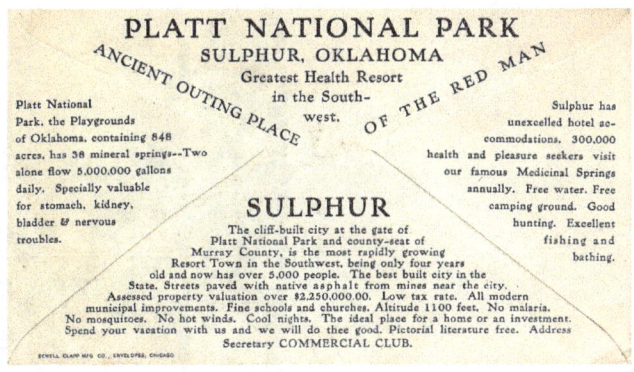

Illustration 147. Postcard

Illustration 148. Sulphur football team. Dave is in the second row, left end.

Illustration 149. Kemper Military Academy football team. Dave is second from right.

Illustration 150. Kemper School program bearing a famous signature. Will Rogers became a celebrated cowboy philosopher, stage and movie actor, philanthropist, and aviator who pioneered advancements in American aviation.
He was Dave's classmate and friend.

Illustration 151. Dave sitting high in the saddle

Illustration 152. Cowboy Dave calf-roping

Illustration 153. Sunday afternoon riding party

Military Service

Member of the 1st United States Volunteer Cavalry, better known as Teddy Roosevelt's Original Rough Riders. Over 2,300 men volunteered within the first twenty-four hours, of which 994 enlisted men and 47 officers were accepted. They mustered May 1 through May 21, 1898. Because of a lack of room in the army ship transports from the port of debarkation, Tampa, Florida, only troops A, B, D, E, F, G, K, and L went to Cuba. David served in company D. The regiment fought at Las Guasimas, and then at the famous San Juan and Kettle Hills. He was shot in the leg with a Mauser bullet during the charge up San Juan Hill. Three days after an Armistice had been declared, the troops went into a quarantine camp at Montauk Point, Long Island (Camp Wikoff), New York. The unit was mustered out of service on September 15, 1898. At the time of muster out, the unit consisted of 52 officers and 1,185 enlisted men.

Illustration 154. Troop D, First Squadron, Roosevelt's Rough Riders

David Victor McClure's Timeline

1898 Spanish American War, April 21, 1898

Dave enlisted March 8, 1898 at Guthrie, Oklahoma
He was honorably discharged September 14, 1898, at Long Island, New York. His enlistment #1581814 Camp Wikoff, Montauk Point, D V. McClure, Oklahoma City, Oklahoma Territory,
Troop D, Roosevelt's Rough Riders, 1st U. S. V. C.

Illustration 155. Teddy Roosevelt and aides

Newspaper Clipping:

"It's not for a moment supposed that the Rough Riders are complaining because they are put to the front in battle. They are not that kind of boys. But their friends at home would suggest that the list of killed and wounded be not made up entirely of Rough Riders. If there is no other regiment that can advance against the terrible fire of the Spanish let the boys go, but if there is another brave regiment in the army let it be put in the van at the next charge on Santiago's fortifications. The Rough Riders have proven themselves heroes. For God's sake, let enough of them come home to tell the story."

Letter from Dave to his parents
March 8, 1898, Oklahoma City

Dear Mama and Papa,

We arrived here alright but was short of provisions. We will likely leave here in a few days to parts of Cuba. Our regiment is the _____ 180 Mexicans will be here then after. Now the Arizona boys are here. Know Mama I have the ____ of a ____ ship. Now tell all my friends hello for me. Both girls and boys. Our horses are very ___. They are poor and ___. Tell papa to take good care of Storey for me. This place here is one of the ___ places in the world. We had a long trip and I was glad to get ___. I will have to close for this time. I hope that you will write soon. I remain your Dear boy, David V. McClure. Tell Veta hello and also Guy. We ___ you ___ him -

Letter from Dave to his parents
June 6, 1898, Tampa, Florida

Dear Papa and Mama,

I am on my way to the transport. We leave for Cuba this afternoon. I have not much time for we are packed up. I will be a good boy and take good care of myself and pray to God to help me. Write to me here and it will be sent to me. Tell Guy he and ___ I want my ___ to him and little Sister, tell them both to write. Now ___ for I would like to hear from home in Cuba. We fixed the war ___ we got there we got some food ___ at best the Regiment but most .... The Regiment are all Gentlemen from start to finish. I won't forget my parents, good ___ and doing war it will help to ___ it better. Mama and Papa Dave is all right. I will have to close, write soon from your loving boy, David. Tell all my friends below address: Tampa, Florida, D. Troop

Letter from Dave to his parents describing the battles. June 25, 1898
Written from Santiago, Cuba

I am alright, yesterday we had a battle. It commenced at 8 am to 10 am. It was a hard fought one. The loss of the Spanish ___ in ___. We started it, six hundred of us and four thousand of them. The R. R. made a rep. at the start. Three men in my squad were wounded and it is terrible to see men falling around you. Then ___ over 700 went like the gallant of old. Never a man flinched or backed out at every command to advance. We went forward, we were the first to raise the U. S. flag and the first to fire a shot. We march about 15 miles a day over their mountains with our nap sack and ___. I am getting into it now. It is hard work. It won't be long before we clean out their outfit then I will come home. Tell all my friends "Hello" for me. I think of them all. I think of you and papa every night and brother and sister. Tell them both hello for me. I send all my love to them and you and papa. Tell Guy to stay at home for we don't want to both be here. Tell him to be a good boy and God will bless him for it. He carried me thru yesterday and the first thing I did was to thank him for it. After the first fire things were as cool as ever. It seemed like part of a game. I will have to close for this time-Goodbye to all and 100 kisses for all-From your most loving son, David

Letter from Dave to his mother
July 15, 1898, Ft. Monroe

Dear Mama and Papa,

I am alright yet and in the United States. I have the measles and a little fever of a Spanish bullet through the left leg. It doesn't amount to anything. It just slid out the skin and the muscle in what sent me here. I am in good health now as I ever was and am in a good place. Know the battle was a hard fought one. I like ____ stared death before it was over with. We went on the firing lines at am July 1 and stood there until Friday with the two and got a cup of coffee for our supper. We _____ and slept on the bare ground. It was pretty hard. _____ it is funny in battle after the first fire things are as cool as ever. I never once thought of getting hit and did not. I never ____ . I will go back to my regiment in a few days. I want to borrow five dollars from Papa. I have all my ____ coming but cannot draw it. Now I have got to ____ ____ things here before I go back and please send the money for I have ____ it in return mail. I will pay you back. Tell that little sister of mine to ____ a good girl and when I come home I will ____ her a lot of things. Tell all my friends hello for me. I will be home someday. How is Miss Grace? Tell her I love her just the same. I will go back in a very few days and then I will be there for some time. But will soon ____ season ____ I guess I will close for this time with all my love. I remain your loving son, David - answer on return mail.

Letter from Mary Ellen to son, Dave
July 28, 1898, Oklahoma City

My Dear Boy, We received your ever welcome letter last evening. Was delighted to hear you were getting along so well, but I am so anxious to see you. Why can't you get a furlough and come home for 30 days. Everyone wants to see a sure enough live Rough Rider. Mrs. Danden was here last evening and said to tell you she is proud that she knows one of the Rough Riders. She would write to you herself but was afraid she would scare a great deal worse than the Spanish did. Mr. Price is going to Washington this week. Said he would go down to see you and maybe you can come home with him. Don't you want to. Tomorrow is the Circus and Mama's 29th anniversary, so of course Papa will have to take me to the circus. Veta is going with Mr. Fiske, one of the survey boys. And this first diversion. She will go with Tom in the evening. There are lots of new girls coming to town and you will be a hero among them when you come home. Walter Bradford has left OK for a year. He is going to school in KC this year. Charley Etters has joined the army. They will leave El Reno next Tuesday. There will be an excursion over to the Ft. next Sunday to let all the folks see the boys before they leave for the war. We can go there and back for 50 cents. Did you get a letter from Jimmie B and Mrs. Sutton? If you did, you do not need to answer them. First mention them in my letter for they would like to know if you received theirs. Daisy and Art are married at last. They have gone to housekeeping on east 5th St. Veta won't let me write any longer so____. We all send our best love and a kiss. I close hoping to see you soon. ____ ____ my darling boy, Mama

Letter from Dave to his parents
August 8, 1898, Fortress Monroe, Virginia

Dear Mama, I received your letter this morning and was more than delighted to hear from home again. I will be there next week. I am coming home on a furlough. Captain Stiles wrote that the ____ asked how I was. I am ever grateful to him for his kindness. Tell Miss Dodson it is all right for her to write. I don't seem____ ___ will ____ . I did not receive ____Bradford letter, but would be very glad to hear from her. Give her my news and all her friends. That I would write them but am coming home so soon that I thought that it would be hardly worthwhile. Give all the masons my best regards. Tell Miss Grace that I love her. Just the same ____ I will. I will close for this time, I remain your loving son, David. PS I received the clippings from the paper and thank you.

Letter from Dave to his parents
Sept. 15, 1898, Broadway Central Hotel, New York

Dear Mama and Papa,

  I am in New York as you see and have had a good time. Today I just got back from Madison Square Garden where I saw an imitation of the different battles with the navy. It was fine. I have got a program of it to bring home with me. I have got my Discharge and am glad of it. I won't be home for a week or ten days for I'm going to stop in Wichita while the fair goes on. Mama, I wish that you would send PW Hunter things to the Central Hotel. Kind of bundle them up first and then in the ____. ____ ____ in don't fail and at once. I will leave here tomorrow night. Don't worry about me for I am all OK. Give all my love and a thousand kisses for you and Papa. Good bye. PS need not answer with ____ you write to Wichita, I remain as ever our loving boy David

El Reno News, Canadian County, Page 6, Col 2

Dave McClure, who was with the Rough Riders in Cuba, has returned to Oklahoma county where he was welcomed with open arms. Dave now sits around on the dry goods boxes and tells the amazed natives how it was all done.

Newspaper clipping

MISS VETA MCCLURE ENTERTAINS,
*Gives a Garden Party in Honor of her Brother,
Just Returned from Santiago.*

One of the most delightful parties ever given in this city was given last night by Miss Veta McClure at her home on the corner of Sixth and Harvey. The party was in honor of her brother, Dave, who just recently returned from the battlefields of Santiago. A platform was erected on the lawn where the guests danced to the sweet music of an orchestra. About the lawn were distributed seats for those who were weary of the dance. Miss Eda Wand presided at the punch bowl. She was dressed in the national colors. The lawn was beautifully decorated in national colors as military as possible. From Fort Reno the following young officers were present: Lieuts, George Fintey, Ira S. Morrison and Sergeant Tom Taylor. The evening was spent very pleasantly by all present.

The letter was written by David McClure (part was dictated by Theodore Miller, part was written by David directly after Theodore's death,) and sent to the mother of Theodore Miller (who was Thomas Edison's brother-in-law). Her name was Mary Valinda (Mrs. Lewis Miller). Letter written from Gibomau, Cuba

Postdate, July 7, 1898.
from Dave McClure,

Mr. Miller, On behalf of your son I write to you. He wishes me to write to you and tell you about his wound. He will be all right I think. He was shot in the left shoulder, and it came out the right one. We will bring him to New York as soon as possible. His wound is a bad one but with his nerve and his strong will he will come out all right. (The following is evidently dictated) Dear Mama, a rather narrow escape but I feel sure I will pull through alright. Ted Berks and Mr. Rosellen have done all that was possible in getting extra things. Mr. Whitney offered to write to you, but Mr. McClure had offered before, so he did so. You must not worry about these things for Dr. Lauer, who is here just now, who is at the head of the Red Cross of America, said I would come out alright soon. He said he was going to write to you himself. They are doing everything that they can for me. I remain your most loving son and will be with you soon. Goodbye (the following is evidently written later) Mr. Miller, allow me to write these few lines. I found your son's acquaintance some time ago when he joined our regiment. Allow me to say that he is one of the most noble and brave boys I ever met. We slept together and fought together.

You have one of the most noble boys he was shot as the charge was made and did not fall out till it was over with. He never flinched free from the Spaniards fire. I think of your son as a brother. To have formed a friendship that cannot be broken. I love him for being so brave and loyal to his country. I will close for this time with all regrets of the one so brave. I remain with him until he is sent home. Very regretfully signed David V. McClure I live at Oklahoma City Oklahoma territory.—From the Thomas A. Edison Papers Collection at Rutgers: [http://edison.rutgers.edu/digital/document/X480A]

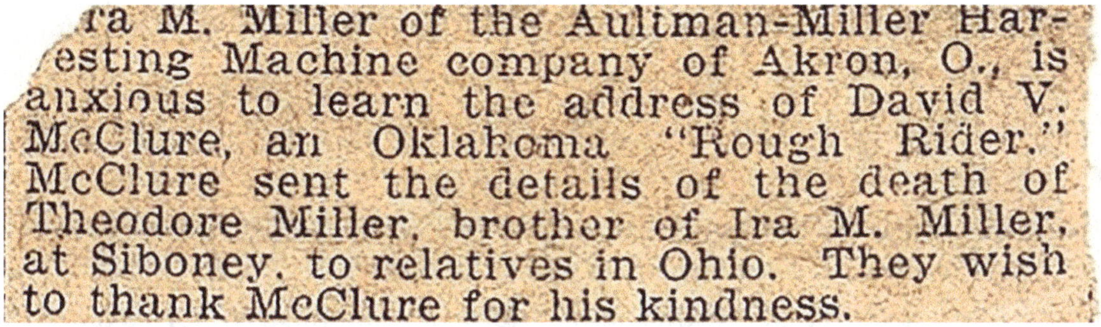

> Ira M. Miller of the Aultman-Miller Harvesting Machine company of Akron, O., is anxious to learn the address of David V. McClure, an Oklahoma "Rough Rider." McClure sent the details of the death of Theodore Miller, brother of Ira M. Miller, at Siboney, to relatives in Ohio. They wish to thank McClure for his kindness.

Illustration 156. Cutout from an Oklahoma newspaper

Letter written to Dave by Mary E. Miller, Oak Place, Akron, Ohio, Sept. 21, 1898

My dear Mr. McClure,

We have heard through your Father that you were wounded and sick at Fortress Monroe. We are exceedingly sorry to learn this news and hope that your wound is healing rapidly and you are able to go home. We are very anxious to know everything possible to be known about our brother, Theodore W. Miller for whom you wrote a letter to us before he died. We know so little of his wound, what he said and talked about while in the hospital and how long he was left in the field hospital and what treatment he received there. Oh, so many things that perhaps you do not know and we will never hear, but we are wanting to ask you these things and would love to hear from you about them. Your own wound and health too. We have succeeded in having the body of our brother returned home and have sent you a copy of his papers containing an account of his funeral service. We trust you are much informed and that you will write to us as fully as possible about what you know of our brother. Very sincerely Mary E. Miller

Letter written to Dave from Dale & Bierer, Attorneys and Counselors at Law

August 1, 1898,

Dave McClure,

Fortress Monroe, Virginia,

My Dear Boy, I Just recently heard of the fact that you were wounded at Santiago and have been sent to your present location to recover from your wound. On yesterday a large number of Guthrie people went over to Fort Reno for the purpose of visiting the Oklahoma battalion which has been organized and are there preparing, as they prepare, to go to Fort Whipple, Arizona, there to be formed into a regiment with other troops from Arizona, New Mexico and the Indian Territory. As we stopped in Oklahoma City on our way over, I saw and had a talk with your father and mother. Your father told me of the particulars as he had received them from you, and also advised me that you had begun to move around, and that you thought you would entirely recover from your wound. My main purpose in writing to you at this time is, first, to scold you for not having let me know about your wound, and second, for the further purpose of advising you to be careful to obey the instructions of the surgeon in charge of your wound. While I am not a doctor or a surgeon, I recognize the fact that if you undertake to use your leg too soon, it may cripple you for life, a condition which ought to be avoided if there is any way possible to do so. I have no doubt the Government is treating you very nicely, and that you are located in a splendid place to recuperate and recover from the effects of the campaign and your wound. I regard it as quite fortunate that you were not wounded until the battle was practically over, because I wanted your Captain and my friends to whom I had recommended you to know and understand that they would find in you a soldier ever ready to do his duty, and the fact that you were young would not be any particular advantage to the Spaniards against whom you were pitted. Your father told me somewhat of the fight as you witnessed it and participated in it. I expect you had a warm time, and that your first experience in battle was of a character to make you understand and know that fighting is not mere fun. I see by the papers that the Spanish Government has sued for peace, and this being true, I do not believe that there will be any more serious fighting between the troops of our Government and Spain. I have no doubt that Spain will accept the very reasonable terms that have been offered. You would have enjoyed being at Fort Reno yesterday. Major Stone, commanding the battalion of four companies, brought the companies out into the parade grounds and gave a good exhibition drill, lasting for about one and one half hours. The boys all did splendidly, considering the length of time they have been practicing. There were three or four thousand people who went on the excursions from different places throughout the territory, and it being a cool, pleasant afternoon they all enjoyed the spectacle very much. Your father and mother did not go over to the Fort, but Veta did, and by the way, Veta is getting to be a very fine appearing young lady. She had her Kodak with her and I saw her taking a number of snapshots. I do not think she can shoot quite as quickly as you can, yet, but she is very industrious in learning the way, neither do I think her firing would be as dangerous to the enemy as yours. Guy was very anxious to get a commission in this battalion and if I had known it in time, I think possibly he could have been placed as second lieutenant. However, I am quite of the opinion that he ought not to go. He has been promised a continuation of the situation in the surveying corps for the Frisco for another year, and by that time he will have become so proficient as a civil engineer that he will always be able to obtain a good position and at a good salary in following that work. Oklahoma City is pushing ahead pretty rapidly. They are building the Oil Mill and Cotton Compress and your father says that the prices of property are stiffening, and that we will soon be able to dispose of property there to a good advantage. I am very glad that you, in going through that battle, were not killed or hurt more seriously than you were. It must have been a terrific fight, both in the thickets and at the charge up the hill at El Caney. The Rough Riders have made quite a reputation for themselves and the people of the country feel that they are well named and that they are as good as any other material ever sent out from any country to do battle. I think you will not get to go to Puerto Rico and probably will not have occasion to do any more fighting, but rather expect that your regiment will be stationed some place in Cuba, perhaps until next spring, when some policy will be devised whereby most of the volunteer soldiers will be discharged from further services in the Army. Oklahoma has raised splendid crops this year. The wheat was pretty good and corn and cotton the best I have ever seen in the territory. I do not know whether this letter will reach you or not. I am going to direct it in such a way that I think it can find you, if not, the loss will not be very great to you. I wanted to let you know that I was thinking of you once in a while and also want you to take such care of yourself as when you get through with this, you will not be a cripple for life. Mrs. Dale sends her best regards also to you and says to be sure and take care of yourself now and obey the instructions of the doctors who have you in charge. With love, I am, as ever, your friend, Frank Dale

Illustration 157. Rough Riders ready for action

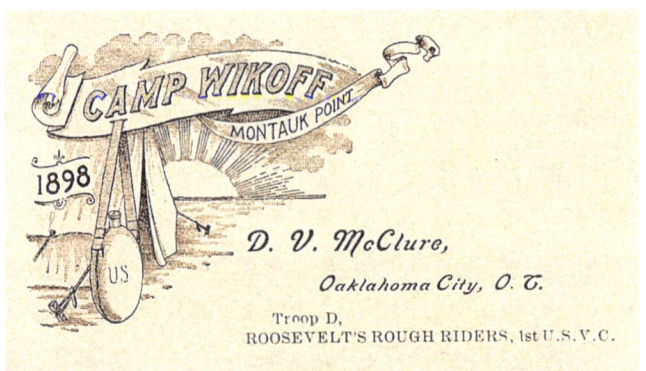

Illustration 158. A soldier's calling card.
Quarantine camp, Camp Wikoff, Montauk Point, Long Island

1899 Letter from Mary Ellen to son, Dave
June 1, Oklahoma City

Dear David,

Veta wrote to you yesterday, but for fear you did not get the letter, I thought I would write again today. Papa has been ____ he is better today and thinks he will go back tomorrow. He has sold the little mules. He will send them up as soon as he goes back. He told me about the ____ you and he made. Dave you must try and do your best. See that the men do their work. The ____ are all ready and Papa __as days. The lumber for this house and I think we have a buzzer for the home. ____ so we will even be able to get dinner there. Veta doesn't want to come at all, she has gone down to select your hat. We will express it to Davis. We like the new hotel fine. Now Dave be a good boy and help Papa all you can. The Dr. says he will never be himself again. I have Dr. Harry Walker doctoring him. He is taking the ____this morning. Dr. says that is the only thing that will do him any good, that he needs no medicine, but that the ____will help him. He had that tooth pulled and I think that will help him. He had a short letter from Guy this week. He is well. Dr. Harry thinks you are one of the finest boys he ever knew. You ought to hear all the nice things he tells Papa about you, but of course Papa won't____hem to you, for fear you will get the big head. I will gladly. My love write and tell me all that news that is ____"gives" ___ time. Your loving Mama

(This letter was written 18 days before the death of Wm. J.)

1900

Illustration 159. Reception dance card

Illustration 160. Dance card cover showing Rough Riders charging up San Juan Hill

Illustration 161. Dapper Dave

1900   The family has been told that Teddy Roosevelt visited the Dave McClure home in Oklahoma City on a subsequent trip to Oklahoma City.

Oklahoma City Times newspaper article

The greatest social event in Oklahoma City's history was the military ball last night honoring Colonel Roosevelt. The Street and Reed building was decorated with a profusion of flags and bunting and made to simulate an army camp. Shortly after midnight Colonel Roosevelt appeared and the band struck up the national airs. The Colonel and Mrs. Lee Van Winkin led the Grand March after which a reception was held. Never before has there been such a brilliant assembly of the fair sex as seen there last night.

Oklahoma City Times newspaper article

There was a rare sport at a roping contest at the park yesterday when champion ropers from Indian Territory, Texas and Oklahoma took part. None was there who excelled over our own Dave McClure, however.

Illustration 162. Roman Racing at Frontier Days, Cheyenne, Wyoming

Illustration 163. Dave bulldogging

Illustration 164. Dave calf roping

Illustration 165. Dave steer roping

1902   Willis Haviland Carrier, chief engineer of the Buffalo Forge Company, devises the first modern air-conditioning system.

1902   Dave became the manager for the famous cowboy, Bill Pickett. He took Bill Pickett to such major events as the 1904 Cheyenne Frontier Days Celebration. (Frenchcreoles.com, page 3.)

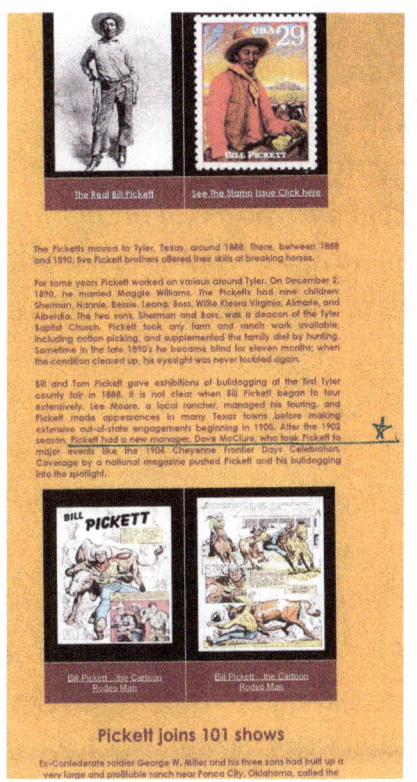

Illustration 166. Program for Bill Pickett's show telling that Dave was his manager

Illustration 167. Dave bulldogging from automobile, Parsons, Kansas, 1905

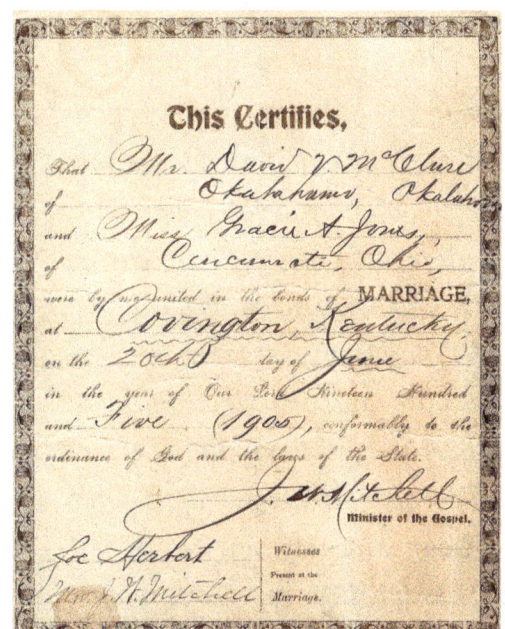

Illustration 168. Dave and Grace's wedding license

Illustration 169. Dave and Grace's wedding photograph

Letter from Dave to Grace, September 27, 1905

My Dear Little Wife, Well Honey, I had another nice day. It was a little warm about noon but there was a good breeze, so my house did not get so warm as one would suppose. _____ would. I could have got to Sulphur by driving a little harder but I thought that this would do for today. I will leave here at about 6:00 am in the morning. I can drive to Sulphur by 9:00am, so my horses will have all day tomorrow to rest before starting to work. Darling, I sure do miss you but we will have to stand it for a few weeks, then we will _____ on being separated many more _____ you ought to be thankful you were not with me last night for I had a battle Royal with bed bugs at the hotel. _____ at Purcell but they finally won and drew me out of the bed. I slept in the corner of the room on the bedspread. But I got _____ with the hotel by showing my sheet and the bedspread. It looks as if I would get a good night not for this in such a nice looking place, but one cannot go by looks. The Hotel food is the best in Purcell and it had all the best bugs that were in Purcell in my room and bed. Well, Darling, don't you worry about the bed bugs for your Papa is big and fast and it will take lots of them to get away with me and you be a good Little Girl and Papa will bring you chewing gum when he comes home. So be good. Kiss mama for me and also kiss yourself about ten thousand times for me with love and kisses to you both. I remain as ever your devoted husband, how does that last word sound to you? By By, XX this is the night kisses

Letter from Grace to Dave, dated October 8, 1905

My Own Dear Boy, I received your sweet letter and I was glad to get it. You bet it is so lonesome here without you. I am so sorry that those nasty bed bugs tried to eat my Papa. I wish I would have been there. I would of killed them and you can bet on that too. Well____ your mama and I went downtown yesterday and I never felt any cheaper in my life. We met _____ and the three of us together and every place we went she would say you had better look at the suits for I will buy you one in every store we went in and she would _____ till we got where a lot of people were and then she would say "would you like me to buy that for you____ those she had bought". Everything I got was why I never felt worse in my life. She was trying to make you look cheap. I guess don't it look that way to you _____ but still she has never bought me anything yet. Dear, I have worked very hard today. Your mother has taken our furniture out of our room. She put the dresser out of the bathroom in there for us and an old couch from the attic and she says that will _____. I am going to do the rinsing tomorrow. I will have to get up at 5:30am and I don't think I will do it all tomorrow knowing the minutes seem hours and hours days to me since you have left. Dear you look around for cheap board as soon as you can so I can come down. Will you dear for I don't like to stay here without you. Dear where did you put the stable lock as we can't find it any place _____ I was over to see Burones get some water and she told me not to do such hard work. Let mother have it _____for she is able to have it done and she says I will break myself down if I don't look out and quit it as the way I am she says little _____ will be very hard on me. I won't think so, do you? Well, Dear this is all I have to say for this time so I will say Good night and be a Good boy. With thousands of kisses to my papa, your loving Wife, Mrs. D. V. McClure

Letter from Dave dated October 2, 1905, and sent from Sulphur Springs, I. T.

My Own Darling Little Sweetheart,

   Your sweet letter arrived this afternoon & you have no idea how glad I was to get it little Darling. You go to the shows and have a good time. It is a pleasure to me to know that my little wife is enjoying herself so don't let it spoil your pleasure just because your Papa is not with you. I am enjoying myself every day working for you. It is really a pleasure to me to work when I think about who I am working for. We went out on the line today. It was awfully muddy and raining today, but that did not stop us. It rained all day yesterday and last night. So you can imagine how it must be to make the rodeo. But I like the world. I have to drive stallions ____ some time and hold the taxi so ____ in some world attached to it. Now Darling you go to the concert & have a good time there. You can tell me all about it when I come home next Sunday. That will do me just as much good as if I was there myself. Well little one this will be all for the present so I will say good night. With ten thousand hugs and kisses I remain as ever your devoted husband, D. V. McClure ps - please give this to Mama Hello Mama why don't you write to someone in a while Mama? I like the work just fine. We were out all day in the rain, but did not get ____ ____. Mama, you take good care of my little Baby for me and act as escort for her. You all must go to ____? lake on everything. Your Loving Son, Dave

1906 Letter dated October 4, Sulphur Springs, I. T.

My Own Darling Little Wife,

   Both of your letters reached me this morning. You have no idea how glad I was to hear from you. I know how lonesome you were last Sunday because it was the longest day for me. But, Dearest, I will try to make it last Sunday. We will be apart. You can come back with me so you can look for me on that early morning train I am sorry ___? the show but you are sure of the joy that is theirs today. Well, dearest, this will be all so. . .

1907   Birth of William John McClure, July 6, Latonia, Covington, Kentucky

Illustration 170. Dave and William John coming home from hospital, Latonia, Kentucky

Illustration 171. Dave arriving by train in Oklahoma City in 1907 with William, six weeks old.

Letter dated September 27, 1907

My Own Dear Little Sweetheart, I have not heard a word from you since I left home. Mr. Clark got a postcard today but me - nothing. Why don't you write or have you and my mail gone astray? I get my ____ hearing tomorrow morning but do not think I will know anything till the first of next week. Well, this will be all for this time. Take good care of Mr. McC tell him to write to Papa has he been ____? the Port ____? I have been sending him some money he might at least ____ manner msg from and write soon. Your Loving husband, Good Night

Newspaper article, June 29

The crowd at Latonia yesterday saw an exhibition of Buffalo riding and Steeplechase riding by Dave McClure on Dell Leath, the red hot favorite for the jumping race. McClure had a winning lead and going over the last infield obstacle Dell Leath did not tarry to jump over it, but ran through it and went to his knees and McClure out of the saddle. It looked as if he was all off with the good thing, when McClure, by a mighty effort, got him on his feet and crawled back in the saddle himself and went on and won the race. Everybody had a good view of the stunt and cowboy Dave deserved a great deal of credit for his quickness of thought and his gameness. When the horse stumbled it looked 100-1 shot that he would go down and that McClure would be spilled, but McClure was equal to the occasion and more quickly than can be written had his mount pointed down the stretch for the final hurdle. Many predicted that his mount would fall at that point but he went over it without a wobble. The race was the fastest one run through the field this season and equaled the mark made by Red Carr two years ago. The big play was concentrated on Dell Leath who not only was bet on at the track but was backed in out of town handbooks and pool rooms. There was nothing to it but Dell Leath after three jumps had been cleared Subador, who was very rank, almost ran out of the second jump and Allen had to take him up to keep him from running all over the course. Subador led over the first two jumps but lost too much ground that McClure forged to the front, going over the water and was never headed after that. There was a battle for the place and Rejectable landed it from Glass Leader who just beat the tiring Subador for the short end of the purse. Garnet fell when Peter Vinegar took the last hurdle but landed in a soft spot. McClure talking of his ride on Dell Leath said he is an awfully hard horse to ride and will toss most any man off, unless he is on the lookout all the time. He did not take off for that jump at all but went right through it and I certainly had a close shave from being spilled. That would have been awful with all the money that was on Dell Leath.

Letter dated September 29, 1907

My Dear Little Sweetheart,

This has surely been a busy day for me. Mr. Clark came over to the house and had dinner with me. We tried to get the kite to the theater. We tried those [rest lost]

1908 He [Dave McClure] was a jockey until 1908, rode rodeos and ranked among the five best rodeo hands of all time.

Illustration 172. Dave Wearing jockey silks of McClure Colors: Cherry red and white

Illustration 173. Dave and son, William (Bill)

Illustration 174. Like father, like son

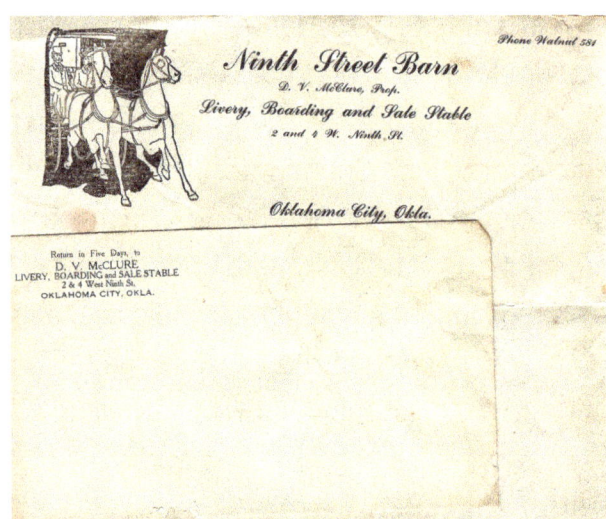
Illustration 175. Stationery for Dave's livery stable, 2nd St. and #4 West 9th Street, Oklahoma City

1910-1945   Receipts of payment every year to the County Treasurer's Office, Murray County, Sulphur, Oklahoma. D.V. McClure paid taxes on two sections of land. Also, Oklahoma County tax receipts for lots in the Maywood Addition. Also, the Britton Lots in Oklahoma County. Also 160 acres in Spring Creek Twp. [the farm at MacArthur and Memorial Roads]

Illustration 176. Dave taking the jumps

Illustration 177. 1910: "The Farm"—McArthur and Memorial

Illustration 178. "The Farm House"

1910   Boy Scouts of America incorporated and founded by Daniel Beard

Illustration 179. Dave (left) in Oklahoma City

Illustration 180. Dave and Bill at the Farm

Dave owned a billiard parlor, as well as a cigar club, in Sulphur Platt National Park, Sulphur, Oklahoma—The Jockey Club Cigar and Billiard Parlor, D. V. McClure, proprietor.

1916

Illustration 181. D. V. McClure, competing in Bromide, Oklahoma, 1916

Illustration 182. Dave McClure roping a steer

1920 Census: Oklahoma State, Oklahoma County; Precinct, Oklahoma City Series T625; Roll 1473; Page 229

[3]David V. McClure, Head, age 40, b. Oklahoma
    Father b. Illinois
    Mother b. Kansas

[3]Grace A. McClure, age 30, Wife b. Ohio
    Father b. Ohio
    Mother b. Ohio

[4]William J. McClure, age 1, Son b. Kentucky

    Father b. Oklahoma
    Mother b. Ohio
[4]Margarett McClure, daughter, b. Oklahoma
[2]Mary E. McClure, Head, age 63, b. Kansas
    Father b. Indiana
    Mother b. Virginia

Illustration 183. Dave's daughter, Veta Ann; mother, Mary Ellen; wife, Grace; David V.; son, William John (Bill)

1925 Letter from Grace to Bill, dated January 17

"My Dear Big Boy!

Just a line to let you know I am feeling fine and Guy Victor is just exciting like you. Your voice and mouth and eyes and just everything. He weighs 6#.

He arrived at 1:15 am. I know you will love him. Papa is so proud of him, you ought to see him out chopping wood. We have had a house full of people ever since Guy came. Mr. Forongrain brought him out his first catch rope and Papa put it in his hand. Yesterday we had a man working but Papa is going to town and see about getting another one as he is worse than Olden, but our worries will soon be over when you get home and Guy gets out this summer. All Papa and I will have to do is sit on the front porch – Ha Ha! For I know you two boys will do things right. I am not going to tell Veta Ann anything about him because she asks me to be very careful of what I wrote to her. So don't you let her know what I have told you. Now be a good boy and study hard and maybe I will run up and see you with heaps of love and kisses, Mama & Papa"

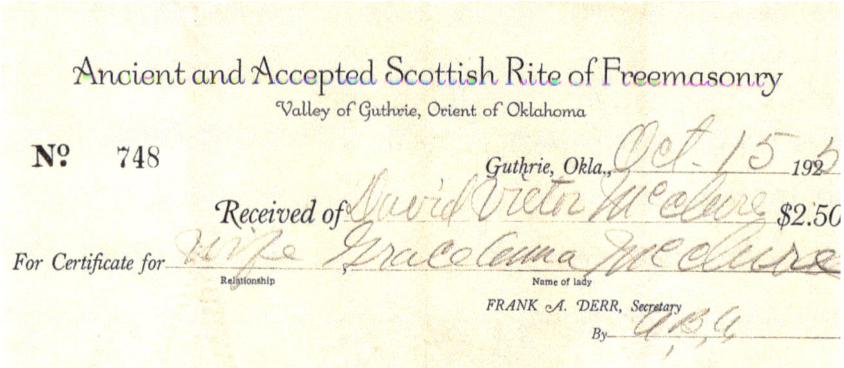

Ancient and Accepted Scottish Rite of Freemasonry
Valley of Guthrie, Orient of Oklahoma

Nº 748 Guthrie, Okla., Oct. 15 1925

Received of David Vreten McClure $2.50

For Certificate for wife (Relationship) Grace Alma McClure (Name of lady)

FRANK A. DERR, Secretary
By

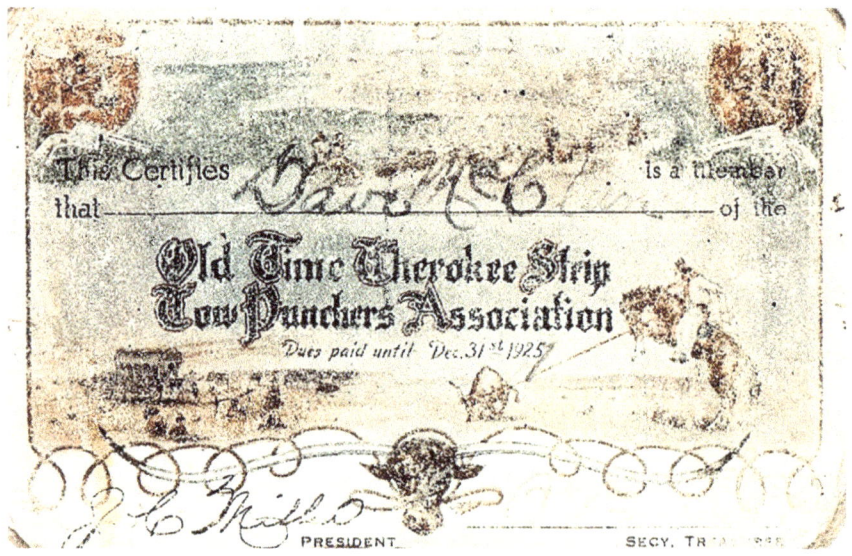

Illustration 184. Dues paid by Dave for Grace's membership in the Scottish Rite

This Certifies that Dave McClure is a member of the

Old Time Cherokee Strip Cow Punchers Association

Dues paid until Dec. 31st 1925

PRESIDENT SECY. TR

Illustration 185. Membership card in Cherokee Strip Association

1926 *The Daily Oklahoman* newspaper article

THE ROUND-UP

Two of the boys arrived here this evening to talk about entirely different subjects, but both of these subjects are of vital interest to all of us. First up to speak, Fog Horn Clancy of Bar C. Ranch, Smithfield, Texas. "Folks, it's about Western men and horses. I'm askin you to listen to me palaver of them. Now, there's Dave McClure of Edmond, Oklahoma, one of the oldest active cowboys of that State, at one time one of the greatest riders of the Southwest and still a very fast steer roper. He is owner of the once undisputed world's champion roping horse, which during its period of roping actively, belonged to the world's champion roper, the late Joe Gardner of Sierra Blanca, Texas."

At the first world's championship rodeo, held at Grant Park, in Chicago in 1920, before the erection of the present Soldiers Field Stadium, horse tents housed the horses which the contestants brought with them for their roping. Joe Gardner was there with his great horse Skunk, a flea-bitten gray. The animal was not good to look upon, but the ropers knew that there was never a swifter, surer, gamer or more sensible cow horse ever turned loose after a longhorn than the ugly gray. And that gray received from the old roper every attention the most aristocratic equine of one of the nation's greatest horse shows could have demanded.

Noticing that the flies were bothering his horse, Gardner employed two attendants, each working an eight-hour shift to fan the flies off of Skunk. And for this kind treatment the great gray rewarded his master by taking him to where his unerring lariat caught the longhorns so fast that, at the end of the nine days' contest, Gardner had outdistanced the field by many seconds and was awarded the capital prize, belt and title of world's champion roper.

A year later Gardner died. He faced death with true championship nerve, and when he was sure that he was leaving the arena of life, he thought of the old gray that had carried him to victory in hundreds of roping contests and determined that his equine pal should not be left unprotected. Among his hundreds of cowboy friends, he remembered one who loved old Skunk almost as much as he did himself. He sent for that friend, Dave McClure, and gave the horse into his keeping. The gray, now twenty-eight years old has long since been pensioned and the setting sun of life of the once powerful fleet-footed gray finds him with little work to do

Once in a while, McClure mounts Skunk and chases a steer, throwing his lariat and missing on purpose just to give the old horse the pleasure of a chase.

Investor in The Deming Investment Co., 45th and Commercial, Oswego, Kansas.

Illustration 186. Oklahoma City trolley, 1926

1927 Work begins on construction of Mount Rushmore, October 1927.

Illustration 187. Card for race #6. Dave McClure, rider #6, at the Denver Fair and Racing Grounds

Illustration 188. Denver Race Association program, 1927

1928 U. S. of A. Bureau of Pensions: It is hereby certified that David V. McClure who was a Corporal, Troop D, 1st United States Volunteer Cavalry at the rate of thirty dollars per month to commence May 26, 1927. #1581814

1929 Stock Market Crash October 18, 1929, and October 24, known as "Black Thursday"

1930

Certificate No. ___ One Share

INCORPORATED UNDER THE LAWS OF THE STATE OF OKLAHOMA

OKLAHOMA CITY SADDLE and POLO CLUB

OKLAHOMA CITY, OKLAHOMA

CERTIFICATE OF MEMBERSHIP

This is to Certify that DAVE McCLURE.

of Edmond Oklahoma.

is a member of the OKLAHOMA CITY SADDLE AND POLO CLUB of Oklahoma City, Oklahoma, having no capital Stock, and is entitled to one vote at each regular and call meeting of the membership. The membership in this corporation is not transferable except by consent of the Board of Directors, and is to be governed in all respects by the Articles of Incorporation and the By-Laws of said Corporation.

Secretary

R. J. Moore
President

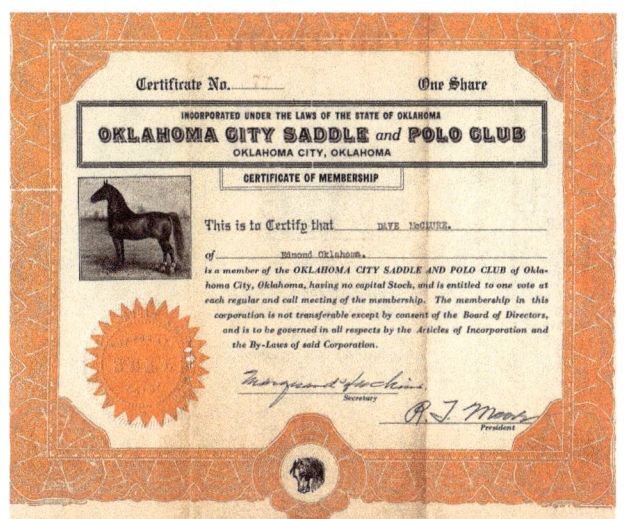

Illustration 189. Oklahoma City Saddle and Polo Club

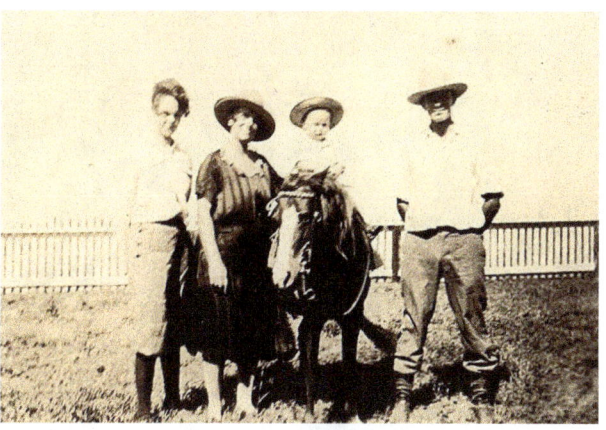

Illustration 190. Dave's daughter, Veta Ann; wife, Grace; son, Guy; Dave

NATIONAL HEADQUARTERS

United Spanish War Veterans

MEMBER AT LARGE

Dec. 2 1930

This is to Certify that

COMRADE David V. McClure

is a member of National Headquarters' Camp and has paid his dues to December 31, 1931.

Commander-in-Chief

No. 80219

Signature of Comrade

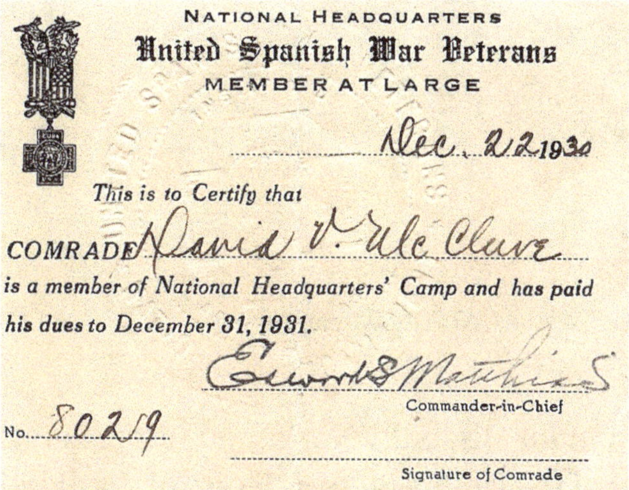

Illustration 191. Dues paying member of Spanish War veterans

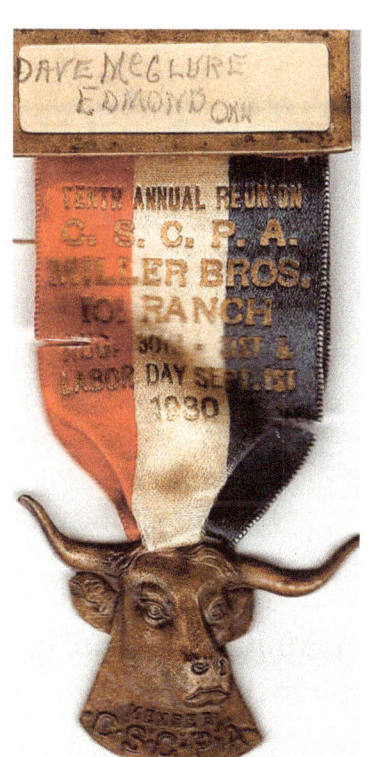

Illustration 192. Reunion of famous Miller Brothers' 101 Ranch

1931 Dave held an immigration card from Estados Unidos Mexicana in Tijuana. This was to race his horses at the Tijuana racetrack.

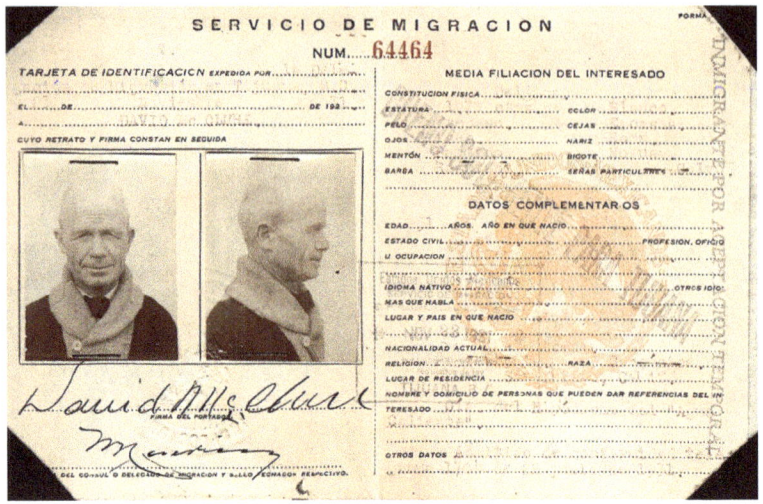

Illustration 193. Mexican migracion passport

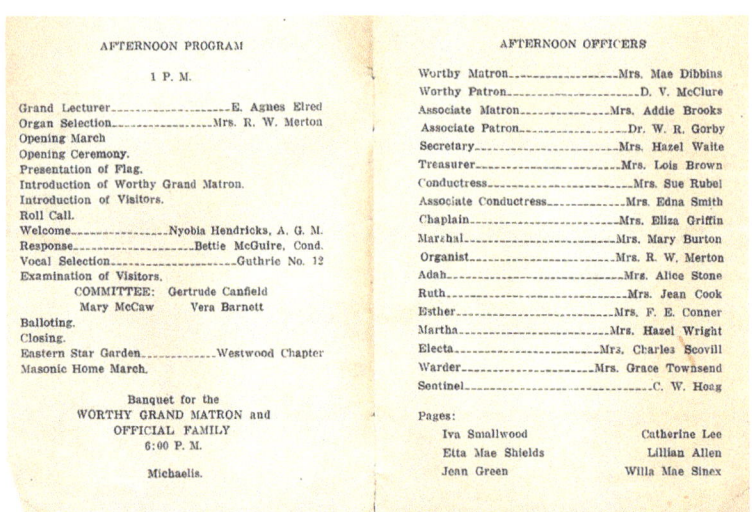

Illustration 194. Dave listed as Worthy Patron of Masonic Lodge

1933 Veteran's Application for Pension for Disability Not The Result of Service in the Active Military or Naval Forces of the United States: Nature of disability: Left leg broken in three places; knee, thigh, and hip. Heart trouble.

1934 Oklahoman Will Rogers called most famous person in America

Membership Card: National Headquarters United Spanish War Veterans, Member at large, Jan. 7, 1933, Comrade David V. McClure #8029

1935 Twenty-Sixth Annual Session, Grand Chapter Order of the Eastern Star, State of Oklahoma; Worthy Matrons—Worthy Patrons Luncheon. Menu: Azure Cocktail, Assorted Relishes, Chicken Croquettes, Supreme, New Persillade Potatoes,

Beans En Blanket, Salad—Spring Vegetable Aspic, Damson Plum Sherbet—Veiled Cake, Hot Rolls, Coffee.

1937 Letter from Veterans Administration, Washington: May 7, 1937

Dear Sir,

Reference is made to your claim for pension. The records of your claim have been carefully considered in accordance with the provisions of the President's Executive Order of January 19, 1934 and you will receive a pension in the amount of $15.00 monthly from January 19, 1934 to March 26, 1934. Appropriate action will be taken at the earliest possible date to adjust your account accordingly. Your present pension of $35.00 monthly will continue as heretofore. Respectfully"

1938 *The Daily Oklahoman* newspaper article

LOCAL FILLY MAY RUN IN DERBY;
Dave McClure's Little Girl Made to Order

There's a Kentucky Derby prospect, a beautiful bay filly, grazing in a pasture five miles west and four north of Britton. Her name is Worthy Matron, and her owner is Dave McClure, a retired steeplechase jockey who still has some records pinned up around the country. His son, Bill, is joint trainer. "If I know anything about horses," said McClure, "this little girl is a racer. If I could build me a horse from the ground up, I'd make her just like this." He ran his hand appraisingly over the firm leg muscles, and down the curve of her back, and explained just how they would change as the "little girl" is worked into prime condition. She will go to Chicago in July to start the rounds of the stake races, leading up to the 1939 Kentucky derby. Her first real tryout will be in the Filly Classic, with $35,000 in prize money. So far Worthy Matron has lived in the serenity of the McClure farm and taken her workouts along the soft, red clay roads in the vicinity. Her only excitement is in the phonograph concerts of martial music, "so she'll get used to bands." The McClures are being super careful with Worthy Matron, for she has that fine balance of blood which is apt to change from spirit and fire into orneriness. Her mother, Preander, by Supremus out of Ausander, had the same disposition but was spoiled, "like a woman having a nervous breakdown," McClure explained. "But it's just that fire and life that makes a winner," he added. We're taking it easy with the Matron here. Never let her get too excited, It's touchy business." McClure bought Preander several years ago in California and bred her to Polante, owned by George Ogle, at the Ogle breeding farm at Waurika. Polante, Worthy Matron's father, was a seven-time winner out of seven starts as a two-year-old, copping $84,000 purse money in one year. He was by Atheline II, out of Polistena. Worthy Matron is 15 hands, 3 inches high now and should measure 16 hands by next May. She weighs about 1,000 pounds and even with working off surplus flesh, should put on another 100 pounds. She will be bigger than the average Derby entry. She is a 2 year old now. The Kentucky classic is for 3-year-olds. All that stands between her and that famed race is a long, hard year, during which her name will become a by-word in racing circles or she will become just another pretty good horse. She already has one blue ribbon for the only show she ever entered—a colt show at Fort Reno, when she was 2 months old. McClure and his son, Bill, expect to have a whole flock of blue ribbons this time next year. Good luck!

The Daily Oklahoman newspaper article, August 20, 1938

DAMP OUTLOOK

To those people the Bluff Creek reservoir would mean more than water in their faucets. It would mean water 20-30 feet deep over their fields and the places where their homes now stand. It would mean the complete obliteration of all they hold most dear—in exchange for its fair value in dollars and cents. The Cecil Larkins won't even have money in exchange, however, for they are tenant farmers of 10 years standing. "It's home to us." said Mrs. Larkins, "but I guess we'll have to move along." It is the only home their daughter, Wilma Jean, 12 years old can remember. George W. Collett won't mind retiring from his farm if they will just let him finish out his fiftieth anniversary next April. He settled on the land in the "run" of '89 and has built the fine-looking farm home. The Dave McClure family whose home is one of the finest in the lake site, say they are just as proud of Oklahoma City as they are of their farm (and their racehorses) so they don't want to stand in the way of anything the city needs. Bill McClure is named after his grandfather who homesteaded a quarter section in what is now Maywood addition and grazed cattle over the proposed lake site before the territory was opened for settlement. They have lived on their farm about 20 years." (This lake/reservoir was never built.)

Illustration 195. David Victor McClure

Illustration 196. Commanding horsemanship

Illustration 197. Dave looking so natural and at ease on a beautiful horse

Illustration 198. Dave and son, Guy, in front of the farmhouse

1938 Newspaper article

FIFTH RACE: WINNER

Society Lady, trained and owned by D.V. McClure, bred by Mr. D.V. McClure, Start good from stall gate. Won driving, second and third the same, Society Lady, was in lead for a half, she came forward when roused entering the stretch and wore down Golden Man midway of the stretch.

Illustration 199. Dave McClure portrayed in the Detroit comic section

Illustration 200. Typical grandstand and crowd at a popular track

Illustration 201. Standing room only on the ground level

Illustration 202. Dave's horse leading the field

Illustration 203. Holding a good lead

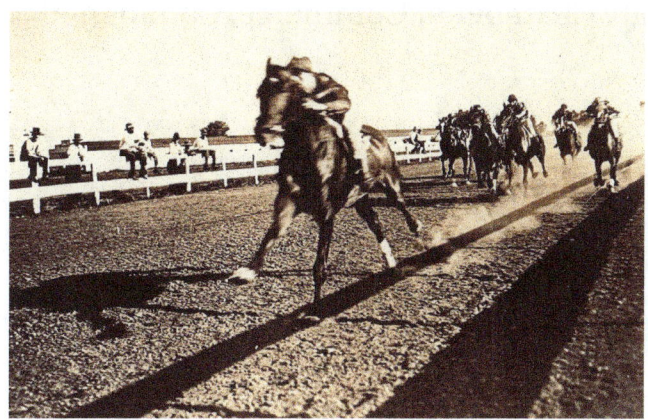

Illustration 204. Thundering toward the finish line

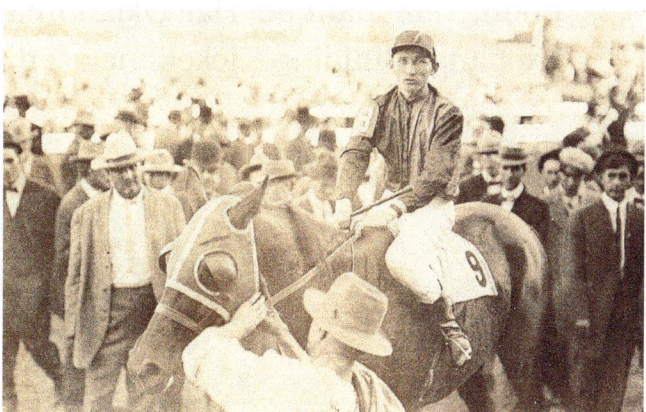

Illustration 205. In the Winners Circle

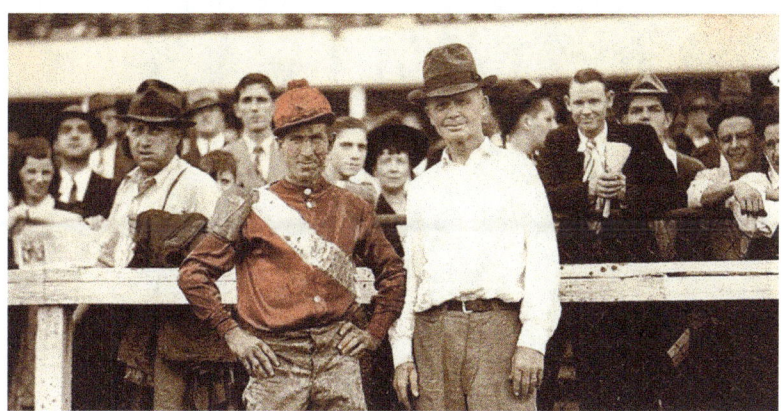

Illustration 206. Dave taking a bow with the jockey

1939

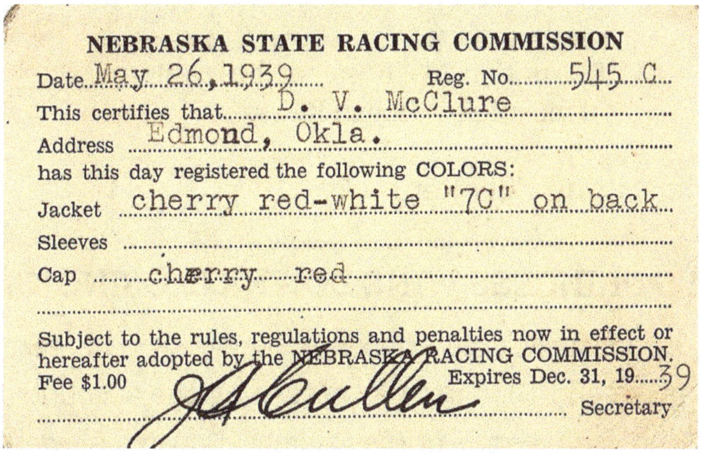

NEBRASKA STATE RACING COMMISSION

Date May 26, 1939 Reg. No. 545 C

This certifies that D. V. McClure

Address Edmond, Okla.

has this day registered the following COLORS:

Jacket cherry red-white "7C" on back

Sleeves

Cap cherry red

Subject to the rules, regulations and penalties now in effect or hereafter adopted by the NEBRASKA RACING COMMISSION.

Fee $1.00 Expires Dec. 31, 19 39

J A Cullen Secretary

Illustration 207. Nebraska race card

Oklahoma City Chamber of Commerce; The Officers and Directors of the Oklahoma City Chamber of Commerce request the Honor and Presence of D. V. McClure at the Founders Day Luncheon Honoring the Pioneers of 1889. A Feature of Oklahoma City's Golden Jubilee; Tuesday, April 18, 1949; 12:25

noon; Main Banquet Hall Oklahoma City Chamber of Commerce, Commerce Exchange Building. Ticket Enclosed

1940

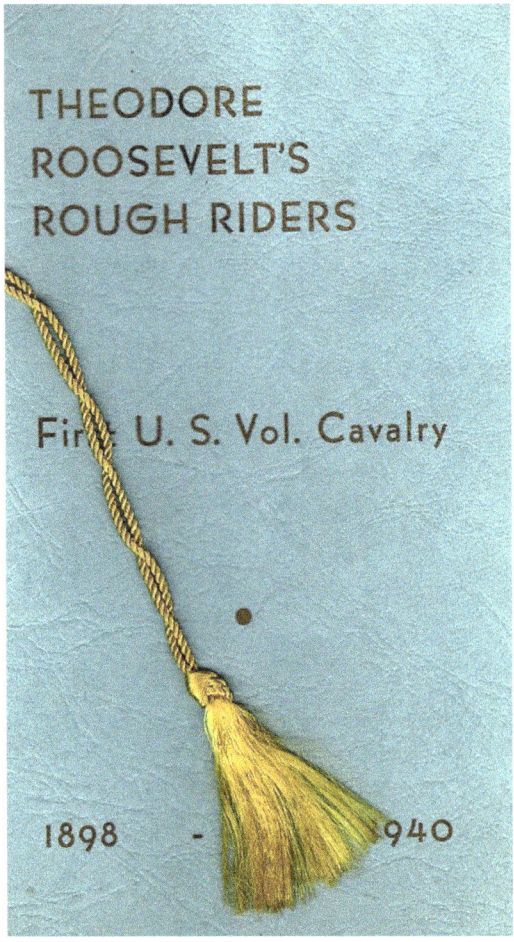

Illustration 208. Roster of the reunion of the original Rough Riders

1942 Newspaper article, Louisville, Kentucky

GOLD PRINCESS WINS DOWNS CLOSING 'GAP'

D. V. McClure's consistent Gold Princess won her second stake of the meeting and her seventh purse and 19 starts this season as she accounted for yesterday's Au Revoire Handicap, feature race of the Churchill Downs getaway program with a crowd of 15,000 on hand to bid the thoroughbreds a Kentucky farewell until spring and climax the best fall meeting in a decade. The speedy daughter of Prince Pam and Gold Nugget stepped the 77 furlongs in 1.24 3/5 within 1 1/5 seconds of the track record to lead Ruth Seidel's Burgee to the wire by two links. Another two links back in third place was JC Ellis Flying Easy. Beautiful to the heavy favorite finished a well beaten 611, excepted the issue and Flying Easy was all first for a good start. Song of War quickly took command, however, followed by Bergie Maid. As the field wound into the stretch, Gold Princess began moving up fast and under W. Bailey's snug ride overtook the leaders and came on to win with something in reserve. The race was worth $1850 to owner McClure and boosted Gold Prince's earnings for the season to $20,160. The winners of two dollar backers received $12.80[4].

1943

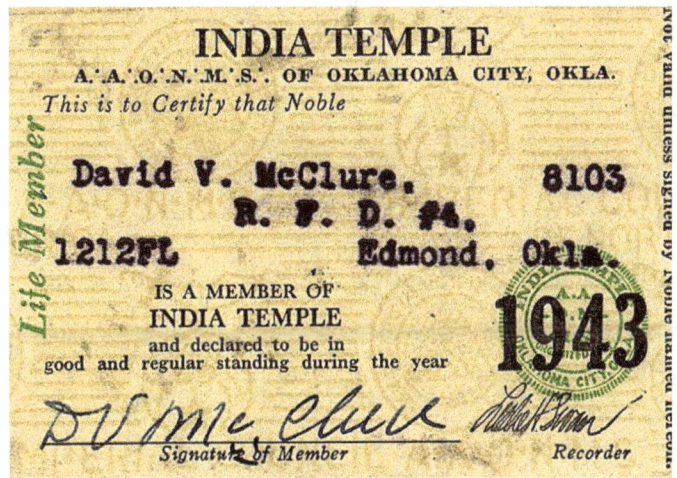

Illustration 209. Membership card

Roosevelt's Rough Riders, Last Man's Club, 1st U.S. Volunteer Cavalry, June 6, 1943

Dear Comrade Dave, Your welcome letters, with check enclosed, reached me yesterday and I am sending you enclosed your paid up card for dues, in our Last Man's Club. At our last Reunion of the Regiment, held in Los Angeles, Calif. I was unanimously elected as President of the Last Man's Club. Bill McGinty of Ripley, Oklahoma was elected Vice President and Leslie C. Chase of Atascadero, California was elected as Secretary-Treasurer of the Club. Am sorry to tell you Dave that our ranks are thinning very fast. One by one our comrades are crossing the Great Divide, and before long tapes will have been blown over the last Rough Rider. We must try and keep in touch with each other, so please write to me often. I sincerely hope you and all yours are enjoying good health. Mrs. Sharland and I are real well at this time. I shall be 73 years of age on March 30 next. Your Friend & Comrade, George H. Sharland, Late of Troop F Roosevelt Rough Rider

---
[4]Adapted text reproduced with permission of *The Louisville Courier Journal*/Courier Journal.com

The Round-Up

TWO of the boys arrived here this evening to talk about entirely different subjects, but both of these subjects are of vital interest to all of us. First, up speaks Fog Horn Clancy, of Bar C Ranch, Smithfield, Texas.

✗

"FOLKS, it's about Western men and horses. I'm askin' you to listen to me palaver of them. Now, there's Dave McClure, of Edmond, Oklahoma, one of the oldest active cowboys of that State, at one time one of the greatest riders of the Southwest and still a very fast steer roper. He is owner of the once undisputed world's champion roping horse which, during its period of roping activity, belonged to the world's champion roper, the late Joe Gardner of Sierra Blanca, Texas.

"At the first world's championship rodeo, held at Grant Park, in Chicago in 1920, before the erection of the present Soldiers Field Stadium, horse tents housed the horses which the contestants brought with them for their roping. Joe Gardner was there with his great horse Skunk, a flea-bitten gray. The animal was not good to look upon, but the ropers knew that there was never a swifter, surer, gamer or more sensible cow horse ever turned loose after a longhorn than the ugly gray. And that gray received from the old roper every attention the most aristocratic equine of one of the nation's greatest horse shows could have demanded.

"Noticing that the flies were bothering his horse, Gardner employed two attendants, each working an eight-hour shift, to fan the flies off of Skunk. And for this kind treatment, the great gray rewarded his master by taking him to where his unerring lariat caught the longhorns so fast that, at the end of the nine days' contest, Gardner had outdistanced the field by many seconds and was awarded the capital prize, belt, and title of world's champion roper.

"A year later Gardner died. He faced death with true championship nerve, and, when he was sure that he was leaving the arena of life, he thought of the old gray that had carried him to victory in hundreds of roping contests and determined that his equine pal should not be left unprotected. Among his hundreds of cowboy friends, he remembered one who loved old Skunk almost as much as he did himself. He sent for that friend, Dave McClure, and

Illustration 210. Account of famous roper horse, Skunk

Newspaper article, Cleveland, Ohio

GOLD PRINCESS WINS BY NECK

Gold Princess goaled 'em in the $5000.00 Moses Cleveland Handicap at the Thistle Downs yesterday, stealing the payoff picture by a chestnut neck on Some Man, the tough "two in a row" thumper that bested Maybe Monday by only a nose for place. With 14,000 getaway-day customers on their feet and in their best voice, old Oklahoma Dave McClure's home-bred daughter of Prince Pan and Gold Nugget hopped to the front on the home pike after Some Man had beaten the top-breaking Maybe Monday back when they were a furlong from the wire. Smartly steered by

Jockey Mike Coffeeville, fourth in the field of nine over the greater portion of the mile and 40 yard ramble, the 9-2 Princes went to the outside for the money drive that got her over in 1.40:3/5 and swelled her earnings for 1942 to $17,000.00. Strictly a three-horse battle it turned out to be on the last lane for all done, fading to sixth, was Beautiful II, the hometown hopes that had forced the pace of Babe Monday for three-quarters. Mrs. E.L. Hopkins' Big Beautiful was the second choice to the Cenini-Marley entry of No Wrinkles and Babe Monday, while Some Man went at 7-2 despite his clicks in two earlier $5,000.00 'caps at the Downs. Third in two sprints while the meeting was young, the Princess hadn't scored since midsummer at Detroit. But old Dave McClure as he said himself had her all freshened up for this heat in which she carried 107 pounds.

Newspaper article, Cleveland, Ohio

GRAND SLAM FOR DAVE

Oklahoma's Dave McClure, our old Thistle Downs friend who likes to tell of the great day back in '98 when he climbed San Juan Hill as one of Colonel Teddy Roosevelt's Rough Riders, had another great day yesterday..... the grizzled Spanish war vets little Gold Princess, a mare that he raised himself on the farm in the former territory of the Indians, went at odds of 17 to 1 in the $17,000 Modesty Handicap at Chicago's Washington Park... And, as Dave himself would say, "there isn't anything that's called her yet!... And it's not so long ago, come to recall, that Gold Princess goaled them at a pretty price and a $10,000 heat at Chicago. . . .Mr. McClure is what the lads around the stables call a spotter. . . .Every now and then he finds a spot for the Princess and, still quoting the stable gang, it's Katie bar the door!

Newspaper article, Cleveland, Ohio

$315,117.00 IS BET ON LAST DAY AT THISTLE DOWNS

Moving on the Thistle Downs pari-mutuel windows yesterday with $315,117. The betters set a record for the Ohio racing season that's now all over. The total was more than $7,000. Higher than the amount wagered a week before but still some $6,000. less than the state high registered at the Downs last Labor Day. :

Newspaper article, Cleveland, Ohio

ROUGH RIDER AT THISTLE

    A kid Rough Rider under Col. Teddy Roosevelt back in '98, Sergeant Dave McClure had to battle his way up San Juan Hill without a horse, but he got there just the same. Now Dave McClure is a bald young fellow of 64, and he has plenty of horse in his home-bred Gold Princess, and a right fair one in his other home-bred, Society Lady, beaten a neck in the Spitfire Handicap at Thistle Down yesterday, but to get back to San Juan Hill: "There being no horses for anybody but the officers," Dave McClure was saying yesterday, "we had to win in a walk. Our horses hadn't been shipped from Tampa, you see, a lot of people don't remember that." "How was the going for that San Juan dash?" somebody asked, "And the betting?" "That was rough and lumpy," Dave McClure replied, "I didn't hear of any betting overnight or otherwise, but I called our gang a cinch. Still and all, though, if there'd been any generalship at all among the Spaniards, they'd have knocked the lot of us off like shootin' ducks. They got me with a wound in the leg the next day, and it was a little after that they decided to put up the flag of truce. Their timing was awful, too." A Gold-Grabbing Princess—This leathery-faced, twinkling-eyed Rough Rider, born and reared in Indian Territory, used to gallop horses across the grassy land on which they built Oklahoma City, where he's lived for many a year. And through 53 racing campaigns he's had his own thoroughbreds under colors, but never another one quite so good, he guesses, as Gold Princess. The Princess, a four-year-old chestnut daughter of his broodmare called Gold Nugget has run into something like $35,000 for Dave McClure. Society Lady, also a daughter of the Nugget, has earned considerably more than her oats, too. She's only three and coming right along. "Now that you've asked about it," he said, "it was quite a kick for a fella in scrambling up San Juan, but I don't suppose I got much more belt out of that than I did out of seeing the Princess get home in front of Miss Dogwood and Signator in the Autumn Handicap at Churchill Downs last year." Miss Dogwood is called the best racing mare in the country now, you know, and Signator the tops of all sprinters, but they didn't have a look-in with the Princess that day. "I knew they wouldn't have a look with her, either – she was SO sharp that day and you could have knocked me over with just about nothing at all when the pay-off figures hung up against her number were $87 for a two-spot. Dave, I said to myself, this game is getting real good." I'd told a little Kentucky girl that waited on me and Mrs. McClure in the track restaurant to have herself a two-dollar bet on the Princess. And when she said she'd made it a rule never to bet any of her money on the races, I handed her two dollars and said, "Well, you have a bet with my compliments." "When I saw her sometime after the race, she tried to give me the two bucks back, "Couldn't break my rule, she said, "But I've got no regrets – not even though $87 is more money than I'll ever need." Dave McClure's listeners insisted on hearing more about San Juan Hill. They'd all seen the Gold Princess. "Well, I'll tell you," he said, "just as I've told my 18 year old boy who is a flight sergeant down in Texas, "These lads in the army today have got more than a little the best of it in a lot of ways. There in Cuba every man was his own cook, and nothing but scarce hardtack and bacon, and coffee that he'd have to grind himself with the butt of a six-shooter. That was something, now, wasn't it?" Nobody wished to argue about that. "But we had pretty fair weather for it," grinned Dave McClure, and the Rough Riders were a fine bunch to be with, and it was worth all the hardship just to be earning the lifelong friendship of a great man like Teddy Roosevelt. Over the public address system came the announcement, "They're at the post!" "Well, that will be enough about '98," said Dave McClure. "Let's move out to the rail and see what all the excitement is about in this heat."

Illustration 211. Pre-race newspaper coverage

Illustration 212. Feature story about Dave

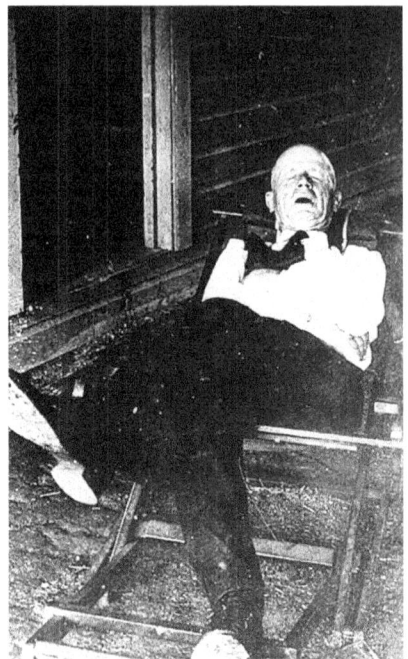
Illustration 213. Afternoon nap time for Dave

1944 Newspaper article, Louisville, Kentucky

D.V. McClure's Gold Princess, a probable starter in Saturday's renewal of the $10,000 Sprint Handicap, will have several engagements at Churchill Downs during the autumn meeting opening on October 21[5].

Newspaper article, November 1, Louisville, Kentucky

D. V. McClure's Gold Princess, who no doubt will accept her engagement Saturday at Churchill Downs in the filly and mare event, the Falls City Handicap, will following that endeavor be shipped to her owner-breeder's farm near Oklahoma City, Okla., along with Generalis. The pair will be rested over the winter[6].

Newspaper article, November 9, Louisville, Kentucky

Top imposed of 115 pounds has been assigned respectively to Miller and Burgers Traffic Court and to D. V. McClure's Gold Princess for Saturday's mile $5000 added Fall City Handicap, Filly and mare highlight at Churchill Downs fall meeting[7].

---
[5] Adapted text reproduced with permission of *The Louisville Courier Journal*/Courier Journal.com
[6] ibid
[7] ibid

December 9: *Blood-Horse* magazine has an article about Dave and his horse, Gold Princess. The article came out two days before his death.

The author recalls the names of a few additional racehorses of Dave's that achieved notable recognition:

Society Lady	Remembering	Jim Boy H
Society Matron	Nick O Time	Whatahoss
Gold Nugget	Me Can	Ol' Blue

Illustration 214. Feature story about Dave and his horses[8]

---
[8]Reproduced courtesy of *Blood-Horse* magazine

Illustration 215. Feature story about Dave's golden filly

Illustration 216. Philanthropic certificate

1944 Letter from The Jesse Chisholm Trail and Memorial Association, Enid, Oklahoma. Dated December 19th, 1944 (just days after Dave's death)

My Dear Old CowBoy Friend,

I am sure happy to tell you we have the Chisholm Marker all completed and it is sitting in the Pellows Monuments Works and will be ready to unveil Sept, 18, 1945 at the Strip Celebration. If you remember some 20 years back at the 101 Ranch we talked about the Marker on the Old Chisholm Trail, and at that time I was one of the committee to help out and I am the only one left of the Old committee. My dream has come true and if we had had some more Dave McClures it would have been completed ten years ago. It will be one of nicest in all the southwest and is made of Melrose granite and weighs nine tons. The Old Cow Boys' names are on the stone. Should you be in Enid, I would be glad to have you call and see it. Yours Very Truly, Ed Stennett, President

Dave McClure's name is listed on this historical monument that tells of the Chisholm Trail and the famous 101 Ranch.

Newspaper article

DAVE MCCLURE, PIONEER CATTLE RAISER, DEAD

Dave McClure, 65, of Britton, died Monday night of a heart attack. A pioneer cattleman, the son of the late William McClure, an '89er and the owner of the Seven C Ranch, he rode the range for his father when as many as 37,000 head of cattle were being run at one time. After the run the senior McClure staked a claim on what is now the Maywood addition, and also two downtown lots. Dave McClure had made his home northwest of Britton for the last 24 years, where he engaged in farming and raising racehorses. His horses were well known on most of the country's race tracks, and in late years he had devoted a large part of his time to taking his horses over the country. His mother, the late Mrs. Mary Ellen McClure, was the first Worthy Grand Matron of the Eastern Star in Indian Territory. Later, McClure served as Worthy Patron for the Britton Eastern Star chapter, an office he held for six years. A brother, the late Guy McClure, was city engineer here at one time. McClure was a thirty-second degree Mason, a Shriner, a member of the '89ers Club and a member of the Presbyterian church. Survivors include his sons, Bill McClure of New Orleans, Lieut. Guy McClure, AAC, now stationed in Mississippi, a daughter, Mrs. Robert Meals of the home address; two grandsons and a sister, Mrs. George Findlay of Washington, D.C. Services will be at 2 p.m. Friday in the Methodist church at Britton, directed by the Sherman funeral home. Burial will be in Fairlawn.

Eulogy by his friend, Cornelius Bowles:

David Victor McClure was born at Atoka, Indian Territory, December 12, 1879, and passed away at his home eight miles northwest of Britton, Dec. 11, 1944. Dave was a great lover of horses and it was through them that he met his wife, Gracie Anna Jones, of Cincinnati, Ohio. While making the western racing circuits as a jockey he met and married his wife. She and Dave had a wonderful time traveling around the first few years of their married life and then they came to Oklahoma, where they have resided ever since. No man could have been more devoted to his family. His next love might be said to be his horses. When Dave talked horses you saw horses. In all our acquaintance with him and all his knowledge of racing we have yet to have ever heard him discuss the race. It was always the horse. When he spoke of the sheen of the coat, the gleam of the eye, the proud carriage of the head, the proud step, the whipping of the mane and tail in the breeze, one saw the particular horse Dave saw. He likes to talk and live again his part in the Spanish American War. The charge up San Juan Hill, the comradery of the men, the love all of them held for their leader Teddy, all these things played a large part in his life. Dave was a man very much alive. Life radiated from him and the most trivial things received as much vitality and force from him as the larger ones. He was charged with energy without affecting one as being nervous or excitable. Life to him was something to be enjoyed and lived. He not only lived but wanted his family to share this life; consequently he made happiness for all around him. His good wife and children attest that he was ever patient and kind with them and did what he could to increase their joy in living. With all Dave's wanderings around following the horses, he always was rooted in Oklahoma and the central part of the state around Oklahoma City. He loved his state. So we think of Dave not as dead but simply gone away for a time as was his wont. He has simply saddled up and ridden away into the sunset. As he looks back we see the twinkling smile and kindly affectionate face. We know he would not be unkind enough to leave us. So all his loved ones and friends shall see him when the sun lights up the west in a final blaze of glory. They shall see him at the nooning as he feeds his stock; they shall remember him in the lodge as he entered so heartily into the work of the lodge; they shall see and, yes, talk with him as he enjoys a friendly chat over the store counter. His dear wife and children shall never fail to remember the clipped, interesting, kindly voice of her husband and their father. What is mortal of Dave shall be laid to rest but he shall still live with us. So until that day, we say "Til we meet again." Dave's love for people was proven by the organizations to which he belonged; Mason, member of the Blue Lodge, Shrine, and Consistory; Patron of the Eastern Star six times and associated Patron four times; a member of the Last Man's Club of the Rough Riders, having been a soldier in Troop D' also a member of the Cherokee Strip Organization and the 89ers. His wife, Gracie Anna, and three children, William, Veta Ann, and Guy Victor remain to mourn the passing of their father. A host of friends shall miss him but be blessed because he lived. Interment will be in Fairlawn Cemetery, Oklahoma City. May his loved ones and friends give thanks that they knew "so great and good a man."

Department of the Army, U.S. Army Military History Research Collections, Carlisle Barracks, Pennsylvania

Dear Mrs. McClure,

Thank you so much for your letter of August 12 offering us the letters, maps, and medal of David McClure concerning service at the turn of the century. We would, indeed, welcome receiving them. To enable them to be sent without charge, a franked mailing label is enclosed. Sincerely,

Magazine article and photo of Dave with Gold Princess, by Lewis H. Walter

It's true that Dave McClure's left leg does seem a bit gimpy these damp mornings when he's in the stall at the Detroit racetrack with Gold Princess, his handicap horse, rubbing her chestnut coat until it glistens like gold in the morning sun. But of course, any man's left leg might be a little bit gimpy if it had stopped a Mouser bullet in that charge up San Juan Hill with Teddy Roosevelt's Rough Riders back in '98. Yes, Dave McClure was with the Rough Riders. THEY TOOK THE RIDGE. They were the glamour boys of '98 and they were the ones who swept up San Juan Hill, took the ridge and the Spanish blockhouse--- and the headlines too. That exploit didn't hurt Teddy a bit in his political career. But Dave McClure wasn't thinking about headlines or a political future as he gnawed at his hardtack and cooked his ration of sowbelly over an open fire. Dave McClure was there for the adventure. Down there in Cuba because there was action. It was only natural that he would be a youngster whose dad in 1870 had bought a huge ranch on the old Chisholm Trail where Oklahoma City now stands. Dave had grown up on the range where his father's cattle could wander from Kansas to Texas and from Arkansas to Texas without a fence to hamper them. Open range it was until April 22, 1889, when the government opened Oklahoma to the pressing hordes of settlers. That was the day when Dave's dad, like hundreds of others, took off with the crack of the pistol at 12 noon in the rush to stake out a claim. And he made it, with relays of cow ponies, to reach his plots on the site of Oklahoma City. Oklahoma City, the rendezvous of cowpunchers, Kickapoo, Cheyenne's and Arapahos was "town" to Dave McClure. That was where he won the first horse race ever run for a purse in Oklahoma when his cow pony "Paddy" in Oklahoma City's first Fourth of July celebration back in 1889. Dave McClure grew up in the saddle. That is why he felt a bit like a fish out of water up there on San Juan Hill with the Spanish bullets whistling around him. Before and since his days with the Rough Riders, Dave McClure has hardly been out of hailing distance of his horse. You can guess that when you sit with him in his tack room out there at the FairGrounds and watch him lean back in his chair to look down the shed-row. Just to see that the groom is giving Gold Princess or her full sister, Society Lady, their correct share of the rations. Of course, you know by looking at the records that this weather-beaten soft spoken Oklahoman never has been away from racing since he came back from Cuba. He was a jockey until 1908, took a whirl at the rodeos and is still ranked as one of the five best rodeo hands of all time. Now he's been training horses for years. WON AT CHURCHILL His ace is Gold Princess, the four-year old filly by Prince Pal from Gold Nugget which Dave bred on his farm outside Oklahoma City. It's a farm that is surrounded by oil derricks and some day soon 60-year old- Dave may be rolling in gold from that oil. It's doubtful, however, that all the gold in the world could give Dave any more enjoyment than this daughter of Gold Nugget. It's a sure bet that Dave will never be any happier than he was last Oct. 31 at Churchill Downs when Gold Princess won the Autumn Handicap, beating the brilliant Miss Dogwood, and breaking the hearts of her hard boot backers. How Dave loves to beat those Kentuckians. Gold Princess, incidentally, makes her first start of the year today in the Langlade Handicap here.

Family Stories and Memories

- David was childhood friends with Will Rogers. The two were classmates at Kemper Military Academy. There was a story told of the two boys playing pranks. At one point they "skipped" school together, were caught, and suspended for a period of time.
- We were told that at one time Teddy Roosevelt was visiting Oklahoma City. He stayed in the home of David and his family [Great-Grandmother Mary Ellen.]
- His father, William John McClure, had the first rodeo arena in Oklahoma City built on his property. We have a photo of David the day he won his first calf roping contest.

- The stadium fell during the first rodeo, and someone was killed.
- His ranch was at the SE corner of Memorial and MacArthur Blvd.
- Many articles appeared in horse racing magazines about David McClure.
- While his horses were running at Latonia Race Track in Covington, Kentucky, he went across the Ohio River to Cincinnati, Ohio, where he met his future wife, Grace Anna Jones. We were told the story that she was a beautiful girl of 16. She was performing on stage. He was smitten, but the story goes that her parents wouldn't let any man "court" her. Dave soon won over her parents. They were married in 1905.

Let us be judged by our actions

Chapter 6
GRACE ANNA (JONES) McCLURE (LOWRANCE)
1889 - 1974

Illustration 217. Grace Anna (Jones) McClure (Lowrance)

[3]Grace lived in the Cincinnati, Ohio, area until she met Dave McClure. As a child she performed on stage singing and dancing under the name "Baby." She had two brothers and a sister. Her father worked for the railroad; her mother was a dramatic arts teacher. Her parents divorced and then her mother supplemented their income as a seamstress and by taking in boarders at their home. Grace's life changed when she married Dave McClure and moved to Oklahoma. She adapted to ranch life. Years later, after Dave's death, she even purchased her own ranch when she married her second husband, Oscar Lowrance—their two ranches were only a few miles from each other.

From the Records
[3]Grace Anna (Jones) McClure (Lowrance)
  b. June 27, 1889, Cincinnati, Ohio
  m. [3]David Victor McClure, June 20, 1905, Cincinnati, Ohio
    Oscar K. Lowrance, Sr., April 29, 1946, Sulphur, Oklahoma
  f. Presbyterian
  d. January 14, 1974; age 84, Sulphur, Oklahoma
    Funeral Thursday, January, 17, Dunn Funeral Home, Oklahoma City
  b. January 17, 1974, Fairlawn Cemetery, Oklahoma City

Clubs:
  Eastern Star Chapter in Britton, Oklahoma
  State 89ers Association

Parents:
  Father: Homer Jones
    b. January 30, 1849
    d. Chillicothe, Ross County, Ohio—or Cincinnati, Hamilton County, Ohio
    m. Rebecca Eveline Armsey, July 4, 1871, Ross County, Ohio
      Homer was a railroad engineer. He ran the "B&O" Hog Engines.
      He divorced Rebecca in the early 1890s. Possibly moved to Indianapolis
      after the divorce.
  Mother: Rebecca Eveline Armsey Jones
    b. September 22, 1849
    m. 1871
    d. April 29, 1916, on a Saturday, Dayton, Montgomery City, Ohio
      Died at the home of George Armsey, 257 S. Paint Street, Dayton, Ohio
        Rebecca was a dramatic arts teacher. After the divorce she rented
        rooms to boarders, sold items door to door, and started a shop
        that did sewing.
    Father: Leonard B. Armsey
      b. 1821
      d. 1892
    Mother: Ann Botkin
      b. 1824
      d. 1899
      b. Chillicothe, Ross County, Ohio, at Greenlawn Cemetery

Siblings

Leonard Franklin Jones
- b. September 1, 1875; Christened June 22, 1877
- d. June 23, 1877
- b. June 24, 1877

Anna (Annie) Lula Jones
- b. September 22, 1877
- m. February 10, 1897, at Covington, Kentucky
    She was a pianist and attended the Cincinnati Conservatory of Music
- d. October 27, 1906

Charles Homer Jones
- b. October 10 (or 15), 1880
- m. March 29, 1900, at Covington, Kentucky
    Charles was an artist. Later he became a Mess Sergeant in Company D, 45th United States Infantry, during World War I. He became an architect.

Children:

[4]William John McClure
- b. July 6, 1907, Latonia, Kentucky
- m. January 3, 1944, Velma Chrystel McClure, Oklahoma City, Oklahoma (Yes, correct maiden name; no relation prior to marriage)
    Children: [5]Mary Ellen McClure, 1945 (Randall)
    [5]Veta Louise McClure, 1948 (Roberts)
- d. February 10, 1970, Aransas Pass, Texas
- b. Fairlawn Cemetery, Oklahoma City, Oklahoma

[4]Veta Ann McClure
- b. March 10, 1912, Oklahoma City, Oklahoma
- m. Robert Wolcott Meals, aka "Three Square"
    - b. ~ 1911, Nova Scotia
    - d. January 2, 1988
        Children: [5]Robert Wolcott Meals ll, 1936
        [5]David Meals, 1940
- d. March 25, 1948, in Ankara, Turkey
- b. Memorial Cemetery, Edmond, Oklahoma

[4]Guy Victor McClure
    b. January 15, 1927, Oklahoma City, Oklahoma
    m. Thamar Perkins
    Children: [5]Charles David, b. January 21, 1953
             [5]Guy Vincent, b. July 20, 1954
             [5]Dewey Allen, b. May 18, 1957
    d. July 18, 1961
    b. Memorial Cemetery, Edmond, Oklahoma

[3]Grace was on stage singing and performing beginning at age 12. At age 16, David saw her perform and wanted to meet her. Her mother was always with Grace when she was on stage and did not allow boys/men to approach her. It was only when David "won over" her mother that he was allowed to meet Grace. On stage she was billed as "Baby." Her favorite song was *Handicap*. Her costume was one like racing colors worn by jockeys. Grace attended Catholic schools. Father Mackey was her priest and teacher.

Ohio Years

Illustration 218. Grace and her brother performing

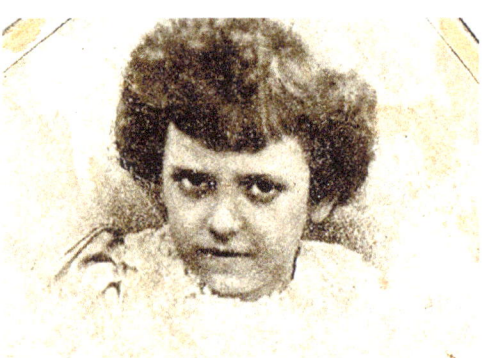

Illustration 219. Young Grace

Illustration 220. Return address on envelope

Illustration 221. Grace in height of fashion hats

Illustration 222. Grace and friend

Illustration 223. Grace (right) and friend and Man in the Moon

Illustration 224. Grace in a "lawn" dress

Grace Anna (Jones) McClure's Timeline

1904 U. S. Army engineers begin work on the Panama Canal on May 4, 1904.

Married David Victor McClure, June 20, 1904, Cincinnati, Ohio
Moved to Oklahoma City, Oklahoma, with her new husband

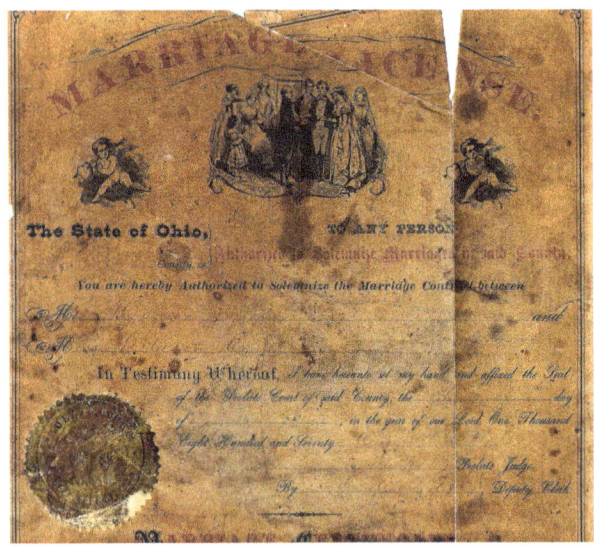

Illustration 225. Grace and David's marriage certificate

Illustration 226. Wedding photograph of Grace and David

Illustration 227. Dave and Grace on honeymoon

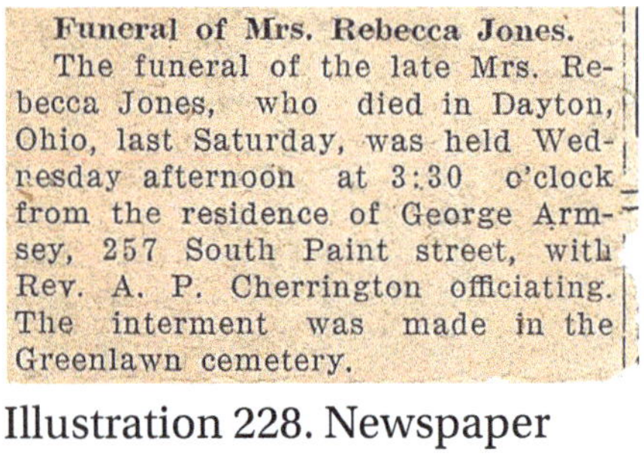

Funeral of Mrs. Rebecca Jones.
The funeral of the late Mrs. Rebecca Jones, who died in Dayton, Ohio, last Saturday, was held Wednesday afternoon at 3:30 o'clock from the residence of George Armsey, 257 South Paint street, with Rev. A. P. Cherrington officiating. The interment was made in the Greenlawn cemetery.

Illustration 228. Newspaper announcement of her mother's funeral

Illustration 229. Grace and David

Illustration 230. Lovely Grace

1907

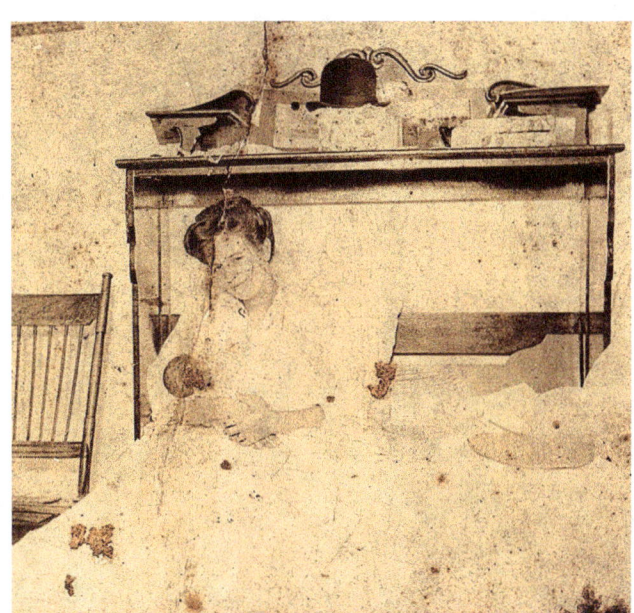

Illustration 231. Birth of first child, William John, July 6, 1907

Illustration 232. Grace with new son, William John

Illustration 233. Dramatic Grace

Illustration 234. Grace in repose

Illustration 235. Grandmother Mary Ellen McClure, Veta Ann, William John, and Grace

Illustration 236. Grace with William John and Veta Ann

Illustration 237. Grace with Veta Ann and William John

1914   World War I, July 28, 1914-November 11, 1918

1916

Illustration 238. Grace's brother, Charles Homer, World War I

Illustration 239. Grace

Illustration 240. Membership in the "Women of '89"

1917   Birth of daughter, Veta Ann

Illustration 241. Visiting Sulphur, Oklahoma: Grace, Veta Ann, William

Illustration 242. Grace and William

1921   March 1, 1921, the first burial held at the Tomb of the Unknown Soldier in Arlington National Cemetery

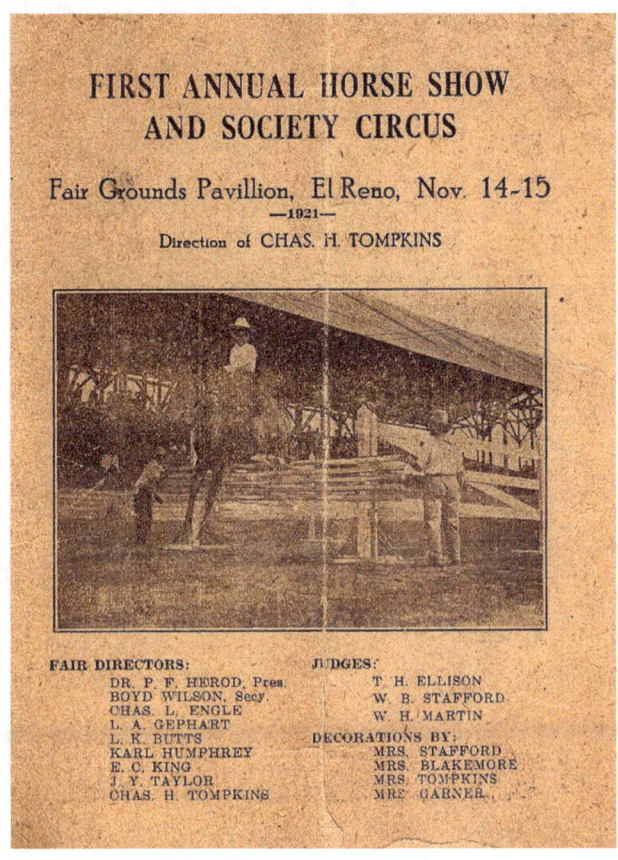

Illustration 243. Horse show Grace participated in

The Daily Oklahoman newspaper article: November 14–15, First Annual Horse Show and Society Circus, El Reno, Oklahoma. Entered in the Class 1 Stallion Division, Mrs. David McClure rode Comet.

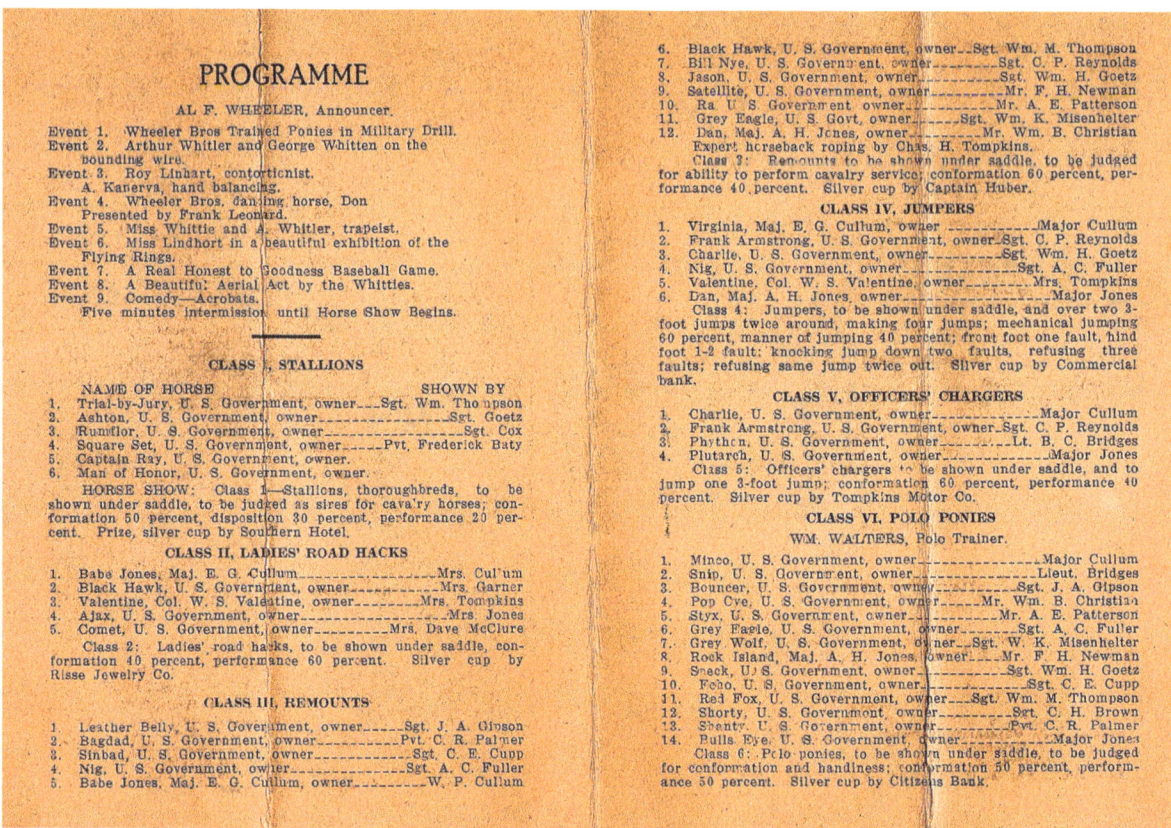

Illustration 244. Horse show program lists Grace as Mrs. Dave McClure competing in Class 11 section.

Illustration 245. Grace could do it all!

Illustration 246. Looking quite at ease

Illustration 247. Grace's friend wearing a fur coat in the hog pen!

Illustration 248. Grace looking content and happy

1923 Warranty Deed, September 29, Grace McClure owned:
Lots: In Block 9: Twenty-nine (29), Thirty (30), Thirty-one (31), Thirty-two (32)
In Block Forty-Six (46): In Block Nine (9): Lots Eight (8), Nine (9), Ten (10), Eleven (11)
All in Britton Heights Addition, Oklahoma City, as shown by the recorded plat

1925   Birth of son, Guy Victor

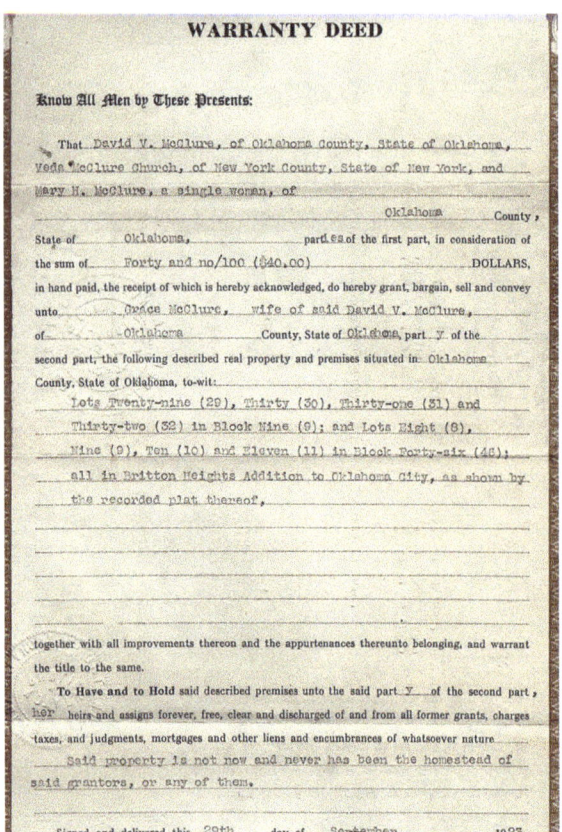

Illustration 249. Real estate deed

Illustration 250. Grace Anna McClure

1936   February 10. State of Kansas, Leavenworth County, Affidavit

   My name is Oscar W. Clark, my present PO is Veterans Administration Hospital Home, Kansas. I desire to state that I have known Charles Jones, formerly Mess Sergeant in Company D, 45th US Infantry during the World War, and have been so acquainted with him since June of 1888, when I was living in Cincinnati, Ohio. I further desire to state that I have known Grace Annie McClure, nee Jones, who at present is a resident of Oklahoma County, Oklahoma and have known her since 1888, when I resided at Cincinnati, Ohio, and I desire to state that I know of my own personal knowledge that the said Charles Jones and Grace Anna McClure, nee Jones, are brother and sister.

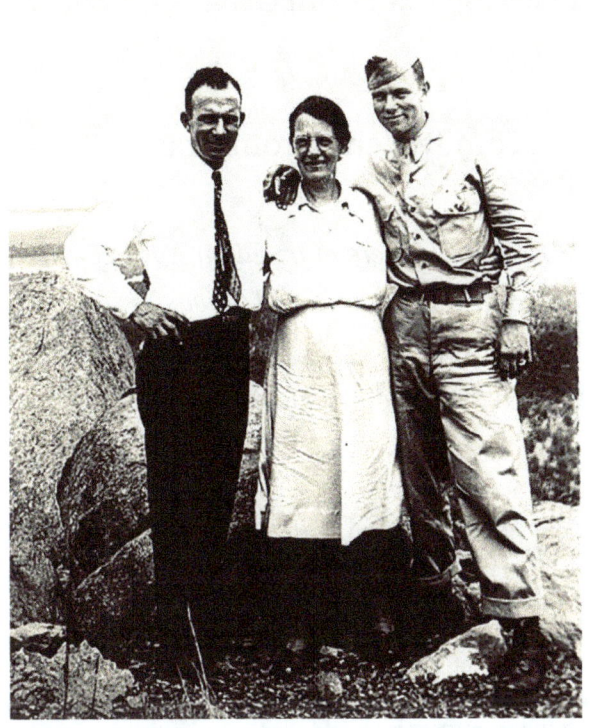

Illustration 251. Grace and her two boys—William John (Bill) and Guy Victor

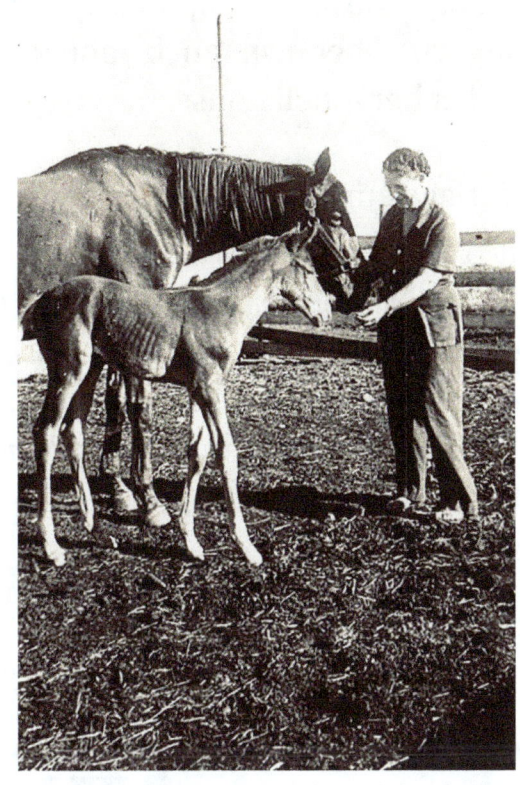

Illustration 252. Grace loved the foals

1944 December 15. [3]David Victor McClure dies.

1946

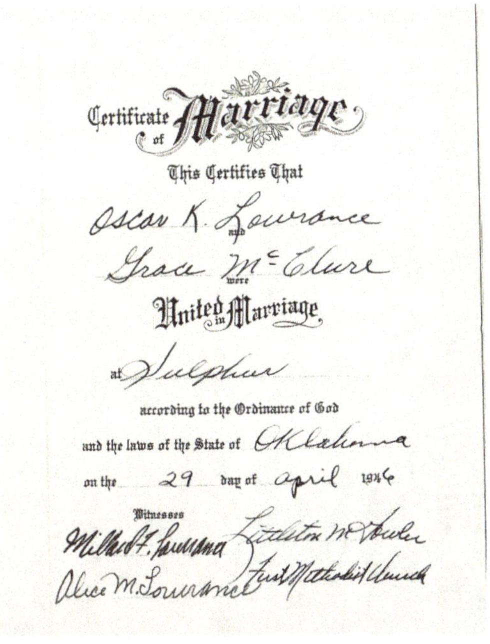

Certificate of Marriage

This Certifies That

Oscar K. Lowrance

and

Grace McClure

were

United in Marriage

at Sulphur

according to the Ordinance of God

and the laws of the State of Oklahoma

on the 29 day of April 1946

Witnesses

Millard F. Lowrance

Littleton M. Fowler

Alice M. Lowrance

First Methodist Church

Illustration 253. Grace's certificate of marriage to Oscar Lowrance

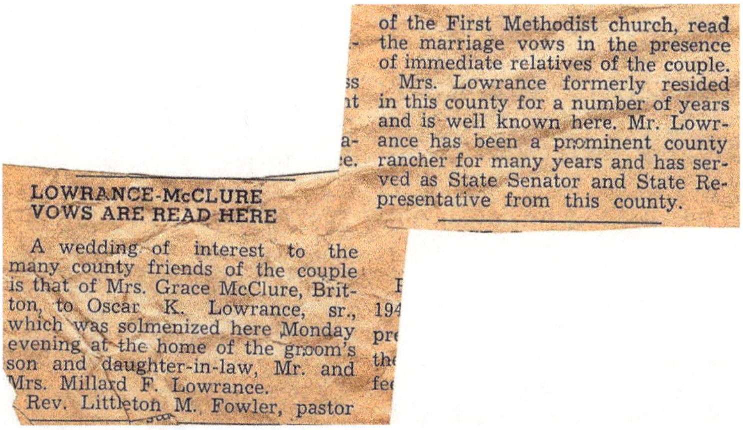

LOWRANCE-McCLURE VOWS ARE READ HERE

A wedding of interest to the many county friends of the couple is that of Mrs. Grace McClure, Britton, to Oscar K. Lowrance, sr., which was solmenized here Monday evening at the home of the groom's son and daughter-in-law, Mr. and Mrs. Millard F. Lowrance.

Rev. Littleton M. Fowler, pastor of the First Methodist church, read the marriage vows in the presence of immediate relatives of the couple.

Mrs. Lowrance formerly resided in this county for a number of years and is well known here. Mr. Lowrance has been a prominent county rancher for many years and has served as State Senator and State Representative from this county.

Illustration 254. Newspaper announcement of McClure-Lowrance wedding

Grace moved to Sulphur, OK, when she married widower Oscar Lowrance. She owned her own ranch about a mile up the road from Oscar's ranch. They lived at her ranch house.

Marriage announcement to the McClure Family: Letter from Grace

My Dear Boy, Chrys, Mary Ellen,

I don't guess you have heard the news but Oscar and I were married on April 29. I know you always liked him and it sure was lonesome being alone and so was he. I am very happy and so is he and I hope you will be too. I am sure_____ will think him fine when she sees him. I am in a hurry right now, so I will write to you later. Heaps of love to all, Mama and Oscar

1964 Newspaper article, Thursday, January 23, Sulphur, Oklahoma

Illustration 255. Feature news article

O.K. LOWRANCE, SR., IS HONORED ON 81ST BIRTHDAY HERE ON SUNDAY 17

O. K. Lowrance, Sr., South of the city, was delightfully surprised Friday evening, January 17, when a group of relatives and friends entertained with a covered dish dinner in celebration of his 81st birthday. The affair was in the home of Mr. and Mrs. Vernon Wells, south of the city, and the decorations were most unusual. The long table was laid with a colorful red and white cloth and old-fashioned coal oil lamps were placed at intervals down the center. During the serving all lights were turned out and the guests ate by lamplight. The guests sang happy birthday to Mr. Lowrance, and the time after dinner was spent visiting. The honored guest received many nice remembrances among them two birthday cakes, one made by Mrs. Lowrance, attractively decorated and topped with eight candles each representing 10 years and another one for one year, totaling 81 years; the other cake, a delicious chocolate, was made by Tommy Wells. Enjoying the occasion with Mr. Lowrance and Mrs. Lowrance, Mr. and Mrs. Vernon Wells, Tommy and Scotty; Mr. and Mrs. Oscar Lowrance, Jr., and Marilyn Sue and Phillip; Mr. and Mrs. Millard Lowrance and Linda; Mr. and Mrs. W. Be. Lowrance, Mr. and Mrs. Joe Taylor, Mr. and Mrs. Bob Lowrance and Bobby Sue, Mr. and Mrs. Esco Chadwick and H. A. Pittman[9].

October 5

Dear Son and Family,

Well, I rented the flat in Keys Apartment House. It has four rooms and a bath; All electric! - so it is a very nice place. I hope you all will like it. It's on the first floor, and has a nice place for my car and pickup. I am going to start moving our things in tomorrow. I was so afraid that Oscar would not like it, but he was just as nice as could be. He said anything I wanted to do was all right with him. I went out and cooked supper tonight and Oscar and I sure did eat! I had fried chicken and we ate it all! Well, it is getting late so I will hang up for now. Heaps of Love, Mama

---

[9]Illustration 255 on facing page and adapted text on this page reproduced courtesy of *Sulphur Times Democrat Archives*

Illustration 256. Grace and Oscar in Sulphur

Illustration 257. Grace and son, Bill

Illustration 258. Bill, Grace, and Oscar

Illustration 259. left to right: granddaughter Veta Louise; Grace; granddaughter Mary Ellen; daughter-in-law Chrystel; and grandson-in-law George Randall

1969 Newspaper article, Sulphur, Oklahoma

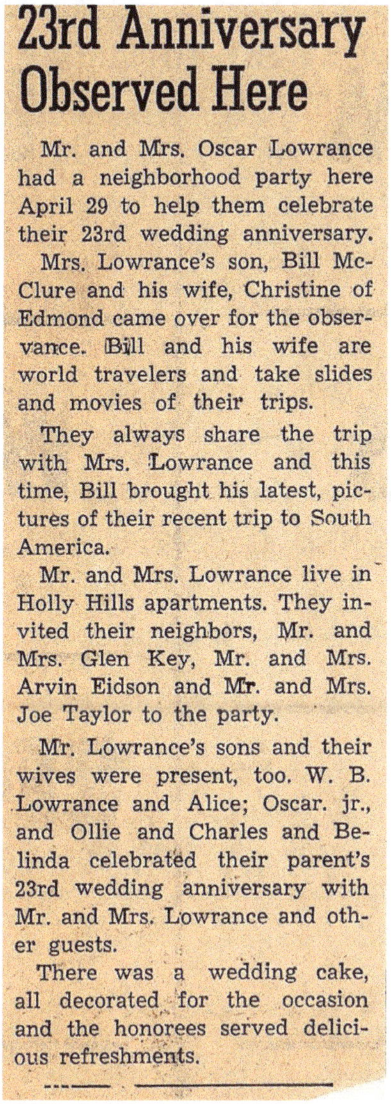

23rd Anniversary Observed Here

Mr. and Mrs. Oscar Lowrance had a neighborhood party here April 29 to help them celebrate their 23rd wedding anniversary.

Mrs. Lowrance's son, Bill McClure and his wife, Christine of Edmond came over for the observance. Bill and his wife are world travelers and take slides and movies of their trips.

They always share the trip with Mrs. Lowrance and this time, Bill brought his latest, pictures of their recent trip to South America.

Mr. and Mrs. Lowrance live in Holly Hills apartments. They invited their neighbors, Mr. and Mrs. Glen Key, Mr. and Mrs. Arvin Eidson and Mr. and Mrs. Joe Taylor to the party.

Mr. Lowrance's sons and their wives were present, too. W. B. Lowrance and Alice; Oscar. jr., and Ollie and Charles and Belinda celebrated their parent's 23rd wedding anniversary with Mr. and Mrs. Lowrance and other guests.

There was a wedding cake, all decorated for the occasion and the honorees served delicious refreshments.

Illustration 260. Anniversary account

23RD ANNIVERSARY OBSERVED HERE

Mr. and Mrs. Oscar Lowrance had a neighborhood party here April 23 to help them celebrate their 23rd wedding anniversary party. Mrs. Lowrance's son, Bill McClure and his wife, Chrys of Edmond came over for the observance. Bill and his wife are world travelers and take slides and movies of their trips. They always share the trip with Mrs. Lowrance and this time, Bill brought his latest pictures of their recent trip to South America. Mr. and Mrs. Lowrance live in Holly Hills Apartments. They invited their neighbors Mr. and Mrs. Glenn Chi, Mr. and Mrs. Arvin Edison, and Mr. and Mrs. Joe Taylor to the party. Mr. Lowrance's sons and their wives were present too. WB Lowrance and Alice, Oscar Junior and Ollie and Charles Lowrance[10].

[10]Illustration 260 and adapted text reproduced courtesy of *Sulphur Times Democrat Archives*

1970s Newspaper article, Sulphur, Oklahoma

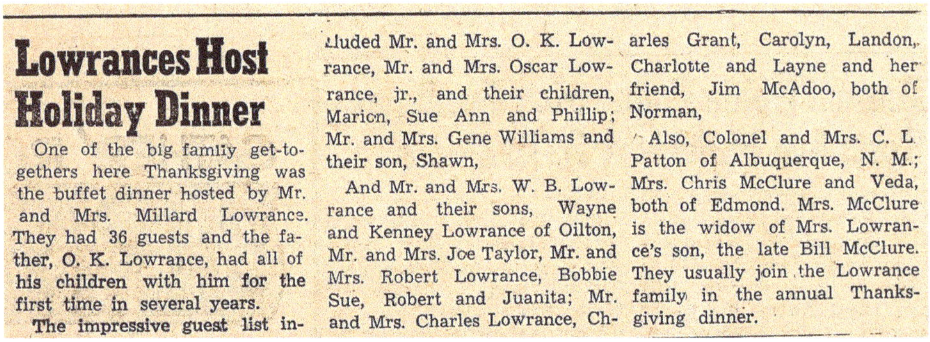

LOWRANCE'S HOST HOLIDAY DINNER

One of the big family get-togethers here Thanksgiving was the buffet dinner hosted by Mr. and Mrs. Millard Lowrance. They had 36 guests and the father, O.K. Lowrance, had all of his children with him for the first time in several years. The impressive guest list included Mr. and Mrs. O.K. Lowrance, Mr. and Mrs. Oscar Lowrance, Jr., and their children, Marion, Sue, Ann, and Phillip. Mr. and Mrs. Gene Williams and their son, Shawn. Mr. and Mrs. W.B. Lowrance and their sons, Wayne and Kenney Lowrance of Oilton, Mr. and Mrs. Joe Taylor, Mr. and Mrs. Robert Lowrance, Bobbie, Sue, Robert and Juanita, Mrs. And Mrs. Charles Lowrance, Charles Grant, Carolyn, Landon, Charlotte, and Layne and her friend, Jim McAdoo, both of Norman. Also, Colonel and Mrs. C.L. Patton of Albuquerque, N.M, Mrs. Chrys McClure and Veta, both of Edmond. Mrs. McClure is the widow of Mrs. Lowrance's son, the late Bill McClure. They usually join the Lowrance family in the annual Thanksgiving dinner[11].

Illustration 261. Thanksgiving celebration

[11] Illustration 261 and adapted text on this page reproduced courtesy of *Sulphur Times Democrat Archives*

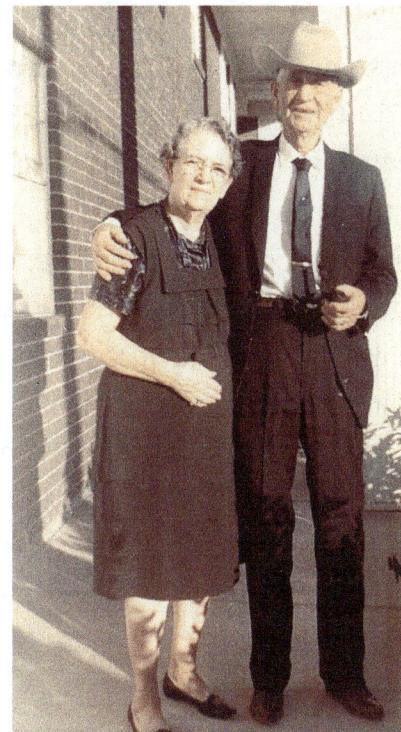

Illustration 262. Grace and Oscar Lowrance

1974

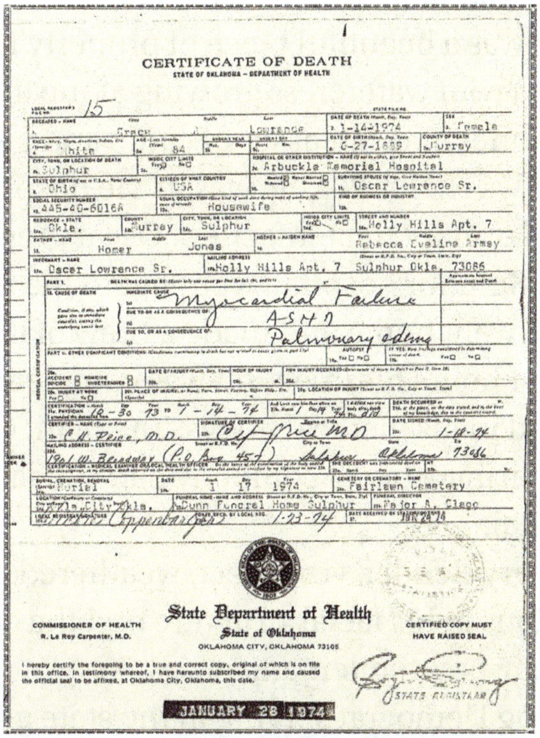

CERTIFICATE OF DEATH

STATE OF OKLAHOMA – DEPARTMENT OF HEALTH

Local Registrar's File No. 15

Deceased – Name: Grace Lowrance

Date of Death: 1-14-1974

Sex: Female

Race: White

Age: 84

Date of Birth: 6-27-1889

County of Death: Murray

City, Town, or Location of Death: Sulphur

Hospital or Other Institution: Arbuckle Memorial Hospital

State of Birth: Ohio

Citizen of What Country: USA

Surviving Spouse: Oscar Lowrance Sr.

Social Security Number: 445-40-6016A

Usual Occupation: Housewife

Residence – State: Okla.

County: Murray

City, Town, or Location: Sulphur

Street and Number: Holly Hills Apt. 7

Father – Name: Homer Jones

Mother – Maiden Name: Rebecca Eveline Armey

Informant – Name: Oscar Lowrance Sr.

Mailing Address: Holly Hills Apt. 7 Sulphur Okla. 73086

Cause of Death – Immediate Cause: Myocardial Failure

Due to, or as a consequence of: ASHD

Due to, or as a consequence of: Pulmonary edema

Certification – Physician: 12-30 73 to 1-14-74

Certifier – Name: C.H. Price, M.D.

Signature of Certifier: C H Price MD

Date Signed: 1-18-74

Mailing Address – Certifier: 1901 W. Broadway (P.O. Box 457) Sulphur Oklahoma 73086

Burial, Cremation, Removal: Burial

Date: 1 17 1974

Cemetery or Crematory – Name: Fairlawn Cemetery

Location: Okla. City Okla.

Funeral Home – Name and Address: Dunn Funeral Home Sulphur

Funeral Director: Major A. Clagg

Date Recd. by Local Reg.: 1-23-74

Date Received by State Registrar: JAN 24 74

State Department of Health

State of Oklahoma

OKLAHOMA CITY, OKLAHOMA 73105

COMMISSIONER OF HEALTH

R. Le Roy Carpenter, M.D.

CERTIFIED COPY MUST HAVE RAISED SEAL

I hereby certify the foregoing to be a true and correct copy, original of which is on file in this office. In testimony whereof, I have hereunto subscribed my name and caused the official seal to be affixed, at Oklahoma City, Oklahoma, this date.

STATE REGISTRAR

JANUARY 28 1974

Illustration 263. Grace's certificate of death, January 14, 1974. She died at age 84 in Sulphur, Oklahoma.

Sulphur newspaper

Rites Scheduled On Thursday for Mrs. Grace Lowrance, 84, wife of Oscar K. Lowrance, Sr., died January 14 here. Mrs. Lowrance had resided in Oklahoma City until coming to Sulphur in 1946. Mrs. Lowrance was born June 27, 1889 in Cincinnati, Ohio. She was a member of the First Presbyterian Church, the Eastern Star chapter in Britton and the state 89ers Association. Funeral services will be held Thursday, January 17 at 10 AM from the chapel of the Dunn funeral home with Reverend C. J. Westhof officiating. Burial will be at Fairlawn cemetery in Oklahoma City at 1:30 PM with Dunn funeral home in charge of arrangements. In addition to her husband, Oscar K. Lowrance, Sr., Mrs. Lowrance is survived by a daughter-in-law, Mrs. William J. McClure, Edmond; a daughter, Mrs. Grace Patton, Sulfur; four sons, W. B. Lowrance, Oscar Lowrance Jr., Robert Lowrance and Charles Lowrance all of Sulfur: seven grandchildren and two great grandchildren[12].

Memories

1. Oscar was a widower and longtime friend of David and Grace. He was a graduate of Oklahoma University. He was also a former Oklahoma State Representative and Oklahoma State Senator. He was part Indian (Chickasaw). His large ranch was about 1 mile south of Grace's ranch in Sulphur. He raised cattle and hogs. It was a beautiful piece of property filled with huge trees. It had beautiful lakes with watercress growing along the sides. There was also a field with lots of bones and carcasses of cattle and pigs.
2. Once when Oscar was in his 70s, he was in the hospital for about two weeks being treated for a urinary tract infection. Oscar grew impatient, checked himself out of the Sulphur hospital, went out to the ranch where he cut some plant material. He went home and made a brew of the plants. Drank the brew and within 24 hours his infection was completely gone. Dr. George was curious and looked in his medical books. The plant Oscar had used is the same plant the pharmaceutical company had used to make medications given in the hospital.
3. Oscar was a tall, very slender, very erect, weathered cowboy. His Indian heritage was obvious in his facial structure and the color of his skin. He was the last of a true cowboy gentleman.
4. Oscar was a lifelong Democrat serving in the state government.
5. His daughters from his first marriage were the first-place winners of the National Barrel Riding competitions for three years in a row.

[12]Adapted text reproduced courtesy of *Sulphur Times Democrat Archives*

6. When Grace married Oscar and moved to Sulphur, she brought with her a ranch hand who had worked for her and David for many years. He was called Ol' Tim. He was a devoted employee/part cowboy who lived in a small house on her ranch. He never talked much, but he kept her ranch running smoothly. Oscar had his hands full running his own ranch—so, Tim pretty much ran Grace's.
7. Grace was a very good rider. One of her favorite horses was a Palomino named *Pumpkin*. He was a large, docile horse with perfect conformation and appearance, with a full white mane and tail. Many of the rodeo queens in southern Oklahoma knew of Pumpkin. Grandmother let several of them borrow Pumpkin to ride in the rodeo parades of the region.
8. When I (Mary Ellen) was in 7th grade, I was allowed to ride the train from Edmond to Davis, Oklahoma, a town seven miles west of Sulphur. Grandmother picked me up and I had two wonderful weeks at her ranch. Most days I spent riding Pumpkin on her ranch. I remember that she took me to the First Presbyterian Church with her. At the time I thought that she was having a good time "showing off her granddaughter." When it was time for me to go home to Edmond, grandmother drove me back to Davis and put me on the train.
9. Sulphur, Oklahoma, is the location of many hot mineral springs. Some of them had a strong odor. There are a lot of parks and picnic areas around the hot springs. It had long been a retreat for Indians in the area. A large stone hotel has been constructed. Sulphur was a destination community.
10. Grandmother Grace had a very fun and infectious laugh. She laughed often. Her hair never turned completely white or gray but always was mostly black with gray in it.

1969

Illustration 264. Oscar Lowrance

Article in T*he Oklahoma Cowman* about Oscar Lowrance. For most of 86 years, Oscar Lowrance had roped and ridden, bulldogged, and skinned broncs. Even in the legislature of the state, he still considered himself "just a Cowboy." This article is included in the family history because it is a good description of ranch life in Indian Territory.

ALWAYS A COWBOY

Dust rose in an orange colored cloud from the arena as a lanky Brahma calf sped along just ahead of the rider on the big roan horse. Suddenly the loop buzzed out of nowhere, snaked around the calf's neck, locked on, and spun him in a heap on the ground. In one fluid motion, the man stepped from the horse, slipped down the rope and was there to latch onto the animal as he staggered to his feet. A quick jerk at the flanks, a grunt and the calf slammed against the ground with a thud. In its legs were caught, the pigging string went twice around and snubbed and up went the arms. 23 seconds. The year was 1967 and the man was Oscar Lowrance, and at the time he was 84 years old. This is 1969 and Oscar Lowrance still ropes a little in competition and has his eye on a win at the old man's roping at Stamford, Texas for this year, a victory that has been eluding him every year since he has been eligible to compete.

"Dammit," he has said with a sparkle in his eye, "my times have been good, and once even stood till there were only two Ropers left, but I've never been able to take a first." Oscar Lowrance is one of a few cowboys left who learned the sport from doing the work back in a time when the events now competed in were just a part of an everyday job. Roping and bulldogging were practiced out of necessity while caring for cattle, and skinning a bronc was something you did to get him ready to put to work. He was born at Boiling Springs, 4 miles south of the present town of Sulphur, January 17, 1883, and from that day to this, has been in his heart nothing but a cowboy. Oscar's father was a white intermarried citizen of the Chickasaw nation and founded the family ranch in 1876. He bought the improvements on a ranch close to the Springs since there was no purchase of land in those days. A man just ran his cattle on an agreed area of range and owned the improvements. There were no fences and the cattle mixed and mingled as they chose and were separated annually during the round up by brand. The elder Lowrance was resented by the Indians, probably, in the main because most whites were a little resented, and also because one of the Indian officials wanted the location where he had made his headquarters. He was harassed for several years until his sons grew old enough to bring the matter to a head and the harassment stopped. Before Oscar Lowrance could walk well he was on horseback and out with the cows. By the time he was 12, he was a hand, and his main job was checking the trail herds passing through for local brands and cutting out the Chickasaw cattle that had joined up with the herds. He had learned to rope on the family sheep and goats as a little kid and he put this skill to good use in his brand checking charge. He would pick up a trail herd from East Texas down for the grass in the Cherokee Strip, and would ride along with it cutting out local ranchers' cattle. If a brand on a particular steer was unreadable, out would come the rope and the rodeo was on. Lowrance would put a loop on him, ride by him in a hurry and "bust" a steer to get the job done. He learned to bulldog the same way, by doing it when he either lacked a rope, or just had a good flat stretch of ground and did it for the sheer joy of doing it. As a youngster, one of Lowrance's jobs was to carry water to the ash hopper to make soap. His mother often said he didn't grow into a big man because he expanded so much effort in this pursuit. He himself allowed that it is hard to imagine the vast amount of water required to make soap this way. He was also responsible for gathering bones out on the range for use in the soap. Another menial chore was the planting of sweet potato shoots just after a rain. This one, Lowrance allowed, he resented thoroughly, especially when the older boys rode off to check cattle and left him with the sweet potatoes. He does remember, however, times when sweet potatoes became the family's staple diet, when meat ran out and game was scarce, and in these times neighboring Indian families were often furnished enough yams to get through on. The family always had plenty of butter and milk to go with them. Lowrance attended the Indian school at Buckhorn, nearby, and was taught by a teacher named Gibbs, who Lowrance remembers as a mean #/'s$&$. He was paid a dollar a month per child and was quite a recruiter. At one time he had 60 kids jammed into the little log schoolhouse, and administered a policy of spare the rod and spoil the child with a ferocity that was hard to believe. His career ended when after an argument, Gibbs went home and got a Winchester and killed a man named Johnson. He immediately left for a healthier area. In 1891, Lowrance went away to another Indian school and found survival on the sowbelly, cornbread and coffee that was the students' staple diet next to impossible. So one night he just left and went back to the ranch. He attended high school in Davis then went to Hargrove College at Ardmore and to the University of Oklahoma in 1903 and '04. In the meantime he spent all his summers and holidays working cattle and perfecting his skills on the back of a horse. One day in 1898 he watched his first steer roping and was interested in the technical aspects of it. He watched how the contestants tied their steers and probably went back to the ranch and practiced until he thought he had it down at least passably. It wasn't until the summer of 1901 that he first tried it in competition, and this was a steer roping at Roth. He competed, tied with a respectable time and won handily. From there on rodeoing became a part of his activities, and he was able to pick up a little money from time to time. He allows that he never expected to win, but that he sure enjoyed it, and his winnings made the thing a paying proposition. In 1904, his brother was running the family place and was spending most of his time on farming and was to a degree letting the cattle go, so Oscar dropped out of school and came home to manage the cattle operation. He was often in the saddle 18 hours a day after that, taking care of from 350 to 400 cows. This was rain or shine, sleet or snow, not many missing many meals but postponing a bunch, and he says that there was a question in his mind as to whether this sort of schedule would ruin his health, but it didn't seem to bother it any. By 1907 he had made a name for himself in rodeo circles, staging a bulldogging exhibition and riding the ranked bronc anybody could find to earn an entry fee for the roping. This was before bulldogging was an event. He did this at Oiltown at a rodeo celebrating statehood and through some chicanery was given a big rank old stag steer to rope. At this time, he didn't ordinarily use a trip, relying on his horse to bust the steer hard enough to allow for a tie. But this steer was quite a bit stouter than usual, and so he changed methods, laid him a trip, and won handily, much to the chagrin of the participants who had gone to the trouble of getting him that particular animal. In 1912, he competed at Calgary, Alberta in what amounted to the world's championship. The finest performers in the nation were there, and Lowrance entered steer roping, bulldogging, and bareback Bronc riding. He did not fare as well as expected in the roping, but was one of the six finalists in bareback bronc riding. In bulldogging he won handily. His first steer went down when he hit him for a really good time, but the second was a little too stout and threatened to carry him right out of the other end of the arena. Despairing of any other way, Lowrance swung his legs and lower body between the steer's four legs and brought him crashing to the ground in a respectable time. He was asked later if this was not a dangerous stunt. "Sure," he said "but there was $500 and a saddle riding on it." He only weighed 135 pounds at the time. In 1914 his boys were getting to an age where he thought big-time rodeo was bad for them and he quit. But a few years later, he started roping calves with them in competition in Oklahoma and has been at it ever since. In 1927 his name was put up for the office of state representative from Murray County. "I didn't run the first time because I really wasn't interested in going, but I carried all three precincts on nothing but my daddy's good name. If the voters had known me personally, I probably would never have won." he said. Before he was through he served three terms in the Oklahoma House and one in the Senate. He was an author of the first bill to provide state aid for weak schools, was co-author of the first Homestead exemption law, and was a strong opponent of legislation providing that clear title could be given to land through a tax sale. This was the heart of the depression, and he was fighting to protect the ranchers' and farmers' interest. He was only out of the legislature one term before the measure passed. Lowrance acknowledges that though he was a Democrat, he was a rebel and was at times a thorn in the side of the governor, especially "Alfalfa" Bill Murray who worked actively for his defeat. He did not get it done and the two men managed to maintain a sort of armed truce throughout their 10 years together. The thought of the old days makes Oscar Lowrance's eyes a bit misty. "It is hard to imagine today what this country was like under the rule of the Chickasaws. It was broad and green and uncrowded. There were no taxes, no fences and no law to speak of, and all things considered, the people got along pretty well together. This was a time when outlaws from all over the country came to Indian Territory to avoid prosecution for their wrongdoings. Many of these became upright citizens of the Indian nations and many died with their boots on in disputes over this or that. Still others continued their outlaw ways and were taken in tow by the U. S. Marshals who were sparsely scattered around the Territory and found justice in Judge Parker's court at Fort Smith. People of the Territory ask few questions about a man's background and even fewer about his disputes as long as they, themselves, weren't directly involved. It was against the law to carry a pistol and those who were arrested with one in their possession were fined $50, but most people carried one anyway," he said. When Oscar's father, W. B. Lowrance was harassed by the Indians in the beginning, he allowed it because he had no choice. The territorial police would come to his place and arrest him on some charge or other, take him to Tishomingo and put him in jail, then release him in a few days with the announcement that the charges, whatever they were, had been dropped. He was never formally charged with anything, and he was never tried for any offense, but over the years spent a good amount of time in jail in this way. When Lowrance and his brother Bob grew into pretty good-sized boys, these incidents continued to happen. And Bob, who is something of a hothead, got fed up with the situation, finagled a deputy sheriff's commission, strapped on a big 45 pistol, took Oscar in tow, and they went down to the courthouse in Tishomingo. There Bob accosted a large group of Indian officials on the street, and insulted them thoroughly and announced in a loud voice that the harassment of their father better stop then and there or he was personally going to deal with it in a way that they would all regret for the rest of their lives, which wouldn't be very long. Oscar said he knew the shooting was about to start since there were about 50 or so Indians in the group, so he found some cover and waited out the harangue, pistol in hand. Bob stood in the middle of the street with his hands at his side and told them off. Then both boys mounted their horses and rode home. Lowrance says he still doesn't see why they weren't killed, but this incident ended the harassment. Life in the Chickasaw nation was good, according to Lowrance, but it demanded a very hardy kind of individual. Everyone helped everyone else as much as they could when times were hard or when illness or misfortune struck one family or another. Lowrance recalls one incident when an unknown Indian rode up to him one day and asked "are you Oscar Lowrance?" He replied that he was. The Indian told him that his wife and child were ill and that he needed six dollars for medicine. Lowrance promptly gave it to him and said that he would never have considered turning him down, though he knew that he would never see the money again. He knew full well that if their positions had been reversed, the Indian would've helped him. Along this same line, there were never any orphans in evidence around the Territory. If a child or children lost their parents, someone always took them into their home and raised them just as if they were their own. It was a fine, free, and exciting time to live. The people were rough and ready and had a spirit that carried them through hard times and gave them an exuberance for living and a will to build a great state. These qualities are evidenced in Oscar Lowrance and those like him who remain. They are the products of their era and this state will be a little less bright and exciting when they are gone. Today, Oscar Lowrance is still a rancher, he goes to work every day and puts in a pretty fair day's work for a youngster of 86. He has cattle and hogs and some sons and a little more help than he had managing the herd back in 1904 and 1905, but he still gives it a fit and is a pretty hard taskmaster. He may ride horseback a little less than before, but he still has his eye for cattle and through it all, he's still just a Cowboy.

[4]Margurite Vinson McClure

Our Mystery Child

No real records exist for Margurite. Here is what we do have:
b. March 10, 1912

On cover of pamphlet: "This score card will give satisfactory results only when used in connection with the explanatory literature which can be accrued from the Better Babies Bureau of the Women's Home Companion, 381 Fourth Avenue, New York City."

Better Babies Standard Score Card (an official health record):
  Entry No. 131, Division 132/3011
  Score: 94%. Age in Months: 31
  City Dweller
  Name: Marguerite Vinson McClure
  City and State: Oklahoma City, Oklahoma
  Street and Number: 1017 N. Central
  Weight at birth: 7 ½ lbs.
  Strong or weak at birth: strong
  2 child
  Breast-fed
  Sleeps alone: No
  If not, with whom: Mother
  Windows open: check, How many: 2
  Father's name: Dave V. McClure
    Occupation: Live stock
  Mother's maiden name: Grace Jones
    Age 25; Nationality, American
    Occupation: Housewife
  Has birth been registered: No
  Contest held at Oklahoma City, Okla.
    By: Oklahoma State Farm & Exposition

Date: September 23rd, October 3rd, 1914

Cradle Roll Certificate

This Certifies that Margurite Vinson McClure was enrolled as a member of the Cradle Roll, Maywood Presbyterian Sunday School of Oklahoma City, Oklahoma on the 18th day of June, 1914. Born on the 10th day of March 1912.

Cradle Roll Promotion Certificate

Certifies that Margurite Vinson McClure, Having reached the required age, is hereby promoted from the Cradle Roll to the Beginners' Department of the Maywood Presbyterian Sunday School of Oklahoma City, Oklahoma. Date June 13, 1915

With a lack of historical evidence, we can only surmise Margurite's place in the family. After reading what we do possess and comparing her information with others, I think that she was the second born child of Guy Vincent and Bernice McAdams McClure. It appears that she spent time with her aunt and uncle, Grace and David McClure and because they list themselves as parents on the health report, I can only assume they thought that kept things simpler. I do remember a few times during my childhood when the name Margurite would be mentioned, but certainly it was a rare occasion.

Let us be judged by our actions

Chapter 7
VETA ELLEAN McCLURE
1881 - 1963

Illustration 265. Veta Ellean McClure

[3]Veta Ellean McClure was born on the 7C Ranch in the Choctaw Nation of Indian Territory. She spent her first eight years on the ranch. The family moved into Oklahoma City April 22, 1889, during the famous land run. She was seventeen years old at the time of her father's death.

With a sparkling personality and a strong will, she was a "larger than life" person. People were drawn to her by her warm personality. She loved life and lived it to the fullest. Her adventuresome life led her over the globe; she "collected" homes. During the Great Depression she was a compulsive buyer of art and artifacts from the great houses and palaces of Europe and China.

From the Records

³Veta Ellean McClure
- b. March 27, 1881, Liberty Hill, Indian Territory
- f. Presbyterian
- d. August 23, 1963, Oklahoma City, Oklahoma
- b. Fairlawn Cemetery, Oklahoma City, Oklahoma, in the McClure family plot

Parents:
- ²William John McClure
  - b. December 7, 1842, Palmyra, Township, Lee County, Illinois
  - d. June 19, 1899, Oklahoma City, Oklahoma
- ²Mary Ellen Kennedy McClure
  - b. December 4, 1855, Kansas
  - d. April 23, Oklahoma City, Oklahoma

Siblings:
- ³Guy Vincent
  - b. December 12, 1877, Silver Lake, Kansas
  - d. October 23, 1918, Oklahoma City, Oklahoma
- ³David Victor
  - b. December 10, 1879, Atoka, Indian Territory
  - d. December 11, 1944, Oklahoma City, Oklahoma

Children: No children from her seven marriages

Education:
- Baird School for Ladies, 1896
- Christian College for Women, Columbia, Missouri, 1900

Politics: Republican

Clubs:
- Women of '89, Settled in Oklahoma, April 22, 1889
- Eastern Star Masonic Lodge

The Seven Marriages of Veta Ellean McClure:

m. March 11, 1903 — Isaac Thomas Jones; Book 6; page 492
Mr. Jones was a member of the Idaho and Colorado bar. They met in the Cripple Creek gold play when she was 22.
b. 1871, Iowa
Brother: Neal Jones, Muscatine, Iowa
Veta Ellean and Isaac divorced a few weeks after their wedding.

m. March 2, 1904 — Lieutenant Leon Roscoe Partridge, Westminster Chapel, Independence, Missouri. Lt. Partridge served in the Fifteenth Regiment Cavalry. Moved to Fort Ethan, Allen, Vermont, on March 26, 1904.
Veta Ellean and Leon divorced in October 1908, New Hampshire.

m. 1910 — E. R. Carhart

m. 1915 (?) — Lt. Col. R. M. Smyth. Smyth graduated West Point 1914 as the most popular man in his class. He served with the 4th Infantry in France during World War I. No records have been found showing he and Veta were ever married.

m. 1918 — Lt. John Harold Muncaster, Washington, D. C.
West Point, 1908
Married in Galveston, Texas

m. 1920 — George Myers Church of New York
    b. 1891, Barton, Missouri
    d. Tarrant, Texas
George went to Ft. Worth, Texas, as a flying instructor at Barron Field. He later served as a flight commander.
He was from the prominent Church family of New York's Chase Manhattan Bank. He was ranked #2 international amateur tennis players in the world. Their wedding trip was to Cuba.
Their divorce is recorded in the Civil Tribunal of the Seine, Paris, France.
1925: Chillicothe *Constitution Tribune*, pg. 19:
    Mrs. George M. Church, whose decree from her New York husband is expected to be handed down October

25, 1925, has stipulated that $35,000.00 paid her immediately on granting the decree and $40,000.00 two weeks later. The final settlement was $3,000,000.00

m. 1933 George Scott Findlay, January 25, 1933, in Southampton, England
b. December 9, 1883
George was from Peterhead in Aberdeenshire, Scotland, where the family home was called "The Links." He was a banker with the Chartered Bank of England and served in Saigon, French Indo-China, Philippines, and India. He met Veta while she was on a tiger hunt in India. His brother, Dr. John Findlay, #83 Chalkwell, Westcliff-on-Sea, England. His brother was an author.
  f. William Findlay
    b. December 4, 1843
    d. March 11, 1914
  m. Isabella Scott Findlay
    b. 1850
    d. October 23, 1873, Peterhead, Scotland

No children were born from Veta Ellean's seven marriages.

Illustration 266. Childhood in Indian Territory and Oklahoma City, Oklahoma Territory

Illustration 267. Veta in Oklahoma City

Illustration 268. Veta and her mother, Mary Ellen Kennedy McClure

Illustration 269. Veta as a young woman

Illustration 270. Veta (front and center) with friends and brother David Victor (back left)

Illustration 271. Demure Veta McClure

Illustration 272. Veta (left) with a friend

Illustration 273. Veta in early Oklahoma City on a boardwalk, the precursor to a sidewalk

Illustration 274. Veta with string of pearls

Veta Ellean McClure's Timeline

1892 Coca-Cola creates its first soft drink.

1896 Baird College, Clinton, Missouri. Bill of receipt for expenses

Dear Mr. McClure,
Please find the above statement of requirements to Mr. McClure and Miss Veta. I wish you could have both heard her recite in her contest — She did splendidly. She will make a fine elocutionist.
With Respect,
K.H. Mina

$210.00	Board and Tuition
$ 25.00	Piano, half year
$ 25.00	Vocal, half year
$ 25.00	China Painting
$ 18.00	Laundry
$ 20.00	Elocution
$ 10.00	Practice, half year
$333.00	

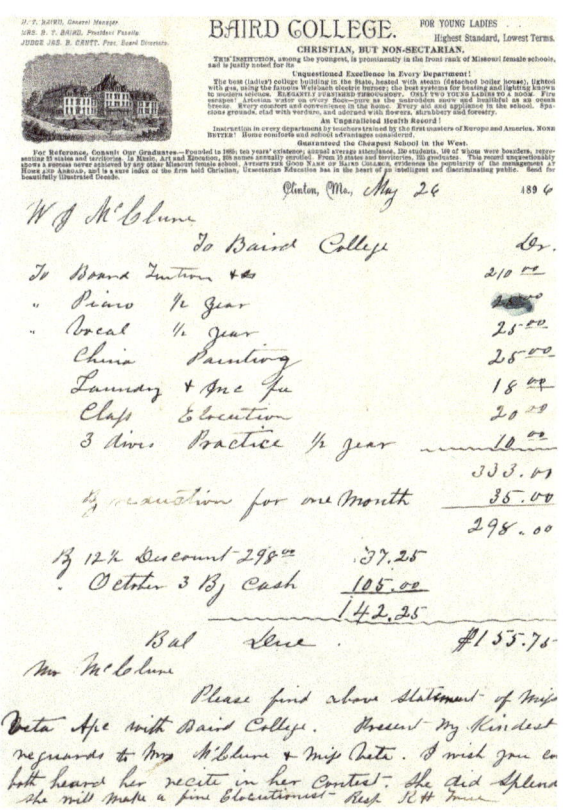

Illustration 275. Charges for one semester at Baird College

Illustration 276. Schoolgirl Veta (second from left, middle row)

1900 February 14, 1900, Christian College, Columbia, Missouri

Bill of school accounts for Veta McClure:

$103.19 Board, heat, light, laundry. Tuition Art, Vocal and Piano, Elocution

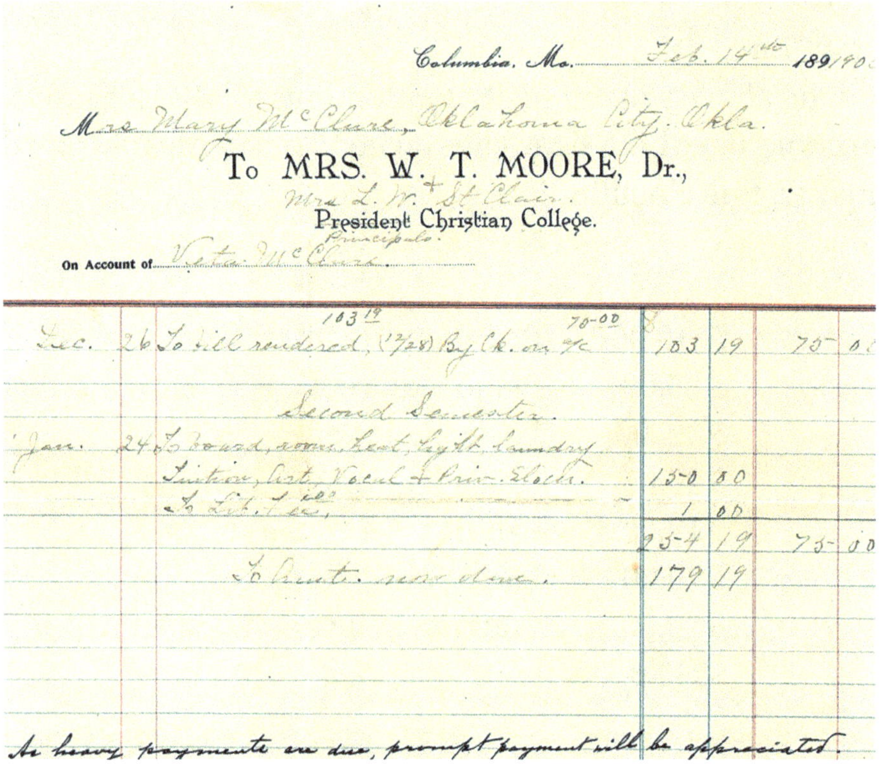

Columbia, Mo. Feb. 14th 1900

Mrs Mary McClure, Oklahoma City, Okla.

To MRS. W. T. MOORE, Dr.,

Mrs L. W. St Clair.

President Christian College.

Principals.

On Account of Veta McClure

Dec.	26	To bill rendered, (12/28) By Ck. on %c	103	19	75	00
		Second Semester.				
Jan.	24	To board, room, heat, light, laundry. Tuition, Art, Vocal + Piano, Eloc.	150	00		
		To Lib. fee,	1	00		
			254	19	75	00
		To Amt. now due.	179	19		

As heavy payments are due, prompt payment will be appreciated.

Illustration 277. Expenses at Christian College

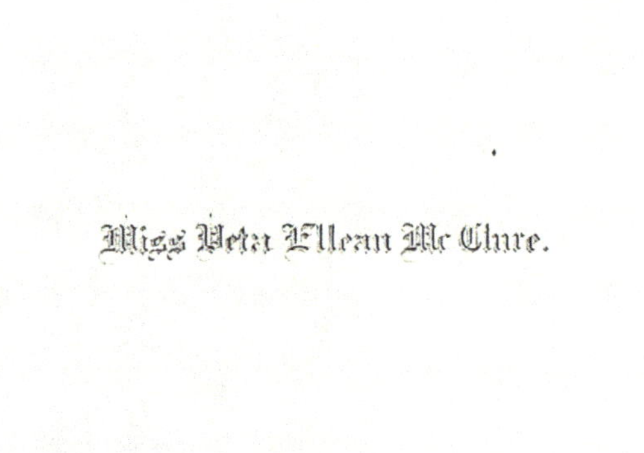

Illustration 278. A proper young lady's "calling card" to be left when visiting friends

Illustration 279. Graduation ceremony from Christian College for Women, Columbia, Missouri

Illustration 280. Veta and mother, Mary Ellen, boarding ship for world cruise, 1900.

Illustration 281. Dressing for dinner aboard ship

Illustration 282. Veta and mother, Mary Ellen, on tour in Europe

1903 First silent film, *The Great Train Robbery*, debuts; Wright Brothers make first sustained flight by a manned heavier-than-air-powered and controlled aircraft.

Article in Oklahoma City newspaper

SOCIETY NEWS AND GOSSIP

On the eleventh day of the month at 9 o'clock in the evening will occur one of the most interesting and brilliant home weddings of the year, when Miss Veta McClure, the beautiful and clever daughter of Mrs. Mary McClure will wed Mr. I.T. Jones of Boise Idaho. The bride's home at which the wedding will occur is admirably adapted to the purpose, being artistically arranged, with a large reception hall which opens with folding doors to the drawing rooms which are long and large and handsomely designed and furnished. Roses and carnations with ferns and smilax will be used in profusion and the bride, who will be unattended, will wear an imported Parisian gown of Rose Point lace over chiffon, built on a taffeta foundation. Mr. G.V. McClure, a brother of the bride of Carmen, O.T. will give her away, and the groom will be attended by Mr. H. Neal P. Jones of Muscatine, Iowa, his brother. After the ceremony and reception, the bride and groom will leave for California points, to be followed by a trip to South Dakota, and will be at home after July 1 at the Idan-ha Hotel in Boise, Idaho. The bride, although educated in the east, is a true daughter of the west and it seems most fitting that of the many suitors for her hand it should be claimed by a western man. Bred in Oklahoma when the vast cattle ranges flourished, her father one of the prominent cattlemen of the early days, who numbered his acres by the thousands and his cattle by the tens of thousands, the romance and charm of the life on the open and breezy ranges has never been forgotten nor ceased to be regretted by Miss McClure. Although a slender and beautiful blonde, she is very athletic, and is as true a hot and intrepid and graceful rider as any of the boys who rode her father's ranges. Mr. Jones was a former resident of Colorado Springs, CO, where he was associated with the Hon. J. W. Ady of federal court fame and tried many celebrated cases being also a prominent club and society man of the town. Later he became interested in mining in the Cripple Creek district, afterwards extending his operations to Deadwood, S. D. and to the Thunder Mountain gold mining district of Idaho, where he has extensive interests. Mr. Jones still finds time to attend to the more important part of his practice, having recently been retained in the famous Stratton will case, which is being so greatly talked about and is of absorbing interest all over the United States. It was while Miss McClure was visiting in Colorado Springs two years ago, they were introduced by a mutual friend, and ever since Mr. Jones has been anxiously urging his suit, which will be happily culminated on Monday, the 11th. Of the two hundred and fifty invitations which have been issued to the wedding, only about seventy are out in the city, the others being sent to out of town friends. Only the most intimate friends of the bride and groom are invited. Of the affairs planned in honor of the wedding, two have been arranged for at Guthrie, on the 8th. Miss Brooks will entertain in the afternoon and Mrs. Reidles will give a large dinner party in the evening. Mr. Jones will be present, stopping off at Guthrie on his way here.

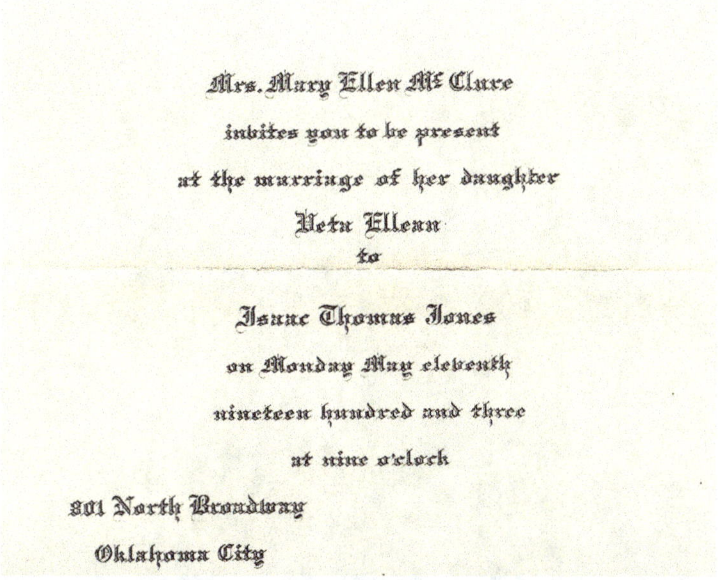

Mrs. Mary Ellen McClure
invites you to be present
at the marriage of her daughter
Veta Elleun
to
Isaac Thomas Jones
on Monday May eleventh
nineteen hundred and three
at nine o'clock
301 North Broadway
Oklahoma City

Illustration 283. Wedding invitation, 1903

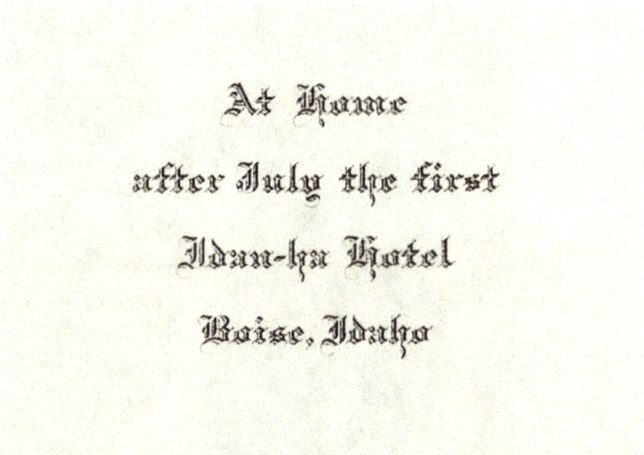

At Home
after July the first
Idan-ha Hotel
Boise, Idaho

Illustration 284. Insert in wedding invitation

1903 newspaper article [headline missing]

The marriage of Miss Veta Ellean McClure and Mr. I.T. Jones, celebrated at the bride's residence last evening at 9 o'clock, was a very brilliant occasion, over seventy-five guests being present. The home was beautifully and elaborately decorated with a profusion of roses and smilax. The back drawing room was adorned in white bride's roses and smilax and broad white satin ribbons. In it, a recess, where the ceremony was performed, was curtained and canopied with smilax, from the center of white was suspended a wedding bell of bride's roses, white also dropped in fragrant clusters on either side, and was illumined with tall white candles in graceful holders. Stately palms banded together with wide satin ribbons of white stood at the sides and white satin cushions lay on the raised dais. An attractive room was the library, done in yellow jonquils and flags, intertwined with smilax. The music room decorations were of pink roses in enormous clusters and intertwined with the smilax portiers, which were tied back with bands of the white satin ribbon. The dining room was another pure white room, with bride's roses everywhere. The table was laid with lace over white silk. Candelabra of heavy silver, holding white candles with white rose shades stood at the four corners, the center being occupied by a large wedding cake. From the smilax wreathed, ribbon looped chandelier was suspended a basket overflowing with bride roses from which bands of tulle were drawn to the four corners of the table and knotted with flowing ends. The hall, a particularly attractive room, held palms.

Illustration 285. Veta's wedding photograph; married I. T. Jones, 1903

Illustration 286. Festooned wedding car

1903 July. *The Daily Oklahoman* newspaper article

DIVORCE FOLLOWS FAST ON HEELS OF MARRIAGE

Matrimonial accidents are not of such a uncommon occurrences that they should cause a furor of excitement, for the records of the divorce courts present many evidences of unlucky alliances; and yet these monuments to the sorrows of affections and faith that have gone amiss, offer few parallels to the number of unfortunate incidents which have occurred in Oklahoma Cities [sic] best society during the past months. It would seem that among a society so strongly fortified matrimonial wrecks of such numbers and such unhappy details would be an impossibility. FADED DREAM OF LOVE. The latest affair of the character and one causing surprise that amounts almost to consternation, is the quickly ended matrimonial venture of one of Oklahoma Cities most prominent and accomplished society girls. Mrs. I. T. Jones, was formerly Miss Veta McClure. Yesterday divorce proceedings were instituted and Mr. Jones waiving issuance and service of summons, the divorce was granted. [paper torn] to support plaintiff and care for her, but that after said marriage instead of supporting plaintiff and furnishing her a home and supplying her with food and clothing, the said defendant insisted on living with the defendant's mother, and, although often requested to do so, defendant neglected, failed and refused to provide plaintiff with a separate home, nor to provide for her living expenses. [torn] gown was of Rosepoint lace that on its foundation of white taffeta drifted snow on gleaming taffeta. The groom looked manly and handsome, the bride was the envy of all her friends. Beautiful gifts were showered upon the pair. The wedding supper was the [paper torn] in town. THE SHORT HONEYMOON on the night of the wedding to the story [paper torn] the wedding was a hastily arranged but brilliant affair and was by all to be a singularly happy and propitious one, as the bride was the most dashing favorite of all ladies in Oklahoma, having beauty, vivacity, dramatic talent and gracious charm. The groom was a possessing appearance, heralded as a man of brilliant legal attainment, a large fortunate mining operator and a popular club and society man to the best society of the west, a favorite with all who knew him. BEGAN WITH A ROMANCE from the beginning there was an unusual touch of romance, commencing with the bride who had made several years of life in Colorado Springs, the residence at the time of the groom. With her and her graces the little girl from Oklahoma made a decided sensation in social circles of the gay resort of the west, and one who felt the power of her charm. Mr. Jones was introduced by a visitor who is well known in society of the Springs, in whose circle he was one of the most flattered favorites. On this, the bride, to use her own words became chesty and indifferent to him, which only served to interest him and he persisted in a quest against all obstacles and finally triumphed over the numerous rivals for her hand, and so the romance culminated with a wedding. Preparations were made, the home was decked in flowers and vines, bridesmaids, flower girls, pages attended the Beautiful bride for her wedding.(paper torn). They traveled to Guthrie and continued their journey from there, (paper torn) and that his illness was surely an excuse to avoid going with her on the morning of her _____ Jones insisted on Mrs. McClure of Oklahoma and her at Guthrie refusing ___ quartered at the Lee Hotel. Mrs. McClure offered to herself to bring his wife from Guthrie if he would promise to take her away at once over the Frisco, as he had said he would do this. She asked Mr. Jones whether he would do this. He replied that he could not do so at once. Mrs. McClure then asked him whether he could take her the day following her arrival home, and he answered no, but he would not be ready so soon. The matter was then dropped and Mr. Jones shortly thereafter left town, without leaving any word or any address. Among other things that Mr. Jones stated during this his final conversation with Mrs. McClure was that he thought "Veta married him merely for the sake of having a big wedding." Mrs. Jones says that this charge is absurd, for if she had desired a showy wedding she would have married a military man and had a wedding attended by a regimental band and officers in uniform, with fluttering regalia and a pageant and attired in robes. Mrs. Jones voiced her sentiments on the subject of intellectual husbands saying that now she "understood ___ ___ talented men always had such stupid wives, because every time they open their mouth they were corrected and snubbed, until finally they tried to make the effort." THE DREG IN THE CUP Although Mr. Jones' conduct remains an inexplicable mystery, a tiny shadow was thrown upon the situation by the bride's statement that if the man only had $1000 then he would gladly have made the most of it. And that if he only had $500 dollars she would have clung to him and sought ___ ___ extremely humble.

Newspaper article

VETA MCCLURE BRIDE AND DIVORCEE

Oklahoma, on or about the eleventh day of May 1903 and ever since have been and are now husband and wife. That the said defendant, Isaac T Jones, has been guilty of gross neglect of duty towards the plaintiff in this. That since the date of said marriage, he has wholly failed to contribute to the support of plaintiff or to furnish her with any money or to provide any home for her, although all of said time well and able bodied and in such condition of health that he could have worked at his profession and earned money and supported plaintiff. That prior to said marriage said defendant informed the plaintiff that he was able. Restoration of her former name of Veta Ellean McClure. Mrs. Jones is represented by Mr. J. H. Everest as her attorney. An Oklahoma girl from infancy, the daughter of a man whose name is synonymous with the growth and enterprise of the city and one whose death is spoken of with regret by all. Miss Veta McClure entered upon life with the most brilliant prospects. Given all the advantages that love and wealth combined could offer, endowed by nature with beauty of face and form, it seemed that the Fates had reserved for her a life unmarred by cloud or storm. But just upon the threshold of womanhood, whose life held out a fairer promise, sorrow has folded her in its sable garments. A few short weeks ago, on May 11 – Miss McClure wedded the man of her choice, but before July had _____ her dream of happiness had faded – (rest of article is lost). With no thought that ever again would she see her husband, and that their parting that morning was the last. Mrs. Jones arrived at Guthrie and was met by her friend, one of the prominent society women. In a sad unhappy sequel to our marriage, but " – and here was reached a crescendo of her woe – " he not only did not have that much money, but he had not gotten so much as $100.00." And it cannot be but conceded. . . .

September 4, 1903. Letter from L.R. Partridge to Veta

My Little Military Lady, To my little military lady,

You are a military girl, because we all think of the red cross as a part of the army, so although your profession is to heal wounds, not make them, you must quote 'Join the Military' if you do as you say you will. I don't know how to write, for great changes here have been effected in a short time, but you surely know me well enough to know that one of my faults is stubbornness, and that I dislike very much to give up that which my heart has been set. Until I see you and obtain permission to speak, allow me to speak, allow me to tell you, "Dear", I am as much your friend tonight as I was January 23, '02 when I sent you another letter. The 14th Cavalry will relieve us early in October, and we will probably arrive in San Francisco November 15. ``Frisco" and the "Presidio" is like home to me, and as for Steiner Street I could tell you stories of two innocent sisters. Little sisters I knew who lived there, that would show you how foolish a person can be and yet not get any prizes. Through some mistake I was not the foolish one, that time, but I must have had some connection for I have never yet heard of any ludicrous incident that couldn't be traced to me somehow. It will be very pleasant for you in 'Frisco if you have friends there for there seems to be something in the atmosphere that drives out all unpleasant thoughts. You can go to the Presidio you know, and see that field where the army went *down to defeat, to the Cliff House, where the army walked you uphill and downhill until you were absolutely worn out, into the Grace Episcopal, on Cal street, where the army was connected to a rabid worship of the middle crest. Then, if you go down Market to Battery St., you will pass a place where the "gallant young officers"— maybe— spoken of by Mrs. Col. Marshall, jumped his horse over a set of fences that had gone down on the slippery pavement (in the parade of July 4, 1901) and cleared all but the head of one of his men. Go to the chutes and pensively observe, from a distance, the comma, the Ferris wheel. See all the sights, old and new, and finally be at home when this army gets back, and when all is over, you will agree with me, that in old 'Frisco many strange and unexpected sights in happening may be encountered. The first foggy day I am in 'Frisco "which will probably be the first day", I will hire a carriage, if I have not forgotten how, and ride around the bluffs to admire the beautiful scenery of the Golden Gate and vicinity. That part of the North American continent looked far prettier to me as one of those days than it ever did on the clearest day California sure experienced. I would like very much, to be accompanied by you on my next trip. Can I? There are lots of things I want to say, but as you know, I cannot, now, but look out for a busy time when I am able to get a reply from you in two seconds, instead of two months. Most important of all, don't let first thoughts and inclinations lead you into any resolve that will naturally influence you after life. I have had disappointment, great and small, and am confident to give you advice and to give advice to anyone under thirty and you, a mere child of twenty one are so young that it seems I must be dreaming that I am trying to deal out a little philosophy, for really, you are too young to be in need of it. You poor little Girl, I don't care for the consequences of this speech; you can count on me till the last toot of Roosevelt's horn, "coming with the millennium" whether you consider yourself single, or married a thousand times. I hope you will receive my letter of August 4 soon enough to show you to burn up those of June 10 and July 18. I probably won't have an opportunity to write to you again from here "for I cannot make it seem right yet". But I will think of you all the time, and no matter how bad the future looks, everything will straighten out if you put your faith in Christ and L. R. Partridge. Pardon address I don't know just how L. R. P.*

1904

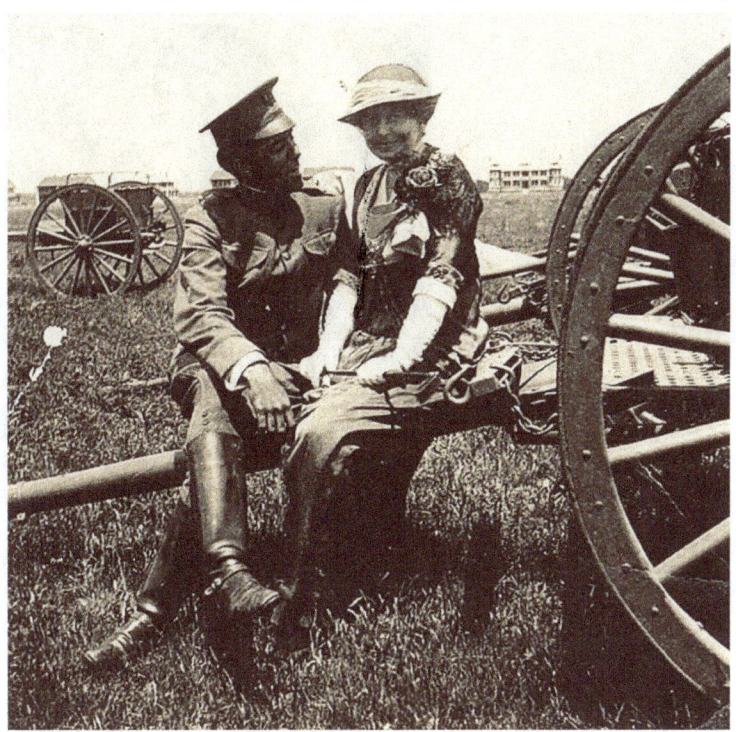

Illustration 287. Lt. Leon Roscoe Partridge, 15th Regiment Cavalry

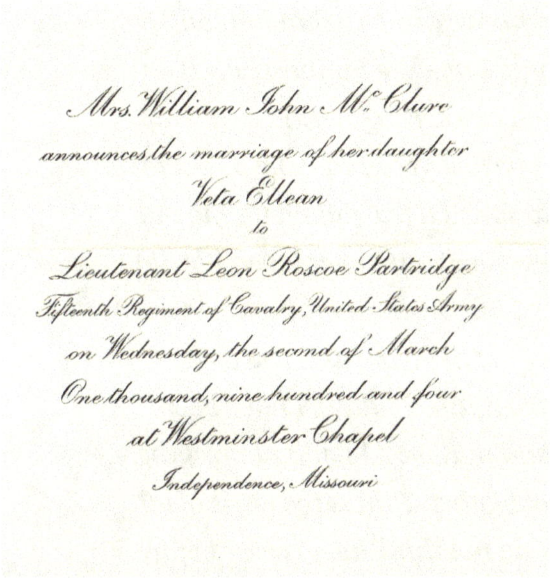

Mrs. William John McClure
announces the marriage of her daughter
Veta Ellean
to
Lieutenant Leon Roscoe Partridge
Fifteenth Regiment of Cavalry, United States Army
on Wednesday, the second of March
One thousand, nine hundred and four
at Westminster Chapel
Independence, Missouri

Illustration 288. Invitation to wedding to Leon Roscoe Partridge, 1904

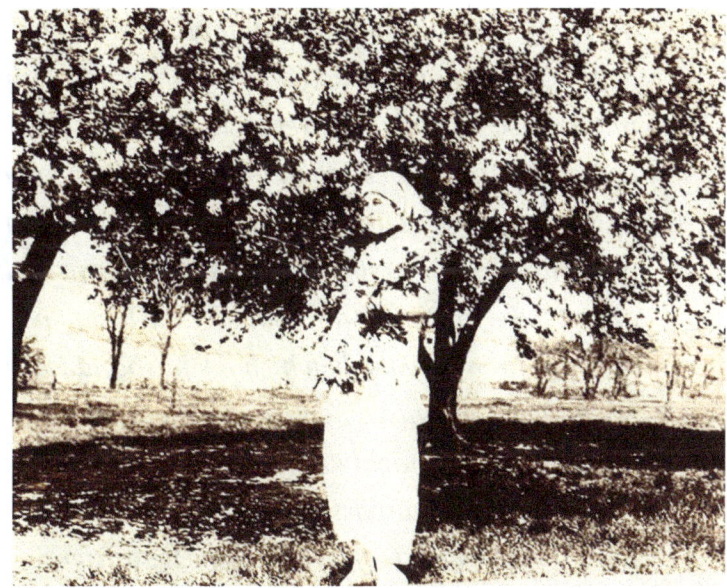

Illustration 289. Wedding photo of Veta in the garden

1904 We have a receipt for dues payment of Eastern Star made out to Veta Partridge.

Mrs. Leon Rosco Partridge

Illustration 290. Calling card to be left at the home of friends

Illustration 291. Veta and mother, Mary Ellen, in Havana, Cuba–1908 or 1909

Letter from Ellen Lorele Carhart, Ann Arbor, MI, January 22, 1910

How suddenly our hopes and plans were overthrown! We are very thankful our dear boy was not attacked on the train where help would have been impossible. It might have proven fatal. Veta will have told you it is a severe case of hernia suddenly became "strangulated" so that the operation could not be delayed. Today he ought to have sat up for the first time. I invited your daughter to spend a few days with me but her heart's love was stronger than her judgment and she went out to her lover. We did expect to be in Denver and Boulder the last of next week but business matters and the message for a new book, which my husband is printing are delaying us a few days. We do not know just when we can leave – but probably within ten days. I have been hoping that you might join your daughter in Denver and that we ALL might meet there. One thing is certain Mrs. McClure, the children love each other. That is the basis of all happy marriages. He has had some dear friends, but I do not think he has ever before asked a woman to be his wife. And he has no doubt at all that Veta is "THE GIRL". We have often spoken of the girl whom he would someday find and love. His ideal is high. I have always talked very plainly to my boy and the fact that he loves his mother and believes in Christian womanhood is not without its value. He is not perfect, but he has a loyal, tender heart, and I believe, good business ability. His tastes are too luxurious for his purse. Perhaps that is an inheritance from his mother. He has no large financial outlook, but he ought to make a comfortable living without difficulty. You know the life of a university professor is one of larger thinking and humble living. We have always had a good house and by careful economy have been able to see something of the world. My own father was a clergymen- one of the old school gentlemen, a direct descendent of one of the signers of the Mayflower compact. On my side, Emory's ancestry is pure New England English and Scotch. His father's side was Dutch, one of the Albany families. If blood tells— and who can doubt it? My son ought to develop into a man of influence and position. Only 25 years old now— "and the best is yet to come". I feel that his future would depend very largely over the woman he marries, for like his father he will depend on her judgment and sympathy if they can be willing to live carefully and prudently to help each other in the growth and character and the making of a beautiful house. I cannot see any reason why they will not be very happy. If your daughter becomes my daughter-in-law I want her to find in me a true and loving friend and helper. Rose writes to me that Veta has everything beautiful. I wonder if she can be content with his modest income. I will be very glad if you would tell me about your family and especially about Veta's life and taste. The children have all repeated that she is sweet, and loveable and elegant,—that is good. But I wish I might know more. I thank you for your very kind letter. It would have been a pleasure to see you in our home if our plans had not failed. Someday surely we want to know each other. Hoping it may be soon and that the dear father who cares for all of his children may especially bless and guide ours in this important crisis of their lives.

    I close with sincere esteem,
    Yours very truly,
    Ellen Lorele Carhart

Illustration 292. Husband No. 3: E. R. Carhart, Ann Arbor, Michigan

Illustration 293. Swimming in the Great Salt Lake

Illustration 294. Mary Ellen McClure, Chicago friends, and Veta in the Great Salt Lake

1917 Spanish Flu pandemic strikes. By 1920 more than 50 million would perish.

Illustration 295. Veta (front left) and friends

1918 Newspaper article

Lt. Col. Smyth was here in the summer and fall of 1917 as a captain of the 4th Infantry. He went overseas with them in April and received his majority in June. About a month later he was again promoted over his files because of his efficiency and courageous gallantry. He graduated from West Point in 1914 and was the most popular man in his class.

Illustration 296. Husband No. 4: Lt. Col. R. M. Smyth, West Point, Class of 1914

Illustration 297. Parade grounds, West Point, New York

Illustration 298. Beautiful chapel at West Point

Illustration 299. Getting ready for the wolf hunt at West Point

Illustration 300. Riding party

Illustration 301. Veta about to drive herself around town

July 4, 1918. Letter from the YMCA headquarters in Paris, France

My Dear Mrs. McClure,

I've been intending to write to you for some time and let you know a little about conditions over here, but first I must tell you the good news that I've been fortunate enough to receive my promotion as a Major. I certainly consider myself a lucky person to have received my majority after only four years service with troops. We left our training area a little over a month ago and were sent by rail to one of the front line sectors. I was still a supply officer when we left and I had my hands full for a while, but after we reached this area things straightened out pretty well and now are going pretty smoothly. I got my majority a few days ago and am now merely hanging around awaiting an assignment. I'd like to stay with the 4th but am afraid that my chances are very small. I wish that you could have the opportunity to see conditions as they really are over here. At times out in the country one can hardly realize that there is any war because everything is so quiet and peaceful and the fields are all under cultivation. But when one goes into a town the war is brought home to you with a vengeance. Up here near the front all of the villages are vacated with the possible exception of two or three people. One sees where the shells have dropped onto the buildings and torn large holes there and everything is in a state of devastation and you can almost constantly hear the sound of the guns either near or at a distance but most of the firing is done at night. As a rule it is very quiet during the day. I don't know where all the people go when they move out and I can't see how they exist because apparently they just pick up and leave practically everything behind. After going into one of the towns and seeing the interior of some of the businesses you can readily see the origin of the expression "Taking French leave". To my mind the most pitiful sight I have seen is to pass a family, which is on the road leaving their house. The party generally consists of one elderly man or couple, women and two or three children; all loaded down with as much as they can carry. And each and all of them with the most fore lone and unhappy expression on their faces imaginable.

We saw quite a bit of that when we first came to this section because it is one in which the Germans had recently made a drive. Our regiment has been under fire a little and everyone has done himself credit. Our casualties have been comparatively small, not any more than one could measurably expect. I was fortunate enough to get to Paris last week. I left in the morning, got there about noon and stayed until noon of the next day. I was on business and didn't get much of an opportunity to see the city as I would have liked to have seen it. The night before I went there the city had been attacked by an air raid. A couple of bombs had dropped near the Louvre. I don't imagine the place is much like it was when you saw it. At night all the lights on the street are extinguished with the exception of one occasional light and it certainly is a weird sight. The night I was there the alarm was given that an air attack was coming but nothing materialized. Veta has written to me that she has been on a visit in Oklahoma. I bet you enjoyed her stay and I hope that she didn't make all of her fleeting calls on you and leave before you had become accustomed to having her with you. I wish I could make myself believe that we would be back to the U.S. before long but I can't see where there is much hope of that.

Sincerely,

R. W. Smyth

Illustration 302. Veta with nephew, William John (Bill) McClure, a student at Kiskiminetas Prep School in Pennsylvania

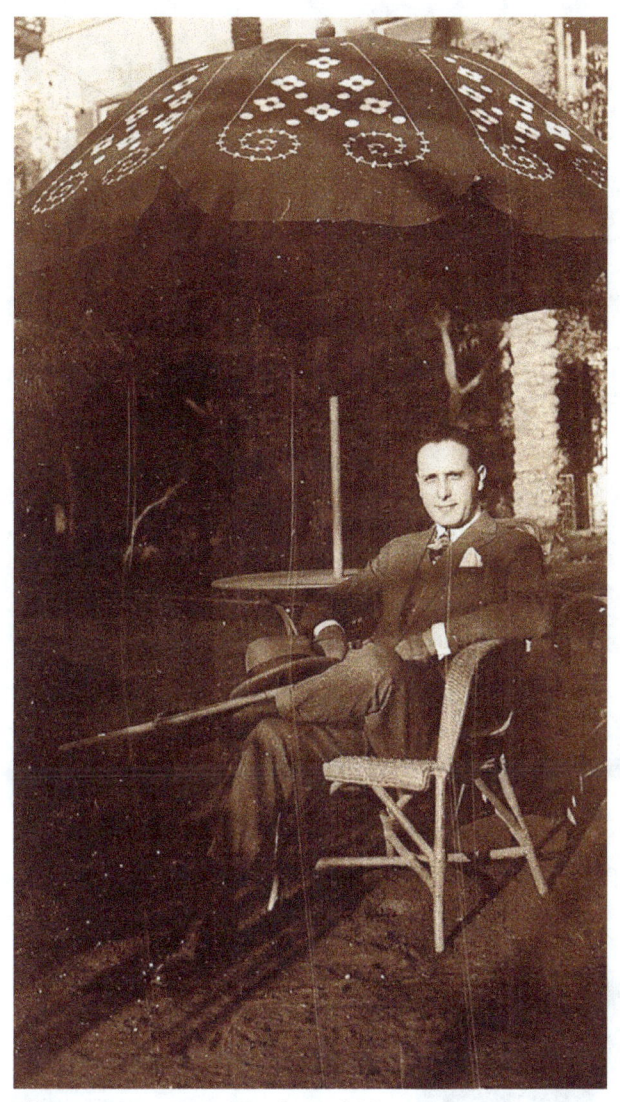

Illustration 303. Husband No. 5: Lt. John Harold Muncaster, Washington, D. C.

Mr. and Mrs. John Harold Muncaster

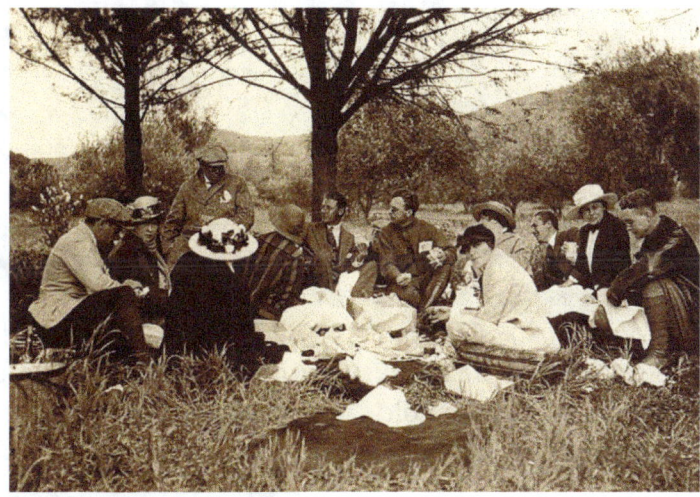

Illustration 304. Calling card

Illustration 305. Picnic

1920 Married George Myers Church

1920 The 19th Amendment becomes law. It gives women the right to vote.

Illustration 306. Husband No. 6: George M. Church at Cripple Creek, Colorado, where each was speculating for gold

Illustration 307. Mugging for the camera at Cripple Creek, Colorado

Illustration 308. Veta McClure Church in pearls

The Daily Oklahoman

FORMER CITY WOMAN MARRIES SIXTH TIME

The marriage of Mrs. Veta McClure Muncaster, daughter of Mrs. Mary E. McClure of 311 West Twelfth Street to George M. Church, wealthy oil man of New York and Texas took place Thursday evening in Eastland Texas, where the bride has resided for the last year. This is the bride's sixth matrimonial venture, her first marriage to I.T. Jones of Colorado Springs, taking place in May, 1903, in Oklahoma City. Within a few weeks Mrs. Jones divorced her husband and six months later married Lieutenant Partridge, U.S.A. in Independence, Missouri. Her third husband was E.R. Carhart of this place. A short time after divorcing Carhart she married R.M. Smyth, followed by Lieutenant John M. Muncaster in Galveston, Texas. During the last few years Mrs. Church has made her home in The East, dividing her time between New York and Washington. Mr. and Mrs. Church will spend their honeymoon in Cuba.

Newspaper article

NOTED TENNIS PLAYER WEDS AT EASTLAND, DINNER GUEST HERE

A wedding of more than unusual interest is that of George M. Church of Fort Worth and Mrs. Veta Muncaster of Washington, D.C. The wedding took place at Eastland Friday night. The wedding came rather as a surprise to Church's many friends in Fort Worth. Mr. And Mrs. Church were the guests at a beautiful wedding dinner given at the Fort Worth Club Saturday evening by H. I. McDonald's. Four couples were present at the dinner. Mr. and Mrs. Church will leave Monday for New York and after an extended visit there they will make a visit to Cuba. George M. Church came to Fort Worth during the war and as an instructor in flying at Barron Field. He was later made flight commander of the field. He is an internationally known tennis player. Mrs. Church is prominent in Washington society and is also very prominent in Oklahoma City, where she formerly lived.

Illustration 309. George M. Church (on bicycle) at Princeton University

Illustration 310. George M. Church, pilot instructor in World War I

Illustration 311. Veta in front seat

Illustration 312. George Myers Church at his family home

Newspaper article in *The Daily Oklahoman* (only partial remains of article)

MRS. MCCLURE CHURCH

An interested and interesting guest at the annual banquet of the '89ers Monday evening in the chamber of commerce rooms will be Mrs. Veta McClure–Church, who is making her first visit here in several years. Mrs. Church, who is the houseguest of her sister (in-law) Mrs. Guy V. McClure, of 210 W. 16th St., is the daughter of the late Mr. and Mrs. William J. McClure, who made the run in '89, and who were prominently identified with the early development of Oklahoma City. Mrs. Church, who has just returned from a trip around the world and who has spent the greater part of the last five years abroad, has decided to establish a permanent home in Washington, D.C. This photograph, in a Spanish fancy dress costume copied from a painting by Fernando Amorsolo, the noted Philippine artist, was taken in Manila, where Mrs. Church spent three months on her last trip.

Illustration 313. Veta painted by Philippine artist Amorsolo, world famous for depicting radiant flesh colors

Illustration 314. Elegant Veta

1922   Soviet Union founded 1917/1922; dissolved in 1991

Illustration 315. Veta and nephew, William John McClure

Illustration 316. Veta and George Myers Church at Green Mountain Falls, Colorado

Illustration 317. Veta's home, Braemar Lodge, Green Mountain Falls, Colorado. It had a six-car garage and separate cabins for guests.

Illustration 318. George and Veta on a Colorado trail ride

Illustration 319. Athens Greece at the Acropolis; Veta and George Church (front right)

Illustration 320. Veta visiting with a fellow traveler in Cairo, Egypt

Illustration 321. Cairo, Egypt

Illustration 322. Pearls and camels at the Great Pyramids of Egypt

Illustration 323. Egypt

Illustration 324. Dressed for the Egyptian desert

1922   Galleria D'Arte, Palazzo, Strozzi, Firenze: March 8, 1922
Mrs. George Myers Church
300 Park Ave., Apt. 5.A, New York

Madam,

According to your wishes we have the honour to send you herewith the list of the various works of Art that interested you so much when you did visit our Gallery and we hope, Madam, to receive soon a nice order from you. As you saw personally all the pieces are first-class, in perfect condition, and any work that you may choose will be carefully packed and we will take good care in order that it may get you in the safest and surest way. Awaiting your most honoured orders we remain, Madam, most obediently yours.

July 14, 1922: Bill of sale to Mrs. George M. Church from Pauly & C. Vinise: 12 Plates, Napoleon; 12 Plates, Napoleon; $2,000.00 Francs

1923   April 21, 1923: Western Union Telegram sent to George M. Church, #300 Park Ave, Apartment Five, N.Y.

MOTHER MET WITH FATAL ACCIDENT COME AT ONCE BRING WILLIAM ANSWER DAVE MCCLURE

May 28, 1923: Envelope addressed to Mrs. George M. Church, 300 Park Ave, Apt. 5a, New York City, From India Temple, Oklahoma City

1927   October 11, 1927: J. Haguenauer, Paris

$ 3,000.00	2 Berglres Louis XIV bois sculpture blanc
$12,000.00	2 Marquises en bois laqué vert veloutés de Glass
$ 4,000.00	2 Tables Louis XVI 150/55, 6 pieds, bois sculpt laque iverie.
$ 1,500.00	1 Table Louis XV bois sculpted
$ 4,000.00	1 Bureau Louis XIV bois sculpté, dessus cuir
$ 600.00	1 Fauteuil de bureau bois sculpté canne
$ 8,000.00	1 Bureau bois de rose et palissandre, avec bronzes
$ 700.00	1 Bauquette Louis XV bois sculptd, garnie en blanc
$ 33,800.00	
$ 1,900.00	2 carcasses de bergere Louis XV
$ 34,700.00 Total	

1927 Letter from the Taj Mahal Hotel, Bombay, 28th September, 1927

Dearest Dave and Grace,

Here I am in India, and enjoying it very much, although it is certainly vastly different from any other part of the world I have been in before. Coming over on the ship I met one of the very wealthy and charming Indian Princes, and he has asked me to his place for a big house party he is giving to the Viceroy of India who is Lord Irwin. Lady Irwin and a large party of her English friends will also be there. This Maharajah has the only lions left in this part of the world. He has a very large estate and in this one jungle there are supposed to be three hundred to four hundred lions. You may have seen pictures of the Prince of Wales, where he had just killed a lion. Well, that picture was taken on this estate. His Palace is in Jamnagar, you can see it on any Indian map. It is in a peninsula, just up from Bombay about 600 miles. He is going to send his Private Railway Saloon up to Delhi for me on 1 November, which is very nice of him, isn't it? You know he reminds me very much of Uncle Mumford Johnson, as I saw him when I was a child. I am also asked to a tiger hunt at Christmas time up in Kashmir, but I think I should go to the races at Calcutta, as everyone in India goes to Calcutta for the Christmas Holidays. I came over from London on one of the finest P. & O. Boats that run out here and so met a lot of charming people. Some I had known before, and some who are friends of friends of mine, so it has made things awfully nice for me. Send this letter to your children at school as I will not have an opportunity to write them just now.

No date (1920s). Letter from "One Nan Chih Tze"

Dear Mrs. Church,

It was a disappointment to hear that you are not coming to Peking. I had been hoping for ages for a nice celebration the day of your arrival. I am sending you ten plates, which I hope you will like. They always come in sets of ten or four and I haven't been able to find more than ten of the same patterns. If I ever find more, I will bring them to you. We never found more than the ten alike & thought you wouldn't think any as pretty as these. When you come, I'll help you find more. This has been a gay winter in spite of all the troubles and general business depression. My aunt came the first of January. She is going home next month, and we are going over in June for the summer so even if I don't see you in China we may meet in New York or perhaps in Paris. I haven't decided yet which way I'll return. I had a miserable trip by Siberia, but it was quick. Have you been having a wonderful time? Do write to me about yourself and all your beaux. Thank you for advising Lieutenant Reibold to call – we liked him so much. With much love and hoping to see you soon somewhere, I am, Most sincerely,

Nellie Husney

1930   November 25. Certificate of Sale from Jung Pao Chai, Jade Store, 17 Jade Street, Peking, China: Sold to M. Church

    Guarantee Stamp dishes are 120 years old; Ching Dynasty
    $ 40.00 4 Piece Gold Porcelain Dishes
    $ 60.00 6 Piece Black Porcelain Dishes
    $100.00

September 3, 1930. Letter from George Findlay, The Links, Peterhead, Aberdeenshire, Scotland

Veta Church,
45th Street & Madison Ave, N.Y.;
Dear Veta,

Last letter I wrote was the "meanest" letter ever, and if I were to write now you would run out of superlatives, so I decided not to. Then came the socks and I knew I had to write and thank you for them. Then our plans began being altered and after long negotiations and telephones we are sailing on Saturday the 13th inst. From Glasgow by the White Star, S.S. Arabia for Montreal. We shall go directly by train to New York and probably meet the "intended" there as we may even have to go to Philadelphia, but that must await our arrival and our destination at the moment is Montreal. Now you know all I know about our intended movements. I shall send you a night cable today telling you of these arrangements. The socks are beautiful, and I thank you ever so much for them. You should not have sent them all the same as you know my queer notion about gifts. I have been some time in acknowledging them, but not so long as some people I know of who haven't even yet acknowledged a small pin I sent at Xmas. The numerous questions in your letters I make no attempt to answer. Not that they are unanswerable but time and space forbid. I am leading an aimless and lazy life which is very amplified to an aimless and lazy person like the writer. He plays golf every day, D.U.W.F. and is now able for 18 holes in the forenoon without undue fatigue. He was arrested by a traffic cop the other day and fined two guineas for driving sister's car "sans" license. I plan, we both plan, to be back here sometime in November, and I shall "winter" in the south somewhere. I trust the Battle crash testament is having beneficial results and if Veta Ann is with you then you will be having a jolly time. Give her my regards and with best wishes & love to yourself, I am most sincerely, George P. S. If there is one thing more than another to which I object it is seeing my own letters again, so don't return this one. P. P. S. You will now remark that "he has said nothing about meeting in New York" Well what can I say? Are you going to be in New York? If so, I of course, would be delighted to see you, and my sister has already written saying she would love to have you come to her wedding. The wedding is to be a very quiet affair and I plan not to figure in it at all except as a distant observer. That's what I plan, and I am not bringing "glad rags" but who knows. We seem to be off again on another letter so this will have to count for two. It gives me another chance to make a better ending than I did before. You doubtless like the last as little as I do.

Love from George

The Daily Oklahoman (no date saved)

TESS TEA TABLE TALK

Well, Veta has been here again for one of her flying visits and left us impressed anew with her vivid personality and the interest she takes in living. I am speaking of Veta McClure Findlay, of course, who with Mr. Findlay arrived here Saturday morning from Washington to spend a day en route to Colorado where they will remain for the summer months. The Findlay's have bought that fine log house built by some prominent Texan; I can't recall his name right now, at Green Mountain Falls. The place is called Braemar Lodge and there, throughout the summer, Veta and Mr. Findlay will entertain their eastern friends. By the way, they also have bought one of those grand old southern mansions in which to spend the early spring months of every year. It is in Charleston, S. C., and was built by a member of the famous old Calhoun family. You know the kind they built in pre-war-pre-Civil War days— a stately white building with classic columns gracing the front of the house, wide upper and lower verandas, 16-foot ceilings, rooms large enough to accommodate a convention, and exquisite paneling of mahogany and walnut. There are state and family dining rooms, immense drawing rooms, 14 bedrooms, and a huge ballroom, to say nothing of the smaller living rooms. Oh, yes, there is an observatory from which one may look out over Charleston Bay, as well as over the city. Sounds like one might be reasonably comfortable there, doesn't it? Veta doesn't know it, but she probably will see more of her Oklahoma City friends there next spring than she sees when she comes here, since each spring finds a greater number trekking that way during blossom time. But getting back to the Colorado cabin: that makes two that Veta owns there now, for surely you remember the years that her mother, the beloved Mrs. Mary E. McClure, went there to spend her summers. Genuine soul that she was, that mountain cabin was dear to her heart, and I fancy that no matter how fine or comfortable the other may be, Veta always will love best the little house that must hold such fond memories for her.

1931 Sunday, March 8. Letter from George Findlay, The Links, Peterhead, Aberdeenshire, Scotland, to Veta

My Dear Veta,

This is the day you are sailing from Shanghai, and I reckon this letter should be in New York before you and say "Hello" to you and "Welcome back to God's own country" I stand gasp at the way you wander around from continent to continent and to think that you have been moving along ever since I saw you in New York in October last. And you seem to like it. Ol' Man River is just not in it with you "movin". Well, where next? I suppose you'll require some time at least in the States to open your mail and all Mary's wonderful son and to attend to your own various and varied interests there, but I hope you have still the intention of coming on to Europe. The last letter to me was from Manila written in January and that was then your idea so I hope you haven't changed plans. It will be good to see you again. I wrote to you from Switzerland, so you know how I spent the winter. It has been two weeks since I came home, and the weather has been awful. Snowstorms & hard frost and feeling like 50 below. My grouchiness and disposition were never good, now they are undoubtedly worse and everybody tells me so and it must be true. Yes, my temper is worse than ever & so is my hearing and altogether I am feeling just "fad". But believe it or not I have become keen on postage stamps. Bought an enormous, nice album for British & British Colonial stamps only and spent hours on the job every day. My next album will be for foreign stamps, and this is where you come in. You are now in America and might be able to get me a fairly large packet of American stamps. I mean at some stamp shop. Also, perhaps some Canadian if you see them. Now I don't want you to spend heaps of money buying up a few post offices for me, but if you do have a spare moment between appointment with the dress maker and the hairdresser you might profitably employ it at a stamp dealer and you will have my undying thanks. From this long story you will see what a keen pillarist I have become. I wish I had asked you to get me some in Shanghai. Sister has been away for two weeks, and mother & I are here alone. Walter (Captain Heanley) is at present in London, and they may both be up here this week sometime. I have just turned on the "radio" and the padre from London is giving thanks for the agreement reached between Lord ____ & Mr. Gandhi. You have seen, of course, that Lord Willingham is to be the next viceroy. I don't know whether I am to be honored with a letter from you from China, but I hope to hear from you from the States and learn of all your affairs. Of Mary, Jay, and Grace & Dave and William. And of your house in Washington and of the status of the big house. You evidently had a wonderful time in Shanghai, and I am longing to hear all about "old" Manila again. I am so pleased to know you are so well and

finding yourself on top of the world. Take care of yourself and don't overdo things.
With Heaps of Love,
    Yours always,
    George
    PS my kind regards to Veta Ann

1932 Two Certificates $1,000.00/each to the Rio Grande Southern Railroad

Dec. 7: Black, Starr & Frost Gorham, Inc., Fifth Avenue Corner 48th St., New York
    March 15 1932

Restring Pearl Necklace	$3.50
Restring Pearl Bracelet	$1.50
Secure Emerald & Diamond Ring	$2.50

June 20 Pearl Necklace Special Cr #883 $59,930.00

June 20

Diamond Ring #D1-1-5454	$22,000.00
PR Clips #D4-2-6446	$9,000.00
Lorgnette #D14-6025	$1,750.00
Sautoir #D60306865	$500.00
Sautoir #D6-2-4726	$13,900.00
Pendant #D7-1-4950	$3,800.00
Brooch #DJ4-2-5121	$700.00
Necklace #D60205121	$700.00
Bracelet #D8-4-6261	$3,650.00
Wrist Watch #DW 1-3-74	$1,500.00
Dress Set: Links, Studs Vest Buttons	$160.00
Wrist Watch #W 95-474	$470.00

Sold to: Mrs. Veta McClure Church, 2222 Mass. Ave. N. W. Washington, D.C.

The Travelers Insurance Company, Branch Office, Washington, D.C.

Itemized	Value Insured
1. Emerald and Diamond Bracelet	$5,000.00
2. Straight Row Diamond Flexible Bracelet	$1,500.00
3. Straight Row Diamond Flexible Bracelet	$1,500.00
4. Straight Row Diamond Flexible Bracelet	$1,500.00

5. Straight Row Sapphire and Diamond Bracelet	$2,000.00
6. Sapphire and Diamond Greek Pattern Bracelet	$12,000.00
7. Diamond Fancy Flexible Bracelet	$5,000.00
8. Pair of Diamond and Emerald Earrings	$2,000.00
9. Diamond (emerald cut) Three Stone Ring	$18,000.00
10. Cabochon Sapphire and Diamond Ring	$3,500.00
11. Cabochon Emerald and Diamond Ring (19 plus carats)	$15,000.00
12. Diamond and Sapphire Ring	$3,000.00
13. Pair of Diamond Hoop Earrings	$600.00
14. Pair of Emerald and Diamond Earrings	$2,500.00
15. Gold Mesh Bag with Forty-two Brilliants and Crest	$2,500.00
16 Gold Cigarette Case Set with Diamond Crest	$1,500.00
17. Diamond Brooch Pin	$1,500.00
18. Diamond Brooch Pin	$2,500.00
19. Alaskan Seal Coat and Baum Martan Trimmings	$2,500.00
20. Baum Marten Muff	$100.00
21. Gray Squirrel Coat	$500.00
22. Gray Squirrel Muff	$50.00
23. Silver Fox Scarf	$100.00
24. Diamond Wrist Watch with Diamond Bracelet	$3,000.00
25. Diamond set Watch with Whole Pearl Bracelet	$1,250.00
26. Pearl Necklace with Diamond Marquise shape snap (#1, #2 and #3 pearls = $10,000.00 each #4 and #5 pearls = $7,500 each Balance of Necklace = $2,000 Diamond Marquise 2.66 carats)	$47,000.00
27. Pearl Bracelet with Diamond and Sapphire Snap (#26 and #27 – Ninety-seven pearls – weight = 720.56 grains)	$3,000.00
28. Russian Sable Scarf	<u>$500.00</u>
Total	$119,100.00

1937-1940 The same Jewelry–Fur Floater Policy with Travelers Insurance

Illustration 325. Veta's bedroom set made by the Queen of Spain's cabinet maker. When it was time to inlay the 24k gold, Veta went to the bank vault, picked up the sheets of gold, and oversaw the work. It was a fourteen-piece bedroom set (sold at auction in 1963).

Illustration 326. Veta (second from right, back row) with trophies of the hunt in India

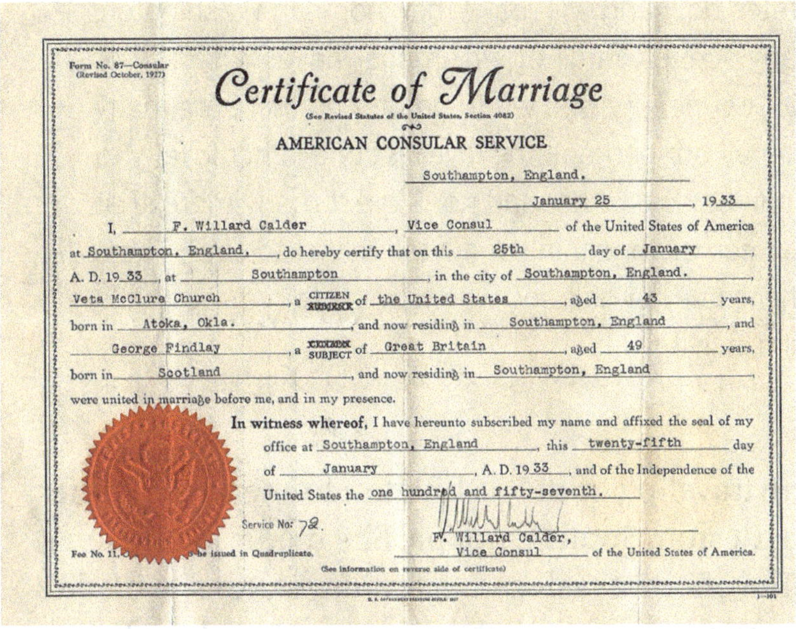

Form No. 87—Consular (Revised October, 1927)

Certificate of Marriage

(See Revised Statutes of the United States, Section 4082)

AMERICAN CONSULAR SERVICE

Southampton, England.

January 25, 1933

I, F. Willard Calder, Vice Consul of the United States of America at Southampton, England, do hereby certify that on this 25th day of January, A. D. 1933, at Southampton, in the city of Southampton, England, Veta McClure Church, a citizen of the United States, aged 43 years, born in Atoka, Okla., and now residing in Southampton, England, and George Findlay, a subject of Great Britain, aged 49 years, born in Scotland, and now residing in Southampton, England were united in marriage before me, and in my presence.

In witness whereof, I have hereunto subscribed my name and affixed the seal of my office at Southampton, England, this twenty-fifth day of January, A. D. 1933, and of the Independence of the United States the one hundred and fifty-seventh.

Service No: 72.

F. Willard Calder,
Vice Consul of the United States of America.

Fee No. 11 ... be issued in Quadruplicate.

(See information on reverse side of certificate)

Illustration 327. Marriage certificate for George Scott Findlay and Veta Church, Southampton, England. George was Veta's husband No. 7.

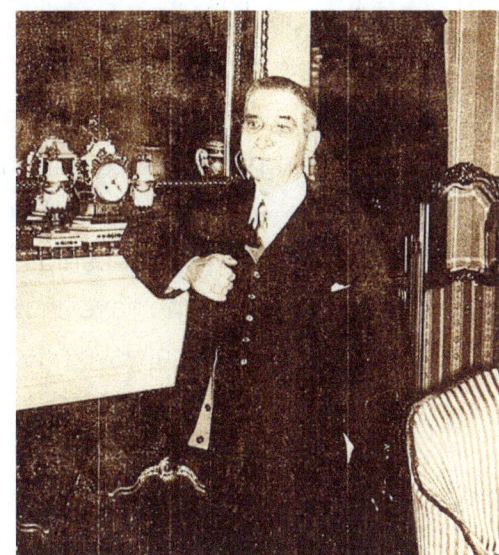

Illustration 328. George Scott Findlay

George Scott Findlay
- Father: William Findlay
  - b. December 4, 1843
  - d. March 11, 1914
- Mother: Isabella Scott Findlay
  - b. 1850
  - m. October 23, 1871, Peterhead, Scotland
- Sister: Jane Scott
- Brother: John Findlay

1933 *The Daily Oklahoman* newspaper society article

TESS' TEA TABLE TALK

What have I heard? Well, several things, but the most exciting is that Veta McClure Church is married. It seems that the wedding took place in January in Southampton, Eng. And that the honeymoon was spent in East Africa with the bridegroom's sister, who is married to an English army officer. Now, this bridegroom is George Findlay, that same interesting Scotsman, who appeared upon the scene when Veta was home for a visit four years ago, and unless I am mistaken, he is a retired banker of the Chartered Bank of England, who hails from Peterhead, Scotland. They, Veta and Mr.

Findlay, are back in the United States now and will make their home in Washington, D. C. I like to think of Veta in many scenes, in all of which she makes a splash or gay color with her vivid personality, her beauty, and warm heart. And there are many lovely things about Veta I like to recall but perhaps the loveliest one is her loyalty to her family and her friends. For it can be said of her and not a great many more, that she is loyal in her friendships. Now, can anyone think of anything finer to say? There are many of us who have known her since her girlhood who wish her more happiness to top the joy she always has found in living. "

1934–36 When Veta and George were traveling from Washington to spend the winter in Florida, they stopped in Charleston, South Carolina. She made an offer on a house at #16 Meeting Street. The offer was refused. A few days later she made a second offer only this time the purchase included the furnishings of the home. That offer was accepted. She owned this 17,000 sq foot home for a few years but grew tired of the constant flow of guests who expected to be entertained. She sold the home but kept the furnishings for herself. This home is called the *Calhoun Mansion* because it was the descendants of John C. Calhoun who owned the house. He never lived in it. It is interesting that the current owner of the home has no interest in seeing the photographs as the Calhoun family left the house. The current "official" guidebook says that they don't know who the owners were in the 1930s. In the 1940s it became a hospital residence where soldiers could recover.

Letters pertaining to the Calhoun house or Calhoun Family:
#1 Letter (no date given) from Mrs. Andrew P. Calhoun, 1324 Inverness Avenue, Pittsburgh, Pennsylvania

My dear Mrs. Findlay,

We often recall our trip to Charleston and mention how much we enjoyed having tea, one afternoon, with you and Mr. Findlay. I am writing this note to ask a favor and if you can grant it words will not be able to express my appreciation. Would you consider selling the portraits of my husbands' grandfather and grandmother, you know he was named for his grandfather and so often speaks of him. They are in the pair of oval gold frames hanging on the right side of your nice reception hall—you have so many, many other portraits, I thought you might not miss these at all. I would like to give them to my husband for Christmas and what a grand surprise it would be. Would you please let me know what you would want for them so I can figure how to meet it. Right now both our children have chickenpox, but one consolation is that by Christmas they'll be all right. With kindest regards to you both, most sincerely

    Eunice C Calhoun

#2 Letter (no date given). From Porter Williamson, 143 Tradd Street, Charleston, South Carolina

Dear Mrs. Findlay,

    After receiving your kind note at the hotel, I went to see Robert _____ and obtained his letter, a copy of which I am enclosing. It is a great pleasure to me to possess the picture you gave me, and I deeply appreciate your kindness. You remember we spoke about a picture of the woman in the lower hall, when we realized you were planning to use it we said_____ it as you had already been so good to us, but should you decide at any future time not to use it, would you bear us in mind and give us the opportunity to buy it. I hope your plans for #16 Meeting St. are working out successfully. Mrs. Williamson joins me in kindest regards

    sincerely yours,
    Porter Williamson

#3 Letter. January 27th from Mrs. Clarence Crittenden Calhoun, Rossdhu Lodge, Chevy Chase, Maryland

My dear Mrs. Findlay

    Mrs. Chambers, the wife of Judge. J. Chambers Thornberg of Charleston. Now I'm in one of where when my husband is Special Assistant with When _____ Mrs. Interested in the Calhoun collection, one of the pictures of

#4 Letter. November 20, 1934, from #53 East 66th Street to Mrs. George Findlay, c/o Carter Hotel, Thermopolis, Wyoming

Dear Mrs. Findlay

    When my wife and I were in Charleston last spring visiting my aunt, Miss Mae L. Wightman of 79 Anson Street, she told us that there was a portrait of my grandfather, painted by my uncle, hanging in the Calhoun house. She had quite a sentimental attachment for the portrait because of its association. Mr. Williams who built the Calhoun House having had the portrait painted because of his friendship with my grandfather. We went down and looked at the painting. It was not hanging presumably because there was a tear in the canvas which seemed dry and brittle. My aunt felt a good deal of concern at the condition of the picture which seemed in danger of completely disintegrating: and I called on Mr. Stoney, who I understood was representing you, asking him whether you would care to sell the portrait. He said that he would take it up with you and let me know. Not having heard from him since, I asked Mr. Henry Williams when he was in New York a few weeks ago, if he knew whether any dispensation had been made of the portrait. Yesterday he wrote to me that Mr. Stoney said he had no authority to sell, but suggested I write directly to you, hence this letter. While I presume the portrait has no commercial value, it has a sentimental value for my family: and if its condition is such that it could be restored and you should care to dispose of it, I should be glad to purchase it for its association at a price which I could afford.

Very truly yours
M. S. Reitman

#5 Letter is a memorandum letter from November 1865, state of South Carolina, Abbeville District. Memorandum of an Agreement between J. Edward Calhoun and Henry R. Freeman

That said Freeman is to have the use of the Roberts field and of the Terrysville field, far as the Bickley burying ground, also, of sufficient ground in the big pasture for a dwelling house with its appropriate lots, for the year 1866 at Rentage of Sixty Dollars, due and payable the first of October, next. Or at the option of said Calhoun, one third of all the grain and one fourth of the cotton he shall raise. He is to keep up the pasture fence along the main road and the Cowan line; not to hire any other hands than the boy and girl, now engaged without the consent of said Calhoun, and especially none of the former slaves that belonged to him. He is not to pasture his cropland without consent of said Calhoun and of his fellow tenants, not to sublet. Said Freeman binds himself under the penalty of a double rentage to horticultural the land, and to cultivate it by rotation of crops in such manner as not to impair its fertility; deliver the crop as gather or harvested to the building on the Millwood Estate, designated by the said Calhoun or his constituted agent, and to send to the blacksmith shop the thresher, the mill, and the gin of the said Calhoun if it required; moveover, the said Freeman is to pay all stamps internal revenue tax and the like incident to and consequent upon transaction connected with this agreement.

Signed this 25 November, 1865
J. Edward Calhoun, Henry R., Freeman

1935   On White House stationery: Mr. and Mrs. George S. Findlay will please present this card at the East Entrance The White House, May 1, 1935 at 4 o'clock. A second card: Mrs. Roosevelt At Home on Wednesday afternoon May the first at four o'clock Garden Party

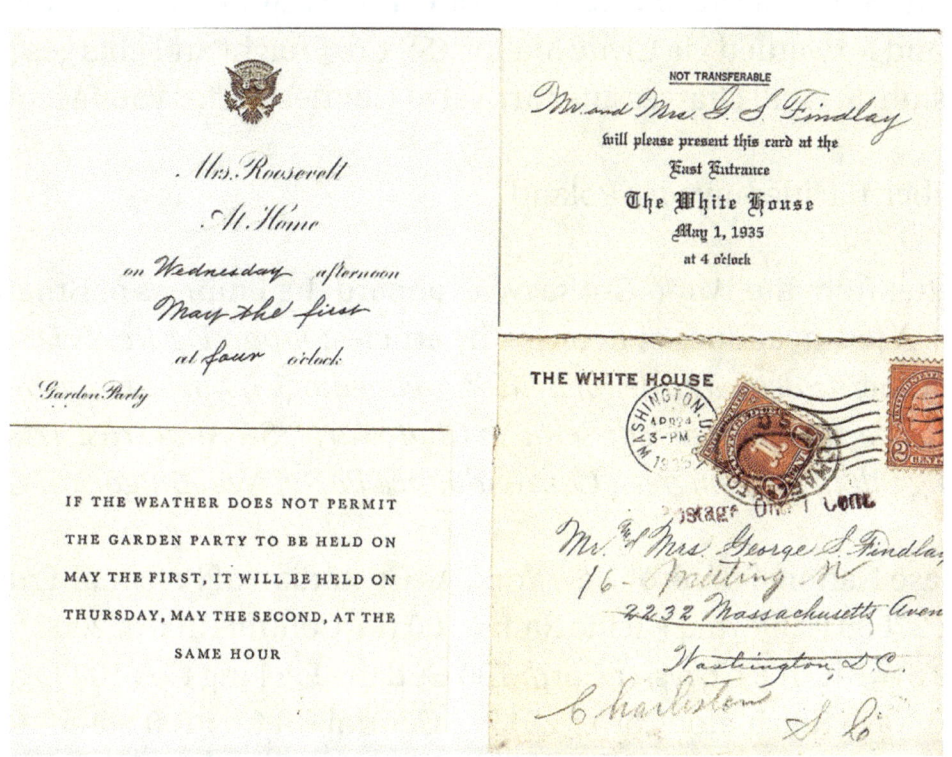

Illustration 329. Invitations to the White House

1936 August 14. Karlovyvary Crystal Glass Works, Ludwig Moser & Sons, LTD., Meierhoffen near Carlsbad, Czechoslovakia, Invoice #119: 1 Punchbowl with 12 mugs cut and engraved, $750.00; 12 Brandy with larger foot hunting- engraved $420.00; 24 Bear glasses hunting – engraved $576.00; 1 set of table glasses 24 places foot gold—etched and edges (top) gold bordered, $600.00; 24 Bear glasses old – German (4 different figures) $384.00; 8 Hock glasses 2/green, 2/violet, 2 pink $120.00; 1 Cocktail set with 8 glasses $160.0 $3,050.00 plus $435.00 Delivery to Charleston insured against all risks in transits

November 6. Karlsbad Kristall. Order #4882: 1 case P.K. 1726, gross weight 93 kg. 1 tea set green 35 pieces, $300.00; 1 tea set pink 35 pieces $300.00; 1 tea set ivory, 35 pieces $300.00; 12 cream soup bowls w/saucers ivory $408.00; 6 service plates $390.00; 2 service plates Cobalt $160.00; 2 wine bottles glass white 24 glasses $305.00;18 water glasses white $416.00; 60 tubes $18.00; 72 cocktail sticks $25.00; 1 beer glass & 2 little vases $20.00; $2,36.00 + $100 packing etc. $2,736.00

November 27. Phoenix Shipping Company, New York Office of Max Gruenhut, Hamburg, Bremen, Rotterdam, Buenos Aires, Foreign Freight Forwarders, 21 State Street New York. Mr. George Findlay, C/O Colonel Pesse Gaston, Citadel Military Academy, Charleston, S.C. Sir: We take pleasure in advising you that the following shipment : 4240 1 cs. Glassware, P.K. 1726 1 cs. Crockery Arrived by ss Hansa and forwarded via Clyde Mallory SS Co. Freight and charges prepaid to Charleston, S. C. all charges after arrival at Charleston for your account.

1939 September 1. Hitler invades Poland.

Newsletter from the *World Cruise News* aboard the Empress of Britain, January 25,1938: A few headlines of noteworthy articles: *Japan Desires Friendly Relations; Jerusalem, Murder of British Archaeologist, Mr. Starkey, by two Arabs who have been apprehended; Spanish Civil War; USA Anti-Trust Trial; The Anti-Lynching Bill in US Congress; Cairo Advance Party; New Bulgarian Cabinet.*

The Chase National Bank of New York, As Custodian of Personal Trust Division Shares: 27000 California Pacific Rail; 2100 NY Central RR Co; 2000 Co Rio Grande SW RR; 100 Chrysler Corp; 100 Cudahy Packing Co.; 100 Liggett & Myers Co.; 600 Nash Kelvinator Corp.; 291 NY Central RR Co.; 100 Standard Brands Inc.; 100 Wesson Oil & Snowdrift; 6 Abstract of Title; 4 Certificate; 2 Deed; 1 Journal Entry Copy OF; 6 Envelope Sealed; 1 Endorsement on Policy; 1 Standard Fire Ins. Co.; 2 Storage & Warehouse Rec.; 19 Travelers Ins Hartford; 10 Travelers Indemnity Co; 1 Travelers Ins Co.

1940s *The Daily Oklahoman* newspaper article (no date)
Letter from Home
Mrs. George Findlay, Colorado Springs, Colorado

Dear Veta,

How do you expect me to write to you when you never let me know where you will be next? From Charlottesville came a note saying you and George were leaving for the "North." Then from somewhere in Illinois came another note saying you would head for the West coast. Immediately after this the races in St. Louis (by the way, did your nephew, William, win many of them with his horses?) but that you would stop over in Colorado Springs en route. Just last week came the news that you had taken a house at Colorado Springs for the summer and were having a grand time visiting old time friends—some from Oklahoma City and some from everywhere, SO, I am sending this letter hoping it will reach you before you change your mind again and leave for some other place. I heard from Ethel Pope (Mrs. Charles B.) that you gave a grand party Sunday at Green Mountain Falls, a real ranch party with guests in cowboy and real ranch costumes. I'd like to hear more about it so please send details. Ethel said she would write to me all about the party but what Ethel says and what she does are very different. I don't think she did it just to break the monotony of summer days, but Irene Brooks (Mrs. William A.) fell part way down the stairs about two weeks ago and has had to wear two casts—continues with local gossip and closes with: Social interest is at a low ebb here right now—too many folk away on vacation trips. But if you will let me know when you finally reach that new (to you but old in years) home in Charlottesville, I'll write to you again and probably will have news by that time.

1941   December 6. An oral story as told by my father, William John McClure, who was visiting his Aunt Veta at her home in Washington D.C. This four-story home backed up to the Japanese Embassy. They shared a back fence. When daddy went to bed, he looked out the bedroom window and saw a big fire burning in the backyard of the Japanese Embassy. Men were running in and out of the house carrying armloads of papers which they piled upon the heap of fire. The next day was the bombing of Pearl Harbor by the Japanese.

February 12. Letterhead, The University of North Carolina, Chapel Hill to Mrs. George Findlay, Thorndale, Taneytown, Maryland

Dear Mrs. Findlay,

    I wish to thank you very much for your kindness and opening up to me through Mr. Henry P. Williams the Calhoun house in Charleston, South Carolina. I got some very excellent photographs of the marble bust of General Duff Green which I hope to use as illustrations in a biography of said Green. Mr. Williams informed me that you had raised with him the question as to where the bust should be placed. At first, I told him that I thought probably Clemson College might be the best place to deposit the bust. After thinking the matter through, however, I have decided, and I wrote to him to this effect, that the University of North Carolina would be the most appropriate place for the bust. I reached this conclusion because of the following things: Duff Green was primarily interested in the development of the South as a section. He devoted his long career to its political and industrial advances and certainly was a figure who would be graded as a sectional or regional leader rather than a state or national. In the second place, he had no direct contact with South Carolina. His only connection being through the inter-marriage of his daughter with the son of John C Calhoun. Hence, there is no logical reason for placing the bust at Clemson. Again, the University of North Carolina has the largest collection of manuscript materials bearing on the agricultural, industrial and political life of the South of any institution in the country. These are to be found in the Southern Historical Collection: and I have personally have an enormous collection of Duff Green manuscripts here at the University. Finally, there are a few places in the South where works of art similar to that of the Hiram Powers bust of Green are on display. At the University we have a rapidly growing art department where Southern students are being taught to appreciate and to contribute to work in painting and sculpturing. It seems to me that a bust by Powers would have a great influence on the young people who are taking training in the field. Furthermore, hundreds of people visit the art department here every week to see the famous paintings and statuary deposited in the art gallery, and the work of Powers would in that way be made known and these people would have the privilege of viewing this work of art. May I ask whether you have made any plans as to the disposal of the books and other historical materials now stored in the Calhoun home? If you have any idea of placing these things in some library, I would like to suggest that you consider this institution. I enclose herewith a little pamphlet concerning the work of our Southern Historical Collection and hope you will give it consideration when you make your plans for the disposal of those things. Again, thanking you for your kindness . . . . I am sincerely yours

    Fletcher M Green

1944   April 27. Letter written from Wichita, Kansas, by Veta to brother Dave and Grace

Our dear Grace and Dave,

    I wrote to you just after I got home from your place – telling you what a good time we had had, and I have not had a word from any of you. Has William gone to Louisville yet? If he hasn't, I do not think he will get away this spring. My teeth were so bad that I went down to Mineral Wells, Texas, to Doctor Zefske and he took the one out that had been giving me so much trouble. Well on the way coming back last Saturday afternoon we were put off the "Rocket" at Wellington and told we would be taken on to Wichita by the "Santa Fe". We stayed in Wellington for three days and then a nice man, a "mason" who lives here brought us home in his car and we had to go through water up to the hubs of the car ever so far. A bridge on the railroad went out just twenty minutes after we went over it going into Wellington. My it was all "awfully scary", but we found a nice little hotel at Wellington, so we were very comfortable. I still think "Challenge Me" will win the Derby. What do you think? What do you hear from Gary? I don't know if we will sell our house here right away or not, but we have to go to Washington on the 12th. If you were going through St Louis just before the Derby in your car, we might go with you. They won't let us go in on the train. Phone me if there is any chance. I know we can't get ready in time now, but I do hate to miss Sat.

    Write soon, Best love to you all, from George and Veta

1945   Letter dated July 5

Return Address, 2156 Wyoming Avenue, N.W., Washington, 8, D.C.
To The Chase National Bank,
45th Street Branch, Madison Avenue, New York, 17, New York
Gentlemen,

I enclose a check of Black Starr & Gorham Inc. in the amount of $15,000.00— check No. 7330—in favor of Veta McClure Findlay which I wish you to place to the credit of my checking account in the name of Veta McClure Church. For the information of your Income Tax Department, I want to inform you that this check does not represent income. It is the return of capital. Kindly acknowledge receipt of this remittance to me here. Yours sincerely,

Veta McClure Findlay

Illustration 330. Veta's home at 2232 Massachusetts Ave N.W., Washington, D.C.

1946   May 31. Check written on The Riggs National Bank, DuPont Circle, $50,000.00 to the order of Veta McClure Church from Veta McClure Findlay

1947   June 6. Edward E. Ayre, Jewelers, The Mayflower, Washington 6, D.C. Mounting Star Ruby and Diamond cluster ring and furnishing 22 round faceted Rubies, mounted in platinum. Star Ruby weighs 11.38 carats, 23 Diamonds 62/100 carats, 22 faceted Rubies 2.53 carats...$785.00. Mounting Diamond circle pin in platinum using Diamonds from your 2 Diamond block bracelets... $630.00.

Dear Mrs. Findlay:

I am enclosing a receipted bill showing in detail the transaction regarding the mounting of the star ruby ring and diamond circle pin. With regard to the setting of the sapphire in your platinum and diamond mounting and the new shank to your emerald ring I find that these two items were entirely separate of the charge for the ruby ring and diamond brooch. The charge for the emerald ring was $20.00 and the alteration to the mounting to take the sapphire was $35.00. The repair to your emerald ring was charged to your account on May 19th last and the sapphire ring charge has been noted on your account today. I beg to apologize for this discrepancy and trust that it won't cause you any inconvenience. I also neglected to ask you to return the receipt, which Mr. Ayre gave you for the various items. Will you kindly do so at your convenience. Thanking you most kindly and trusting that we may have the pleasure of serving you again, we are.

1947-1948 *The Daily Oklahoman* newspaper society column

TEA TABLE TALK
by Irene Bowers Sells

With the Christmas rush what it is at our house each year, the Christmas cards that arrive daily for a fortnight before the Great Day dawns are given a hasty reading. There is appreciation of these expressions of friendliness and a warm glow enkindled in my heart, but there is no time to sit myself down by the fire and let the warmth of that friendliness sink well into my soul—no time to reminisce over the days and hours spent with those who sent them. So, being snowbound one day last week, I took that opportunity to re-read the Christmas greetings and warm my heart at their glow. This leisurely reading, even though a second one, is most satisfactory. When I have finished with it, I feel very much closer to those friends, far and near, who remembered me with kind words at the Yuletide. Just as gay and just as colorful as the woman who sent it was the one that came from Veta McClure Findlay, who, by the way, lives now at 1009 East Brow Road, Lookout Mountain, Tenn. Probably it would be safer if I said Veta lived there when she sent the Christmas card. She has a way of buying houses here and there and almost everywhere, lives in them a while, then buys another place and moves on. Veta was one of my girlhood friends here, one of the most beautiful women Oklahoma ever claimed for her own, generous and warm-hearted. She has lived in many places and known many folks and friends since she left Oklahoma City, but she still has a warm spot in her heart for the friends of her youth and never forgets them.

1947-1948 *The Daily Oklahoman* newspaper society column

Veta McClure and her husband, George Findlay, have gone to Glenwood Springs, Colo., not because it was too hot here for them but it was just time to go someplace. Between bridge games Veta will look at the scenery —which is wonderful—and George will swim in the pool of heated water.

1955 Jonas Salk's polio vaccine declared safe and effective

No date given. Letter written from the Barbizon-Plaza Hotel, Central Park South New York

My dear children,

It was so nice to hear your voices a little while ago. I am lonesome already. I do think your Mother's Day cards are so cute. I never know where you find them. I am sending you this article about Margaret Williams, as I thought you all would enjoy it. We only have time for a note as we are going over to Radio City to see Maurice Chevalier in "Count Your Blessings," rather he is in the stage show. Our trunks came through all right and are now over at the Cunard Pier. We have booked our passage home on the Queen Elizabeth, July 2nd and will arrive here in New York July 7th, which should get us home about July 9th. We will only stay at the Skirvin two nights and go on out to Colorado where we hope you will come later. Our best love to all,

Uncle George and Aunt Veta

PS Hope Mary Ellen and Veta Lou get along well with their dancing. Write to me about it.

Illustration 331. Veta at home and dressed to go out

Illustration 332. In Veta's living room sits the last Steinway played by Paderewski on his final concert tour in the United States.

1950s No date given. Tea Table Talk society column in *The Daily Oklahoman*

BUT THEN PLANNING IS PLEASURE
by Irene Bowers Sells

Robert Burns certainly said a mouthful when he spoke of "The best laid plans of mice and men going astray." For instance: there are the plans of Veta McClure and her husband, George Findlay. They were all made for a trip around the world to countries visited before by Mr. and Mrs. Findlay, but they just wanted to go someplace, and the world seemed an inviting place in which to roam. All plans were completed: the house, duly arranged for a long period of unoccupancy, trunks were packed and on the way to New York, and Veta and George were in the hotel for their last night in Oklahoma City. What happened next? That night Veta had a heart attack, one severe enough that the doctor said all plans for traveling must be canceled, so Veta and George are still in the hotel. Their home has been restored, and as soon as Veta is able they will go back there. But in the meantime, Veta is keeping busy in her bed at the hotel by reading brochures on other lands and it is hard to tell where she will decide to go. But her trunks are packed, so I feel sure that as soon as the doctor gives the "go" signal, Veta will be on her way. In the meantime, the Findlay house has been de-moth-balled, and all is ready for their return. Veta probably will not consult me about her plans but if she does, I shall insist that she go someplace where that blue woolen scarf that

Kate and I gave her for Christmas can be worn. As I write this it looks like the best place to wear that scarf is Oklahoma and I suspect that is just where Veta will wear it.

1950 Handwritten letter from the Cunard White Star

Well my dear Children,

We are now on our way to Cairo and are continuing to have a grand time. You have both been dears about writing and we are ever so glad to receive your letters and to know you are all well. I am so anxious to get your next letter so as to know what you are going to do. Where have you sent your horses? This picture shows you how the Zulu children look. You know in Paris, you address us care of the Chase National Bank. Just one month more of this wonderful cruise and then we will be in Paris.

Lots of love to you all,

Devotedly, Aunt Veta, February 27th

Illustration 333. Veta and George in St. Mark's Square, Venice

1950 Two certificates: 100 Shares of the Gobel Brewing Company

1956 U.S. Dept. of Interior; Assignment of Overriding Royalty, December 6, 1956, between Trident Company and Mrs. George Findlay, three percent (03) County Pike, Colorado, 8 South, 58 West

Illustration 334. Veta's passport photo

Illustration 335. Newsmakers Veta and George visit to Oklahoma City reported in *The Daily Oklahoman*

1956 Letterhead: Commonwealth of Virginia, Virginia Museum of Fine Arts, Boulevard and Grove Ave., Richmond VA September 19, 1956

Mrs. George Scott Findlay
214 Rugby Road
Charlottesville, Virginia
Dear Mrs. Findlay:

We have been referred to you in connection with a painting in your possession, a portrait of "John Calhoun" by Colonel John Trumbull. In mentioning your portrait to Professor Theodore Sizer of Yale University, the foremost respected authority on the work of Trumbull, Professor Sizer expressed a strong desire to have a photograph of the painting. Professor Sizer is interested in studying this work and, if a photograph is available, I would greatly appreciate receiving a copy from you. We append Professor Sizer's address below. If, however, you should prefer to send the photograph to us we would be most willing to forward it to Yale ourselves.

Thank you very, Sincerely yours,

Pinkney Near, Curator: Professor Theodore Sizer, Department of the History of Art, Yale University, New Haven, Connecticut.

1957 January 2

Dear Chrys and William,

This is just a note to let you know we arrived safely here yesterday afternoon—New Year's Day. We spent Monday night at Wichita Falls, Texas, and went up to Veta's friend's house after dinner, and stayed until nearly midnight and then back to the Kemp Hotel. It was only 90 miles to Mineral Wells, and we arrived in time for lunch. We hope you all had a very happy New Year's Day. Veta sends her love to you all and she will write soon. Our rooms are 522 and 524 and Veta is planning a massage and dress making a dress-alteration and we will likely be here for about at least a week.

Best love to you all from Aunt Veta and Uncle George

1957 *The Daily Oklahoman* newspaper article

LETTER FROM HOME

Dear Myrtle,

I wish you could have been here all this week and joined with us, taking out of storage our memories of the days Oklahoma City and we were young. Why this delving into the past? Well, mostly because Veta McClure and her likeable husband, George Findlay, arrived to bring together what is left of us old-timers. Then, just for good measure Helen Gloyd (Mrs. John M.R. Lyeth) arrived from New York and Miriam Richardson (Mrs. John Dumars of Topeka) arrived for a brief visit. Veta had just bought a new house—or rather another old house—in Charlottesville, Virginia. And after moving into it decided she needed a rest and since she hadn't been home (this IS STILL home to Veta even though she has wandered all over the world) she decided to head toward Oklahoma City. We have been getting together in small groups to talk about the old days and how much fun it has been! Bill and Irene Brooks (Mr. and Mrs. A.) got us together Sunday evening and I wish you might have joined us in recalling this and that and the other person and event. Betty Lou Sims and her husband, Dr. Leslie Westfall, brought together practically the same group Wednesday evening and there have been and will be, other small parties for Veta and Mr. Findlay. They were the guests of Dr. and Mrs. Moorman (Lewis J.) Tuesday evening when the Moormans invited a handful of folks in to meet informally our former American Ambassador to Turkey, George C. McGee, after the annual Y.M.C.A. dinner at which Mr. McGee was the speaker. Fred and Eddie Jones, who, of course, had not known Veta in the old days but who had met her and Mr. Findlay in Washington through Mike and Mary Ellen Monroney, entertained at a small dinner, and Mary Rumsey (Mrs. Joseph F.) also has planned a dinner for the Findlays although her acquaintance with them dates back only two or three years when they were on the same Caronia cruise to South Africa. I don't know how you feel about it but I have been intrigued by Veta's purchases of houses. She always buys them for a home and DOES live in each one a while but soon there is another. You will remember that she bought a fine old place on Church Street in Charleston, S. C., lived there a while then bought a big place at Pinehurst, N.C., another estate in Maryland, a home on Lookout Mountain at Chattanooga, Tenn., three houses in Washington into which she moved from time to time and one of which she still keeps for her Washington home, then a famous old house in Charlottesville became the first one that was not large enough. It seems to me, too, that not many years ago she bought a huge place in Wichita and lived there a while. Miriam came down from Topeka especially for the meeting of the Five O'clock Tea Club (of which you still are a member.) I believe it was held Thursday with Ruby Richardson (Mrs. George Woodward) at the Aberdeen Hotel. (Article continues with local gossip.)

1957 July 29. Letter addressed to Mrs. George Findlay in Colorado Springs, Colorado

Dearest,

I was so glad to hear from you. Irene told me you had her information. She's OK, but I didn't know how to reach you. Your letter sounds like you are moving to the Antlers from this address, so I hope you get it. Mike wasn't too ill but in about March, he felt tired and didn't want to do much at night. Then in April he was tired and depressed, and it grew worse in May. So, he decided to go to the Naval Hospital and get a thorough check up. They found his temperature comes up every afternoon around four and stayed up a degree until he went to bed. It was a low-grade infection that he had picked up somewhere, but it had gotten him in a run-down condition and he had lost 12 pounds. At this time now, he is full of beans and pep and ready to go. I knew something must be wrong. The summer hasn't been too bad here, and our house is completely air conditioned, so we never suffer from the heat. And our garden at night is delightful with the light my eyes can see through the trees. Lots of people are gone, so everything now is informal. Most of the diplomats are still here and we've had several dinners in the garden. I'm sticking it out here and not going to Nantucket as Mike is a delegate to the Inter-Parkway Union which meets in London on September 10 and we are going over for that. After it's over we are motoring on up through Scotland, then fly to Denmark and home. Next year the meeting is in Rio and that will be a long trip so we won't take too long this time. Everything fails, compared to the Far East. I have lost my good senses over the far-eastern influences. Can't wait to get back there. Would actually like a Japanese type of house, filled with Buddhas and old scrolls and my wonderful China, you gave me. Downing, "the jeweler from Cairo" was here exhibiting King Farouk's jewels. More later and now we are looking forward to seeing you in the fall and I love you.

Mary Ellen (Monroney)

1957 Letter

Return Address: United States Senate, Washington, D.C.
addressed to: Mrs. George Findlay,
22 West Buena Ventura, Colorado Springs, Colo.
Aug. 20, 1957
Dearest Aunt Veta,

How darling of you all to send me this most useful traveling sewing kit. I've always needed one. But forget it until I am in some queer place and need it badly. Since writing to you the other day – Mike's plans have been changed somewhat and he is going to the Atomic Energy World Meeting in Vienna after the London Conference, then to Moscow. Did I give you our plans? First to Germany, London, Finland, Denmark, Holland and the conference for a week in London. There are so many parties given for us, we will be dead. So we are going to the Bernese Alps and the Italian lakes and Venice for 10 days. Then Mike flies to Vienna for the Atomic Peace Conference. Then the senators are flying to Moscow. I don't like them flying on non-scheduled planes, and an Air Force plane at that, but Mike says they will be alerted all along the way, and a Russian pilot will be on board to communicate with the Russians. But just some smart aleck Russian pilot could mean the end of them. I will go to Florence and Rome and get on the Independence at Naples. Mike will get on at Cassius. It's a wonderful trip but I can't get excited over anything after Hong Kong. All the movie people are here, Sophia Loren, Cary Grant, Jane Russell, Bob Hope and the most wonderful producer Richard Rogers who produced "Oklahoma", "Carousel", "The King and I", "Porgy and Bess", etc. I took him to the senator's largo and he loved it. Tonight, we are going to a party at the Italian Embassy for Sophia Lauren. The children are fine, but I feel like a dirty dog, not taking them to Nantucket. Sharon is so darling and lovable, and Alex is such a devil but cute. Really more personality than Sharon, but Sharon is an angel and so full of love and sweetness. I do hope your little baby is all well by now with ever so much love and we will write along the way.

    M. E. (Monroney)

1958 Airmail Special Delivery letter to
Mrs. George Findlay, c/o M.S. Britannica, Cunard Line,
Pier 92, New York, New York
From Mary Ellen Monroney

Dearest Aunt Veta and George,

    I wish I knew where you were staying in New York, and we would surely call you. I would be so happy to be going. I would be beside myself. I'm a born sailor!! I'd go anywhere to be going. I do hope the weather will be nice – and you enjoy the crowd on board. I think that makes a lot of difference on a cruise like this - you know all the staff and it will be like home. I feel that way about the Independence. There is so much going on now- too much. Balls, dinners and receptions. We go when we feel like it. Everyone adores Mike's Italian red silk dinner jacket. Even Douglas Fairbanks wants one like it. I had a luncheon for Todd Rockefeller last week. And he knows antiques and china. And I was so proud of the celadon bowl. I have it on my low Chinese coffee table. I simply love it. My first piece of celadon. I have a vase in storage at Hong Kong, but no telling when I'll get it. Please promise me this, when you give Mary, William and the girls your things, please tell them the value of it and explain what the porcelain and china is worth. You have so many priceless things that with the gift you must tell them the value of it. So many people do not realize what they are getting. I know H____ didn't know - until I took her in tow!! And now she is beginning to really realize these valuable old things. I have been asked to go on a commuter trip to DuPont's, but I don't think I know *everything yet. I saw Mary Bradley the other night – she looks fine and Caesar has been put on this new board to reorganize the Pentagon. Sharon continues to be the delight of my life. So sweet and precious and comforting— but Alice is a Hellion! Do plan to stop here on your way home and see us . We want you to—so much. Drop us a card from the different ports—and know we are missing you very much. I am so happy for you and will be thinking of you sailing out of the harbor.*

   Yours truly,

   Mary Ellen (Monroney)

1958 Assignment of Overriding Royalty: Zephyr Drilling Corp., Tulsa, OK, William O Antonides and Mrs. George Findlay, 1815 N. Hudson, Oklahoma City, Oklahoma. Assign One-Eighty (1/8) override royalty and one-half (1/2 of all oil, gas and other hydrocarbon substances, which may be produced and saved from the premises . . . .

1959 June. *The Daily Oklahoman* newspaper society article

LETTER FROM HOME
Mrs. George S. Findlay, R.M.SS Caronia,
Witty, S.A., 5 Plaza Medinaceli, Barcelona, Spain

Dear Veta,

   I hadn't intended to write to you so soon but, after all, your cruise will end in ten days and you will be visiting George's relatives in England. Then I had some news that simply wouldn't keep until your arrival here in July. SO—you get another letter from me—two letters on one cruise—quite a record for me. The bit of news I know would interest you particularly is that Mike and Mary Ellen Monroney (Senator and Mrs. A.S.) are the proud grandparents of a boy— Mike Monroney, born to Mike Jr. and his wife, Teddi, on May 1. (the article of gossip news continues—one interesting note for history is the following) This should have provided enough excitement in the Monroney family but just prior to that, Senator and Mrs. Monroney gave a dinner party to honor former President Truman. It was a small dinner party, the kind the Monroneys usually give, but it got a lot of publicity. Since you have been sailing the Mediterranean, you may not have kept in touch with the U.S. news so I had better tell you that the Monroney dinner made front page news because following the dinner, Sam Rayburn, also a guest, took Mr. Truman back to his hotel and en route they discussed Democratic presidential candidates for 1960. They decided upon majority leader Lyndon Johnson, who was of course, the favorite of Mr. Rayburn, and Senator Stuart Symington, from Mr. Truman's own state of Missouri.

1959 July 2

Mr. W. G. Antonides, Antonides & Company,
P. O. Box 30, Glenwood Springs, Colorado.

My dear Bill,

 Thank you so much for your letter yesterday. It was so kind of you to take us down to Billy Ellen's and we did appreciate your kindness. Uncle George and I did enjoy meeting your family and they are both precious. Bill, I did not have time to figure this deal out—I was so upset about William. After going over the entire deal I think it is too much to pay for down-right "Wildcat", Royalty. I will do this and stick to it. I will pay you $500.00 (five hundred dollars) for one third of your three per cent holding. I feel under the circumstances I should not invest that—but if you need the money and want to sell at that price, and if it will help you out a little, I will be very glad to take a chance on that much. I am sending these papers back to you to change if you wish to do so—but I do feel it is a very big gamble even for this small amount. Our William is very ill, and I may have to go to Oklahoma any day. I will leave a check with Uncle George as he can send it to you at once if you wish to accept my offer. Bill dear, I do wish I could do more, but I think at best it is a very poor gamble, for they may all decide not to put a test hole there, and we will just be sitting with a nice piece of Mountain side. Of course, for your sake I hope that will not be the case. With love to you all,

 Devotedly,
 Veta McClure Findlay.

1959 December 7

Harry Winston, Inc.,
7 East 52st St., New York, 22, N.Y.

Gentlemen,

 This is to confirm the same by me and the purchase by you today of the following articles of jewelry at the prices indicated. One Emerald Ring weighing 18.00 cts., $12,000.00. I warrant that I am the owner of the items enumerated, which are unencumbered, and that I have the sole right to sell them. I acknowledge receipt of your check for $12,000.00 in full payment for all items listed above,

 Very truly yours,
 Veta McClure Findlay,
 1815 N. Hudson,
 Oklahoma City, Okla.

1960 The Travelers Insurance Company, Hartford Connecticut: April 15, 1960

Nuclear Exclusion Clause: It is understood and agreed that this Company shall not be liable for loss by nuclear reaction or nuclear radiation or radioactive contamination, all whether controls are uncontrolled and whether such loss be direct or indirect.

1962 Letter sent to Mrs. George Findlay, 1815 N. Hudson, Oklahoma City, from 2760 Thirty-second Street, N. W., Washington 8, D.C.

Dearest Aunt Veta,

I would have written days ago, but I was so tired when I got home, I slept for 14 hours the first two nights. Mike was in the hospital resting, so I had all the week to . . .

———

1962 February 28. Letter written by Veta Louise McClure, mailed to Tucson, Arizona

Dear Aunt Veta and Uncle George, and Yank, too,

It sure is lucky thing Yank isn't here to walk with family. Everything is covered with ice. I hope you stay in your bed where it's nice and warm and not get out in this weather. At the state wrestling tournament our wrestling boys came in first. Everyone was sure happy. Our wrestling coach was chosen to tour Japan this summer. They will choose eight boys from Colorado and Oklahoma to go. We hope about four boys from Edmond will get to go. Today in science we were just calmly sitting there and talking. All at once one of the girls screamed and a little mouse ran across the floor. All the girls stood on their chairs and just screamed. Our principal came running down the hall to see what was wrong. When we told him, he just stood there and laughed. I hope you both are feeling okay, and Mr. Yank is behaving himself. Be sure and write.

Loads of Love,
Veta Lou

1962 November 23

Dearest aunt Veta,

I would have written days ago, but I was so tired when I got home, I slept for 14 hours the first two nights. Mike was in the hospital resting so I had all the unpacking to do. Then all the people descended on me. The swimming pool man to clean the pool and it looks so pretty and clean now. To nurserymen from Maryland with plants to set out. These are from Maurice Ramsey. Windows to be clean, flat floors to be waxed, gutters to be clean and I was so tired I didn't think I couldn't think. I would forget. I didn't go out to see Mike until I brought him home and he looks fine but needs some weight. I got home with the beautiful porcelain. Brought it on the plane and kept it on the seat next to me. Everyone wanted to know what was so precious that I kept beside me. It is so beautiful, I am fixing a place for it to show. I really am Chinese, and love it. All the Chinese things look so well with the 18th century things. Thank you from the bottom of my heart and if you ever should want them back for Veta and or Mary Ellen let me know. These things are yours and I am just using them. When I die I will let Veta Lou and Mary Ellen have them. I enjoyed my trip around the states, and next time will go around and speak, as they all want to know about Washington etc. My life here, what I do, who I meet etc. We had a very good Thanksgiving. Just the family and an old friend, who is ambassador to Tunis home on leave. We leave tomorrow for the Bahamas. Our address there is quite large, Harbor Island, British Bahamas. There is no phone, just mail and cables. We have to spend the night in Nassau. I'll write to you from there as we are staying at a favorite friend's Plantation. Do you have your friends write to me and let me know how you are? You always look good to me. Thank you for all you do for me and remember I love you deeply.

Love to all the family,
M. E. (Monroney)

1963 Two checks written on April 16, 1963, each for $25.00; one to Mary Ellen McClure, the second to Veta Lou McClure; and two checks written May 28, 1963, each for $50.00; one to Mary Ellen McClure, and one to Veta Lou McClure.

1963 *The Daily Oklahoman*, Saturday, August 24

MRS. FINDLAY, FIRST SETTLER'S DAUGHTER, DIES

Mrs. Veta McClure Findlay, 1815 N. Hudson, died Friday at the Sheraton–Oklahoma Hotel. Services are pending with Hahn-Cook Funeral Home. Mrs. Findlay was born in Liberty Hill, Indian Territory, and was a member of First Presbyterian Church and Eastern Star. She is the last surviving child of William J. McClure, first legal settler in Oklahoma City. Survivors include her husband, George, of the home.

1963 October 2. Letter from The Caledonian Hotel, Edinburgh, Scotland

Dear Chrys & Bill,

We have just returned from a summer in the British Isles, Scandinavia, and Paris. When we opened our mail here was your note with the sad reminder of Veta's passing on August 23. We are so sorry to hear of this; Veta was one of our very warm and close friends for such a long time. I called her or tried to see George and Veta each time I was

in Oklahoma City or any of the other places they lived. I knew she was far from well but just didn't expect her passing to be so soon. I am very sorry that we were away and could not have come to Oklahoma City. I talked with Lucille Bowers and Herman soon after learning of her passing to find out the particulars. I am sure that you will miss her a lot and also know you will have a terrific assignment taking care of her great number of valuables and properties everywhere. No one had such a collection of great and priceless possessions as Veta. I have always enjoyed seeing her things and wished for just a few of such lovely things. I am sure that to dispose of such a valuable collection will be a great assignment to you all. European museums did not have more priceless things than Veta owned. I can recall places we have been that would love to have some of her things to complete their collections. Some of the china that Josephine once owned and greatly desired by the French Government Veta possessed as well as other things I can recall. You are very kind and thoughtful to let us know about Veta's passing. Thank you very very much. How is George and where is he now? It is too bad that he is so elderly and his hearing so impaired. If he is in Oklahoma City, please give him our Best Regards,
    Yours truly,
    Dorothy and John Paynter

1963   Offered At Auction: Open House Viewing, Saturday November 30, 1-4 pm and Sunday, December 1. Sale of furnishings begins at 9:30 am December 2nd, 3rd, and 4th. The late Mrs. Findlay, daughter of one of the leading pioneer families, who came to Oklahoma before the run, was a world traveler, maintained a residence in Paris for 7 years, lived in India for many years, maintained a Park Avenue apartment in New York, a residence in Washington, D. C., and several years ago returned to her native Oklahoma where she established her North Hudson home. She purchased the old John C. Calhoun home in Charleston, South Carolina, in the 20s, together with the Calhoun paintings contained therein. Many of the paintings offered will be from the Calhoun collection. We can describe only briefly a small portion of this collection; therefore, we invite you to attend an open house on Saturday and Sunday preceding the auction. On Dec. 2, a fee of $5.00 will be required from each registering guest. This $5.00 is for rental of a chair and may be applied on any purchase. No one will be admitted this day without a chair as there will be no standing room.

Offered At Auction

the residence of the late
Mrs. Veta McClure Findlay

1815 North Hudson, Oklahoma City, Oklahoma
Auction of real estate offered promptly
Monday, December 2nd   9:00 A.M. at the residence
Consult Mr. Bill McClure, Edmond, for appointment to see interior
Open House Sat. and Sun. preceding the auction 1:00-4:00

> Immediately following auction of real estate, the luxurious contents of this lovely home, together with the furnishings of Mrs. Findlay's Washington, D.C. home, will be auctioned to the highest bidder (see following pages for description of contents).
>
> Contents Liquidated By
> MARY MILES CLANTON

Twelve room Georgian brick, over 6,000 sq. ft. of floor space, tile roof, corner lot, 150 ft. on Hudson and 180 ft. on N.W. 18th St. Living room 16½x29, Dining room 15½x24½, Club room 26x28½ with parquet floors and bar, 3½ baths, 5 fireplaces, 4 bedrooms and 2 sitting rooms, library, large foyer, hardwood floors, downstairs draped, steam heat, full basement. Lovely grounds, big trees, shrubbery, sunken garden, circle drive, swimming pool 45x18, 3 car garage with modern apartment, fall-out shelter.
Immediate possession
Sale subject to approval of court. Successful bidder will be required to deposit 10% of sale price with clerk.

Illustration 336. Sale of Veta's Oklahoma City home after her death on August 23, 1963. The liquidation sale lasted three days. Jackie Kennedy sent representatives to buy for her.

Veta's Known Addresses:

1882–1889	7C Ranch,	Indian Territory
1889	7th & Broadway	Oklahoma City, Oklahoma Territory
1900	# 311 West 12th St.,	Oklahoma City, Oklahoma Territory

1921	# 300 Park Avenue	New York City, New York
1923	Rue Cambon	Paris, France (7 years)
1935	# 2232 Massachusetts Ave. N. W.	Washington, D.C.
1937	Braemar Lodge	Green Mountain Falls, Colorado
1937	# 16 Meeting Street, Calhoun House	Charleston, South Carolina
1941	Thorndale	Taneytown, Maryland
1942	# N. Roosevelt Ave.	Wichita, Kansas
1947	# 1109 East Brow Road	Lookout Mountain, Tennesee
1954	# 214 Rugby Rd.	Charlottesville, Virginia
1955	# 1 University Circle	Charlottesville, Virginia
1958	#1815 N. Hudson	Oklahoma City, Oklahoma

Illustration 337. George Scott Findlay

Illustration 338. "The Links": The Findlay family home in Peterhead, Aberdeen, Scotland

Illustration 339. George Scott Findlay and his father, William Findlay

Illustration 340. The Findlays

Illustration 341. The Findlay clan

Illustration 342. Saigon opera house in Vietnam during the time George was a banker with the Chartered Bank of England

Illustration 343. The Saigon Cathedral

Illustration 344. Saigon harbor

Illustration 345. Officers of the Chartered Bank of England and employees. George stands in back row, jacket open and wearing a vest.

Illustration 346. Vietnamese river life

Illustration 347. Vietnamese junk boat

Illustration 348. George (center) Swimming in Saigon

Illustration 349. "The Old Boys Club" in Manilla

Illustration 350. George S. Findlay (right front)

Correspondence about the 24,000-square-foot house at Number 16 Meeting Street, Charleston, South Carolina: Veta bought the house and all its furnishings from the family descendents of John C. Calhoun, Vice President of the United States.

Extremely hard-to-read penmanship explains the blanks that appear here in this reprint of the letters. The letters are important because they verify that Veta bought the house and its furnishings from the Calhoun family. As of 2022, the Calhoun Mansion was still standing, owned by investors.

Mrs. Clarence Crittenden
Rossdhu Lodge, Chevy Chase, Maryland

My dear Mrs. Findlay,

    Mrs. Tremblers, the wife of Judge Tremblers ____ go ___ of Charleston now is the ____ of Justice here when my husband is Special Assistant to the _____. Mrs. M_____ to me by her husband this way of the Presidential Inauguration. She told me that you and your husband had purchased the former "Calhoun Mansion" and I had done it over most _____. So I ____ conceived the idea that you might possibly be interested in the ____ of Calhoun ____ which were one of the ____ of the ____ ____ which I built as a ____ and ___ in while I was Mrs. Andrew _____ of Charleston. In addition to the ____ ___ in the ____ ____ I ensure there is a____ ___ ___ of ____mahogany ____cooler which belonged also to John C. Calhoun. When my first husband was ____ also his mother'___ Frank Martin Calhoun. My _____ husband is of ___ ____ Parrish not of ____ of the Calhoun's of Scotland. -____ ____ ___ ___ but has the ____ and was "the war of succession" We have most of the ____ . ___ where we have no ____ for the mansion ____ ____ of which I will be ____ to ___ it goes all in the last ____. As I hear you also are ____ Scotch. I am ___ that ____ ____. Of the ___ Bonnie ____ Charlie gives me by one of my Scotch ___ only around which I haven't a ___ with me the I remain only where ___ but I will ____

    Sincerely,
    T. B. Calhoun

Letter from Mrs. Andrew P. Calhoun, 1324 Inverness Avenue, Pittsburgh, Pennsylvania

My dear Mrs. Findlay,

    We often recall our trip to Charleston and mention how much we enjoyed having tea, one afternoon, with you and Mr. Findlay. I am writing this note to ask a favor and if you can grant it words will not be able to express my appreciation. Would you consider selling the portraits of my husband's grandfather and grandmother, you know he was named for his grandfather and so often speaks of him. They are in the pair of oval gold frames hanging on the right side of your reception hall – you have so many, many other portraits. I thought you might not miss these at all. I would like to give them to my husband for Christmas and what a grand surprise it would be. Would you please let me know what you would want for them so I can figure how to meet it. Right now both our children have chickenpox but one consolation is that by Christmas they'll be all right. With kindest regards to you both.

    Most sincerely,
    Eunice C Calhoun
    Wednesday, December 3

Letter: from 143 Tradd Street, Charleston, South Carolina

Dear Mrs. Findlay,

After receiving your kind note at the hotel, I went to see Robert Manigaul and obtained his letter, a copy of which I enclose. It is a great pleasure to me to possess this picture you gave me and I deeply appreciate your kindness. You remember we spoke about a picture of the woman in the lower hall, when we realized you were planning to use it we said no more about it as you had already been so good to us but should you decide at any future time not to use it would you bear us in your mind and give us the opportunity of buying it. I hope your plans for 16 Meeting St. are working out successfully. Mrs. Williamson joins me in kindest regards.

Sincerely yours, Porter Williamson

Letter from 53 East 66th Street, November 26, 1934, to Mrs. George Findlay, c/o Carter Hotel, Thermopolis, Wyoming

Dear Mrs. Findlay,

When my wife and I were in Charleston last spring visiting my aunt, Miss Mae L. Reitman of 79 Anson St., she told us there was a portrait of my grandfather, painted by my uncle, hanging in the Calhoun mansion. She had quite a sentimental attachment for the portrait because of its associations. Mr. Williams who built the Calhoun House having had the portrait painted because of his friendship for my grandfather. We went down and looked at the painting. It was not hanging presumably because there was a tear in the canvas, which seemed dry and brittle. My aunt felt a good deal of concern at the condition of the picture which seemed in danger of completely disintegrating and I called on Mr. Stoney, who I understood was representing you, asking him whether you would care to sell the portrait. He said that he would take it up with you and let me know. Not having heard from him since, I asked Mr. Henry Williams when he was in New York a few weeks ago, if he knew whether any disposition had been made of the portrait. Yesterday he wrote me that Mr. Stoney said he had no authority to sell, but suggested I write directly to you—hence this letter. While I presume the portrait has no commercial value, it has sentimental value for my family: and if its condition is such that it could be restored and you should care to dispose of it, I should be glad to purchase it for its association at a price which I could afford.

Very truly yours,
M. S. Reitman

Letter from the Commonwealth of Virginia, Virginia Museum of Fine Arts, Boulevard and Grove Ave., Richmond, September 19, 1956

Mrs. George Scott Findlay.

We have been referred to you in connection with a painting in your possession, a portrait of "John Calhoun" by Colonel John Trumbull. In mentioning your portrait to Professor Theodore Sizer of Yale University, the foremost authority on the work of Trumbull, Professor Sizer expressed a strong desire to have a photograph of the painting. Professor Sizer is interested in studying this work and, if a photograph is available, would greatly appreciate receiving a copy from you. We append Professor Sizer's address below. If, however, you should prefer to send the photograph to us we would be most willing to forward it to Yale University ourselves. Thank you very much, Sincerely yours,

Pinkney Near,
Curator, Professor Theodore Sizer
Department of the History of Art
Yale University, New Haven, Connecticut

Letter found in the Calhoun papers (presumed to be Calhoun family) Liverpool, 3rd October, 1840

Dear Father,

I received your letter of 11 September and I am surprised that my letters have not reached you. Have written to Susan, Adam, and yourself. Since my last have investigated the highlands, of Scotland which are a perfect destination when the miserable season___ these are considered ___not repaid one for the inconvenience attending the town. Edinburgh offers so many enticements that I remained a week there. It is the most___city that I've visited and was more respectfully entertained than in any other place except Belfast which is the only place I would care to visit again. on this side of the water. My reception there was all that could be desired, for the most ____is a fine fellow his wife the____ are lively. This set have my attention, to me. Mrs. Conway has lost all claim to good looks, but haha, of the ladies just coming out that would pass it down. Miss James, is fancy and Stephanie who have in ___ in '38 with the Maywood lands, is a good looking young woman in her own. ___ to evaluate for all civilians, have most a number of my fellow citizens have b___ Captain W. Williams and Mr. Tom Hall ___heard of ___a more walking in Paris also ___ ___ ___who are making quite a fling of it ___ ___ engaged. He's ___ to return home as a ___ I am informed that he was seen in good society there. I shall sail on the 11th in the ___ for New York and do not leave there. Come by with my Richard there is something to be made out of any one's home. All the prospects of searching a perfect wife suffer. And loss which I can only attainable to my ___ weird it's destiny. I see suffering but endure hardship. In people. I will make an effort to get something. [Rest of letter is lost.]

The Calhoun Mansion #16 Meeting Street, Charleston, South Carolina, with original furnishings when purchased by Veta

Illustration 351. Entry Vestibule of the Calhoun Mansion

When Veta purchased the house, she asked her nephew, William John, to inspect it. He found a latch hidden behind a wood panel in the entry. The latch opened an entry to a secret tunnel. Its purpose was to offer an escape route to Charleston Harbor if the city was attacked by the British. The edge of the harbor lay close to the house in 1878, the year the house was built. Today the harbor has receded a noticeable distance.

Illustration 352. Garden on south side of #16 Meeting Street in Charleston, South Carolina

Illustration 353. Entry of #16 Meeting Street

Illustration 354. Calhoun Drawing Room

Illustration 355. Calhoun Sitting Room

Illustration 356. Calhoun Sitting Room

Illustration 357. Library at #16 Meeting Street

Illustration 358. Calhoun Bedroom

1954-1963

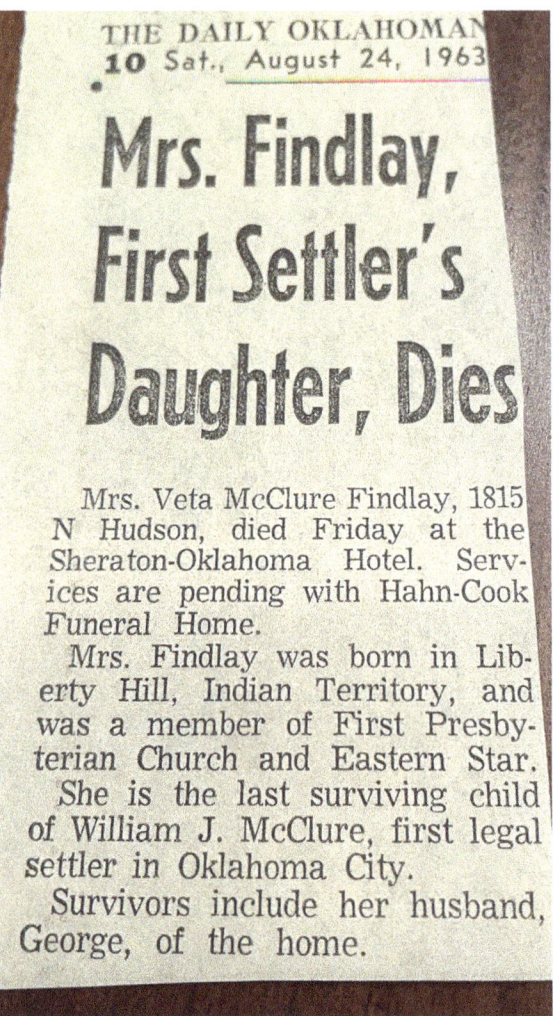

Illustration 359. Veta's obituary

Around 1954, Veta and George "came home" to Oklahoma City. She purchased the beautiful, Georgian home at the southwest corner of 18th and Hudson (1815 N. Hudson). She surrounded herself with exquisite paintings, tapestries, carpets. and furniture gathered over her lifetime. She still gave elegant dinner parties, but her circle of friends was getting smaller. She was outliving many of her childhood friends.

During this decade—she, Bill, Chrys, and the girls established a ritual of sharing Sunday lunch with each other. After lunch they would always spend Sunday afternoon together at her house, having lively, interesting conversations.

Holiday dinners were elaborate affairs with crystal, china, silver and appropriate centerpieces. It was always a grand affair. Veta knew no other way to entertain.

She and George hired a driver to take them to Lookout Mountain, Tennessee, in the summer of 1963. When they returned from that trip, they stayed in the

Biltmore Hotel until their house could be "opened". Opening entailed taking off the white sheets that covered all the upholstered furniture and removing the large galvanized tubs of water from each room. The sheets and the tubs of water were standard practice built on a lifetime of protecting fine furnishings. The sheets protected against dust and fading. The tubs of water provided humidity to keep the furniture from drying out and cracking and splitting.

On August 23, 1963, while still in the Biltmore Hotel [news article on facing page wrongly states the Sheraton-Oklahoma Hotel], Veta succumbed to an apparent heart attack at age 82.

Her life was colorfully lived. Her energy and boldness embodied the prairie frontier of her youth. She was a daughter of Oklahoma and the world.

Let us be judged by our actions

Chapter 8
WILLIAM JOHN McCLURE
1907 - 1970

Illustration 360. William John McClure

[4]William John (Bill) McClure was the first of three children born to David and Grace McClure. Bill attended early elementary grades in Oklahoma City, then attended military academies from about fifth grade forward. He had an aptitude for mathematics and was a gifted athlete, competing in several sports. He was awarded a scholarship to play football at University of Kansas. He was also a consummate horseman, having been in the saddle since an early age.

Much like his Aunt Veta, Bill had a large outgoing personality. He was accepting and inclusive of all people, never judging a person on anything other than a person's character. This brought him friends from all walks of life.

He devoted his life to his family and created a home that became the gathering spot for the friends of both of his daughters. He was on a golf course in Texas practicing for an "old timers" tournament when he had a fatal heart attack and died in 1970 at age 63.

From the Records
[4]**William John McClure**
  b. July 6, 1907, Covington, Kenton County, Kentucky
  m. January 3, 1944, Chrystel McClure
    (McClure is correct maiden name), Oklahoma City, Oklahoma
  f. Presbyterian
  d. February 10, 1970, age 63, Aransas Pass, Texas.
    Cause— Acute Coronary Occlusion
  b. February 13, 1970, Fairlawn Cemetery, Oklahoma City, Oklahoma
    Baggerly Funeral Home, Edmond, Oklahoma

Early Life:
   Bill's parents had purchased the 160 acres at the southeast corner of MacArthur and Memorial Roads NW of Oklahoma City. The farm consisted of a large two-story home, a caretaker's house, a horse barn, a hay barn, a small shed for equipment, a pigpen, a henhouse, and a full horse racetrack. The home was encompassed by white fences and lined with large lilac bushes on the north and west perimeter of the yard. In addition to pastures there was a large alfalfa field.
   Bill's mother Grace was his Boy Scout leader. Summers were spent in Green Mountain Falls, Colorado, where his grandmother had built a home called "House of Seven Gables." It was built at the same time a large resort hotel was built in conjunction with the railroad construction around 1880. The hotel was to help this area of Colorado become a summer destination for people in the Great Plains to escape intense summer heat.

Education:
   Bill attended primary grades at Classen School, Oklahoma City. Following in the family tradition of military school, he entered Howe Military School in Howe, Indiana, for elementary school. For middle school he went to Kiskiminetas Boys Prep School near Pittsburgh, Pennsylvania. Then, for high school and two years of college, he attended Kemper Military School in Boonville, Missouri. It was while at Kemper that he won the most athletic awards

in the school's history. His record held for more than 40 years. He lettered in football, baseball, swimming, track, and wrestling.

Military:

Bill was too young for World War I and too old for World War II. During the Second World War, he oversaw the building of war ships in Baltimore, Maryland. During that time, he ran his horses at nearby tracks.

Bachelor years:

Through his Aunt Veta, Bill met and dated the movie stars Betty Davis and Rita Hayworth. He said that Rita Hayworth was part of a family from Mexico who performed in nightclubs. They were very protective of young Rita but did allow her to go out with him. This happened before she became a movie star. He traveled the world during his bachelor years. And ran a thoroughbred racehorse business. His horses ran the major tracks of the era — Churchill Downs, Hawthorne, Aqueduct, Belmont Park, Fairmount Park, Arlington Park, among others in the eastern United States and Toronto, Canada. In addition, he invested in and was involved in home construction and entrepreneurial ventures with his father.

Marriage:

Bill was 36 years old and Chrystel McClure (maiden name) was 30 years old when they married in 1944. Neither had been married previously. It all happened because they had the same last name. Their good friends in Oklahoma City, Greg and Virginia Duggan, thought they would be a good couple. The Duggans had a dinner party to introduce them. Chrystel was living and working in Dallas at that time. She went to Oklahoma City just for this party. Family stories were that—during the evening—William looked at Chrys and said, "You are the woman I have been waiting for." They were married two weeks later at his family ranch home at the southeast corner of MacArthur and Memorial Boulevard. Cy Hess sang *I Love You Truly*. Chrys notified her parents by Western Union Telegram that she had married "an Oklahoma cowboy!"

Children:

Two daughters were born to Bill and Chrys. Mary Ellen was born in 1945 in Chicago Heights, Illinois. She always joked that she was "born in a stable" because they had been watching Bill's horses run at Arlington Park when she was born. (They did make it to the hospital for her birth.) In 1948, Veta Louise was born in Louisville, Kentucky. This time his horses were running at Churchill Downs.

Organizations: 89ers Association, Masons

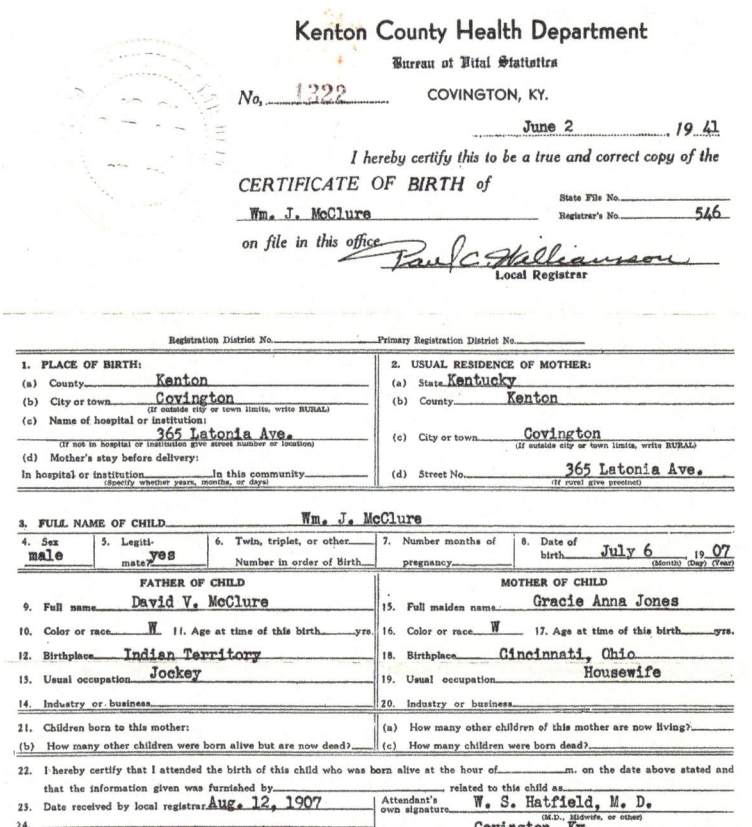

Illustration 361. William John's birth certificate

Illustration 362. Six-week-old William and his dad, Dave, arriving Oklahoma City by train

1907 Bill was born in Covington, Kentucky, because his father had horses racing at Latonia Racetrack. Dave and Grace's ranch was at the southeast corner of MacArthur and Memorial Boulevard, Oklahoma City. This was where Bill grew up. He attended his early primary grades at Classen Grade School. Grace was his Cub Scout den leader. We still have a small "tom-tom" that was a project he made while a Cub Scout. His grandmother, Mary Ellen, owned a home (the House of Seven Gables in Green Mountain Falls, Colorado). Most of his early summers were spent there. In those days (before air conditioning) people from the hot Great Plains who could move to the cooler mountains did so. One family story handed down tells of the family staying at Green Mountain until close to Thanksgiving. They had a ham hanging on a back screened porch to cure. During the night a bear broke down the screens and door to get the ham.

1907   Oklahoma becomes the 46th state in the union.

Illustration 363. William and mother, Grace

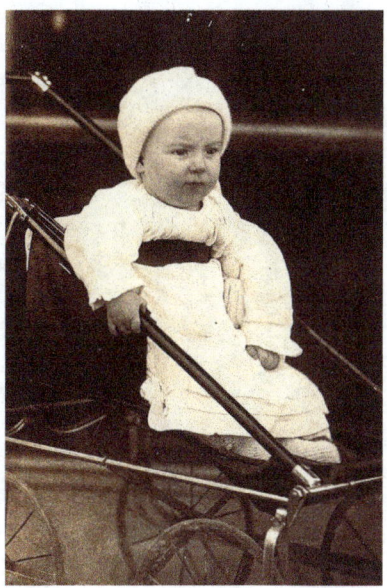

Illustration 364. Baby William

1908

Illustration 365. William and grandmother, Mary Ellen

Illustration 366. William John McClure, July 6, 1908, the day he turned one year old. He rode four miles that day.

1908   Henry Ford introduces the Ford Model T automobile.

Illustration 367. Grandmother Mary Ellen and Baby William

Illustration 368. Toddler William and furry friend on grandmother's front porch

Illustration 369. A toddler already riding and using a crop, baby William

Illustration 370. Proud Dave with young William

Illustration 371. William about two years old

1909   President McKinley assassinated; Vice President Theodore Roosebelt becomes the 26th President.

Illustration 372. William

Illustration 373. He even rode a donkey.

Illustration 374. Grace, William, and Dave

Illustration 375. William at his folks' ranch in the early 1900s, corner of MacArthur and Memorial Boulevard, Oklahoma City. The fenced yard gives William a safe place to ride alone on the 160-acre ranch.

Illustration 376. William and little sister, Veta Ann

Illustration 377. Veta Ann and big brother, William

1912   *Titanic* ocean liner sinks in the North Atlantic; Oreo cookies invented; Fenway Park opens in Boston; New Mexico enters Union as the 47th state.

1913   Woodrow Wilson becomes U.S. President.

Illustration 378. William, age six, 1913

Illustration 379. William, now seven

Illustration 380. William, 1913

1913   16th Amendment becomes law, creating an income tax.

1914   World War I begins.

1915   German U-boat sinks passenger ship *RMS Lusitania*, contributing indirectly to the U.S. entering World War I.

1917   Spanish Flu pandemic strikes. By 1920 the dead numbered between 20 million and 50 million, possibly as high as 100 million.

1918   World War I ends.

Illustration 381. William, leaving on train for school

Illustration 382. William in uniform of Howe Military Academy

1923 Letter written by William to his grandmother. Postmarked Indiana, January 5, 1923

"Dear Grandmother,

I thought I would drop you a few lines. I was skating today and did really well. I had lots of fun too, but a few falls that hurt a little but kept right on. Dear Grandmother, I was very disappointed when I was home. For you did not say anything about the breakfast room windows. I was sure that would be the first thing you would see. The first morning I was there, but I guess you have got used to it by now. It was two days to get here, but they did not say anything for I came from so far away. Basketball has started and I have not got my trunk yet that has my clothes in it, so I don't get to play till I get it. Must leave off for this time with Love and Kisses,

Your Most Loving Grandson William

Illustration 383. Howe Military Academy football team. William (back row—fourth from right)

Illustration 384. William wearing Howe Military Academy letter sweater

Illustration 385. William's first letter sweater

Illustration 386. William at rest on Howe's campus

1923   Letter written from Howe, Indiana, from William to his grandmother

Dear Grandmother,

Just a few lines for I promised you I would write every week, but I have been so busy with my examinations I have had hardly time for everything. The Blake Midgets are still undefeated and yesterday we beat the daylights out of them 7 to 4 and now we have only one more game to play. I guess I will stay here for my Easter vacation, I will have a good time and from today it is only 75 days till I will be home. Well, I will quit for this time with love and kisses, Write soon.

From your Most Loving Grandson,
William

1924   Ellis Island closed as an entry point for immigration

1925   Scopes (Monkey) Trial, July 10-21 in Dayton, Tennessee

1926 William attends the Kiskiminetas Boarding School in Saltsburg, Pennsylvania, 30 miles east of Pittsburgh. Kiski (as it is fondly called) is one of America's oldest boys' boarding schools, founded in 1888. It enrolls young gentlemen from all over the world who wish to prepare for the rigors of the nation's best universities. Kiski's 360-acre campus overlooks the small town of Saltsburg, Pennsylvania. Kiski's dynamic faculty employs technology every day. About 200 boys and 40 faculty and administrators live on the beautifully wooded campus. William loved to play golf even in the Pennsylvania wintertime snows, when he would use a red golf ball.

Illustration 387. Aunt Veta and William

Illustration 388. Aunt Veta and William

Illustration 389. Uncle George Myers Church and William

Illustration 390. George M. Church and William

Illustration 391. William growing up

1927 Model A Ford introduced

Letter dated April 17

Dear Dad and Mother,

I received your letter Friday and your package yesterday and thank you very much for the box. I have not much to say this time for the reason that I said everything in my other letters this week. Just what is the matter with my boots you never say a word about them, and I have asked you about them in every letter that I have written to you or are you just keeping something from me that you don't want me to know. I went to church this morning and everyone there was all decked out in their new spring rags and they definitely did look nice, only I would have liked it much better if you and I had been home and gone to church with you all and GUY old boy, I guess you all are busy to go to church today, but next summer you may expect to go to church every Sunday and we will be able to take Guy and get him started. We are going to Lexington next week to play them in ball, that is Wentworth, and we are going to give them some work if they try to best us. Well, I will have to stop for this time, but I will write soon, and I hope you will do the same because I do like to hear from you all, Your older Son,

Letter written to his mother and father—no date—but on Kemper letterhead

Dear Mother and Dad,

I received your dear letter yesterday and I certainly was glad to get it, because things were beginning to get rather dull around this place. Excuse the typewriter but I am trying to learn how to use one and I thought that I would try by writing to you because I know you will not mind if I write with this machine to you, to answer your letter. Things are going perfect around here now, school is in full speed and each day is drawing us a day closer to Christmas vacation and my roommate just said that there is only 91 more days til we start home, and if that doesn't sound good, I would like to know what dose [sic], because that means home sweet home, and also a dear Dad and Mother I will get to see, so if that does not make a fellow feel perfect I would like to know what dose [sic]. There have been four new boys run off in the last three days because they were so homesick and they could not stay away from their girls any longer. It has only rained about half of the time since I have been here- so you know just about what it has been, I can hardly wait til it is time to come home, for one reason is to see the new house and how things are arranged. Well, I guess this will be about all for this time with heaps of love and kisses to all.

Love, William

ps – Please write as often as you can.

Boonville newspaper, no date given

T. K Hitch, A. J. McGuire, W. F. Blackmon, M. S. Francis, C. M. Ferguson, W. H. Frye, W .H. Ramey, E. W. Paype, C. B. Emmitt, W. J. McClure, and T. R. Taylor, Kemper cadets attending the R.O.T.C. camp at Fort Leavenworth, Kansas this summer drove to Boonville Saturday evening in decrepit Ford owned by McClure and Traylor returned to camp last night. The boys reported an uneventful trip down except for a little difficulty in climbing hills and a 3 ½" rain, they encountered near Leavenworth, which gave them a real drenching.[13]

---

[13]Adapted text reproduced courtesy of *Boonville Daily News* and CherryRoad Media

Illustration 392. Athlete William

Illustration 393. William in football uniform of Kemper Military Academy

Illustration 394. Gridiron gladiators

Illustration 395. Gridiron action

KEMPER GRIDMEN WIN CONFERENCE GAME HERE 8...

Yellow Jackets Score Tw... Touchdowns to Lutheran's One.

CADETS PLAY FAST BAL...

Hard Contest Scheduled This Week With Ducks From C. B. C.

Conference Standing

	W.	L.	Pct.
Kemper M. S.	1	0	1000
Wentworth M. A.	1	0	1000
Rockhurst Col.	0	1	000
St. Pauls Col.	0	1	000
Chillicothe B. C.	0	0	000

Crashing through the line at will, striking the ends for long gains, and hurling long passes with perfection the Yellow Jackets displayed a powerful offense last Friday when they defeated the Saint Pauls College eleven of Concordia, Mo., 83-7. So powerful were the ground gaining plays of the Forner men that they scored two touchdowns in each of the first two quarters and four in each of the last two periods. The only scoring of the invaders came in the last of the first half when the Lutheran quarterback took the ball on Kemper's kickoff after a touchdown and ran through the entire cadet team for their lone score of the game.

The local men started the game with a rush, driving the invaders back to their one yard line but all in vain for Kemper fumbled the ball and Saint Pauls recovered. Again the cadets on gaining possession of the oval carried it within scoring distance but repeated their sad performance of a minute before, fumbling the ball. The invaders were forced to kick and this time the Kemper men set themselves to score. Two line plunges brought first down and the possibility of a score. A long end run and two cross-bucks placed the soldiers for a third time in a scoring position. This time the ball was given to McClure and the tiny halfback darted across the line for six points and Holmes added the seventh with a neat try for point, a thing which he did not miss in ten chances offered him during the game. Gordon scored the second touchdown by picking up a fumble made by the Lutheran's and dashing across the line, Holmes kicking goal.

Second Quarter

KEMPER WINS 83 TO 7

(Continued from page 1)

...tra point.

The second half opened with the cadets making another march down the field. With Winberg, Lashley, McClure ripping off long gains the army men brought the ball within scoring distance in six downs and on the seventh W. L. Johnston plunged across for the fifth touchdown. Holmes kicked goal. A long pass Johnston to Tarr took the ball to the two-yard line and Winberg hurdled the pile for another six points. Again Holmes drop-kicked for the extra point, a thing which he did successfully on all of the remaining touchdowns. Again the aerial attack was completed, for with two passes, McClure to Johnston and McClure to Holmes, the oval was in position for the plunging Winberg to score and he did. On the next play Lashley caught the kickoff, started up the field, suddenly reversed his direction and with Holmes cutting down the only dangerous man, the speedy half ran the rest of the way across ... opposed.

REPRODUCED COURTESY *BOONVILLE DAILY NEWS* AND CHERRYROAD MEDIA

Illustration 396. Sports news

Illustration 397. Kemper baseball team. William (front row, third from right)

345

Illustration 398. Kemper's baseball catcher, William

Illustration 399. William in Kemper togs

Illustration 400. Military School track team (William at end, left)

Illustration 401. Kemper Military School swim team (William back row, right)

1927 Newspaper article, Boonville, Missouri

YELLOW JACKETS HOLD FAST LEAD

The Yellow Jackets of Kemper advanced another notch forward toward the championship when they defeated St. Paul of Concordia by the decisive score of 33-6. The Yellow Jackets were not forced to play their best, keeping themselves in trim for the hard task to come next Saturday when Rockhurst, also a leader, is to be met in Kansas City. This will be the hard game, and Kemper has great hopes of breaking over the line with another victory which will assure them the championship for this year. First Quarter: St. Paul won the toss and chose to defend the west goal. McClure kicked off for Kemper to St. Paul's 19-yard yard line and ball returned to St. Paul's 36-yard line. Pass incomplete. Five yards around the right end. Fullback thrown for loss by Black. St. Paul kicked to Kemper's 28-yard line. McClure returned the ball to Kemper's own 48-yard line. McClure 1 yard line at right end. Van Dyne 3 yards at left tackle. McClure punted to St. Paul's 21-yard line. St. Paul's pass incomplete. St. Paul netted 2 yards at right end, 2 yards over left tackle and punted to Kemper's 44-yard line. McClure returned the ball to St. Paul's 48-yard line.

McClure made it first down through left guard. Ball on the St. Paul's 40 yard line. McClure 3 yards at center. McClure over the center for touchdown. His try for point by drop kick failed. McClure kicked off to St. Paul's 15-yard line. McClure played stellar ball for Kemper, ripping off yardage at will. (This is a portion of a long article in which he is named many times).[14]

1928 Penicillin discovered

Letter written on Kemper stationary

My dear Mother and Dad,

I have not written for several days, and I guess you know more about that than I do, but I also know about you so that is swell, isn't it? All I have been thinking of is the game here against Wentworth. We have everything at stake and every one of the men are going to battle to the last. We'll give those guys a real wholloping. Everybody will be there, so will the Wentworth battalion; it will be a battle royal between two of the oldest rivals in this part of the country. I will wire you the results of the game as soon as I can. It will be about six o'clock. You know about our other games with Rockhurst. The weather delay, we were just off around three____? At about six the grandstand teams at Kemper. Say, I think I will have to have a gift for Missy Jamison for ____. As and you can get things that

---
[14]Adapted text reproduced courtesy of *Boonville Daily News* and CherryRoad Media

are so much nicer and get them cheaper. Will you give me a real nice present and send it to me? A real good looking compact or whatever you think, and a little something for the son too? (ha ha). I received my baseball and thank you for sending it. I think it is very good looking myself. Well, this will be all for this time, but write soon and Hello Guy Old Boy,

Love,
William

Illustration 402. Kemper military exercises. William (back row, third from right)

Illustration 404. William, commissioned Second Lieutenant

Illustration 403. William (left) at military camp

Illustration 405. Buddies (William second from right)

Illustration 406. Boys being boys

Illustration 407. Class picture, Kemper Military School (William in second row, second from left)

Kemper Military School, Boonville, Missouri

"This is to certify that Cadet W.J. McClure has achieved the following distinction during the school year of 1928-1929: Member of K Club, President; Member of Student Council; Lieutenant; Letters in Football, Baseball, Swimming, and Indoor Track; Member of Class Graduating from Junior College."

Article in Edmond, Oklahoma, newspaper

Boonville, Mo., Dec. 4—Reward for four years of distinguished work in the military department was given by authorities of Kemper Military school to William J. McClure, son of Mr. and Mrs. D.V. McClure of Edmond. According to an order from the school's superintendent, Lieutenant Col. A. M. Elliott, Cadet McClure was commissioned a second lieutenant, being promoted from the rank of sergeant.[15]

William John graduated Kemper Military Military Academy High School May 29, 1927, and Kemper Military College, May 21, 1929.

William set more athletic records than any other student at Kemper. His records stood unbroken for 40 years. He was offered a scholarship to play football at Kansas University, but turned it down to go into entrepreneurial ventures with his dad.

Illustration 408. William's graduation photo

1929 Wall Street Stock Market Crash

---
[15] Adapted text reproduced with permission of *Edmond Sun*/CNHI, LLC

Illustration 409. A pickup football game in Sulphur, Oklahoma (halfback William in back row, left)

After graduation, William joined the family businesses of ranching, raising thoroughbred horses, construction, and oil. Some of the ranch land was in Sulphur, as well as Oklahoma City.

1930 Beginning of the Dust Bowl. The drought lasted until 1936.

1931 Grand Secretary's Certificate of membership in the Most Worshipful Grand Lodge, A.F. & A.M. of the State of Oklahoma: Wm. John McClure was awarded a Master Mason in good standing of Britton Lodge, January 1, 1931.

1937 Economic recession continues

Illustration 410. William's passport photos

Passport issued to William John McClure. Stamps for Great Britain, France, Suez Canal, Egypt, Italy; several stamps not legible

Newspaper article dated January 13, 1937

FORMER BRITTON RESIDENT LEAVES ON CRUISE OF WORLD

William McClure, well known thirty-year-old son of Mr. and Mrs. Dave McClure left with his aunt and uncle, Mr. and Mrs. George Findlay, on a five month's world tour on the Empress of Britain at 11a.m. Saturday from New York City. Traveling via the Mediterranean, on the largest British steamer afloat, Mr. McClure will visit more than 108 ports and places which will include Gibraltar, Algiers, Monaco, Naples, and Athens and a special trip to Jerusalem and Cairo. In private trains the former local resident will cross India to Delhi, and the Taj Mahal, stopping to spend a week visiting in the home of his uncle's brother. An inland journey to Peiping, the ports of the Orient, and three weeks' stay in Paris where he will also visit the world-famous Monte Carlo, are among Mr. McClure's globetrotting stops. Being a horse fancier, he will attend the Grand National Steeplechase held in London, England during his three weeks' stay there. This race will cover four and a half miles of the most difficult riding from the leading contestants of America, and the Continent. Mr. McClure will enjoy the tour in the company of Mr. and Mrs. Findlay who have previously circumnavigated the globe four times also living in Bombay, India for many years where Mr. Findlay was connected with the London Bank. Well known in this part of the country, Mr. McClure attended the local schools before enrolling in Kemper Military School in Boonville, Mo., where he completed six years' work. His many friends wish him a successful and very pleasant journey and are looking forward to his return.

A separate newspaper article without a date

When asked what was the most interesting place he saw on his recent trip around the world. . . 'Home!'

1937 Letter from Grace Anna Jones McClure (Bill's mother)

My Dear Big Boy, Veta and George,

Just a line to thank you for that wonderful letter. I wish you could have seen Daddy, he surely looked nice in his tux. I fixed the blue dress over and wore it. I had all Grand Officers to install. They gave me more lovely presents. I surely was surprised. The chapter

gave a bouquet for me and there were over a hundred and everything was decorated with flowers, and they gave me a big bunch of red roses and made me a crown of white & red rose buds. And put it on my head. Dr. Philips gave me a silver purse and you and Guy gave me a lovely evening handkerchief and so many other things, but no one will ever know how proud I was of Daddy. Goldie shaking hands with me. She sure is growing. Daddy says he sure thinks she is fine. He stands and looks at her and shakes his head and sighs and I am sure he likes her as well as Matron. (a reference to two horses Gold Princess and Worthy Matron) I am sure of it—everything is fine here. Baby came finish & she runs a bucket full. Give Aunt Veta & Uncle Geo my best wishes and heaps of love too. Guy is at school, so he won't get in on this letter. Have a good time and be good to Aunt Veta—answer and tell us all about what you are seeing.

Love,
Mama

1938 Seabiscuit defeats War Admiral at Pimlico Race Course.

January 18, 1938. Letter Addressed to Mr. W.J. McClure c/o American Express Co, Rome, Italy

Dear Son, Veta and George,

It is just a little over a week since you sailed but it seems like a month. Everything is okay here at home. For the past two weeks, we have had real spring weather. Son, your message to your mother was fine and did she feel proud of it. It got her! Guy asked her, after she was installed as Worthy Matron, if he could approach the east. Guy said he had been talking with Mr. Johnson and he said "while you are serving as Worthy Matron, Daddy and I would probably have to get up and cook our own breakfast and eat a cold dinner. But we won't have to do that will we, Mama?" Your mother said, "why no son". Guy said "well then here is a little gift from Bud and me. We wish you a happy and prosperous year." Guy acted and talked like he was about to cry. He did not have to, his mother did it for him. It was the best and brightest thing Britton Chapter has ever pulled off. We had entertainment from Mo 10 Chapter, also from Myrtle Chapter and they were fine. None of our chapter knew who they were or that they were going to ___everything. And were they surprised! Horses are doing fine. Prander will bring a colt this spring. Do not forget to send Miles cards as he enjoys them very much. Just think of everyone you know in this part of the country, and they are asking about you. They see by the papers that you are having some storms in that part of the world. Hope you are missing them. Have you been feeding the fish? Mama and Guy join me in sending Love and best wishes to all of you,

Daddy

Illustration 411. William, Aunt Veta, and Uncle George in Venice

Illustration 412. William at top of Acropolis, Athens, Greece

Illustration 413. William in Egypt

Illustration 414. William visiting the pyramids of Egypt

1939 May 26. William holds a membership card from the Nebraska State Racing Commission.

1939 Newspaper article in *The Courier* (Louisville, Kentucky) *Journal*

Churchill Downs Visitors: photograph of Mrs. Jay Willingham, Lookout Mountain, Tenn., and Mr. William McClure, Oklahoma City (cousins—author's insert) and owner of Ranch 7C, prefaced the Kentucky Derby with a week's racing at the Downs.[16]

Illustration 415. William in Taneytown, Maryland

1941 William lived in Taneytown, Carroll County, Maryland, where he boarded his horses, so letters were addressed to R. F. D. Taneytown. Taneytown was founded in 1754, named after Raphael Taney, who had one of the first land grants. George Washington once wrote, "Tan-nee town is but a small place with only the Street through which the road passes. The buildings are principally of wood."

---

[16]Reproduced with permission of the *Louisville Courier Journal*/Courier-Journal.com

Illustration 416. Taneytown, Maryland, where William boarded his horses

Illustration 417. Driveway view of Taneytown, Maryland, horse farm

1943 This letter began a friendship that lasted the lifetime of both William and Chrys. The C. W. McClures of Ohio began following Bill McClure's horses because they had the same last name.

East Cleveland, Ohio
November 1, 1943
Dear Mr. McClure,

Congratulations on the fine performance of Gold Princess last Saturday. It has often been said that a good horse was one that did what was asked of it. Since this is especially true of the Princess, I believe that without further proof of her quality she should be made a Queen. I would like to have a picture of her. With the best wishes for the best of luck I am sincerely yours.

C. W. McClure

Illustration 418. William exercising his race horse in Toronto, Canada

1943 Letter from the Selective Service System, August 16

Dear Mr. McClure:

Upon reference to your letter of February 23, 1942 we find that you had made an application for active duty to the Adjutant General's office, however, we have never received notice as to whether or not you were accepted. We would appreciate your letting us have an official notice either from your Commanding Officer or from the Adjutant General's office as to your present status in as much as we are required to keep our records up to date.

For the Board,
Margaret Martin, Clerk

1944 January 3. Oklahoma City, Oklahoma. William marries Chrystel McClure (correct maiden name).

Illustration 419. William, Chrys, and *Remembering*

Illustration 420. William, Chrys, and friends (the Harpers) with thoroughbred *Remembering* in winner's circle, Hot Springs, Arkansas

Illustration 421. Gusher well, an investment with Deardorf Oil Company

1961-1970 Lots of awards for golf tournaments

1961 Part of a Letter from Aunt Veta Findlay dated November 9

My Dearest Children,

You have both been so good about writing and I have been very bad – but, I have just not felt well at all. Today I am feeling a little better. Mary went over to the "Southern Club" and won $80.00 playing roulette. She was on top of the world. I did not go with her, as I just did not feel like it. Everyone is just scared to death over here at Little Rock. I think we will most likely have war in the next three months. I want to go out to El Paso, Texas in about two weeks. I thought you could motor down to Fort Worth on Saturday and stay that night with us then go back on Sunday. The doctors say I cannot be where I will get any cold air this winter. We want to see all of you. We are lonesome to see each of you. I will pay the bill. Mary sends her best love – so does Uncle George – so do I.

Devotedly,
Aunt Veta.

1961 *Arkansas Gazette* newspaper article, November 13

YOU CAN SURVIVE ATOMIC ATTACK
Be Careful to Store Everything You Need

To draw up a list of essentials needed in a fallout shelter, imagine you are actually living in it for 48 hours, or two weeks. Do you find you have plenty of canned foods – and no can opener? Put one aside, now. A jar of instant coffee, but no cup or glass? Hot coffee, or warmed milk for a baby, could be morale boosters. If power is knocked out, have you thought of providing a supply of canned heat which burns without smoke, or a camp stove if your shelter has enough room for it? I have a friend who built a $25,000 shelter, perhaps the best ever built. He has stocked it well and gone on to add a set of the Encyclopedia Britannica as a choice of reading matter, The Bible, a dictionary, Shakespeare, current novels, your selection of books taking relatively little space can help adults pass the boring time, even if the shelter only permits reading by daylight. For insurance take sleeping pills, too. Ask your doctor what kind. But let's look at the true essentials for survival in your shelter. I'd list highest the transistor radio, radiation meter, flashlights, candles, and plenty of spare batteries, checked at intervals for age and condition. Check whether your shelter needs an aerial for your radio. They could be especially important in rural or farm areas, and in underground shelters. Add a shovel, even an ax and pick, in case your shelter collapses and you must dig your way out. And a broom to sweep out fallout dust and a first aid kit. Let me emphasize again, that the main thing in protecting yourself is an understanding of what you might face, what these weapons might do, and then having the equipment to deal with situations. You need water. Your shelter should have a minimum of five gallons of bottled water per person using the shelter. Plan a 14-day supply, go easy on the water, at the outset. Some bottled water could be left just outside the entrance of a cramped shelter, but within easy reach. Cover it with paper or plastic film, which would hold off any fallout dust settling down—then flip off the paper or film and bring the water inside. Xrays from the fallout will not harm the water one iota, nor make it radioactive and the same thing holds for food too. You must not eat the dust itself, but the radiation doesn't hurt the food. Wash the food or open a can and it will be safe. If you run out of water, tap water still is safe if your supply comes from deep wells. Do you have blankets, sleeping bags, Extra blankets, games and toys. You need toilet or sanitary facilities. Don't overlook plates, knives, forks, and spoons. One essential of life is oxygen, and I am considering putting a tank of oxygen in my shelter in case of a firestorm from a bombing. That's a subject to be considered later."

WILLARD F. LIBBY, *YOU CAN SURVIVE ATOMIC ATTACK* (ASSOCIATED PRESS, 1961)

1963 Letter from second cousin, Mickey Willingham, Macon, Georgia, August 29. Mickey was the son of Mary Hortense (McClure) and her husband, Jay Willingham. Mickey was the owner of Georgia Coating Clay Company, mines in the Georgia townships of Franklinton, Dry Branch, Fitzpatrick, and Jeffersonville. He was the son of Mary and Jay Willingham, Chattanooga, Georgia.

> *Dear Chrys and Bill,*
>
> *This is merely a note to express my sincere appreciation for the many nice and thoughtful things you both did for us on our visit to Oklahoma. In fact, the three of us left yesterday a lot richer for having been with you and gotten to know all your family (including Margaret) so well. I consider all the McClures not only my relatives now, but warm, genuine friends as well which is really more important to me anyway. Thank you again everyone, for making our stay such a memorable one and please make a sincere, concerted effort to visit us in Macon in the near future.*
>
> *Love to all,*
> *Mickey*

1965 Passport issued to William J. McClure. Stamps: France, Spain, Italy, Austria, Switzerland, Germany, Belgium, England, Scotland, Wales

1960-1970

By 1960 William John had retired from his many business enterprises; For the next decade he and Chrystel traveled to Europe, Mexico, and widely across the United States. He kept close ties with the McClure clan, always making himself available to help family members with whatever chore they needed done. He was active in the men's group at First Presbyterian Church, Edmond, OK. He loved people from all walks of life, was never a self-promoter, but always ready to give anyone a helping hand. In 1970 he and Chrystel were spending the winter at Aransas Pass on the Texas Gulf coast. After breakfast in his motor home, he went out to play a round of golf. He was a good athlete and loved to compete. This particular morning he was going out to fine-tune his game for the upcoming Old Timer's Golf Tournament in Las Vegas. It was a typical February morning in Aransas Pass, mildly cool and breezy. He was playing ahead of a foursome. They watched him line up his next shot in the fairway. Suddenly he collapsed. The foursome rushed to him, but they were too late. A heart attack had ended his life at age 63.

1968 Life member in good standing of Oklahoma Historical Society

1970 *The Daily Oklahoman* newspaper article

McCLURE RITES ARE HELD FEB. 13.

Services were held Feb. 13, 1970 at Baggerly Funeral Home Chapel for William J. (Bill) McClure, 63, 606 Timber Lane, who died Feb. 10 while playing golf at Rockport, Texas. Burial was in Fairlawn Cemetery, Oklahoma City. A native of Latonia, Ky., (not true – just born there) he lived most of his life in the Edmond, Oklahoma City area, where his family pioneered. A member of First Presbyterian Church, he was a retired rancher and investor. He belonged to the Edmond Lodge AFAM #37 in the Guthrie Consistory. He is survived by his wife, Chrystel of the home; two daughters, Mrs. Mary Ellen Randall, St. Louis, Mo., and Miss Veta Lou McClure of Stillwater and his mother, Mrs. Grace Lowrance who lives in Sulphur.

Let us be judged by our actions

Chapter 9
V. CHRYSTEL McCLURE
1913 - 1985

Illustration 422. V. Chrystel McClure

[4]Chrystel was the second child born to Hugh and Mary Alice McClure in Lowell, Arkansas. Her father was the railroad station master in Rogers, Arkansas. Her grandfather had drawn the plat plans for the town of Lowell, had brought the first telephone lines and the first electric lines into town. The main street in Lowell is named McClure Avenue.

Chrystel attended school in Rogers. Upon high school graduation she went to nursing school in Fayetteville. During her freshman year she contracted whooping cough and diphtheria, at the same time. She went home for six months to recover.

After that period, she went to business school. She became a secretary for an insurance firm in Nevada, Missouri. The president of that office was asked to be CEO of the holding insurance company in Dallas. He asked Chrystel to move to Dallas as his secretary.

In Dallas she met a good friend, Virginia Duggan. During the ensuing years, Virginia and Greg Duggan moved to Oklahoma City. Here they became friends of Bill McClure. They thought it was cute that Bill and Chrystel shared the same last name, although no familial relationship existed. So they planned a dinner party in Oklahoma City and invited Bill and Chrystel McClure. That night Bill told Chrys that she was the woman he had been waiting to marry. Two weeks later they married.

Chrys and Bill were married 26 years until Bill's death in 1970. Her life with Bill was full of adventure and excitement—thoroughbred racehorses, travel, and the birth of two daughters. She was a full-time homemaker. Chrys's top priority was her family and her home. She was a warm loving mother and created a home environment that was inviting, and at the same time a sanctuary for her family and friends.

From the Records
[4]V. Chrystel McClure
   b. 1913, August 5, 1913, Lowell, Arkansas
  m. 1944, January 3, 1944, William John McClure, Oklahoma City, Oklahoma
    f. Presbyterian
  d. 1985, August 3, 1985, Edmond, Oklahoma
   b. Fairlawn Cemetery, Oklahoma City, Oklahoma

Parents:
   Father: Hugh Brown McClure, railroad station master in Rogers, Arkansas
   Mother: Mary Alice Bishop McClure, well-know for skits she wrote and read over radio stations in Rogers, Arkansas

Siblings:
   Elmo died in a car accident near Pittsburg, Kansas, at age 23.
   John Samuel (wife, Sally)
   Mary Alice McClure Slate (husband, Joseph)
   Jack (Hugh Bishop) (wife, Sally)
   Margaret Louise McClure (never married)

Children:
[5]Mary Ellen McClure Randall (husband, George R.)
[5]Veta Louise McClure Roberts (husband, Thomas R.)

Organizations:
'89er Association
Church Women
Ladies Investment Club
Volunteer at the Edmond Hospital

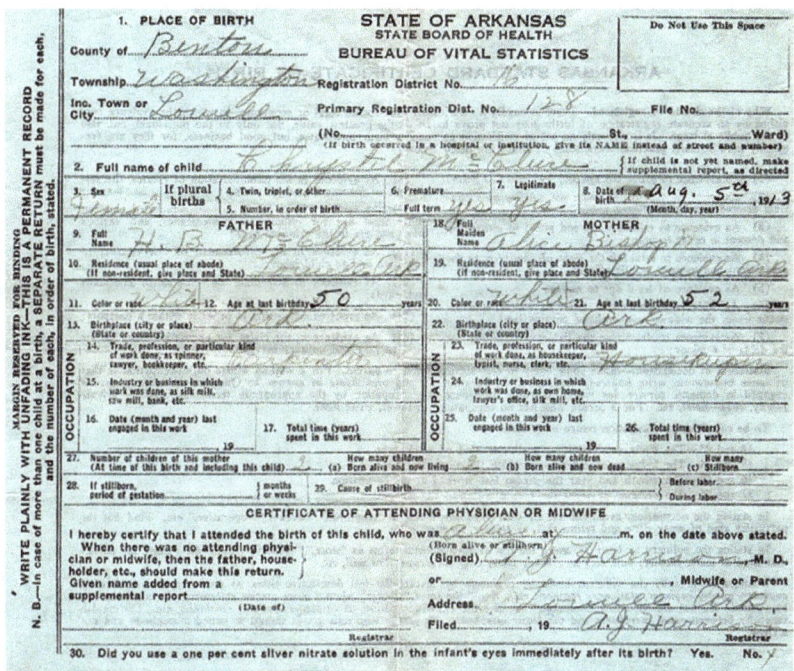

Illustration 423. Birth certificate, 1913

V. Chrystel McClure's Timeline

1913 16th Amendment passed, creating income tax

1914 World War 1 begins.

1915 *RMS Lusitania* sunk by German U-boat

1916 General Pershing fails in quest of rebel Pancho Villa, in Mexico.

1917 Spanish Flu strikes the world—by 1920 well over 50 million persons perished.

1918 World War 1 ends.

1919 18th Amendment passed, prohibiting the legal making or selling of alcohol

1920 19th Amendment adopted, giving women the right to vote

1921   Race riots in Tulsa, Oklahoma

1922   The Soviet Union founded

1924   Ellis Island closed as an entry point for immigration

1925   Scopes Monkey Trial

1926   First television demonstrated; SAT testing begun; Winnie-the-Pooh published

1927   Model A Ford rolled out; Charles Lindbergh, the first pilot to solo across the Atlantic Ocean

1928   Penicillin discovered; Amelia Earhart, the first woman pilot to solo across the Atlantic Ocean

1929   Wall Street stock-market crash, onset of Great Depression

1930   Debut of Mickey Mouse comic strip

Illustration 424. Elmo, Mary Alice, mother Mary Alice, Chrystel, and cousin Genevieve Bishop

Illustration 425. Mary Alice with Elmo (left), Chrystel (second from left) and friends

1931   The Star Spangled Banner adopted as U.S. National Anthem; the Dust Bowl

1932   Worldwide economic depression; Radio Music Hall opened

1933   21st Amendment repealed; Adolf Hitler named dictator; Albert Einstein settled in the U.S.A.

1934   Dust Bowl, 300 million acres damaged by drought; Ritz Crackers invented

1935   Hoover Dam (1930-1936) built; Social Security started, August 14

Illustration 426. Chrystel (left), Elmo, Mary Alice, Genevieve

Illustration 427. Mary Alice (left) and Chrystel

Illustration 428. Elmo and Chrystel with their grandmother, Lizzy McClure

Illustration 429. Lowell, Arkansas, train depot where Chrystel's father, Hugh, was the station master. During WWII and early 50s, he came out of retirement to become station master in Bokhoma, Oklahoma. This was located in a major timber area. The war effort needed timber for ship construction.

Illustration 430. Chrystel (front row, fourth from left) with her elementary school class

Illustration 431. Chrystel (front row, third from left) with junior high school class

Illustration 432. Chrystel backing up cousin Genevieve for a bull ride

1936 Turing Machine invented by Alan Turing; electricity brought to rural areas of the U.S.A.

1937 Economic recession bleak; Kix Corn Puffs introduced

1938 War Admiral defeated by Seabiscuit at Pimlico Race Course; Czechoslovakia invaded by Hitler

1939 Europe caught up in WWII; Debut of nylon stockings, traffic yield signs, and *Wizard of Oz* movie

Illustration 433. Chrystel's (second row, third from left) graduating class from Rogers High School–1933

Illustration 434. Chrystel's graduation, 1933

Illustration 435. Chrystel (right) and friend

Illustration 436. Chrystel (left) dating 1930s style

Illustration 437. Chrystel's too cute for this guy!

Illustration 438. Off to nursing school for Chrystel

Illustration 439. Chrystel and friend at nursing school in Fort Smith, Arkansas

Illustration 440. Chrystel (left) with life-long friend, Catherine Graham Looney

Illustration 441. White dresses, white sidewalls. Chrystel (left)

Illustration 442. Chrystel on break from work in Nevada, Missouri

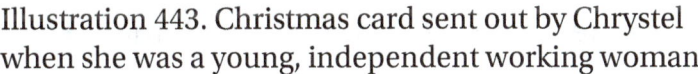

Illustration 443. Christmas card sent out by Chrystel when she was a young, independent working woman

Illustration 444. Young career woman Chrystel

1940 Winston Churchill named England's Prime Minister; Estonia, Latvia and Lithuania annexed by U.S.S.R.

1941 U.S thrown into World War II following Japanese bombing of Pearl Harbor

1942 Manhattan Project started; corn dogs invented; Atomic power discovered

Illustration 445. Chrystel with one of the loves of her life, animals

Illustration 446. Chrystel (left) on a sunny stroll in Dallas, Texas

1943 Synthetic rubber invented; rationing begun on food, shoes, paper; meat drippings proven popular in cooking during WWII rationing

1944 GI Bill of Rights passed; kidney dialysis machine invented; Normandy, France, invaded by Allied troops on June 6

1945 World War II ended; United Nations established; one-third of U. S. citizens living in poverty, most have no running water

1946 Mensa Society created; UNICEF created; Nuremberg War Trials; UNESCO

1947 Cold War begun; Creation of Israel voted on by United Nations; National Security Act adopted, creating the Central Intelligence Agency (CIA)

1948 Mahatma Gandhi murdered; Israel proclaimed an official state

1949 Mao Zedong named chairman; Geneva Conventions supplemented with two protocols relating to protection of victims of armed conflict; Volkswagen Beetle arrives in U.S.

Illustration 447. Chrsytel at Fort Sill, Oklahoma, during visit to her brothers Sam and Jack who were training in the Army artillery during World War II.

Illustration 448. Chrystel in 1940s with cousin Edwin Bishop, a colonel in the Air Force

Illustration 449. Chrystel and her brother, John Samuel McClure

Illustration 450. Chrystel's family members: sister Mary Alice (left); brother and sister-in-law Sam and Sally; and father, Hugh McClure

Illustration 451. Sister Mary Alice, brother Sam (holding Betty whose relationship to the family is unknown), with Chrystel (right)

Illustration 452. Chrystel inspecting an artillery at Fort Sill, Oklahoma

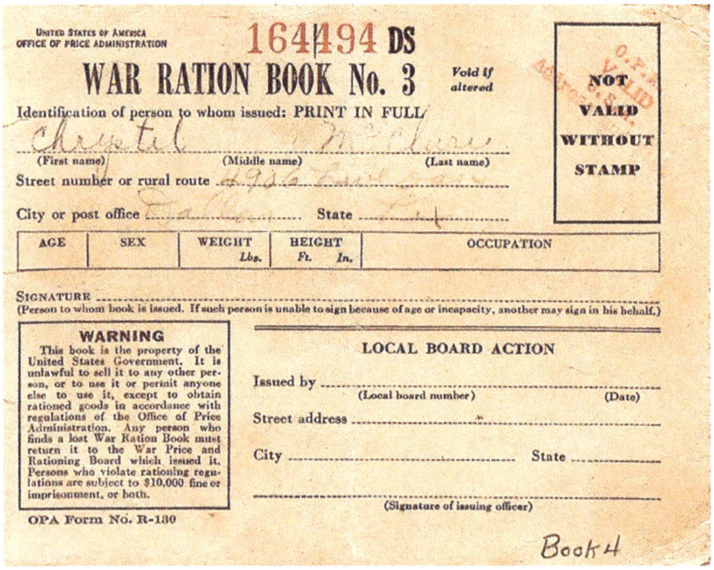
UNITED STATES OF AMERICA
OFFICE OF PRICE ADMINISTRATION

164494 DS

WAR RATION BOOK No. 3

Void if altered

NOT VALID WITHOUT STAMP

Identification of person to whom issued: PRINT IN FULL

Chrystel McClure

(First name) (Middle name) (Last name)

Street number or rural route

City or post office Dallas State

AGE	SEX	WEIGHT Lbs.	HEIGHT Ft. In.	OCCUPATION

SIGNATURE

(Person to whom book is issued. If such person is unable to sign because of age or incapacity, another may sign in his behalf.)

WARNING

This book is the property of the United States Government. It is unlawful to sell it to any other person, or to use it or permit anyone else to use it, except to obtain rationed goods in accordance with regulations of the Office of Price Administration. Any person who finds a lost War Ration Book must return it to the War Price and Rationing Board which issued it. Persons who violate rationing regulations are subject to $10,000 fine or imprisonment, or both.

OPA Form No. R-130

LOCAL BOARD ACTION

Issued by (Local board number) (Date)

Street address

City State

(Signature of issuing officer)

Book 4

Illustration 453. Ration Book for food during World War II

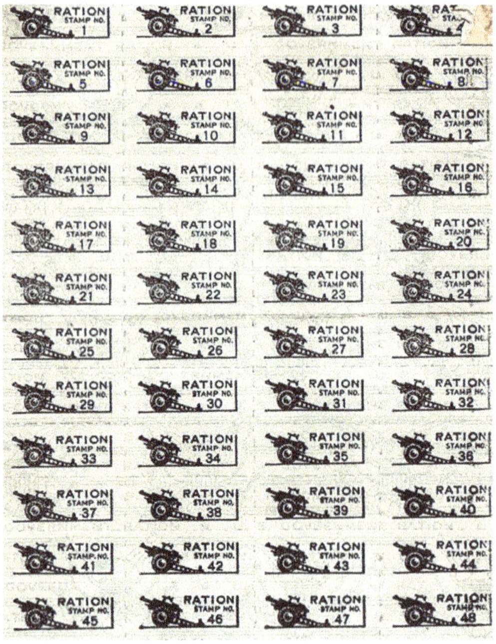

Illustration 454. Ration stamps during World War II

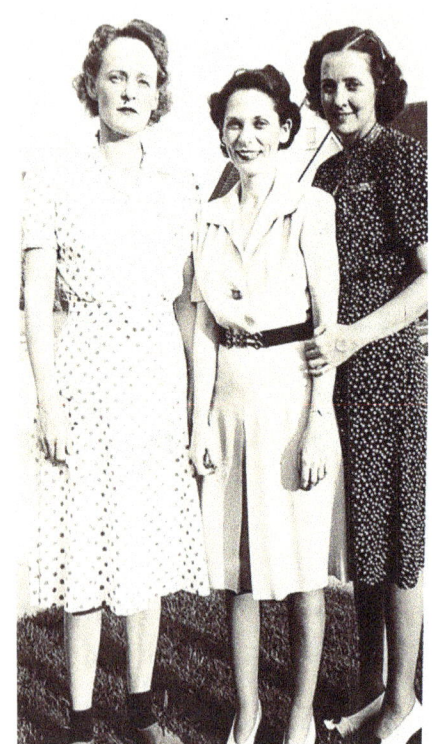

Illustration 455. Chrystel (center)1940s war years in Dallas, Texas

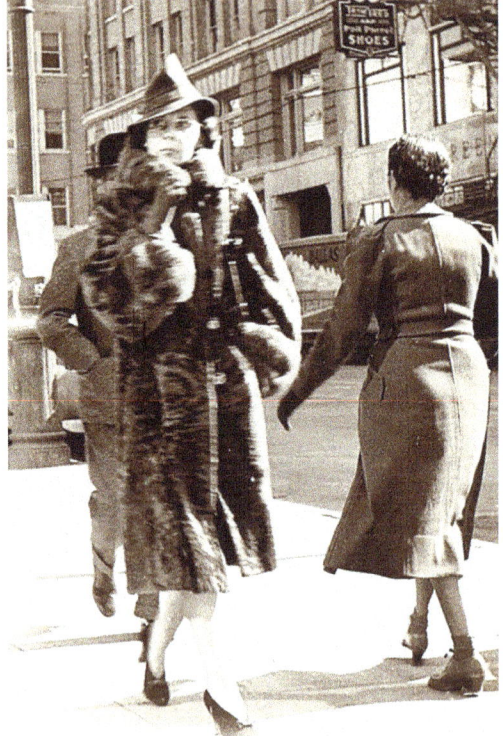

Illustration 456. Fashionable career woman about town in Dallas, Texas

Illustration 457. Chrystel (left) strolling in Dallas, Texas

Illustration 458. Chrystel and William dating in 1940s

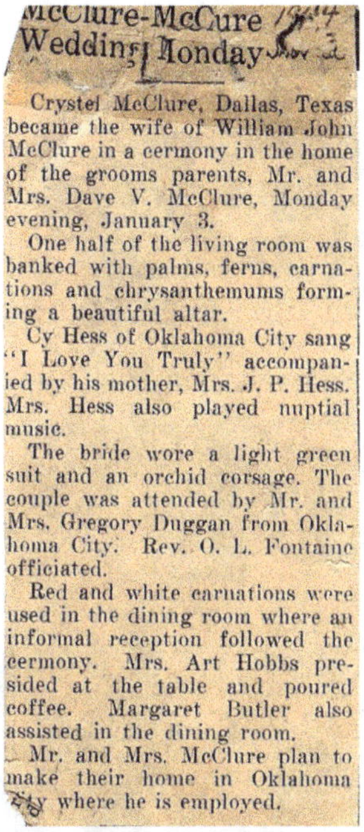

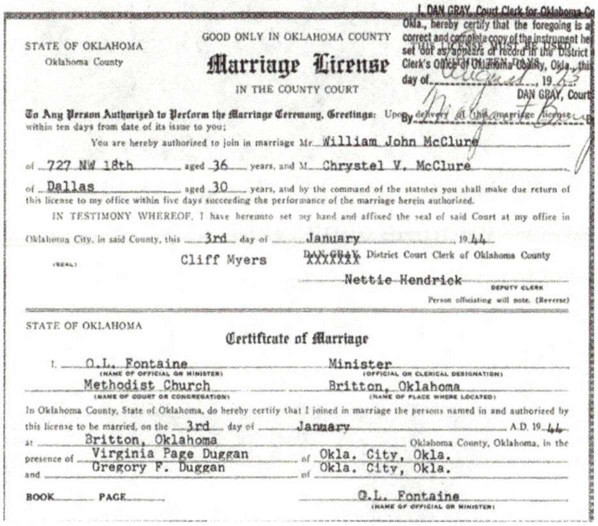

Illustration 460. Chrystel and William's marriage license

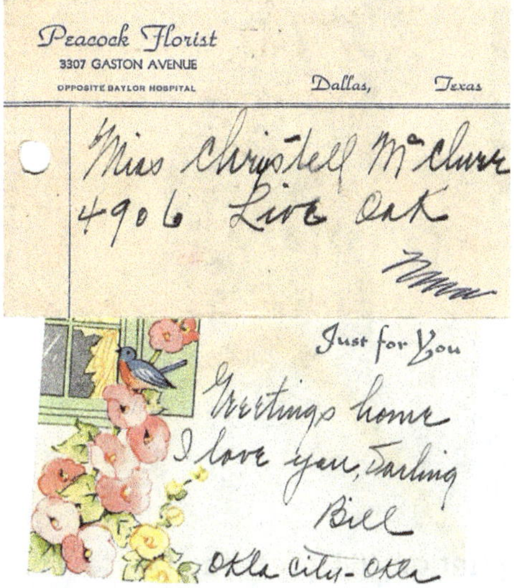

Illustration 459. News account of Chrystel and William's marriage

Illustration 461. Note sent to Chrystel from husband Bill

Illustration 462. Chrystel and Bill's wedding photograph

Illustration 463. Chrystel and Bill on their wedding day. It was typical for wartime brides to wear suits for their wedding.

Illustration 464. Wedding Day for Chrystel and Bill, January 3, 1944

Illustration 465. Newlyweds

Illustration 466. Chrystel and Bill on honeymoon in Colorado

Illustration 467. Honeymoon high, Bill on Royal Gorge Bridge

Illustration 468. Chrystel tempting fate at Garden of the Gods, Colorado Springs

Illustration 469. Honeymooners stepping out

Illustration 470. Honeymooners relaxing

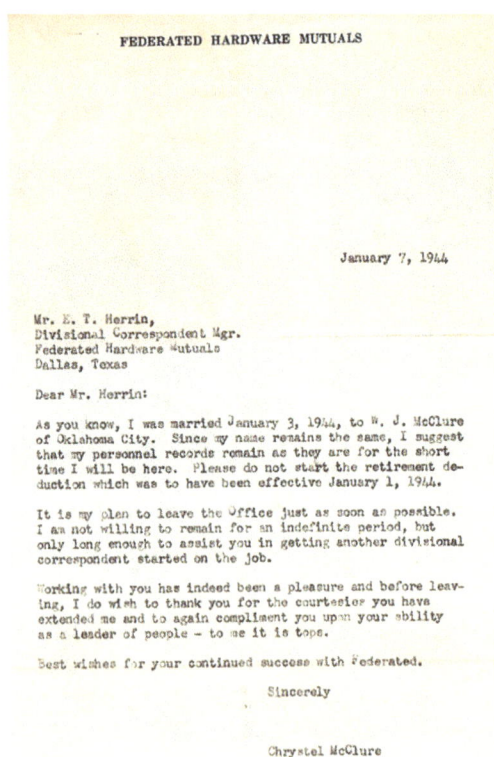

Illustration 471. Chrystel's job resignation letter

Illustration 472. Chrystel and Bill in the early years

Illustration 473. Chrystel and mother, Mary Alice Bishop McClure

Illustration 474. Chrystel becoming a horse woman

Illustration 475. Height of 1940 fashion

Illustration 476. Siblings (left to right): Hugh Jack, Margaret Louise, John Samuel, Mary Alice, and Chrystel. Parents: (on right) Hugh and Mary Alice

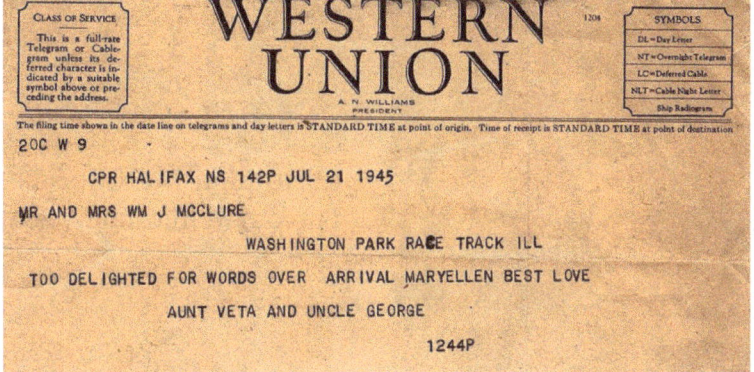

Illustration 477. Telegraphed message congratulating Chrystel and Bill on birth of their first child

Illustration 478. Newborn Mary Ellen at the stables

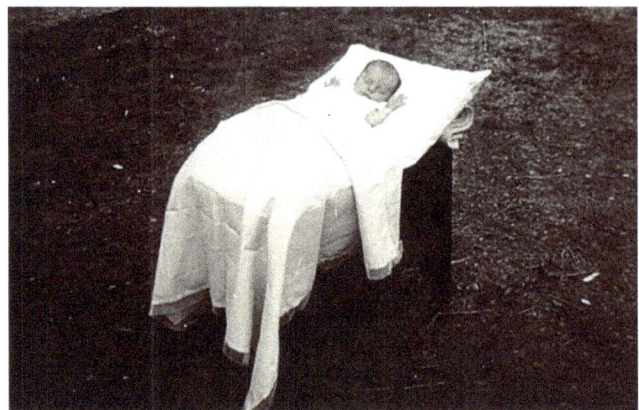

Illustration 479. Mary Ellen afternoon nap at the stable

Illustration 480. Bill, 2-year-old Mary Ellen, and Chrystel in Detroit, Michigan

Illustration 481. Chrystel and Mary Ellen at the Lincoln Memorial, Washington, D. C.

Illustration 482. George S. Findlay, Chrystel, and 3-year-old Mary Ellen, Christmas at Lookout Mountain, Tennessee

Illustration 483. Chrystel, Mary Ellen, and Margaret at an overlook in Hot Springs, Arkansas

Illustration 484. Friend Virginia Duggan, Chrystel, and Mary Ellen

Illustration 485. Chrystel at home in Edmond, Oklahoma

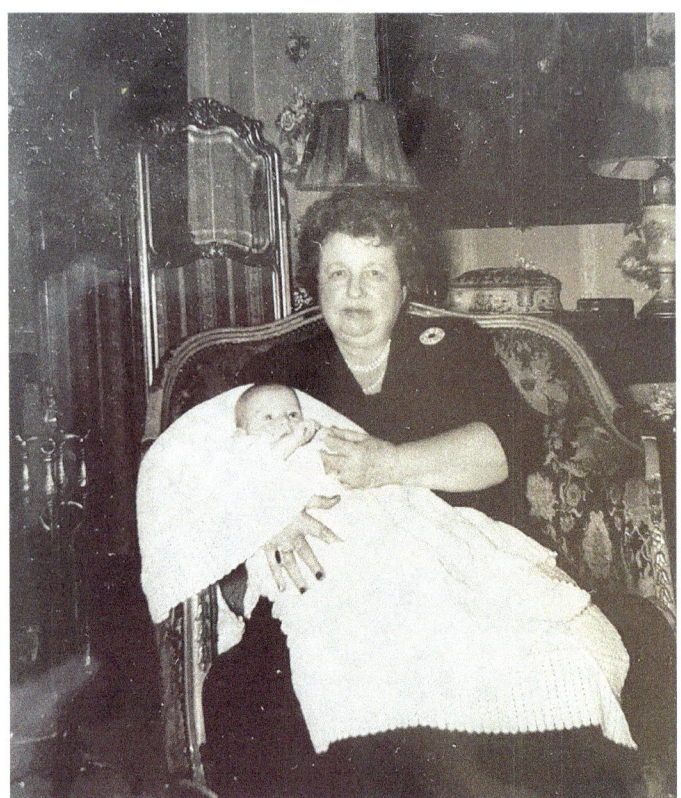

Illustration 486. Veta Findlay with great niece, Veta Louise McClure

Illustration 487. 18-month-old Veta Louise and sister Mary Ellen

Illustration 488. Mary Ellen and Veta Louise

Illustration 489. Veta Louise's first birthday celebrated with Mary Ellen

1950 Korean War start-up; racquetball invented by Joseph Sobek

1951 Term rock 'n' roll coined by Cleveland disc jockey Alan Freed

1952 Polio epidemic across USA; Dwight D. Eisenhower elected President; Elizabeth II crowned Queen

1953 Korean War ended; Death of Stalin; DNA double helix discovered

1954 Elvis Presley career launched; *Brown vs. Brown*, court case making racial segregation of children in public schools unconstitutional; Polio vaccine inoculations begun on large-scale

1955 Bus boycott sparked by Rosa Parks, civil rights icon; Udall, Kansas, tornado

1956 Dwight D. Eisenhower elected to second term; Construction of U.S. Interstate Highway System underway

1957 Bubble wrap invented by Alfred Fielding and Marc Chavannes; 1957 Asian flu outbreak globally; Sputnik launched by the Soviet Union

1958 NASA formed; Nikita Khrushchev named premier of the Soviet Union; instant ramen noodles invented by Momofuku Ando

1959 Cuba taken over by Fidel Castro; Statehood for Alaska and Hawaii

Illustration 490. Veta Louise posing while gathering blossoms

1950s

Illustration 491. Veta Louise, Chrystel, and Mary Ellen dressed for church, 1951

Illustration 492. Dress Alikes: Chrystel, Veta Louise, Margaret, and Mary Ellen at Manitou Springs, Colorado

Illustration 493. Chrystel at home with Veta Louise and Mary Ellen

Illustration 494. Visiting sister Mary Alice (middle) in St. Louis, Missouri: Margaret (left, back row) and Chrystel (right, back row) with Mary Ellen (left) and Veta Louise

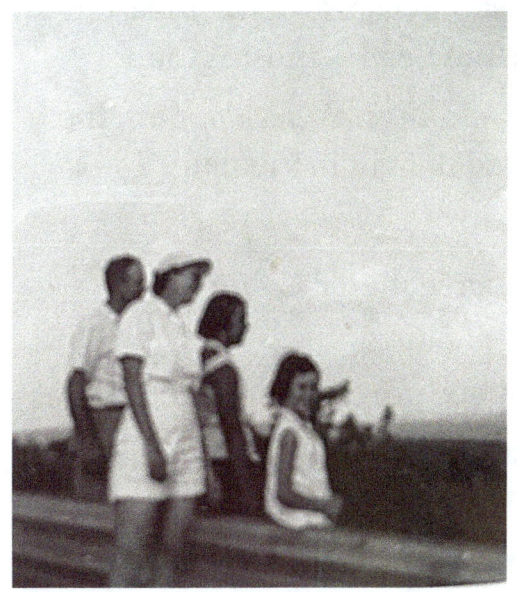

Illustration 495. Admiring scenery

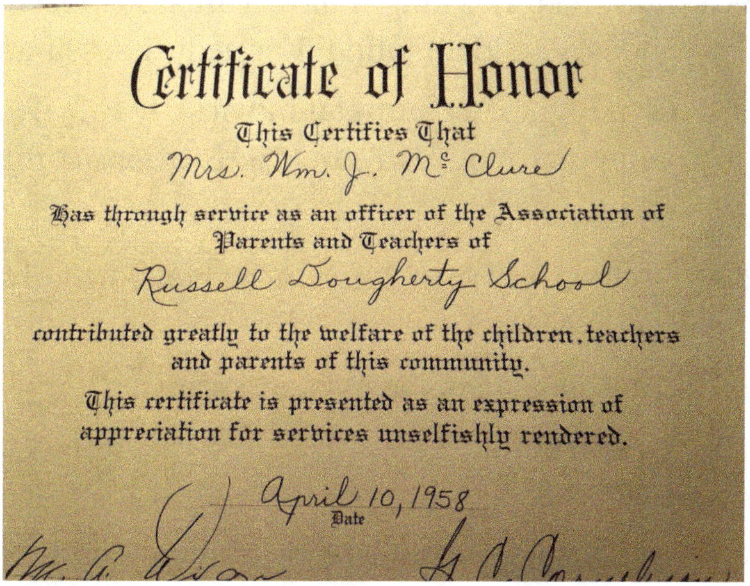

Certificate of Honor

This Certifies That

Mrs. Wm. J. McClure

Has through service as an officer of the Association of Parents and Teachers of

Russell Dougherty School

contributed greatly to the welfare of the children, teachers and parents of this community.

This certificate is presented as an expression of appreciation for services unselfishly rendered.

April 10, 1958

Date

Illustration 496. Testimony to Chrystel's active participation in girls' education

1960 The Twist dance craze; J.F.K. elected President

1961 Berlin Wall built; Peace Corps Act of 1961

1962 Taco Bell founded; Nick Holonyak operated the first visible LED device; Cuban Missile Crisis

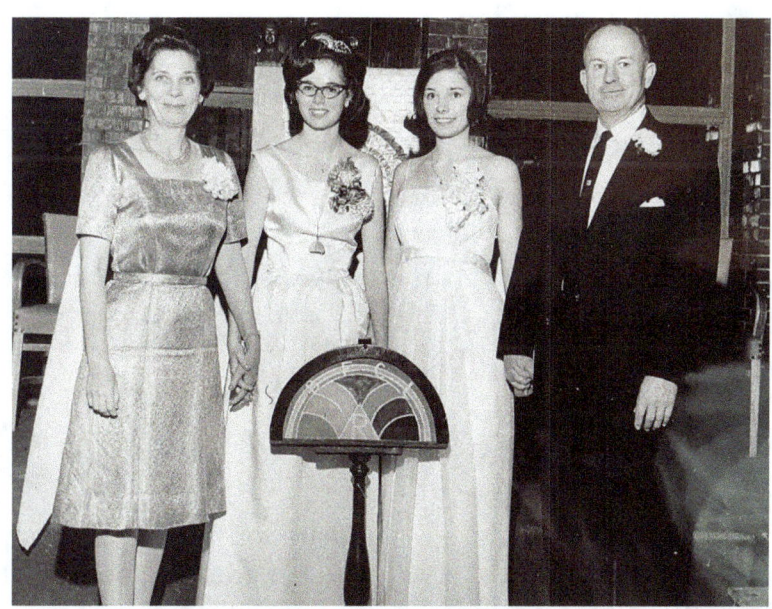

Illustration 497. 1964 installation of Veta Louise (second from left) as Worthy Advisor of the Rainbow Girls chapter in Edmond, Oklahoma. With her are sister Mary Ellen and her father and mother, Bill and Chrystel.

1963 Martin Luther King "I have a dream" speech; first official use of five digit ZIP codes; President John F. Kennedy assassinated; The Beatles music group

1964 Civil Rights Act; popular movies *My Fair Lady, Goldfinger, Mary Poppins*; the computer mouse invented; U.S. troops committed to fight in Vietnam

1965 St. Louis Arch completed

1966 Council for World Mission formed, formerly Congregational Council for World Mission

1967 Arab-Israeli Six Day War and war riots; Apollo space program launched

1968 Martin Luther King and Robert F. Kennedy murdered; 911 Emergency Number first used

1969 Neil Armstrong walk on the moon; Woodstock music festival held in New York; Debut of *Sesame Street* on PBS television station

1970 Prince Sihanouk of Cambodia removed from office as head of state

1971 26th Amendment, voting age lowered to age 18; Debut of Disney World in Florida and Nasdaq Stock Market founded

1972 Watergate break-in reported; Hobby Lobby's first store opened

1973 U. S. troops withdrawn from Vietnam; Abortion made legal by *Roe v. Wade;* U.S. stymied by Oil Crisis

Illustration 498. Celebration dinner at Veta's house: Mary Ellen holding her daughter, Courtney Chrystel; Margaret; young George William; Veta Louise standing beside her mother, Chrystel; and Mary Ellen's husband, George Randall

Illustration 499. Chrystel enjoying playtime with her grandchildren, Courtney Chrystel and George William

1974 Terra-cotta warriors discovered; Rubik's Cube introduced

1975 Saigon taken by North Vietnamese; Cambodia overtaken by Khmer Rouge; Tiger Woods born

1976 U. S. Bicentennial celebrated; Jimmy Carter elected U.S. president; Apple I computer invented

1977 Elvis Presley dead at age 42

1978 Seasat, U.S. surveillance satellite launched

1979 Khmer Rouge rule ended; Three Mile Island nuclear accident

Illustration 500. Chrystel with grandson Thomas Jason and his mother, Veta Louise

Illustration 501. Chrystel enjoying her grandchildren, George William (left), Thomas Jason, and Courtney Chrystel

Illustration 502. Chrystel with Veta Louise and Thomas Jason, 1976

Illustration 503. Chrystel and tulips in Amsterdam, capital of the Netherlands

Illustration 504. Chrystel standing on the corner of Second and McClure Avenue in Lowell, Arkansas. Her grandfather, J. H. McClure founded the town in the 1800s and laid out the streets and electric and phone lines.

Illustration 505. Chrystel in Greece

Illustration 506. Chrystel with friend Helen Granzow

1980 Winter Olympic Games held in Moscow; One-child policy begun in China

1981 Iran Hostage Crisis ended; Ronald Reagan elected President

1982 Independence granted to Canada by the Canada Act

1983 Sally Ride honored as the first American woman in space; Microsoft Word launched

1984 Indira Gandhi assassinated; Ronald Reagan elected to a second term

1985 Mexico City earthquake, 5,000 people killed

1986 Space Shuttle Challenger disaster; Chernobyl nuclear facility disaster

1987 Stock Market crisis known as Black Monday

1989 San Francisco Bay struck by 6.9-point earthquake; George H. Bush elected president; Chinese army opposed by student protestors in Tiananmen Square, Beijing, China

Illustration 507. Chrystel with her four precious grandchildren—her Pride and Joy— George William, Courtney Chrystel, Emily Louise, Thomas Jason

Illustration 508. Chrystel with her two daughters, Mary Ellen and Veta Louise

Illustration 509. Chrystel (front, left) and sister Margaret visiting Veta Louise and Rick and their children, Emily (hiding) and Jason in Bahrain

Illustration 510. Chrystel with Veta and Rick's houseboy during her six-month visit in Bahrain

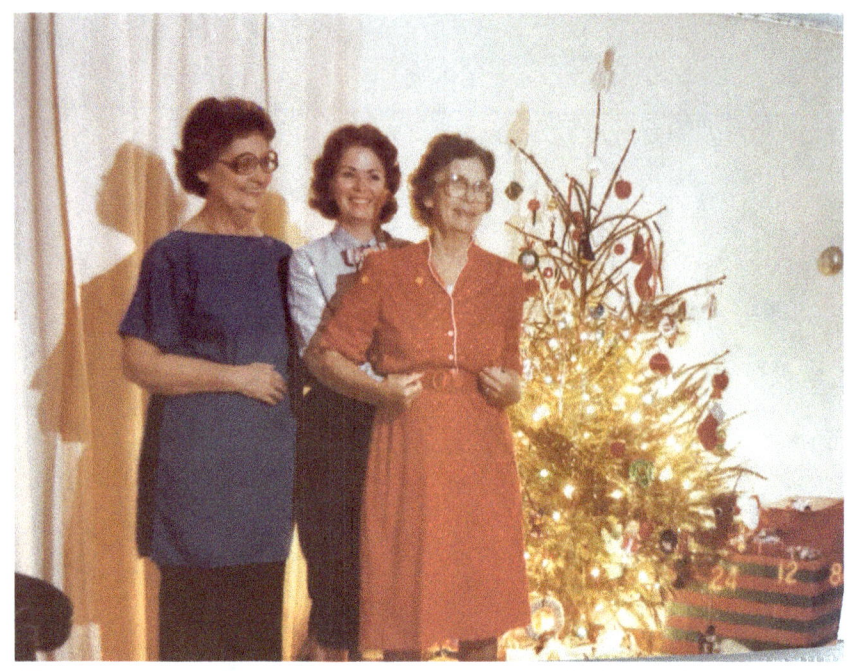

Illustration 511. Margaret, Veta Louise, and Chrystel in Manama, Bahrain, with scrawny desert Christmas tree

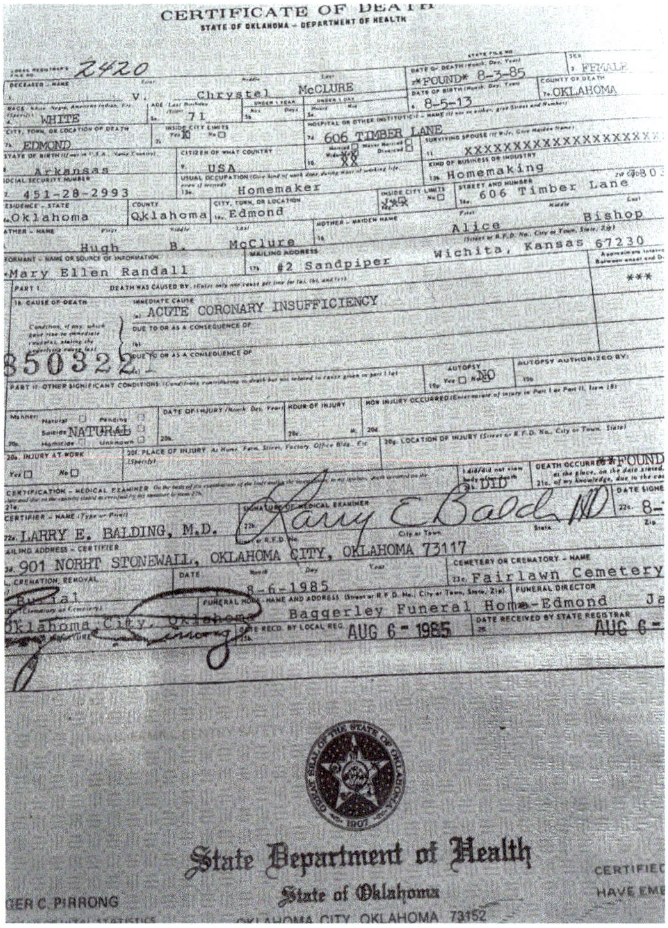

CERTIFICATE OF DEATH
STATE OF OKLAHOMA – DEPARTMENT OF HEALTH

2420

DECEASED – NAME: V. Chrystel McCLURE
SEX: FEMALE
DATE OF DEATH: *FOUND* 8-3-85
COUNTY OF DEATH: OKLAHOMA
RACE: WHITE
AGE: 71
DATE OF BIRTH: 8-5-13
CITY, TOWN, OR LOCATION OF DEATH: EDMOND
INSIDE CITY LIMITS: Yes
HOSPITAL OR OTHER INSTITUTION: 606 TIMBER LANE
STATE OF BIRTH: Arkansas
CITIZEN OF WHAT COUNTRY: USA
SURVIVING SPOUSE: XXXXXXXXXXXXXXXXXX
SOCIAL SECURITY NUMBER: 451-28-2993
USUAL OCCUPATION: Homemaker
KIND OF BUSINESS OR INDUSTRY: Homemaking
RESIDENCE – STATE: Oklahoma
COUNTY: Oklahoma
CITY, TOWN, OR LOCATION: Edmond
STREET AND NUMBER: 606 Timber Lane
FATHER – NAME: Hugh B. McClure
MOTHER – MAIDEN NAME: Alice Bishop
INFORMANT – NAME OR SOURCE OF INFORMATION: Mary Ellen Randall
MAILING ADDRESS: #2 Sandpiper Wichita, Kansas 67230
PART I. DEATH WAS CAUSED BY:
IMMEDIATE CAUSE (a) ACUTE CORONARY INSUFFICIENCY
DUE TO OR AS A CONSEQUENCE OF (b)
DUE TO OR AS A CONSEQUENCE OF (c)
850322
PART II. OTHER SIGNIFICANT CONDITIONS
AUTOPSY: NO
AUTOPSY AUTHORIZED BY:
MANNER: NATURAL
DATE OF INJURY / HOUR OF INJURY / HOW INJURY OCCURRED
PLACE OF INJURY / LOCATION OF INJURY
INJURY AT WORK: Yes ☐ No ☐
I did/did not view body after death: DID
DEATH OCCURRED: **FOUND
CERTIFICATION – MEDICAL EXAMINER
SIGNATURE OF MEDICAL EXAMINER: Larry E Balding MD
CERTIFIER – NAME: LARRY E. BALDING, M.D.
MAILING ADDRESS – CERTIFIER: 901 NORHT STONEWALL, OKLAHOMA CITY, OKLAHOMA 73117
BURIAL, CREMATION, REMOVAL: Burial
DATE: 8-6-1985
CEMETERY OR CREMATORY – NAME: Fairlawn Cemetery
LOCATION: Oklahoma City, Oklahoma
FUNERAL HOME – NAME AND ADDRESS: Baggerley Funeral Home-Edmond
FUNERAL DIRECTOR: Ja
DATE RECD. BY LOCAL REG.: AUG 6 - 1985
DATE RECEIVED BY STATE REGISTRAR: AUG 6 -

State Department of Health
State of Oklahoma
OKLAHOMA CITY, OKLAHOMA 73152
GER C. PIRRONG
CERTIFIED
HAVE EM

Illustration 512. Chrystel's death certificate

Area Death

McClure

Chrystel McClure, 71, Edmond, died Saturday. Services were held at 10 a.m. today in the Baggerley Memorial Chapel with burial in the Fairlawn Cemetery, Oklahoma City, under the direction of the Baggerley Funeral Home.

McClure was born Aug. 5, 1913 in Lowell, Ark. to Hugh and Alice McClure.

After marrying William John McClure on Jan. 3, 1944 in Oklahoma City, they made their home in Edmond. She was preceded in death by her husband in 1970, who was a son of a pioneer cattleman's family. His grandfather was the first white settler in Oklahoma.

She was a life member of the 89ers Association, and very interested in the historical aspect of Oklahoma, and with the Oklahoma Historical Society. She was a member of the First Presbyterian Church of Edmond.

Survivors include two daughters, Mary Allen Randall, Wichita, Kan., and Veta Roberts, Duncan; a brother, J.S. McClure, Tulsa; two sisters, Margaret McClure, Edmond, and Mary Slate, Irving, Texas; two sons-in-law, George R. Randall, Wichita, Kan., and Thomas R. Roberts, Duncan; four grandchildren, George William Randall, Courtney Chrystel Randall, Thomas Jason Roberts, Emily Louise Roberts.

REPRODUCED WITH PERMISSION OF EDMOND SUN/CNHI, LLC

Illustration 513. Chrystel's obit in the *Edmond Sun* newspaper

Illustration 514. Chrystel's grave, Fairlawn Cemetery, Oklahoma City

Let us be judged by our actions

Chapter 10
VETA ANN McCLURE MEALS
1912 - 1948

Illustration 515. Veta Ann McClure Meals

[4]Veta Ann was the second child born to David and Grace. She lived most of her young life in Oklahoma City. As a young adult, she traveled the world. She met and married Col. Robert Meals. Their life led them to all points of the globe. Robert was stationed in Istanbul, Turkey, when Veta Ann suddenly became ill. Her hair turned white within a two-week time period. When her casket was returned to the USA, the government would not allow the casket to be opened. The cause of her death remains a mystery.

From the Records

[4]Veta Ann McClure Meals
  b. March 10, 1912
  m. Col. Robert Wolcott Meals—West Point graduate, 1933,
    who attained the rank of general in the U.S. Army
    b. 1910
    d. 1988
      Meals' parents were:
      Charles A. Meals and Pauline Meals
      67 Mulberry Street, Springfield, Massachusetts
  d. March 25, 1948, in Ankara, Turkey
  b. Memorial Park, Edmond, Oklahoma, Section 4—northwest corner near pond; 20x20 inside

Children:
    [5]Robert W.—called Bobby—West Point graduate, 1958
      b. May 8, 1936–2017
      m. Martha
      d. July 22, 2017—cancer (obituary at end of Veta's story)
    [5]David A.
      b. September 27, 1942

Parents:
    [3]David Victor McClure 1879–1944
    [3]Grace Anna Armsey McClure 1889–1974

Siblings:
    [4]William John McClure 1907–1970
    [4]Guy Victor McClure 1927–1961

Education:
    Christian College for Women, Columbia, Missouri

Illustration 516. Veta Ann, born 1912

Veta Ann McClure Meals' Timeline

1912 *Titantic* ocean liner sunk after hitting North Atlantic iceberg

Illustration 517. Baby Veta Ann with grandmother, Mary Ellen (left); brother William; and mother Grace (right)

Illustration 518. Veta Ann, mother Grace, and brother William

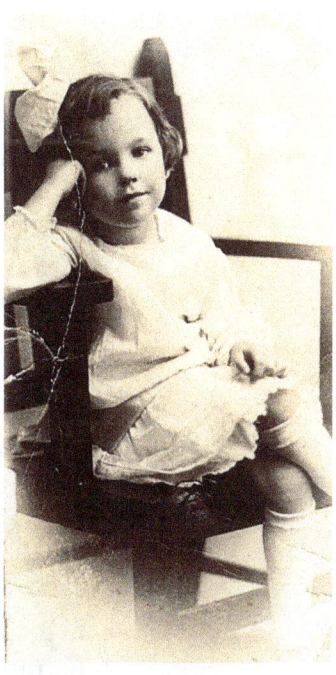

Illustration 519. Pensive little girl, Veta Ann

1918-1928

Illustration 520. Veta Ann in driver's seat

Illustration 521. Preteen Veta Ann and her mother Grace

Illustration 522. Grace and her two children, Veta Ann and William, at Sulphur Springs, Oklahoma

Illustration 523. Veta Ann, schoolgirl

Illustration 524. Veta Ann and parents, Dave and Grace McClure

Illustration 526. Veta Ann's passport photo

Illustration 525. Stylish Veta Ann

1920s Letter, no date, from Veta Ann to her brother

My Dear Brother,

I hope you had a very pleasant trip. I also wish you a very happy birthday. I will send you your present soon. I must close.

With Love,
Veta Ann

1931 *The Daily Oklahoman* newspaper article (May 4) with a photograph of 19-year-old Veta Ann

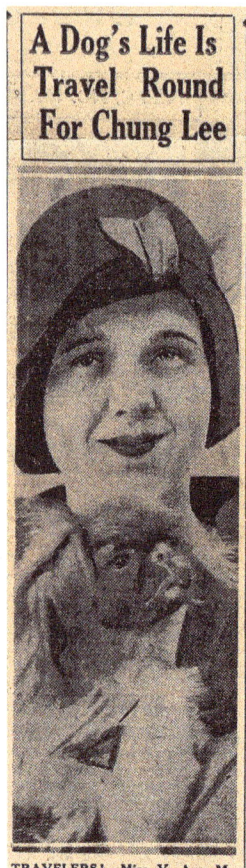

Illustration 527.

TRAVELERS!—Miss V. Ann McClure with her dog, Chung Lee, which she plans to make the most traveled dog in the world.

Every dog has his day, but Chung Lee, bright eyed Pekinese owned by Miss Veta Ann McClure of Washington D.C., has a lot of them ahead.

And what days they will be– for Chung's mistress announced yesterday that she plans to take him to every country in the world!

Miss McClure with her aunt Mrs. V. McClure Church, prominent in Washington D. C. and New York society, arrived in Seattle yesterday from the Orient on the liner *President Jefferson*.

"I'm going to see that Chung Lee visits every country across both the Pacific and Atlantic," Miss McClure said as she gave the appreciative Pekinese a hug. They left last night for New York.

Illustration 528. Aboard ship with Chung Lee

Illustration 529. Very fashionable Veta Ann

1933 The envelope of this letter was postmarked from West Point, February 13, from R. W. Meals

"B" Co. U. S. A. C. West Point, N. Y., addressed to Miss Ann McClure,
Route 3, Box 181, Edmond, Oklahoma:
Darling Ann,

Speaking of blizzards we must've had the tail end of one. Saturday morning when I woke up there was about 8 inches of snow on the ground, and it had not stopped snowing. The temperature at the time was below freezing and did the wind blow? I spent at least ¾ of an hour in the trunk room looking for my galoshes amid much dust and muttered growling. I had put them away last year and it required much straining of memory to locate them. There were 267 men walking the area yesterday and with an insufficient O. G. It took some time to post them. I walked all of 15 minutes. Which reminds me, I picked up two more demerits at Saturday inspection which makes a total of five for the month. I am certainly glad this month is short for I am pulling after all my worth to keep the total below 10 so that I can take a weekend with you dear. I got 16.1 out of 18.0 in Engineering, 8.3 out of 9.0 Ordinance, 5.2 out of 6.0 in Economics, and 8.4 out of 9.0 in Law. I was not policed in engineering so I must be gaining back my lost files. I expect by now you have received your mother's letter as she said in her letter that she would write to you on the fifth. I imagine that you are rather cut off from the world just at present if you get your promised blizzard. Dearest I am just as lonesome as you and even though I am busy most of the time. They say that work helps but it doesn't since I keep thinking of the 2000+ miles that separate us and of the many days before I shall see you again. I do so hope that your father will say yes to you and that you will again be hitting the rails early in March for a long stay chez les grandes. I hope next summer to be able to see you further on my way out to the coast for duty. With conditions as they are at present with Congress planning a 1/3 cut in the Navy appropriation things look pretty bleak and the probability of our getting a good furlough is small indeed. I have yet to hear from Mrs. Church. She most probably is out of range of cables apparently. Be good and play a lot of solitaire, work a lot of crossword puzzles etc. and the time will pass a lot faster.

I love you,
Three -Square

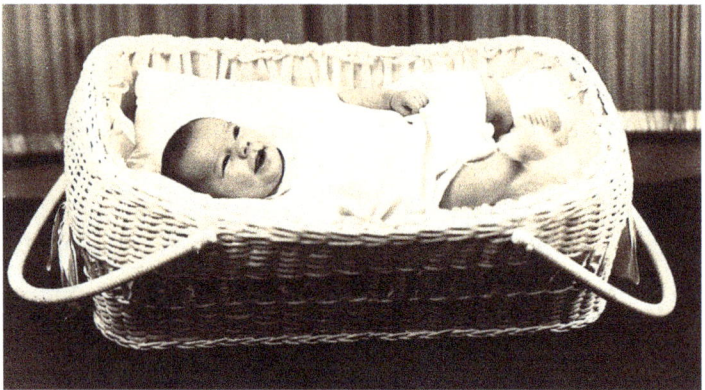

Illustration 530. Baby Robert Meals, born in 1936

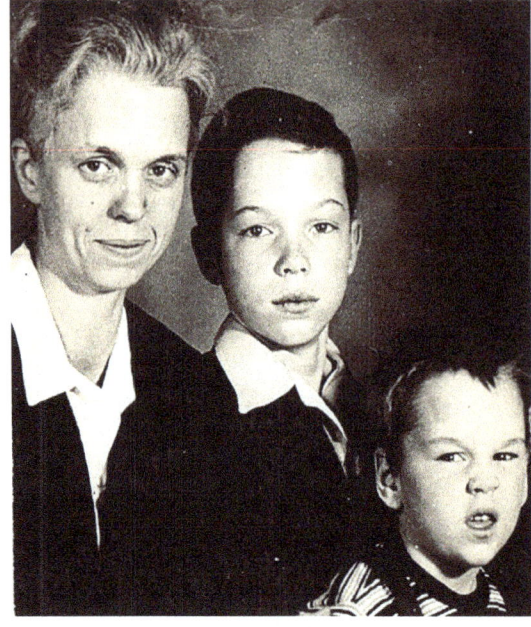

Illustration 531. Veta Ann with her two boys, Robert (Bobby) and David

Illustration 532. Veta Ann, circa 1948

1948   March 29 letter from Mrs. Charles A. Meals, 67 Mulberry Street, Springfield 5, Massachusetts. Letter written to Veta McClure Findlay about the death of her niece, Veta Ann McClure Meals

> *My Dear Veta,*
>
> *I just received your letter and I hasten to answer it although I really have very little to tell you besides what you already know. I have talked with Washington and they have promised to telephone me when they hear more. If Robert comes in on an army plane, he will land in Westover. It's very near here and I will then see him. I have no idea where or when the funeral will be. But when I find out I will send you a wire. It is all very complicated and distressing. As to the children, I want to help in any way possible of course but until I see Robert. I wouldn't know what to tell you. Happy has wired me his willingness to help with the children and I would be very glad if Robert would consent to have him, and Susie take Bobby. They would give him much love, intelligent care and have infinite patience with him. Perhaps later I could help out by joining them. In a way I really felt that a younger person should deal with children, but I would be glad to help out. It's really up to Robert. And after I see him, I can be more intelligent about the whole thing. I promise to write to you and if I find out about the services in time, I will wire you. My best to George and love to you and thank you for writing to me hastily, Pauline*
> *PS please excuse the envelope, but I am writing at the hospital and seem to have no others.*

1948   At 36 years of age Veta Ann McClure Meals died in Ankara, Turkey, where her husband, Robert W. Meals was serving the U. S. Army. The story told to the family was that she became ill with a flu-like disease, within two weeks her dark hair turned white, and she died. Her casket was not allowed to be opened within the United States. Burial at Memorial Park Cemetery, Edmond, Oklahoma. Her grave is Lot #4, across from the Memorial Reflecting Pool.

Illustration 533. Robert (Bobby) Meals with cousin, Mary Ellen McClure (circa 1949)

Obituary, St. Helena, California

ROBERT WOLCOTT MEALS JR. 1926–2017

Robert Wolcott Meals, Jr. passed peacefully from this world to the next on July 22nd, 2017, after a brave battle against cancer, at home with his loving family at his side. Bob was born in San Francisco in 1936 to Captain Robert and Veta Meals. When he was eight years old, Bob had the experience that would determine the rest of his life: his uncle Guy V. McClure took him up in an airplane for the first time, and that amazing adventure sealed his destiny. Bobby attended The United States Military Academy at West Point, New York, and immediately upon graduating in 1958 he entered US Air Force pilot training. Bob served honorably for 28 years in the Air Force. After his military retirement, he went on to a 20+ year second career which he also loved, as a flight simulator instructor for the KC10 program. For Bob, being in the world of aviation was more than just a career he loved, it was a calling, and he remained true to this calling for as long as he was physically able. Bob leaves behind his loving wife, Martha Meals, his son, Robert Wolcott Meals 3rd, and his daughter Joan Hawki, son-in-law Dennis Hawki, his grandson Garrett Hawki, granddaughter Jodi Hawki, and his brother David Meals. Memorial service will take place September 15, 11 am at Grace Episcopal Church in St. Helena, California.

Let us be judged by our actions

Chapter 11
GUY VICTOR McCLURE
1925 - 1961

Illustration 534. Guy Victor McClure

[4]Guy Victor was the youngest child born to David and Grace. He lived most of his early life at the family farm. His early interest in airplanes and motorcycles remained with him his entire life. Guy loved anything that flew or went fast. He was an avid pilot, both private and military—even model airplanes. He became a flight instructor during World War II. Like the other McClure men, he loved competition. He was a ranked motorcycle competitor, setting several records. Guy died of a heart attack at the early age of 36, leaving his young wife and three sons.

From the Records
[4]Guy Victor McClure
  b. January 15, 1925
  m. Thamar Perkins
  d. July 18, 1961
  b. Memorial Park Cemetery, Edmond, Oklahoma
    Section 41-southeast corner of tower

Parents:
  Father: [3]David Victor McClure, b. December 10, 1879, Atoka, Indian Territory
  Mother: [3]Grace Anna Jones, b. June 27, 1889, Cincinnati, Ohio

Siblings:
  [4]William John (Bill) McClure, b. July 6, 1907, Latonia, Kentucky
  [4]Veta Ann McClure (Meals), b. March. 10, 1912, Oklahoma City

Children:
  [5]Charles David, b. January 24, 1953, Oklahoma City, Oklahoma
    m. Judy
    Children:
      Matthew Charles, b. January 27, 1977, Denton, Texas
  [5]Guy Vincent, b. July 10, 1954, Oklahoma City, Oklahoma
    m. Wendy
    Children:
      Kati Rae, Cody, Wyoming
      b. December 12,1989
      Guy Tanner, Cody, Wyoming
      b. October 31,1993
  [5]Dewey Allen, b. May 18, 1957, Oklahoma City, Oklahoma
    m. Lisa
    Children:
      Megan, b. March 4, 1985
      Emily, b. October 13, 1983
      Sam Zachary, b. January 11, 1988

Education:
  Putnam City (Oklahoma) High School

Texas A & M 1943–1944
Military Aviation Training Schools

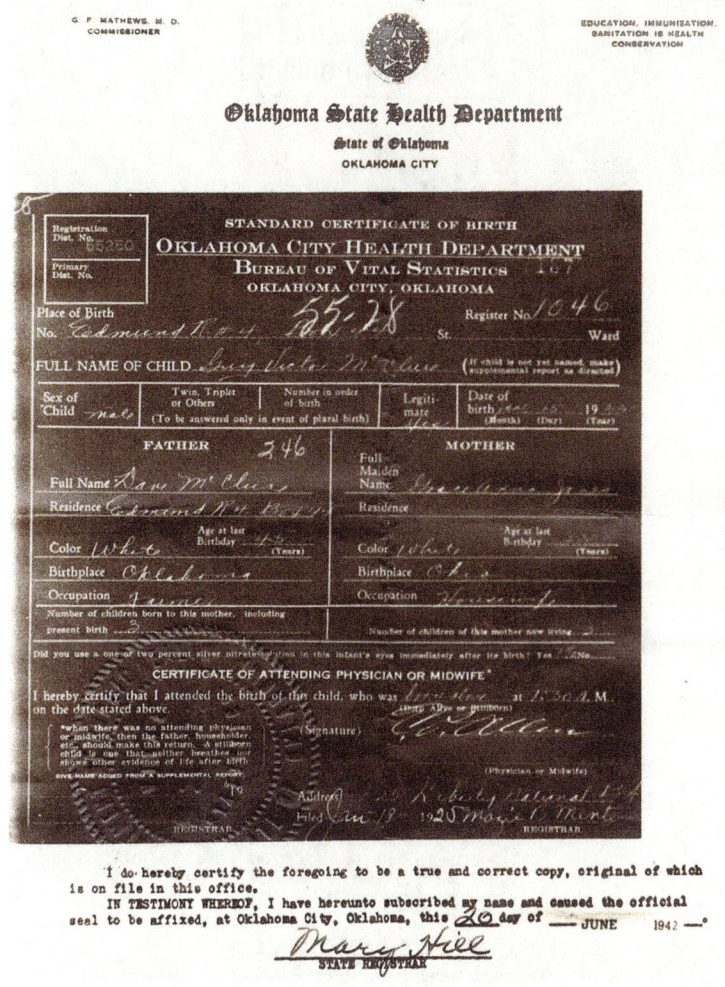

Illustration 535. Guy Victor's birth certificate

Illustration 536. Guy Victor McClure, two years old

Illustration 537. Guy Victor's Sunday School enrollment card

Guy Victor McClure's Timeline

1930 *The Daily Oklahoman* newspaper article and photograph

Illustration 538. *The Daily Oklahoman* newspaper article

YOUNG, BUT HE IS REAL COWPUNCHER

Guy McClure, 5 years old, son of Mr. and Mrs. Dave McClure, who live 15 miles northwest of Oklahoma City, is the youngest "cowpuncher" attending the Southwest American Livestock show at the coliseum. Guy is nothing if not confident, having been a horseman since his legs were long enough to straddle a pony. He's right at home in the rodeo arena and rather resents not being permitted to ride wild Brahma steers. His forebears were pioneers in Oklahoma, having come here many years before the state was opened to settlement.

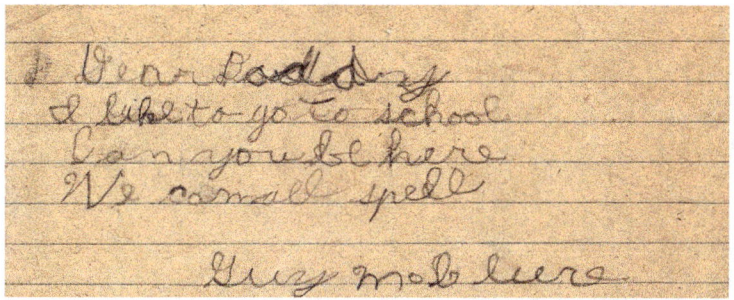

Illustration 539. Note written by Guy Victor to his father, David

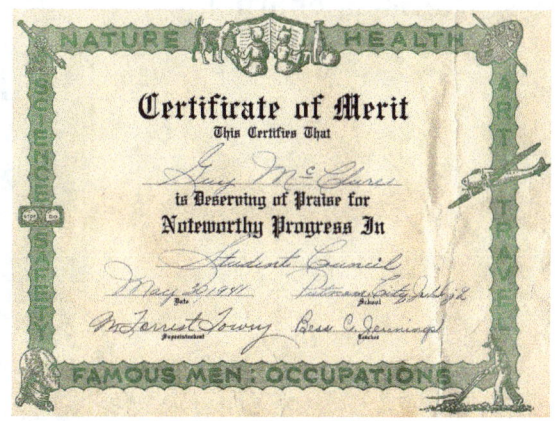

Illustration 540. Guy Victor's Student Council Certificate of Merit

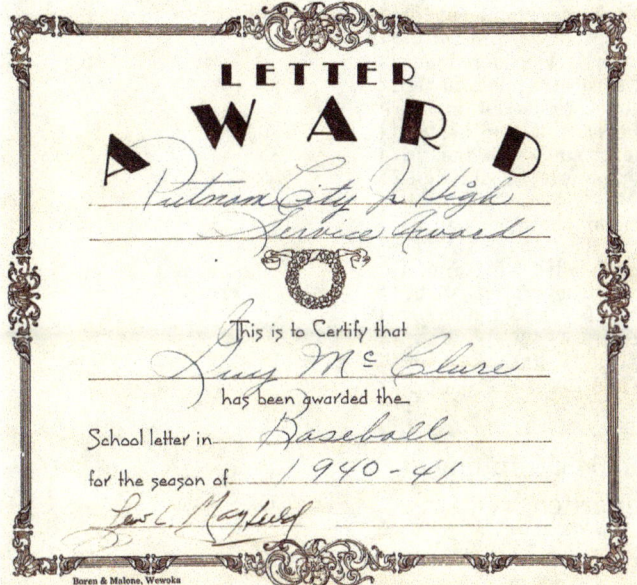

Illustration 541. School baseball letter for Guy Victor at Putnam City Junior High School

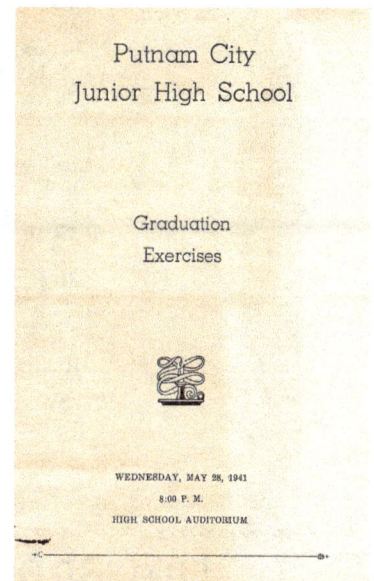

Illustration 542. Guy Victor's graduation program from Putnam City Junior High in Oklahoma City, 1941

1941 Newspaper article

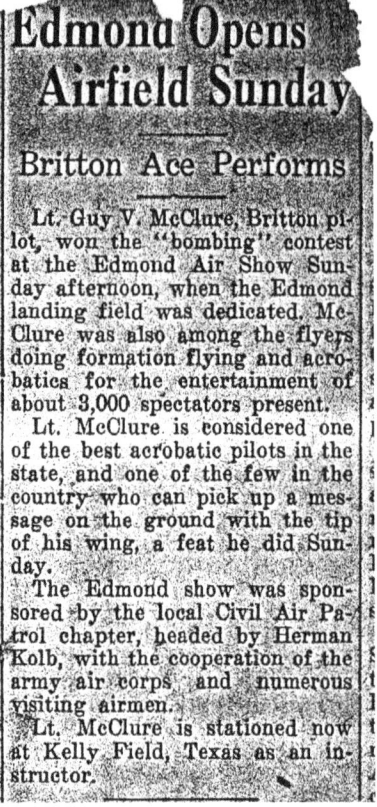

Illustration 543. Clipping of newspaper article

EDMOND OPENS AIRFIELD SUNDAY
Britton Ace Performs

Lt. Guy V. McClure, Britton pilot, won the "bombing contest" at the Edmond Airshow Sunday afternoon, when the Edmond landing field was dedicated. McClure was also among the flyers doing formation flying and acrobatics for the entertainment of about 3,000 spectators present.

Lt. McClure is considered one of the best aerobatic pilots in the state, and one of the few in the country who can pick up a message on the ground with the tip of his wing, a feat he did Sunday. The Edmond show was sponsored by the local Civil Air Patrol chapter, headed by Herman Caliber, with the cooperation of the army air corps and numerous visiting airmen.

Lt. McClure is stationed now at Kelly Field, Texas as an instructor.[17]

---

[17] Illustration 543 and adapted text reproduced with permission of *Edmond Sun*/CNHI, LLC

1943 October 25. A form letter all new soldiers sent home

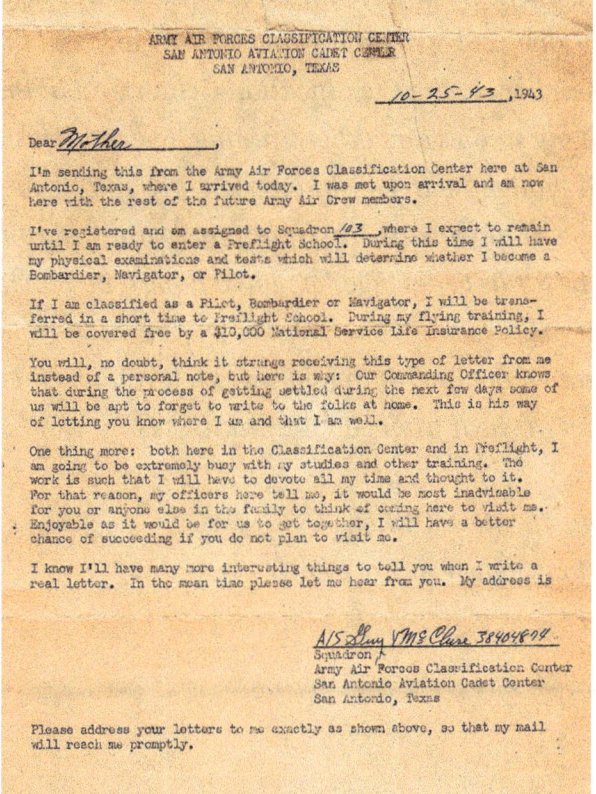

Illustration 544. Army form letter for sending home

Army Air Force Classification Center,
San Antonio Aviation Cadet Center,
San Antonio, Texas
10-25-43, 1943
Dear Mother,

I'm sending this from the Army Air Force Classification Center here at San Antonio, Texas, for I arrived today. I was met upon arrival and I am now here with the rest of the future Army Air Crew members.

I've registered and I am assigned to Squadron 103 , where I expect to remain until I am ready to enter a pre-flight school. During this time, I will have my physical examinations and tests which will determine whether I become a Bombardier, Navigator, or Pilot.

If I am classified as a Pilot, Bombardier or Navigator, I will be transferred in a short time to Preflight School. During my flying training, I will be covered free by a $10,000 National Service Life Insurance Policy.

You will, no doubt, think it's strange receiving this type of letter from me instead of a *personal note, but here is why: Our Commanding Officer knows that during the process of getting settled during the next few days some of us will be apt to forget to write to the folks at home. This is his way of letting you know where I am and that I am well.*

One thing more: both here in the Classification Center and in Preflight, I am going to be extremely busy with my studies and other training. The work is such that I will have to devote all my time and thought to it. For that reason, my officers here tell me, it would be most inadvisable for you or anyone else in the family to think of coming here to visit me. Enjoyable as it would be for us to get together, I will have a better chance of succeeding if you do not plan to visit me.

I know I'll have many more interesting things to tell you when I write a real letter. In the meantime, please let me hear from you. My address is

Squadron
Army Air Force Classification Center,
San Antonio Aviation Cadet Control Center,
San Antonio, Texas

1945 Letter

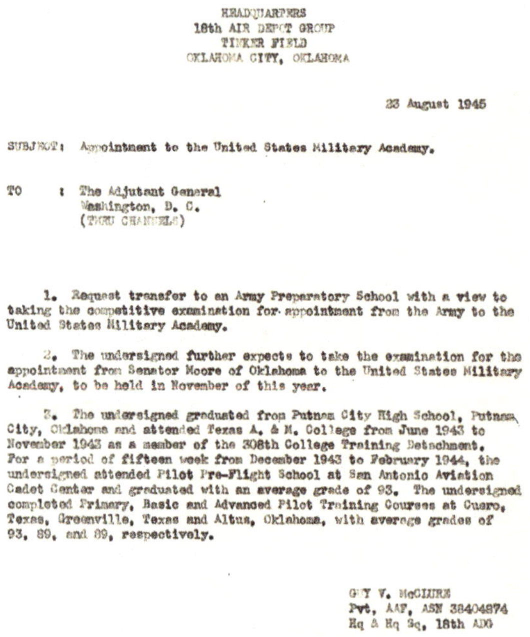

Illustration 545. Guy's letter requesting transfer to Army prep school

Headquarters,
18th Air Depot Group
Tinker Field,
Oklahoma City, Oklahoma.
Subject: Appointment to the United States Military Academy.
To: The Adjutant General, Washington, D.C.

1. Request transfer to an Army Preparatory School with a view to taking the competitive examination for appointment from the Army to the United States Military Academy.

2. The undersigned further expects to take the examination for the appointment from Senator Mears of Oklahoma to the United States Military Academy, to be held in November of this year.

3. The undersigned graduated from Putman City High School, Putman City Oklahoma and attended Texas A&M College from June 1943 to November 1944 as a member of the 306 College Training Detachment. For a period of 15 weeks from December 1943 to February 1944, the undersigned attended Pilot Pre-Flight School at San Antonio Aviation Cadet Center and graduated with an average grade of 93. The undersigned completed primary, basic and advanced pilot training courses at Cuero, Texas, Greenville, Texas and Altus, Oklahoma, with average grades of 93, 99, and 89, respectively.

Signed,
Guy V. McClure Pvt, AAF, Air Force ASN 38404874 Eq & Hq Sq. 18th ADG

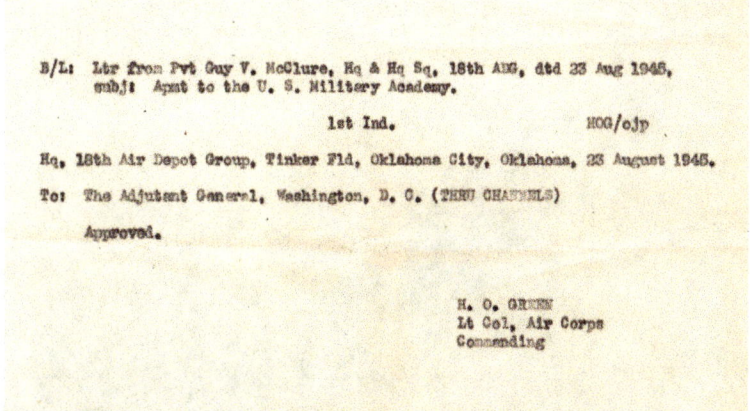

Illustration 546. Oklahoma City, 1945. West Point application approved

Illustration 547. Guy Victor as a young aviator

Illustration 548. Guy Victor, military pilot, World War II

Illustration 549. Guy Victor as military pilot

Illustration 550. Guy Victor returning with prize from hunting wolves from his plane

Illustration 551. Coyote killed from the air by pilot Guy Victor who used a pistol

1946 *The Daily Oklahoman*, September 4

Illustration 552. Article in the *Oklahoma City Times*

SOONERS TAKE NATIONAL MODEL PLANE AWARDS

Oklahoma winners in the national model airplane meet, held Monday in Wichita, Kansas. Arrived home late Tuesday. . .tired but happy and by early Wednesday, were busy showing off their gleaming trophies.

Donald Leaf, 16, of 2812 NW. 24th, walked off with first place in the class A junior free flight for gas models. Leaf's plane, a Mercury, with a 42-inch wingspan, stayed aloft for a total of 5½ minutes for three flights. He was awarded the Tiger Products championship trophy, and also the Tiger Products championship perpetual trophy, which he will be permitted to keep for one year, at which time it will be passed on to the next winner of the class A Junior Free-Flight.

His First National Meet

This was the first national meet Donald, the son of Mr. and Mrs. Hubert Leaf, had ever entered. His father, by the way, won honorable mention in the best finish class with a plastic model plane.

Guy V. McClure, 21, of route three, Edmond, entered Monday's meet, which was also his first national, and came home with the coveted Model Airplane News trophy.

McClure entered and won the class C open, with a Vagabond gas Model plane with a 76-inch wingspan. His plane was in the air for a total of 37 minutes, 52 seconds and "four tenths" he adds, for three flights.

"On one flight," said McClure. "My plane was in the air for 33 minutes and 52 seconds. I had the fastest climbing plane there."

Has Fast-Climbing Model

McClure's plane has an Orwick motor, and according to his estimates "will climb 1,500 feet in 20 seconds."

Fred Whiting III, 16, of 426 NW. 33rd, won 5th place. in class B senior. Whitting won with a Baby Sailplane, having a wingspan of four feet. His plane is scaled down 1/3 the size of a Comet Sailplane, and was in the air for 10 minutes and 23 seconds for three flights.

"And," laughed Whiting, "my prize was a big box of screwdrivers. Don't ask me why."

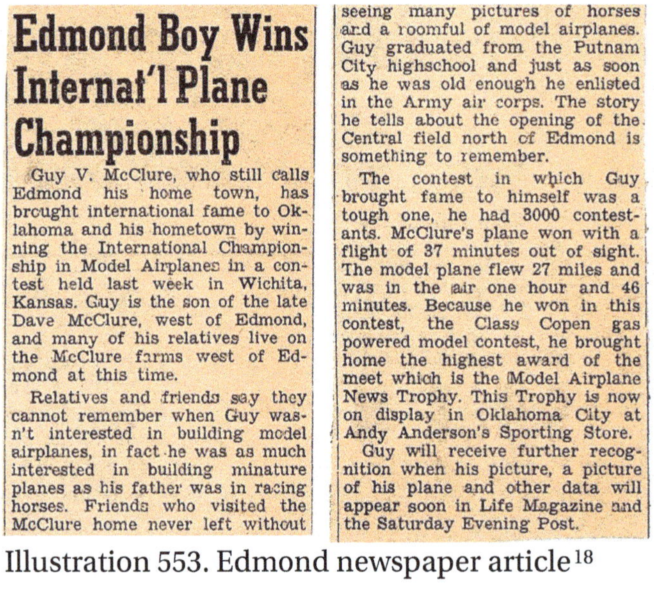

◇◇

Edmond Boy Wins Internat'l Plane Championship

Guy V. McClure, who still calls Edmond his home town, has brought international fame to Oklahoma and his hometown by winning the International Championship in Model Airplanes in a contest held last week in Wichita, Kansas. Guy is the son of the late Dave McClure, west of Edmond, and many of his relatives live on the McClure farms west of Edmond at this time.

Relatives and friends say they cannot remember when Guy wasn't interested in building model airplanes, in fact he was as much interested in building minature planes as his father was in racing horses. Friends who visited the McClure home never left without seeing many pictures of horses and a roomful of model airplanes. Guy graduated from the Putnam City highschool and just as soon as he was old enough he enlisted in the Army air corps. The story he tells about the opening of the Central field north of Edmond is something to remember.

The contest in which Guy brought fame to himself was a tough one, he had 3000 contestants. McClure's plane won with a flight of 37 minutes out of sight. The model plane flew 27 miles and was in the air one hour and 46 minutes. Because he won in this contest, the Class C open gas powered model contest, he brought home the highest award of the meet which is the Model Airplane News Trophy. This Trophy is now on display in Oklahoma City at Andy Anderson's Sporting Store.

Guy will receive further recognition when his picture, a picture of his plane and other data will appear soon in Life Magazine and the Saturday Evening Post.

Illustration 553. Edmond newspaper article[18]

---

[18]Illustration 553 and adapted text on page 417 reproduced with permission of *Edmond Sun*/CNHI,LCC

Illustration 554. Guy Victor in motorcycle race

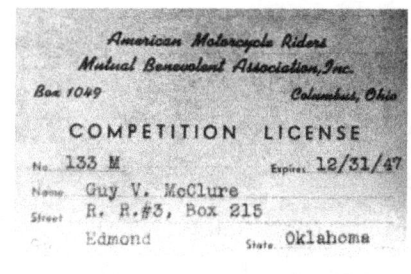

Illustration 555. Card carrying member

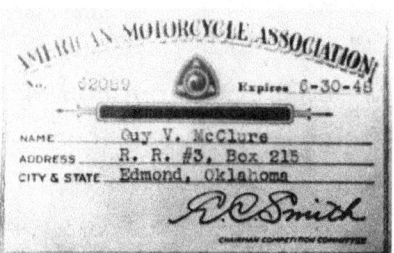

Illustration 556. Guy's license to compete in motorcycle races

EDMOND BOY WINS INTERNAT'L PLANE CHAMPIONSHIP

Guy V. McClure, who still calls Edmond his hometown, has brought international fame to Oklahoma and his hometown by winning the International Championship and Model Airplane in a contest held last week in Wichita, Kansas. Guy is the son of the late Dave McClure, west of Edmond, and many of his relatives live on the McClure farm west of Edmond at this time.

Relatives and friends say they cannot remember when Guy wasn't interested in building model airplanes, in fact he was as much interested in building miniature planes as his father was in racing horses. Friends who visited the McClure home never left without seeing many pictures of horses in a room full of model airplanes. Guy graduated from the Putman City high school and just as soon as he was old enough he enlisted in the Army Air Corps. The story he tells about the opening of the central field north of Edmond is something to remember.

The contest in which Guy brought fame to himself was a tough one, he had 3000 contestants. McClure's plane won. It was a flight of 37 minutes out of sight. The model plane flew 27 miles and was in the air one hour and 46 minutes. Because he won in this contest, the Class C Open gas powered model contest, he brought home the highest award of the meet which is the Model Airplane News Trophy. This Trophy is now on display in Oklahoma City at Andy Anderson's Sporting Store.

Guy will receive further recognition when his picture, a picture of his plane and other data will appear soon in Life Magazine and the Saturday Evening Post.

1961 Obituary in *The Daily Oklahoman* newspaper

Guy V. McClure Services for Guy V. McClure, 36, of 13200 N. MacArthur, who died Tuesday of a heart attack, will be at 10 a.m. Thursday in Village Christian Church. Burial will be in Memorial Park Cemetery under direction of Schurman funeral home. McClure was a lifelong resident and was chief supervisor of industrial engineering at Tinker Air Force Base, where he had been employed since 1951. He was descended from a colorful local family. McClure's grandfather was the first legal settler of Oklahoma City when he bought and settled on Bill Chisholm's ranch in 1867. His father, David Victor McClure, was the youngest member of Teddy Roosevelt's Rough Riders in the Spanish- American war of 1898, and later became a prominent rancher here. Surviving are his wife, Thamer, and his three sons Charles, Guy, and Dewey, all of the home; a brother Bill, Edmond; his mother, Mrs. Oscar Lowrance, Sulphur, and an aunt, Mrs. Veta McClure Findlay, 1815 N. Hudson.

July 18 Obituary

RITES SET FOR TINKER EMPLOYEE

A chief supervisor of industrial engineering at Tinker Air Force Base and a lifetime resident of Oklahoma, Guy Victor McClure died Tuesday of a heart attack in Baptist Hospital. McClure, 36, of 13200 N. MacArthur, had suffered a previous attack three years ago. At that time, he was hospitalized for about two months.

Started in 1951

He started to work at Tinker in March of 1951 as an engine tester. Later that year he was transferred to the supply department and into industrial engineering. In 1955 he became chief of the facility's engineering. This was later changed to chief supervisor of industrial engineering. McClure's grandfather was the first legal settler in Oklahoma City. In 1867, he bought and settled on the Bill Chisholm ranch.

Rites tentative

Services will be 10 a.m. Thursday at Village Christian Church. Burial will be in Memorial Cemetery; Sherman funeral home is in charge. Surviving are his wife, Thamar; three sons, Charles, Guy, and Dewey, all of the home; a brother Bill, Edmond; his mother, Mrs. Oscar Lowrance, Sulphur; and an aunt, Mrs. Veta McClure Findlay, 1815 N. Hudson.

Let us be judged by our actions

About the Author

Mary Ellen (McClure) Randall

Former business owner, historian at heart, and designated keeper of family records—Mary Ellen (McClure) Randall has lived most of her life on the Great Plains of Oklahoma and Kansas. She has passed on her love of story, history, people, and place to her two children, eight grandchildren, and (so far) five great grandchildren.

Appendix 1
WHO ARE THESE McCLURES?

Lost in time are the names and other identifying facts about the McClure ancestors appearing in these tintypes and photographs.

Do you bear a resemblance to any of these persons?

Even though your lineage may seem to lie outside the McClure ancestral line, you may be looking at a past link to your present self.

Ask yourself: Are my family roots somehow an offshoot of the McClure family tree? To explore that possibility, please contact Mary Ellen McClure Randall at: McClure1889@gmail.com.

(1) (2) (3)

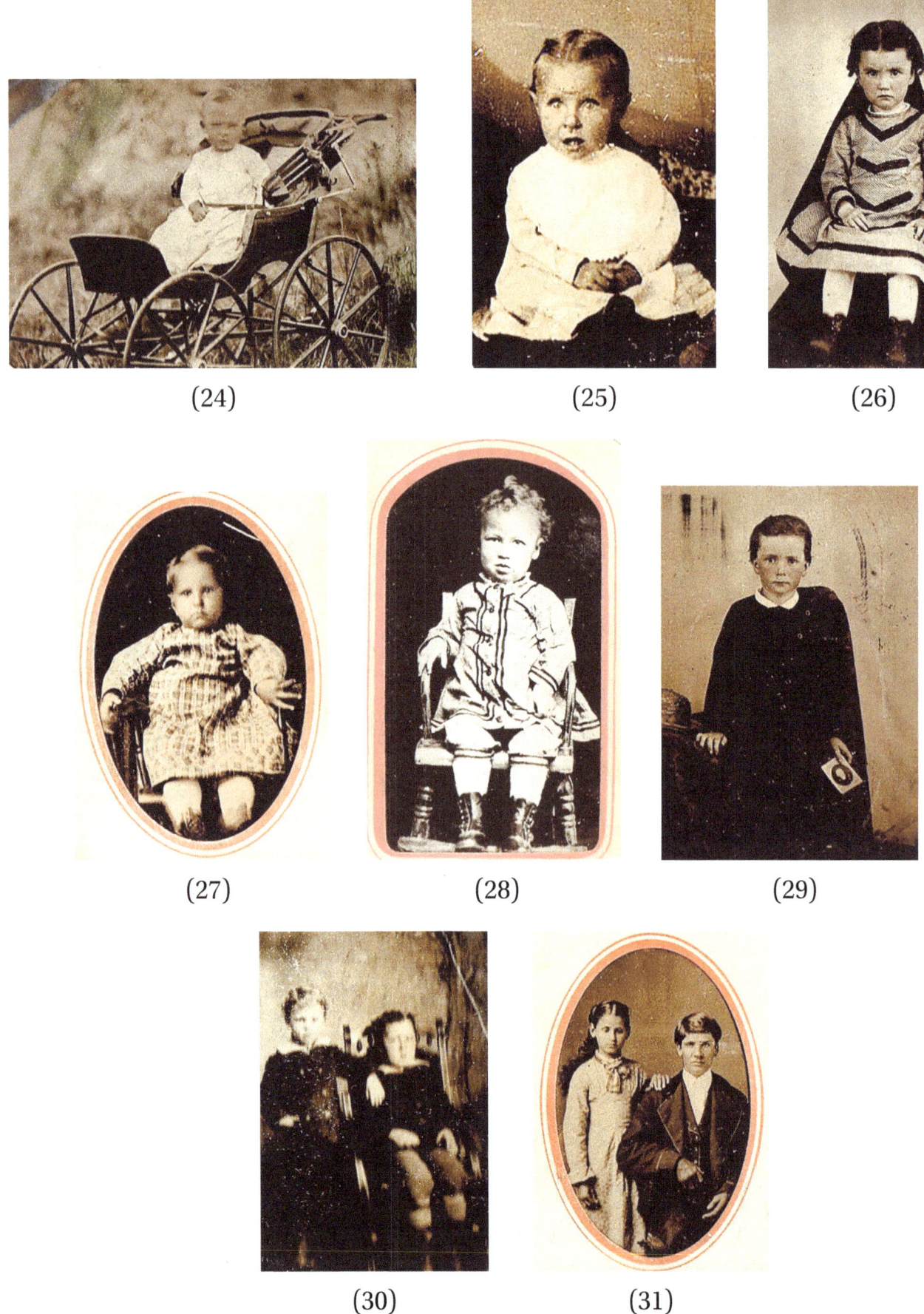

Sources

Books
And Satan Came Also by Albert McRill
Boom Town by Sam Anderson
1889, The Boomer Movement, The Land Run and Early Oklahoma City by Michael Hightower
Born Grown by Roy Stewart
The Oklahoma Land Rush of 1889 by Stan Hoig
The Chronicles of Oklahoma, Volumes XLVIII, November 1, 1970; and Volume LVIII, Number 1, Fall 1980
The Crowded Hour by Clay Risen
Heart of the Promised Land Oklahoma County by Bob L. Blackburn
Reminiscences of 89ers by the 89ers
The Story of Oklahoma by Muriel Wright
The Story of Oklahoma City by Angela C. Scott

Libraries, Museums, Foundations
Ulster Historical Foundation Mormon Library
    Film 020, 369: McClure Family, Lancaster, Pennsylvania
    Film 599.202; McClure Family, miscellaneous Illinois Families

Original Sources
First person letters, deeds, newspaper articles, photographs from collection of the author

Public Records
Historical real estate records filed by County and obtained from the Register of Deeds office

Websites
Ancestry.com
Ancestryireland.com
www.familysearch.org/eng/library/FHC/frameset_the_asp
www.familysearch.org/eng/Library/FHLC/frameset_fhlc.asp
Family Search, Family History Center Locator
HeritageQuestOnline web page
[www.usgennet.org/usa/topic/historical/1908k_2_8.htm]

Design and digital production by
Felton Stroud, Stroud Design, Inc.
Composed in the Utopia Std font family

Printed on 50# gsm paper, perfect
bound and case laminate

Printed and case bound by IngramSpark

www.ingramcontent.com/pod-product-compliance
Lightning Source LLC
Chambersburg PA
CBHW060537010526
44119CB00005B/180